Textbook of Psychology

FOURTH EDITION

Textbook of Psychology

FOURTH EDITION

D. O. HEBB
D. C. DONDERI

 LAWRENCE ERLBAUM ASSOCIATES, PUBLISHERS
1987   Hillsdale, New Jersey   London

Lawrence Erlbaum Associates, Inc., Publishers
365 Broadway
Hillsdale, New Jersey 07642

Library of Congress Cataloging-in-Publication Data

Hebb, D. O. (Donald Olding)
   Textbook of psychology.

   Bibliography: p.
   Includes index.
   1. Psychology.   I. Donderi, D. C.   II. Title.
BF121.H35   1987   150   86-23931
ISBN 0-89859-934-2

To the Crosbies and the Donderis,
especially S.N.C., D.C.D., A.M.D.
and V.H.D.

Contents

From the Preface to the First Edition

This book is meant both for the student who will go on to further courses in the subject and for the one who takes only one, the "terminal," course. Both pedagogically and professionally, it seems to me that the terminal course should be no less scientific than the one which is an introduction to further work.

If psychology is a science, it should be presented as a science; it is at least as interesting, intellectually, as its applications, and I surely do not need to argue here that basic science is in the long run a very practical training. We would not think at the graduate level of turning out practitioners without a thorough basic training; we insist instead that a critical understanding is vital to the professional psychologist. Training in methods only, it is agreed, is a mistake. But if we give a first course which is primarily concerned with personal adjustment and the like, we are making precisely that mistake. The function of the course instead should be to develop critical understanding, to prepare the student to evaluate his later reading in the field of method, and prepare him also to understand the new methods that will be developed after he has left his "terminal" course. Valuable as the practical methods of psychology now are, I believe that those of the future will be more valuable still; if so, the theoretical and academic course is—as I have said—the most practical one in the long run.

D. O. Hebb

Preface to the Fourth Edition

This edition retains the direction, goals and structure of the previous ones. We believe that an introductory psychology textbook should be written to explain mind and behavior. All of us eventually may live more happily in a better world because of the work of psychologists, among others. But an important first step to achieving this goal is to transmit a knowledge of psychological principles to the student. Then, intellectually equipped, he or she can worry about life adjustment and social problems.

The nervous systems of small invertebrates are yielding beautifully to studies that describe the functions of single neurons or small groups of nerve cells. But the discovery of more neurotransmitters and more neurohumoral influences on behavior makes the structure and function of the nervous systems of higher animals even more difficult to understand. The cell assembly ideas that underlie our exposition are, we believe, still a sound basis for understanding the function of the nervous system of higher animals in relation to mind and behavior. Recent developments of cell assembly theory in the field of mathematical biology have strengthened this conviction.

In the last ten years much has been learned about language and thought. Although the differences between humans and other primates in ease and flexibility of communication are striking, the complexity of primate communication is far greater than was previously realized. This strengthens the evidence that the neural and mental processes of humans and other primates are similar, a theme that recurs throughout this book.

Certain aspects of human thought have begun to yield to logical analysis based on the use of computers. These computer simulations frequently include processes, like expectancies, that are capabilities that cell assembly theory assigns to humans and to some other animals. These developments are also reviewed in this edition.

The McGill University Psychology Department provided the setting for the preparation of this edition. We thank Barbara Watson at McGill, who typed most of the manuscript. We also thank our colleagues at McGill, who directly or indirectly have contributed to the development of some of the ideas in this book and who for many years have provided a stimulating environment for research and thought.

D. O. Hebb
D. C. Donderi

1

Psychology and Human Behavior

The object of this book is to introduce you to the scientific study of the human mind and behavior. That is essentially what psychology is about. Psychologists study animals too, and they are fascinating, but the main reason for studying them is to understand human behavior.

Our concern is with scientific psychology and fundamental principles. Each year more is learned about human nature, and you will want to follow the evolution of psychological knowledge and theory. A good understanding of fundamental principles is the best preparation to follow developments in psychological knowledge and to understand the changes in how that knowledge is applied.

STUDYING THE MIND

How are we to study the mind? Your own mind is not open to inspection. It was once supposed that you could look inward at any time and know what you were thinking. In 1820 the German philosopher Herbart realized that there is much that is going on in your mind about which you know nothing at all. Sigmund Freud, in about 1900, made this a central part of his theory. Like Herbart, Freud assumed that unpleasant things, things you do not like or are ashamed of, are suppressed and kept in the unconscious. Freud, like others at that time, thought that all other mental processes were available for examination. But now it is clear that introspection, or "looking inward," does not exist for *any* mental processes. You are not conscious of your consciousness. You are conscious of your body of your speech and "inner speech," and of the world around you, but not of what is going on *inside* your mind.[1]

We said before that you are not conscious of your thoughts. But imagery is a part of thought (chapter 5), and you may believe that you are at least conscious of your imagery. Not so. Try this small experiment: Look for a few seconds at a bright object. Now look away toward a plain wall. You see a dark patch, corresponding in shape to the bright object. Where does this dark patch seem to be? It is outside you, not inside. You know the dark patch doesn't correspond to a real object, because you feel nothing when you put your hand out to touch it; besides the dark patch moves as your eyes move. You conclude that there is nothing outside and that what you see is just an image caused by some activity of your visual system. You are right, but you have *inferred* the truth, not directly observed it. You are conscious of something outside yourself, and *not* of the mental process that generated the false image.

So we can learn about the mind only indirectly, from knowing how human beings are made and what they say and do. There is complicated machinery inside. We can find out something about how it works by stimulating it in different ways and seeing what output follows a given input. But the mechanisms are indeed complex, and psychology has a long way to go before the problem is solved—if it is ever completely solved. In principle, however, the method is straightforward: you must learn about others' mental processes—and even about your own, much of the time—from what they say and do. The great American philosopher C. S. Peirce (1958) said that he knew what he thought only when he heard himself speak or when he found himself acting on a conclusion his mind had come to. (Peirce, 1958).

Clearly Freud was right in supposing that you can be thinking something and not know that you are thinking it. It is common to hear someone say, "I don't know how I could have forgotten" or "I don't know what got into me" about something done or not done. Freud took his ideas further, suggested that by laughing at someone you show you

---

[1]One modern theory goes so far as to suggest that early human beings thought their own "inner speech" came from outside—as messages from the gods. See Jaynes, J. (1977). *The Origin of Consciousness in the Breakdown of the Bicameral Mind.* Boston: Houghton Mifflin, or "Consciousness and the voices of the mind" (1986) by the same author in *Canadian Psychology, 27,* 128–139.

dislike him; that if you can't remember a name, or how to pronounce it, you may dislike him even though you *think* you like him. These are examples of how one may use behavior to make inferences about thought. Inferences of this kind are not always true: before one could be sure, one would have to examine the person's behavior further. Laughter is not always malicious; simple forgetting does occur. But though we would not now generalize as much as Freud did when he proposed these ideas, we should see that in proposing them Freud was exploring the problem of how to think objectively in studying the mind. When he went so far as to study his own unconscious in this way—for example, when he himself forgot a name—he was clearly a pioneer in the development of objective psychological methods.

MIND OR SOUL?

Now for the nature of mind itself: What is it? What does it consist of? We will take for granted, as a working assumption, that mind is a function of the brain and not something that can exist apart from the brain. We will assume that thought and consciousness arose in the course of evolution. They are not activities that we alone are capable of. Dogs and cats, monkeys and chimpanzees also think and have minds.

Speaking very generally, there are two theories of mind. One in its clearest form is *animistic*, a theory of demonic possession. It assumes that the body is inhabited by an entity, a demon known as the mind or soul. Less extreme (and less clear) forms of the same theory simply are called *dualistic*. They assert only that mind is not physical, and is separate from the workings of the body. The second theory is *physiological* or *mechanistic*. It assumes that mind is a bodily process, the activity of the brain or some part of that activity. This is *monistic* theory. Modern psychology works with monistic theory, and we will do the same in this book. It is a working assumption. Both theories are intellectually respectable—there are thinkers of the highest ability to be found on each side of the question. It is essential that you understand that a scientific theory should never be "believed." A scientific theory is best thought of as a sophisticated statement of ignorance, a way of formulating possible ideas so that they can be tested, rather than a statement of final truth. In the case of psychology, the working theory is to assume that a separate soul does not exist. There is no conflict here between religion and scientific method. Science approaches truth by a series of approximations and psychology is in no position to be dogmatic about the correctness of its notions about the nature of mind.

PSYCHOLOGICAL RESEARCH

Learning

The foregoing discussion will have more meaning if we look now at some areas of psychological research. Psychologists do not spend all their time trying to settle outsize questions like What is mind? or Is there a soul? They usually study easier topics, like learning, motivation, perception, intelligence, or memory—all of which must be understood if we are to understand the mind.

The first, and main, area of research is learning. The distinctive mark of the psychologist is an interest in learning. Learning may seem very simple to you, because you have been doing it all your life. But do research? Learning is just a matter of repetition. Practice makes perfect. The more often you catch a ball, the better you are at catching it; the more you read, the more you will remember . . .

Or will you? That last statement may sound right, but it is a trap. Learning is not so simple. There are better ways to learn more and to remember more than by repetition. Human learning is very peculiar in a number of respects. We will come back to it in later chapters, but here we can give you some idea of how much there is still to find out about learning—even about study methods.

Let's take a moment to look at study methods. (For a fuller account, see the study methods section of chapter 6.) It may be true that the more you read this textbook the better you will remember it. But it is not true that simply reading it over and over is a sensible way to learn. You will get better results with less pain from a different method. Less than half your time should be spent reading; more than half, making notes, or trying to reorganize what you have read, or trying to recall it.

Stop reading at this point and look through the whole of this first chapter to find out why the parts are arranged as they are. Read the headings, sample the text, look at the Summary, and see if the organization of the chapter makes sense. If not, sample more of the text and try again. How would you organize these points? Instead of just reading and trying to remember, find out what the pattern of ideas is. You will remember more not by trying to remember but by just trying to understand. This method is easier as well as more efficient. It's also easier to talk yourself into study when you do it this way. This is how you should approach any new chapter or any new book. Look for the main picture and the details will look after themselves.

Nevertheless, there are times when straight memorization is necessary. When you are studying the anatomy of the brain, you must be able to name the twelve cranial nerves. In biology, you must know the classification scheme of kingdom, phylum, and so on. Many generations ago students discovered something that psychologists still cannot explain to their own satisfaction: learning more is sometimes easier than learning less. Instead of pounding away at *olfactory, optic,* and the names of the other ten nerves till they can be repeated, you add something: a short ditty that goes as follows "On old Olympus' tufted top, a fat-armed German viewed a hop." The first letter of each word is the first letter of the twelve cranial nerves: olfactory, optic, oculomotor, trochlear, trigeminal, abducens, facial, auditory, glossopharyngeal, vagus, accessory, hypoglossus. Similarly, "King Peter came over from Germany seeking fortune" will organize and help recall kingdom, phylum, class, order, family, genus, species, and form. Most English-speaking people learn the number of days in each month with the familiar jingle "Thirty days hath September. . . ." Eventually you know that November has thirty days without having to go through the rhyme, but it is easier to start by learning the rhyme. In the case of the cranial nerves, it is quite clear that by adding something to the task, the task becomes easier. One must learn those anatomical names, glossopharyngeal and the rest, in the end; yet they are easier to learn with the jingle. This surely is a surprising state of affairs. Orators and actors have used mnemonics like these from ancient times. Papyrus was an expensive luxury, and wax tablets were too heavy for lecture notes, so there was a higher value on good memory. The practice of mnemonics is not new; but the theory is still poorly understood.

Another example of a learning problem aided by a mnemonic is learning to tell your left hand from your right. Many people all their lives have to stop and think a moment before knowing what to do when someone says "Take the next turn to the right." This should be simple: All you have to do is to associate the sound of the word "right" with a movement of the right hand or moving the eyes to the right. Why is there trouble? Partly at least because of the symmetry of the body, the similarity of the left and right sides. In learning to tell left from right, children learn more than they have to, and in this case the "more" causes trouble. What is learned first is not to associate the word "left" with a particular hand or side, but with sidedness, with one of the dimensions of the body in space. Children also begin to learn to name the right and left sides of someone facing them, which of course is opposite to their own left and right. The result of all of this is confusion (see Fig. 1.1).

Learning is cumulative. Daily routines like tying shoelaces or counting change include many acts that were at first learned with difficulty but which are now done without thought or effort. Learning these acts need not be specifically recalled in order for them to be done in the

FIGURE 1.1. Children learn the differences between p and q, b and d very slowly when they begin to learn to write the alphabet. Not only do they mix up the left–right direction in writing single letters, they sometimes confuse the direction for writing entire words. One of the authors recalls visiting a kindergarten where children were painting. Two children shared a single large easel, one child on each side. At one easel, a girl finished her painting first, and wrote her name—CATHY—in large letters at the upper left-hand corner of her paper. The other girl at the same easel finished later. Not knowing where to write her name, she looked around the easel at Cathy's painting, and then wrote her own name in the upper *right*-hand corner of her own painting and directly opposite to Cathy's name, and starting at the same place, wrote inward from the edge ᴀBBƎᗡ

right way at the right time. In discussing memory later on, we will see that what can be recalled has certainly been learned, but not everything that has been learned need be recalled. We shall also see later that "recall" is no respecter of history—you may "recall" things that never really happened—and that the brain mechanisms for learning and for recalling may be very different.

Learning is like the tip of an iceberg. When something new is learned, it is usually only the specific associations or the specific relationships that are new; the ideas or words or actions are usually not new at all. Most people reading this book had to be told (or had to hear) only once the name of the person elected president or prime minister of their country; "one-trial" learning was sufficient both to establish and to maintain a new association between two well-learned words or phrases: the candidate and the office.

It appears that the human brain does not do simple things in a simple way. This makes the world very interesting for psychologists, but there are drawbacks. If you meet someone who thinks that learning is easy to understand, ask why it is so hard to learn which side is left, and which side is right.

Experimental Neurosis

Consider mental disorder in a dog. Though this example involves an animal lower than man and cannot prove anything about human behavior, it does show that failure in a learning problem can produce a serious problem in some animals and suggests the possibility that similar problems may happen with human beings.

An experimenter in the laboratory of the great Russian physiologist Pavlov, using the method of conditioned reflexes (see chapter 2), was trying to find out how small a difference the dog could detect between two objects. He taught the dog that food would be given following the sight of one object but not following the sight of another. No punishment was given if the dog failed to discriminate between the objects. The objects were made more and more alike until, after several days of failing to discriminate, the dog's behavior suddenly changed. Instead of coming eagerly to the experimental room, the dog struggled to avoid it. Instead of standing quietly in the apparatus, waiting for the next signal to appear, he bit and howled. Discrimination disappeared. The experimenter went back to easier forms of the problem, which the dog had solved previously, but this had little effect on the changed behavior. The disturbance never completely disappeared; even after a long rest, the dog became excited again if he was put back into the experimental room.

It is remarkable that a simple perceptual conflict should have such drastic and long-lasting effects. No pain was involved, nor fear of pain. Might a human neurotic disturbance be produced in the same way, when something learned in childhood, say, conflicts with some adult experience? Is neurosis all a product of learning? Before leaping to that conclusion, we must take one more fact into account: only a few dogs, perhaps 1%, developed a neurosis in that experimental situation. It seems there must be a special susceptibility for the breakdown to occur. Here we are dealing with an interaction between experience and a particular hereditary disposition. But the phenomenon does remind us that small differences can have large effects when we are dealing with something as complex as the brain. Human beings are more vulnerable to emotional experience than dogs, as we will see later (chapter 11), and so conceivably the human susceptibility to neurotic breakdown following minor stress may also be more widespread and not limited to a small proportion of the population.

Hyperactivity

The interplay of biology and experience characterizes the puzzling childhood disorder commonly called hyperactivity, a disorder affecting more boys than girls. Some children cannot stay still; they cannot sit quietly and listen. They fidget, they move restlessly from one thing to another. They react impulsively to tasks or to questions, doing or saying the first thing that comes to mind. They respond to the obvious and to the immediate; to search for a subtlety or plan a careful investigation is beyond them. Paradoxically, the young school children who match this description may have normal IQs; when tested by a patient psychologist, they show that they can reason and remember at least as well as the average child of their age. Older hyperactives may score lower on IQ tests—and thereby hangs a tale.

The onset of hyperactivity is early. Parents recognize unusual restlessness and distractability in their children before they reach school age. Research with hyperactive children first focused on the observation that they were easily distracted by novel or highly noticeable stimuli. It was thought that they needed more varied and more stimulating input to maintain normal alertness because there was a deficiency in the intensity of the internal mechanism that kept them alert. It was also thought that this deficiency is correctable by increased stimulation—of interesting sights, sounds, and movements, which, if they are lacking in the environment, the hyperactive child will personally produce.

As is characteristic of science, further research corrected the first idea. It now appears that hyperactive children are no more or less generally alert to their environment than normal children. Their problem is that they do not appropriately concentrate their attention. For example, when a well-motivated schoolgirl hears the teacher say, "Now, I am going to spell DOG," she stops fidgeting, becomes attentive, and concentrates on remembering the letters. A well-motivated hyperactive boy cannot direct or maintain his alertness: He may at first sit still, but he cannot sustain the inhibition of fidgeting and other responses long enough to pay attention to the letters. These observations are substantiated by physiological evidence. The hyperactive boy shows brain waves (EEG) and skin conductance (GSR) patterns which demonstrate that he is *as* alert as the normal child, but that he cannot concentrate his alertness and attention for long in response to what, for normal children, are attention-getting and attention-concentrating signals and instructions (Douglas & Peters, 1979).

The cumulative result of years of failure to concentrate alertness in school is, of course, that the hyperactive child learns less than other children even though, when his attention is concentrated, he has the demonstrated capacity to learn as well as the normal child (Thorley, 1984). Children who learn less eventually are less well prepared to succeed in life, and they score lower on IQ tests. Both results are seen in hyperactive older children and young adults.

The symptoms of hyperactivity are alleviated in some children when they receive regular supplements of a drug that acts as a neurotransmitter, or chemical messenger, in parts of the brain apparently responsible for the salutary effects of rewards. Some hyperactive children also respond well to learning situations that provide praise or reward after every response (a little reflection will demonstrate how unusual this is in the ordinary world). Another tentative theory, then, is that in hyperactive children the brain mechanisms that normally allow the expectation of reward or success to concentrate alertness on the task at hand are inefficient: not because of any insufficiency of reward in the hyperactive child's life, but because there is a biological deficit in the function of this system for attention and reward in the hyperactive child. The deficiency in this system is at least partially overcome when an extra dose of the system's neurotransmitter chemical is provided (a biological therapy) or when extra reward is provided (a psychological therapy). A great deal more must be learned about hyperactivity before this or any other theory can be confidently advanced to explain this disorder.

THE OBJECTIVE APPROACH TO BEHAVIOR

We have been looking at problems where the objective study of behavior takes on practical significance. A main reason for insisting on objectivity is the need to keep inferences separate from facts, to distinguish between theory and evidence. Theories may differ, but it is no good arguing about theory if there is no agreement on the facts. Psychology is behavioristic, which means that it uses what people do or say as evidence. What people do or say can be observed by others, and so agreement concerning the facts is possible. The essence of a good observation for scientific purposes is that anyone properly trained can make the observation and so test its accuracy.

Most of the time we do not split hairs about what is subjective and what is objective. Pain is technically subjective, a "private" event that no one else can know about directly. But the report of pain by the person who feels it, saying Ouch!, screwing up the face and jerking the hand back from the sharp object that caused pain—is a report of behavior. What the person does is observable and objective and permits a reliable inference that pain is occurring. Similarly, although an afterimage is subjective and can only be observed by one person, the report of afterimages in certain conditions is so consistent that we can be certain that under these conditions afterimages do occur. We can, then, take for granted that there is pain when someone receives a burn and that there is an afterimage when someone stares at a bright object. In such cases, we need not quibble about whether the evidence is subjective or objective. Nonetheless, where there is doubt or when one must choose between two hypotheses, it is the objective evidence that carries greater weight.

Speech, which includes reports of subjective experience, is a most important form of objective behavior. Facial expression is also an important form of objective behavior in social communication. The muscles of the face can convey annoyance or pleasure or absent-mindedness. Blushing (caused by changes in muscle tension in the blood vessels just under the skin) is behavior indicating embarrassment or anger (though we call it "flushing" when it is due to anger). Breathing is behavior, and changes of breathing are part of the behavioral evidence used in the so-called lie detector methods (which are really emotion detecting). Behavior does not consist only of using the big muscles of arms and legs—to fight, to run away, to find food, to play games—nor of these plus the finer muscles of the fingers. It is the activity of all of the muscles of the body, plus glandular secretions such as mouth-watering (secretion of saliva), tears, and sweat.

Behavior is also the interaction between animals or people. A great deal can be learned about people or animals by unobtrusively watching and recording what they do in natural or contrived groups. This technique can be used to study communications among small groups of people trying to solve a common problem, for example, or the behavior of infant monkeys deprived of maternal care.

Behavior tells us what is going on in the mind only when we take account of the circumstances in which it occurs. We must keep track of the *stimuli* or the *stimulus situation* as well as the response made to stimulation. We must keep track also of the temporal pattern of behavior: what follows what, the relation of what the subject does now to what was being done before or what will be done next. The great american psychologist William James insisted that mental events are not discrete and separate from one another but form a flow, which he called "the stream of thought" (James, 1892). The same is true of behavior. The flow of a stream may be smooth or tumultuous, it may meander gently in part of its course and elsewhere pour over the rocks with great violence, but it is a continuity.

So behavior has to be understood in terms of the circumstances in which it appears and its pattern over periods of time. For example, not answering when spoken to means one thing when you are watching TV, something else when you are not busy, especially if your silence is followed by walking out and slamming the door. For someone who is usually quiet at parties, not talking much is normal; for someone who is usually the life of the party, exactly the same behavior may mean depression, annoyance, or preoccupation with an important problem. Silence cannot show what the disturbance is, but it does indicate a disturbance. This example illustrates (a) that mild feelings and emotions are not recognized so much by present behavior as by contrast; (my good humor is apparent not because I act in a polite way but because I am more polite than usual) and (b) that doing nothing—being silent, not moving, failing to respond—can be a most important feature of the behavioral pattern. By definition, doing nothing is not behavior, but it has meaning by contrast with past behavior.

This may sound more complex, more intimidating, than it really is. Everyone makes judgments based on behavior patterns every day. Since infancy, we have all learned from behavioral patterns in everyday life to infer what goes on in another person's mind, often wrongly, but very often correctly, especially when we can observe also what is happening to the other person at the time (what stimuli precede his responses). The inference from behavior is not a matter of simply seeing a smile and knowing that the smiler is happy but a complex judgment from all relevant data.

DEFINITION OF TERMS

We can now attempt some definitions, with commentary to avoid misunderstanding. Of course, the same word can mean different things to different people: the word mind, for example, may mean a ghostly, immaterial agent in one book, be dismissed as a meaningless term in another, and be defined as a brain process in a third. You must therefore learn how certain fundamental terms are used here.

Behavior, as a psychological term, may be defined as the publicly observable activity of muscle or glands of external secretion, as manifested, for example, in movements of parts of the body or the appearance of tears, sweat, saliva, and so forth. This does not include glands of internal secretion (endocrine glands), whose activity is not directly observable. We know of the thyroid gland's activity, for example, only by inference, either as the result of elaborate chemical analyses or by observing the changes that occur a week or so after the gland is injured. But we know of the tear gland's activity directly because we can see it. Behavior is the factual basis of psychology, and we do not include in the definition anything that is not at least potentially observable.

Psychology, then, is defined as the study of the more complex forms of organization in behavior. This includes the study of such processes as learning, emotion, or perception, which are involved in organizing the behavior. *Integration* or *organization* means the combination of different segments of behavior in relation to each other and to external events impinging on the organism.

Psychology is not defined here simply as the study of behavior, as is often done. Such a definition would include too much. It is the physiologist, not the psychologist, who studies the units of behavior—for example, the mechanism of glandular secretion—and who has obtained our knowledge of the integration of reflexes, an outstanding example being Sherrington's (1906) *Integrative Action of the Nervous System* (a work that has had profound effect on psychological thought). Hubel and Wiesel (1962) undertook a detailed analysis of the function of individual cells in the visual system of cats and monkeys. This is brilliant physiology,[2] and it has had a profound effect on thinking about the psychology of visual perception (see chapter 12).

We cannot draw a really sharp line between psychology and physiology. We can say that the physiologist is mostly concerned with the functioning of the different parts of the body and the segments of behavior that these parts exhibit; the psychologist, with the functioning of the whole organism and the way in which the segments of behavior are coordinated to form complex actions and sequences of action. The focus of psychology is on the patterns of behavior shown by the whole animal of a higher species in adjusting to his environment over appreciable periods of time. To say the same thing in a different way, psychology is concerned with the mental processes of higher animals.

If psychology cannot be sharply distinguished from physiology, it is even less easily distinguishable from ethology. In fact, ethologists investigate behavior in the same way that some animal psychologists do. Psychologists, however, though they claimed all behavior for their

---

[2]For which they won the Nobel Prize in physiology and medicine in 1981 along with Roger Sperry, a noted neuroscientist.

province, left large regions unexplored. They did little with species other than a few mammals (mostly rats, monkeys, and people) or with the problem of instinctive behavior (going so far, in fact, as to deny its existence). In the meantime, students of evolution were discovering that differences in behavior sometimes were the key to an evolutionary sequence, and they became aware, as psychologists did not, of the problem of the evolution of the striking and beautifully coordinated patterns of behavior in birds, fish, and invertebrates (Hinde, 1970; Lorenz, 1952).

The parts of physiology, ethology, and psychology concerned with the organization of segments of behavior and their origin in the brain or nervous system are frequently grouped together as *neuroscience*, science whose emphasis is on the study of the function of the central nervous system. To simplify the biological task, neuroscientists frequently study animals whose nervous systems are relatively simple and whose behavior is consequently also relatively simple: frogs, snails, salamanders, cockroaches and worms are typical examples. Psychologists, then, share their interest in the organization of behavior with other scientists, who specialize in either the complex behavior of species that psychologists have neglected or the function of the nervous system in animals whose behavior is simpler than that of the cat, dog, ape, or human. But there is more to know in psychology than one person can master, and today there is an effective collaboration between all the specialties, each complementing the other's work.

SUMMARY

Psychology used to be called the study of mind; today it is usually called the study of behavior. If, however, it is the mind that determines the complex behavior of higher animals, both definitions are approximately correct. In modern psychology, mind is considered to be brain activity or some part of it (though this is only a working assumption) and is studied by objective methods. Mental events are known theoretically, being inferred from behavior, which includes speaking and writing. In such a framework, the study of animals has a natural part, both for its own sake and for the light it casts on human behavior.

Use of objective methods is necessary because in science it is essential to be able to confirm the facts on which a theory is based. Private events are those that are peculiar to one person; they cannot be observed by anyone else and consequently they are unsatisfactory as scientific evidence. Also, it is known that introspection, direct observation of one's own mental processes, is not possible. But a verbal report of a private event is public or objective evidence, on which theory can be based, and certain private events like the afterimage are so uniformly reported that we know they exist. Using objective methods has not handicapped psychology but instead has made it more effective.

Psychology, of course, uses other evidence in constructing theory. It builds on the basic sciences of physics and chemistry, and on the anatomy and physiology of the sense organs, nervous system, and muscles.

GUIDE TO STUDY

In reviewing, note that you will not fully understand this first chapter until you have a fair understanding of the later chapters. You should read through the text several times, each time with a more complete understanding. Read the whole book, skipping or skimming as necessary, well in advance of the lectures or assignments and without attempting detailed study. Then plan to work seriously through the book twice, as suggested above.

It may be a help, in mastering this chapter, to proceed as follows. Make sure you understand and can answer the following questions:

How did Freud make a contribution to objective psychology?

Why is a sensation of pain less satisfactory, as scientific evidence, than talking about it?

What are the two kinds of theory of mind?

How does one distinguish animism and dualism from mechanism and monism?

Which theory of mind is used in this book?

In what sense is it correct to "believe" a scientific theory?

What is a temporal pattern, and how can it make doing nothing an important feature of behavior?

With respect to learning and the study method, how should you approach a new textbook?

Do these questions that you are now reading fit in with the recommended method?

Why is the old rhyme "Thirty days hath September . . ." of psychological interest?

What is surprising about one treatment of hyperactivity?

Finally, what is surprising about the cause of neurosis in Pavlov's dog?

NOTES AND GENERAL REFERENCES

Psychology as a science is scarcely old enough to have a history, although as a branch of philosophy or religion it is as old as civilization. Alfred Binet, Hermann Ebbinghaus, Sigmund Freud, Lloyd Morgan, Ivan Pavlov and Edward L. Thorndike are all great names in the history of scientific psychology. The lives of these men and outlines of their work can be found in E. G. Boring (1957) *History of Experimental Psychology*, New York: Appleton-Century-Crofts. For Binet's work, see chapter 9 of this text. A good account of Freud's ideas is given in C. S. Hall (1954) *A Primer of Freudian Psychology*, New York: World. The idea that consciousness is inferred, but not observed directly, is discussed in E. G. Boring (1953). A history of introspection. *Psychological Bulletin, 50*, 169–189. We will return in the following chapter to Pavlov's work, but he has given a very readable account of it himself in his *Lectures on Conditioned Reflexes* (1928), trans. H. L. Gantt. New York: International Publishers. The report of experimental neurosis is on page 342 of that book. See also Pavlov's *Conditioned Reflexes* (1960), New York: Dover, p. 290 (Originally published in 1927). There has been no recent compilation, in a single source, of the basic facts and approaches of experimental psychology. The following books provide authoritative historical background information: Stevens, S. S., Ed. (1951) *Handbook of Experimental Psychology*. New York: Wiley. The 36 chapters by different authors range from neuroanatomy to the higher processes of human thought. Woodworth, R. S. and Schlosberg, H. (1954) *Experimental Psychology*. New York: Holt. An excellent integration of classical topics such as imagery and imageless thought, with a modern approach to theory. The 1971 revision cited below has become very "sensory" and has lost the special values of the earlier edition. Kling, J. W. and Riggs, L. A., Eds. (1971) *Woodworth and Schlosberg's Experimental Psychology*. New York: Holt, Rinehart and Winston.

OTHER REFERENCES

Douglas, V. I., Peters, K. G. (1979). Toward a clearer definition of the attentional deficit of hyperactive children. In G. A. Hale & M. Lewis (Eds.) *Attention and the Development of Cognitive Skills*. New York: Plenum Press.

Hinde, R. A. (1970). *Animal Behavior (2nd Ed.)*. New York: McGraw-Hill.

Hubel, D. H. & Wiesel, T. N. (1962). Receptive fields, binocular interaction and functional architecture in the cat's visual cortex. *Journal of Physiology*. (London), *160*, 106–154.

James, W. (1961). *Psychology: Briefer Course*. New York: Harper. (Original work published in 1892)

Lorenz, K. Z. (1952). *King Solomon's Ring*. New York: Thomas Y. Crowell.

Peirce, C. S. (1958). Questions concerning certain faculties claimed for Man. In Wiener, P.

P. Ed. *Values in a Universe of Chance: Selected Writings of C. S. Peirce.* Garden City, NY: Doubleday.

Sherrington, C. S. (1906). *Integrative Action of the Nervous System.* New Haven: Yale University Press.

Thorley, G. (1984). Review of follow-up and follow-back studies of childhood hyperactivity. *Psychological Bulletin, 96,* 116–132.

CHAPTER 2

Conditioning and Learning

In our systematic examination of behavior and behavior theory, we begin with the phenomena of learning. Learning involves all aspects of psychology, and in the following chapters we will return to it repeatedly. The other chief influence on behavior is heredity. Heredity determines what sort of brain, sense organs, and motor equipment we have: these, in turn, set the limits on what we can learn. Learning and heredity interact closely (in chapter 7 we consider some details of their interaction).

DEVELOPING IDEAS ABOUT LEARNING

Ebbinghaus' Nonsense Syllables

We saw in chapter 1 that human learning is surprisingly complex, but in 1886 Hermann Ebbinghaus found a way of avoiding some of the complexities, and so opened up the topic for study. Theories about how learning takes place had been discussed since the time of Aristotle, but the process seemed too elusive and subtle to be studied in the laboratory. Ebbinghaus changed all this by inventing a new kind of material for people to learn and then showing how to use this material to study human learning.

Ebbinghaus' invention was the *nonsense syllable*, a short combination of letters such as *dak, wom, cib, nuv*. He made up lists of such syllables to memorize. Using such lists, he was able to study the rate of learning, by finding out how many times a list has to be read over before it can be repeated correctly. He also was able to study the rate of forgetting, which was what mainly interested him. Figure 2.1 shows the rate of forgetting: very fast at first, then becoming very slow (see also Fig. 6.2a). The rate of forgetting, (or whether forgetting occurs at all) is influenced by many factors; the shape of the forgetting curve, for example, depends on the kind of material and the conditions in which the material is learned.

Thorndike's Puzzle Box

Very soon after Ebbinghaus did his research, other psychologists began applying the experimental method to learning. Edward L. Thorndike's

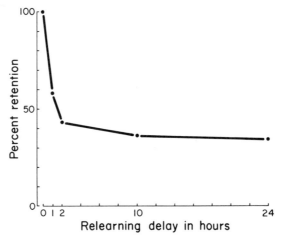

FIGURE 2.1. Ebbinghaus' own performance in remembering nonsense syllables. He first memorized a list of nonsense syllables and counted the number of times he had to read it through before the list was completely learned. Then, after a short delay, he relearned the list until he could again recite it perfectly; again, he kept track of the number of times necessary to read it through the second time before it was completely relearned. The reduction in the number of readings required the second time, compared to the number of readings required the first time, measures the *retention* at the delay interval chosen. Retention is the advantage in learning a second time conferred by previous learning.

The data in this graph were obtained by Ebbinghaus with different lists on different occasions; it is the average result from many separate lists at each interval. The retention is expressed as a percentage: 0% retention means that as many readings were required the second time as the first; 100% retention means that no new readings were required to recite the list perfectly the second time.

early experiments were done with animals, but few experiments have had more influence on our ideas about people. What he did, very simply, was to put hungry cats into boxes with food outside. In one box, the cat had to press a lever, which opened the door; in another the cat had to pull a loop of string; and so on. As the cats became quicker and quicker with practice, learning was measured by the change in the time it took to escape on successive trials (Fig. 2.2). Learning in tasks like these can also be measured by counting "errors"—false moves made on each trial—or by counting the number of trials needed to achieve an errorless performance.

No one really cares much about how long it takes a cat to pull a string

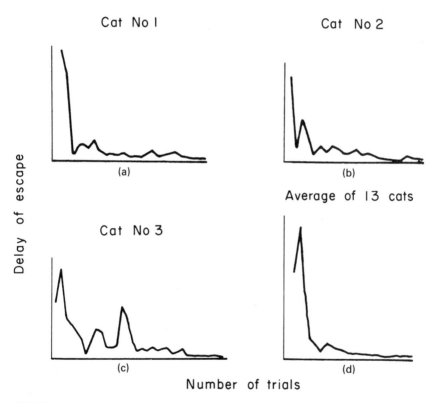

FIGURE 2.2. Thorndike's cats learning to escape from boxes. The time between the cat's confinement and escape was recorded on each of 24 successive trials. The time per trial for three cats is shown in (a), (b), and (c); the average time per trial taken by 13 cats to solve the same problem is shown in (d). Notice how rapidly and consistently the escape occurs on later trials following long and irregular times on the first few trials; notice also how regular the averaged result is compared to the individual data. Although averages over individuals do give a typical performance, they frequently conceal interesting individual variations.

to open a door to get to food. But Thorndike's experiments led him to look in a new way at learning and thinking—*any* learning or thinking, not only the cats'—and this raised fundamental questions that have since had a dominant influence in psychology. Not that Thorndike's views were generally accepted—on the contrary, they gave rise to violent argument. On one side were those psychologists who more or less agreed with his ideas but were apt to make them more extreme. On the other side were the majority of psychologists, who strongly disagreed. Today we have recovered from these extremes and can see better what Thorndike's contribution to knowledge was.

The first question he raised was whether cats have minds and mental processes. Do they think about the situation and then decide what to do, or is there some simpler way in which animals learn? Lloyd Morgan, another student of animal psychology, had thought that learning was possible only if an animal was conscious. He thought the animal would have to remember the pleasure that followed a correct response and the lack of pleasure or the pain following an incorrect one.

Watching his cats, Thorndike thought their learning was very mechanical and that they showed little intelligence or thought. It seemed to him that the cat's brain somehow made a connection between stimulus and response, so that when the cat saw a loop of string and learned to pull it, or saw a wooden button and learned to turn it, a message would go straight from the cat's eye to his paw and no thinking would occur. The two possibilities are diagrammed in Fig. 2.3. Because of Thorndike, psychologists came to realize the importance of the kind of connection that is represented by line A-B in Fig. 2.3. This is the S-R formula, a fundamental idea in psychology, which will be discussed again in chapter 5. Furthermore, cats *do* think. They are capable of delayed response, which, as we will see in chapter 5, is evidence of the ability to think. But Thorndike was right to raise the question, since at that time there was no proof at all that any animals except humans could think. One result of his work was to stimulate others to find the proof.

Thorndike's second main question was, Why does an animal learn some responses and not others? When is a connection like A-B in Fig. 2.3 formed? When a human or other animal is learning to make some response, many wrong moves are made. Yet they are not remembered and repeated. The more often the wrong response is made, the less likely it is to be made again, so mere repetition is not enough. Thorndike proposed that there is another factor operating—a special effect of reward or punishment. He said that when a connection like A-B operates and the cat gets to the food, *the effect of this reward* is to strengthen A-B. When the cat looks at the loop of string and then pulls it, food

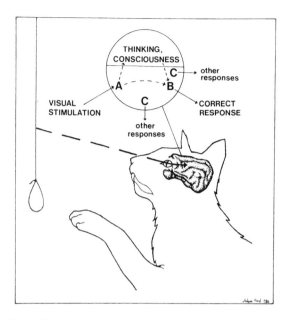

FIGURE 2.3. Thorndike's question about learning and the mind. Suppose that the large circle represents the cat's brain. When the cat sees a loop of string in a puzzle box, the brain has received excitation from the eye. How does this produce the correct response? Two different possibilities: (1) the excitation goes to a part of the brain where there is thinking and consciousness, and this mental activity then excites the motor path leading to the response; (2) a much simpler possibility is that A gets connected directly with B, a stimulus-response connection with no thinking involved—the stimulus excites the response directly. Learning then has nothing to do with the mind but consists of making S-R connections.

follows, so that the next time the cat is more likely to pull the loop or even to pull it sooner. On the other hand, if a connection A-C (Fig. 2.3) should operate, there is no reward and the connection is not strengthened. Thus, as trials go on, A-B becomes stronger and stronger. Thorndike's *law of effect* was that an S-R connection is strengthened if it is active and a pleasant state of affairs follows, but it is weakened if an unpleasant state of affairs follows. In modern psychology Thorndike's "effect" is referred to as *reinforcement*, a concept to which we will return.

Pavlov's Conditioned Reflexes

Shortly after Thorndike began experimenting, Ivan Petrovitch Pavlov in Russia turned to the study of conditioned reflexes. He was already famous for his studies of digestion; now, in 1902, he began a second career of research on the brain that made him even more famous.

Pavlov's experimental arrangement is illustrated in Fig. 2.4. He

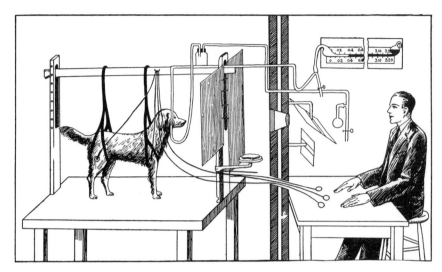

FIGURE 2.4. Pavlov's procedure for Type-S conditioning. Dog and experimenter are in separate rooms. The controls for stimulating the dog's skin and for feeding the dog are in front of the experimenter's hands. Note the attachments on shoulder and thigh, and the food dish, which can be made to swing into the dog's reach. Attached to the dog's cheek is a tube which leads to a gauge at upper right, by which the salivary secretion is measured. The sequence of events on each trial was as follows: First, the dog experienced a conditioned stimulus (a touch on the skin). Shortly afterwards (the sooner the better) the food dish (the unconditioned stimulus) was moved into the dog's reach. The dog salivated (unconditioned response), and ate. The dish was moved out of the way. After an irregular delay, the procedure was repeated. After ten to fifteen repetitions, the dog's saliva began to flow (conditioned response) when his skin was touched (conditioned stimulus). (From Pavlov, 1960. Reproduced by permission.)

almost always used a dog's secretion of saliva as the response to be studied. The stimulus to be conditioned was most often a sound—a bell, a buzzer, a metronome ticking at a particular rate—but he also used visual and touch stimuli. The dog in Fig. 2.4 is shown with attachments for mechanically stimulating (scratching) his shoulder and thigh, but these were not the only stimuli used. To collect saliva, Pavlov made a minor operation to let one of the salivary glands secrete outward into a small cup cemented to the dog's cheek.

Pavlov proceeded as follows. Some more or less neutral stimulus, such as the sound of the buzzer, was presented repeatedly, each time followed by food. (A buzzer or metronome is "neutral" since it does not excite the dog to make any strong response and by itself would soon be disregarded.) The buzzer was sounded for 15 sec, and then food was moved into the dog's reach while the buzzer continued for another 15 sec. This sequence, buzzer followed by food, was repeated at irregular intervals about 10 times in a 1-hour session. By perhaps the 15th or 20th trial in the second session, the dog would begin to secrete some saliva on hearing the buzzer, before the food appeared; on the 40th trial, he would do so copiously and reliably. A *conditioned reflex* had been established.

In this procedure, the neutral stimulus is the *conditioned stimulus* (CS); food in the mouth is the *unconditioned stimulus* (UCS); the secretion of saliva when food is in the mouth is the *unconditioned response* (UCR); and the secretion of saliva as a response to the neutral stimulus (before the food appears) is the *conditioned response* (CR). In other experiments, the UCS might be electric shock applied to the dog's paw, the UCR lifting the paw. Or, with a human subject, the UCS might be a puff of air hitting the cheek near the eye, and the UCR would then be an eyeblink.

The UCS-UCR sequence is the operation of an *unconditioned reflex*, which simply means that the response is not learned. The stimulus evokes the response because of inherited connections in the nervous system—connections that are determined by the subject's heredity and normal growth processes. Examples are the constriction of the pupil when the eye is exposed to bright light, coughing when the throat is irritated, sweating in warm air and shivering in cold air, and pulling back the hand from a painful contact. The salivary reflex does not seem a likely prospect for the study of learning, but Pavlov showed that, in fact, it was a very good one.

TYPE-S CONDITIONING

The learning Pavlov studied was quite different from the learning Thorndike was studying in the United States at about the same time. No doubt this was due partly to the fact that one man studied cats, the other, dogs; but the main reason was a difference of method. Pavlov measured salivation, which is a glandular response. He limited all other activity by his animal. Thorndike worked with muscular responses, which are more closely controlled by higher brain centers (that is, they are voluntary rather than involuntary; chapter 3), and his animals could move around more freely. Pavlov's procedure is now known as *Type-S conditioning*, Thorndike's as *Type-R conditioning*.

In Type-S conditioning, the experimenter uses a UCS to control the response to be conditioned. In Type-R conditioning, there is no UCS; the experimenter waits until the response occurs, more or less by chance, and then rewards it. In Type-S conditioning, the response is elicited by stimulation, when the experimenter wants it to occur; in

Type-R conditioning, the response is emitted by the subject and is not the result of any particular stimulation. Pavlov wanted to make an association between the sound of a bell (for example) and the secretion of saliva; he rang the bell and then *made* the dog salivate (by giving him food). To make an association between seeing a loop of string and pulling it, Thorndike had to wait till the cat happened to pull the string—and then he rewarded the cat with food. In the Type-S case, food is both a stimulus and a reward; in the Type-R case, food is a reward only. Type-S conditioning attaches old responses to new stimuli; Type-R develops new response patterns, sometimes to familiar stimuli and sometimes to unfamiliar ones.

One of Pavlov's important discoveries is *generalization*. Let us suppose that a dog's first CR has been established, the CS being a tone of 500 Hz (Herz, the metric system name for cycles per second). Now a new stimulus is presented: a tone of 600 Hz. The dog secretes saliva. Why? He is hearing this new tone for the first time. The answer is that dogs, like people, generalize: having learned to make a response in one situation, they will make the same response in other more or less similar situations. The dog does not confuse 600 Hz with 500 Hz: he can distinguish such tones perfectly well, as Pavlov also showed. By continuing to feed the dog following 500 Hz, but never feeding following 600 Hz, 400 Hz, and so on, Pavlov could readily get a dog to a stage at which the CR was always elicited by the 500 Hz tone and never elicited by any of the other tones.

Another important item is Pavlov's demonstration of *inhibition*. When the 600 Hz tone is presented and the dog does not respond, as in the preceding example, you might think that the response has gradually weakened and disappeared. Pavlov showed that the connection between stimulus and response is still there, but inhibited. A sudden, unexpected noise can break up the inhibition temporarily (this is known as *disinhibition*), and now the 600 Hz tone will elicit salivation again. The inhibition is extensive when it is present: it not only prevents response to the 600 Hz tone, but also prevents other responses. For example, if the 500 Hz tone is presented immediately after the 600 Hz tone, the 500 Hz tone will not elicit salivation. A negative CS—one that is not followed by the UCS—sets up in the dog's brain an inhibitory state that takes several minutes to disappear.

Inhibition also appears in the *extinction* of a CR with massed trials. After a CR has been well established, it can be extinguished by presenting the CS by itself (without the UCS) about eight times, at 3- or 4-minute intervals. Afterwards there is no salivation to the CS, and other CRs are affected as well. The CR is not wiped out but only subject to a temporary inhibition, for when the animal is brought back to the experimental room next day the CR reappears.

TYPE-R CONDITIONING

Reinforcement

Type-R conditioning is so named because of the emphasis it puts on the selection of a particular *response* from several possible ones (whereas the S of Type-S points to the importance of the conditioned and unconditioned stimulus). But another good reason for the Type-R name is the large part that *reinforcement* plays in Type-R conditioning. Before we go into this, let us define some terms.

Reinforcement in its general sense is an event immediately following a response that increases the probability that the response will be repeated when the subject is in the same situation again. The increased probability means that the response is being learned.

Primary reinforcement is the satisfaction of some biologically primitive need: food when hungry, escape from painful stimulation, and sexual satisfaction are examples.

Secondary reinforcement is sensory stimulation associated with primary reinforcement. Having occurred at the same time or just before primary reinforcement, it has acquired some of the same power to promote learning. Examples are the smell of food or sound of the dinner bell, the sight of a chair when one is tired of standing, the first touch of a cool breeze on a hot day (before it has time to do any cooling; the actual cooling, when one is too warm, is primary reinforcement).

The modern development of Type-R conditioning is chiefly the work of B. F. Skinner. It is in following his procedures that the nature of reinforcement, and its effectiveness, becomes clearest.

Procedure.   Put a pigeon into a box with a button on the wall and a delivery chute for grain, or put a rat into a similar box with a bar or lever sticking out of the wall and a device for dropping food pellets into the box (consider Fig. 2.5b; for the pigeon, see Fig. 2.5a). The food can be supplied by hand or automatically. Then wait. The hungry animal moves about the box, pecking at the walls and floor or sniffing in corners and investigating anything investigable. Sooner or later the bird pecks the button, or the rat rests on the bar and depresses it. Immediately food appears. The animal eats and then resumes its investigation. The same sequence of events is repeated as soon as the

FIGURE 2.5a.   Pigeon in a Skinner box, discriminating a brighter from a darker spot of light. At left a choice is being made (the darker spot is obscured by the bird's beak); at right, the bird receives food following a correct choice. (Photographs by Roy DeCarava, from D. S. Blough, July, 1961, *Scientific American.*)

FIGURE 2.5b.   Rats in a Skinner box, one about to press. The original caption in the Columbia Jester read, "Boy, have I got this guy conditioned! Every time I press the bar he drops in a piece of food." (From Skinner, 1959. Reproduced by permission.)

animal again makes contact with the button or bar, and before long the animal begins making the response systematically as soon as it is put into the apparatus.

The animal is conditioned. There is not one CS but many—visual, olfactory, tactual—simply from exposure to the experimental chamber itself. And the CR does not need to have any natural connection with the reinforcement that is used (whereas a salivary CR is related to eating and withdrawal is related to pain). Thus, this method easily allows us to condition any behavior in the animal's repertoire. Also, it is possible to reinforce only every second or third or tenth response, thus producing more responses per minute than if the animal got a piece of food every time and stopped to eat it. With this procedure, which is called *partial reinforcement*, very high rates of responding can be obtained.

What we have been talking about here, of course, is primary reinforcement (food for a hungry animal). The role of secondary reinforcement is next seen in a procedure that uses Type-R conditioning to *shape up* new forms of behavior: behavior that is not in the animal's original repertoire, though each individual action of the complex is.

The first step is to make a *secondary reinforcer* of some easily produced noise. The noise is made and then food is given, repeatedly, until the animal looks for food as soon as the noise is heard. When the animal makes any movement toward where you want him to go, or performs the first of the sequence of actions you want him to perform, you make the noise instantly and follow it with the food. After a few repetitions, the first part of the movement you want is being made reliably. Wait till the animal moves a little farther toward the desired goal, then give the secondary reinforcement (make the noise) again, and feed; and so on.

Here the practical importance of secondary reinforcement is that it can be given at once, as soon as the right movement is made. Primary reinforcement takes longer to produce. The secret of shaping up is to reinforce, without delay, the first slight movement in the right direction, then, when this is established, the slight further movement that takes the animal a step closer, and so on. To do this efficiently requires skill. The skilled operator can manipulate an animal's behavior—establishing a new pattern of behavior in a matter of minutes, or extinguishing one and substituting another with equal speed—in an almost miraculous manner. Even beginners, with care, can produce surprising results by consciously using secondary reinforcement. You must separate it from the primary reinforcement, which is also necessary (otherwise the secondary reinforcement loses its effect) but which is more difficult to present rapidly.

LATENT LEARNING

The learning we have considered so far is by no means representative of the range of ordinary human learning. For the purposes of the laboratory—especially in earlier exploratory stages when the field was new and no one knew what complications might turn up—it was desirable to study well-defined tasks, with definite responses in clear stimulus situations. It was also a great advantage to study simple memorization like Ebbinghaus' rote learning task. (Rote learning means learning by heart, or simple memorization, as distinct from learning in which the ideas matter rather than the exact words.) But important as memorization may be (in mastery of the multiplication table, for example, or learning the names of people at a meeting) and fundamental as conditioning is in adapting to the environment, there are other forms of learning.

Having a human brain predisposes one to certain kinds of learning that involve no apparent response at the time the learning occurs. This is called *latent learning*. A simple example will help to make latent learning clear. A girl watching an exciting TV program makes no move when the phone rings, and someone else answers. Did she hear? Two minutes later, during a commercial, she asks who called. She did hear, a stimulus had its effect on brain activity, and the brain activity caused a response later. Learning had occurred, but there was no evidence of it at the time. As we will see, latent learning can be found in some nonhuman animals, but it occurs constantly in the waking hours of human beings. It is of fundamental importance in human behavior.

There are several forms of latent learning to be considered. The first is delayed conditioning.

Delayed Conditioning

Learning in the laboratory is easier to study when the response to be learned and the reinforcement occur at about the same time. But the real world is not a laboratory. Suppose a wild rat samples a new food. The food was poisoned and 12 hours later the rat sickens but recovers. The pain and general distress suffered half a day later is enough to teach the rat, on one trial, to avoid the strange food tasted earlier. The distress is not associated with the sights and sounds that occurred immediately before the sickness. The rat learns instead to avoid the unusual food eaten long before the sickness, but does not learn to avoid the everyday sights and sounds that just preceded his getting sick, nor to avoid foods usually eaten. Learning is selective in time and mode: certain things will be learned in preference to others (for example, the association of an unusual taste or odor with an illness, rather than a sight or a noise) even if the delay is great.

Perceptual Learning

Perceptual learning can be defined as a lasting change in the perception of an object or event resulting from earlier perceptions of the same thing or related things. The change is primarily in the direction of a clearer or more distinctive perception, but in some cases the clearer perception of one aspect of the object means that other aspects are seen less clearly.

An example of an increased distinctiveness with practice comes from study of the *two-point limen,* a measure of ability to discriminate points on the skin. With the subject blindfolded, the skin is touched sometimes with one, sometimes with two points (points such as those of a pair of dividers). Each time, the subject is asked to report whether one or two points were felt. On the most sensitive areas—the tip of the tongue, the tip of the forefinger, and the lips—the subject can tell that two separate spots were touched even when there is only one millimeter or so between them (1 mm. for tongue, 2 mm. for fingertip); on the upper arm or back the spots must be 40 to 70 mm. apart. For our present purposes, however, the important thing is that prolonged testing in any area will decrease the two-point limen to half or less of its original value. Repeated sensory input has changed the functioning of the central processes involved in the perception. By definition, this is perceptual learning.

An experiment by R. W. Leeper shows how learning can make the perception of an object clearer in one way and less clear in another. Figure 2.6 shows drawings of an old woman, a young woman, and a composite of the old and the young woman. The composite drawing is an *ambiguous figure,* which may be seen as either an old woman or a young woman. (For another example of an ambiguous figure, see chapter 12, Fig. 12.6a.) The subjects of the experiment were college students. One group was shown only the composite drawing for 15 sec; one group was first shown the old woman for 30 sec and then the composite drawing for 15 sec; and one group was shown the young woman for 30 sec and then the composite drawing for 15 sec. Thirty-five percent of those who saw only the composite drawing saw it as an old woman and 65% saw it as a young woman. But of those who were shown the drawing of the old woman first, 97% saw an old woman in the composite drawing and of those who saw the drawing of the young woman first, 100% saw a young woman in the composite drawing. Clearly, the perceptions of the ambiguous figure were affected by

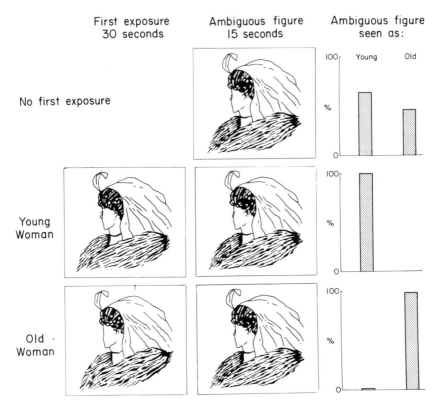

FIGURE 2.6.   The ambiguous figure (center panel) was redrawn from a cartoon in *Puck*, 1915 (title, "My wife and mother-in-law"). It was rescued for psychology by E. G. Boring (1930) and used by Leeper (1935) in his perceptual learning experiment. The first exposure panels each accentuate one of the two ways of seeing the center panel. The results of the first exposure conditions on seeing the center panel are reported in the graphs at the right of the figure.

previous experience. It is also clear that perceiving one of the two aspects of the picture first means that, on the average, the second aspect is less well perceived. In another experiment, with a different ambiguous figure, Leeper (1935) found that some of his subjects saw both aspects of the figure. Perception of one does not always preclude perception of the other. Thus perceptual learning may make a given perception more difficult, or may interfere with one perception by strengthening another.

Learning Set

Learning set is another example of latent learning. The difference between slow and fast learning is often not the learner's ability, but, rather, previous experience with what is to be learned. This is shown in demonstrating *learning set*. A typical demonstration employs a problem that is easy for human adults, but difficult for monkeys. Two different objects—say a cross and a circle—are displayed (Fig. 2.7). The monkey picks up one of the two objects and if the correct object was lifted, eats a raisin found underneath. Picking up the wrong object ends the trial without a reinforcement.

Each pair of objects is presented six times. A learning set demonstration consists of the successive presentation of many different pairs of objects. At first, the monkey learns by trial-and-error to choose one of the two objects. Performance improves over the six trials, but the improvement is slow. After 10 or 20 pairs of objects, however, the monkey shows *one-trial learning*. If he picks up the correct object on the first trial, the same object will be picked up on the next five trials. If he picks up the wrong object on the first trial—as will happen by chance half of the time—he switches to the correct object on each of the next five trials. Over a long series of problems with the same task but with different pairs of objects, the monkey gradually improves from trial-and-error to one-trial learning. Learning set is, in part, an example of perceptual learning. The monkey has learned to attend to the relevant characteristics of the stimulus set on each trial, and to ignore the many aspects of the stimulus environment that are either constant over many trials or which vary from one trial to the next, but which are irrelevant in every case.

S-S LEARNING

Association of Ideas

"Association of ideas" is a 19th century term, but the time has come to put it back to work again. The reason for its disappearance was the earlier doubt that ideas and thought exist at all. We have seen that Thorndike raised this question about cats. John B. Watson (1930) took it further and suggested that human thinking is only a series of tiny muscular contractions, each contraction providing a stimulus to the next one, so that in thinking one is really talking to oneself under one's breath. In that case ideas would not exist, and because of this doubt the term *idea* practically disappeared from psychology. We now know, however, that ideas do exist as special processes in the brain, and we know also that connections can be set up between them. The classical term "association of ideas" thus becomes useful again. *S-S learning*, or stimulus-stimulus association, has much the same significance. Its

Testing Apparatus for Learning Set

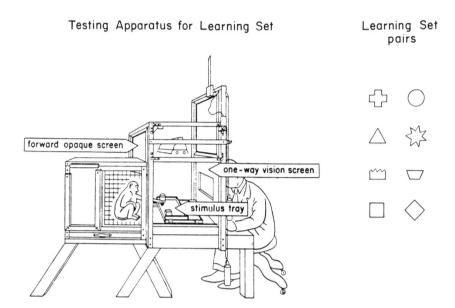

Learning Set pairs

Learning Set Performance

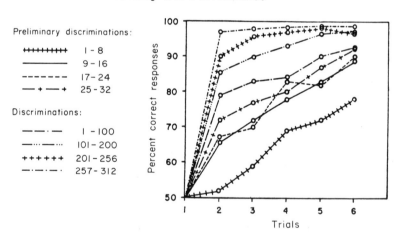

FIGURE 2.7. Learning set. A monkey is shown two different objects, and is allowed to pick up one or the other, but not both. The positions of the objects change from trial to trial, but one object always covers a raisin. Each pair of objects is presented on six successive trials, and is then replaced by another pair.

The graph shows the change in trial-to-trial performance on successive blocks of discrimination learning set problems. The last block shows one-trial learning: Once a correct response is made, it is maintained on the remaining trials with that pair. (From Harlow, 1949. Adapted by permission.)

value lies in its clear distinction of S-S from S-R learning and its direct reference to laboratory procedures. It is clearly shown in the fundamentally important demonstration of *sensory preconditioning* by W. J. Brogden (1939).

With a dog as subject, the first step is to present an association between two sensory events, such as a light and a sound. The light and a buzzer are presented together some six to ten times for this purpose. This is represented in the first diagram of Fig. 2.8. Next, the light is made the CS for an avoidance CR, which is lifting the paw to avoid electric shock (second diagram). Then comes the crucial test. The buzzer is presented, and the dog lifts his paw. Why? The buzzer is not the CS. The only answer seems to be the one represented in the third diagram of Fig. 2.8: the central process or brain activity excited by the buzzer has become connected with the central process excited by the light. The latter is part of the conditioned-reflex pathway, so the sound of the buzzer is able to evoke the response.

A number of *control procedures* (see chapter 8) have been employed to show that this is what actually happens. For example, for half the subjects, the light is made the CS; for the other half, the buzzer. In another example, groups are exposed to both light and buzzer, but without pairing these stimuli. It is clear that sensory preconditioning is a genuine phenomenon. It also seems that the explanation is the sort of connection between brain processes that is diagrammed in Fig. 2.8.

In the sensory preconditioning experiment we also have the perfect example of latent learning. After the two stimuli, light and sound, have been presented together several times, learning has occurred but there is still no evidence of it. Only the later test shows that the dogs had made the association between the two sensory events. Such associa-

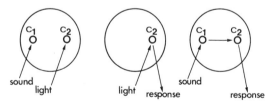

FIGURE 2.8.   The large circles represent the brain at three different stages in the sensory preconditioning experiment. The first diagram represents the simultaneous presentation of auditory and visual stimuli: C_1 and C_2 are the "central processes" aroused together by the two stimuli. In the second stage, the light is made the CS for a conditioned avoidance response; the sound is not presented, so it is not a CS. But in the third stage, the sound is presented without the light and evokes the CR. The explanation must be that there is a connection between C_1 and C_2 (shown by an arrow in the third diagram) owing to the earlier presentation of sound and light together, in stage 1.

tions are common in humans. The associations between thunder and lightning, knife and fork (or the smell of food and eating), mosquitoes and an itching skin, dark clouds and rain, are obvious examples of the S-S learning that human beings are extremely good at and that is very important in our behavior.

Modern Conditioning Theory

The scientific tradition followed by Thorndike and Pavlov was to describe learning in the simplest possible way. The tradition of scientific simplicity still motivates the psychologists who study learning. S-S learning can now be described by using simple mathematical expressions which incorporate the familiar components of Type-S conditioning, the CS and the UCS, in new ways. Learning is still assumed to be an association between the CS and the UCS, resulting in a CR which occurs in response to the CS. We have seen how Brogden's experiments made this idea acceptable. In the mathematical expressions, the CS and the UCS are relabeled and recombined in order to explain some phenomena unknown by Thorndike and Pavlov.

The basic mathematical expression for S-S learning is

$$\Delta V_a = A(L - \Sigma V).$$

The first term, ΔV_a, symbolizes the change in the strength of the learned association between a CS and the UCS on a single trial in which the CS (for example, a light) is paired with the UCS (for example, a shock). The second term, A, measures the intensity of the CS (in this case, the visibility of the light, determined by its position and brightness). The third term, L, sets the maximum amount of associative strength (or learning) which can occur between any CS and the UCS. It depends on the UCS. If the intensity of the UCS, (for example, a mild shock), is increased, L increases; if the UCS (the shock) is reduced, L decreases. The last term, ΣV, measures the accumulated strength of the learned associations between the UCS and *all* of the CSs present on a trial. It summarizes the results of the previous conditioning trials.

Suppose that a light and a tone are both present as CSs on the same trial, with shock as the UCS. Then the equation tells us that the change in associative strength (learning) between the light CS and the shock UCS caused by one trial can be found by multiplying the visibility of the light (A) times the difference between the maximum learning possible for the given level of shock UCS (L), and the *total* learning already accumulated between both the light CS *and* the tone CS, and the shock UCS on previous trials (ΣV). Another similar expression will establish the change in learned association between the tone and the shock.

Using equations like these, some very unexpected predictions have been confirmed. In one experiment, two CSs (a light and a tone) were each *separately* associated with a shock as UCS. The learning for each CS was carried to completion, so that the total amount learned for each CS-UCS pair was equal to L. Then a *combined* CS consisting of both light and tone was presented together and paired with the same shock UCS. Later testing of each CS separately showed that the association between each CS (presented separately) and the UCS had been weakened. In other words, even though each CS had been presented more often (both alone and in combination) with the same UCS, the strength of the association between each CS (presented alone) and the UCS had *decreased*.

Knowledge: A Preparation for Response

The last form of learning to be discussed is an important feature of higher behavior, and of human behavior particularly. It is the acquisition of *knowledge*. Computer scientists have begun to take a serious interest in this form of human learning. They want to create "expert systems" which are computer libraries of useful knowledge about specific topics: for example the diagnosis of illness, along with computer programs which provide access to this knowledge like the access available to you when an "expert" answers your questions in his or her area of expertise.

In dealing with a familiar object or event, which in the past has been encountered in different situations and responded to in different ways, the higher animal has learned not one but a number of ways of reacting to it. When an object is perceived and its position or its size or its color is remembered, further learning has occurred.

But what kind of learning? Not learning to do something, for in most such cases (and this is something that is happening to the normal human being all the time) one never does anything more and before long forgets the event completely. Yet in another sense, one has acquired a great many *potential* responses to other stimuli depending on what may happen to one later. You learn that "msec" means milliseconds, or "amp" mean amperes, and (if you don't move your lips when you read) you make no response at the time. But in later situations, such as during a physics exam or while you are using printed instructions on a new piece of equipment, your behavior is different from what it would have been without this knowledge.

Another example, perhaps clearer: Looking for glue in a friend's workshop, I see a screwdriver lying under a pile of shavings. Having no use for the tool I do no more than let my eye rest on it for a moment and go on with my search. But if my friend should say, "Is the screwdriver on the bench?" I would at once say, "Yes" without having to look first. If he should say, "The screwdriver must have been left outside," I would answer, "No, it's here." If I should find the glue but could not get the lid off, I would reach directly for the screwdriver instead of looking for it first or getting out the pocket knife I might otherwise have used. And so forth. Perceiving the screwdriver, knowing that it is on the bench, has changed the response I would make to each of a large class of potential stimulations (it is not possible to list them all). Also, there is no definitive way of reacting to a screwdriver (which may be used to drive screws or remove them, to pry cans open or to pierce them, to prop open windows, to close electrical circuits, or to throw at cats). So the learning is not learning to do any particular thing—it is not an incomplete S-R connection. What it really amounts to is changing some of the connections in the brain, so that now any of a number of later stimuli will produce a different response from what it would have otherwise.

THE DISTINCTION BETWEEN LEARNING AND PERFORMANCE

Implicit in the preceding discussion is a distinction that should be made explicit: the distinction between learning and performance, or between learning and learned behavior. The distinction applies to all learning, not just to latent learning. Learning is not something we see or observe directly. Instead, it is something inferred from behavior: a presumed change in the nervous system that produces changes in performance. Psychologists sometimes try to define learning as the behavioral change itself, but this is unsatisfactory. For example, a rat is trained to press a bar for food; then we feed him to satiety and put him back in the apparatus, and we find that the behavioral change (bar-pressing) has disappeared. If learning is a change of behavior, then we must say that the learning has ceased to exist—but this is wrong, for when we make the rat hungry again, he presses at once, without having slowly to acquire the habit all over again. The learning is a neural change, which continues to exist when the animal is not hungry but it makes itself evident only under the proper conditions.

This logical distinction is essential. In sensory preconditioning, learning occurs without giving any evidence that it is happening, until a later test is made. The learning can only be shown by making the test. The distinction between learning and performance is also essential for understanding the acquisition of knowledge. You see another car driver get stuck on an icy hill: can I tell if you have learned anything? Have you retained whatever you might have learned? Only later, when I see you putting on chains for driving in icy weather, or telling someone else about chains, or taking care to avoid the icy hill, do I have the behavioral evidence.

In sensory preconditioning and the acquisition of knowledge the difference between learning and performance is inescapable, but it is important in S-R learning also. The distinction must be made if you are to think clearly about learning, and, in a later chapter, if you are to think clearly about memory and forgetting.

SUMMARY

This chapter begins by reminding you that learning and heredity are closely related. The chapter outlines the start of research on learning by giving a brief account of the work of three men: Ebbinghaus—human learning (memorization), 1885; Thorndike—cats in problem boxes, 1898; and Pavlov—conditioned salivation in dogs, 1902. All three lines of research have continued, and form a large part of modern experimental psychology. It was Pavlov who produced the most interesting data (Pavlovian inhibition, for example), Thorndike who asked the most interesting questions (Have cats got minds? Why does one connection form in the brain, and not another?). Pavlov's method is Type-S conditioning; Thorndike's "trial-and-error learning" can be regarded as Type-R conditioning; and Skinner showed how this latter method can be used to shape new forms of behavior by an efficient use of primary and secondary reinforcement. Ebbinghaus, Thorndike and Pavlov designed research methods that dominated the study of learning for nearly a century, and their work established a vocabulary for learning: conditioned stimulus, unconditioned stimulus, conditioned response, unconditioned response, reinforcement, and the rest. But there is more to learning than Type-R and Type-S conditioning. Several *latent learning* situations are reviewed: delayed conditioning, perceptual learning, learning set, the association of ideas, and the acquisition of knowledge. Learning often occurs without response, and is only demonstrated by a modification of response made much later. In such situations it becomes apparent that learning and performance are different. The same distinction is important in any kind of learning. Learning itself is a change in the organization of the brain; performance is the response or responses determined by the changed brain organization.

GUIDE TO STUDY

Be able to define each of the following terms *in its correct context*, illustrating how it is used in describing learning:

CS
UCS
CR
UCR
Type-S Conditioning
Type-R Conditioning
Primary reinforcement
Secondary reinforcement
Latent learning
S-S learning
Sensory preconditioning
S-R learning
ΔV
L
ΣV

Be able to describe the contributions of each of the following people to the study of learning:

Ebbinghaus
Thorndike
Lloyd Morgan
Pavlov
Skinner

NOTES AND GENERAL REFERENCES

The work of Ebbinghaus and Thorndike is discussed in many texts, but a good account of each can be found in Woodworth, R. S. and Schlosberg, H. (1954). *Experimental Psychology*. New York: Holt, Rinehart, and Winston.

Conditioning

Pavlov, I. P. (1960). *Conditioned Reflexes*. New York: Dover. (Originally published 1927).
Skinner, B. F. (1961). *Cumulative Record*. New York: Appleton-Century-Crofts. This is a collection of papers that vary in technical difficulty. The student's attention is drawn particularly to "A case history in the scientific method" and "How to teach animals," but the whole book is valuable.

Sensory Preconditioning

Brogden, W. J. (1939). Sensory Preconditioning. *Journal of Experimental Psychology*, 25, 323–332. The original report.

Seidel, R. J. (1959). A review of sensory preconditioning. *Psychological Bulletin, 56,* 58–73. The interpretation of Brogden's results as a form of S-S conditioning raised doubts, but this review (with the following paper by Tyler) dispelled them.

Tyler, V. O. (1962). Sensory integration with and without reinforcement. *Journal of Experimental Psychology, 63,* 381–386.

Perceptual Learning

Boring, E. G. (1930). A new ambiguous figure. *American Journal of Psychology, 42,* 444–445.

Gibson, J. J., & Gibson, E. J. (1955). Perceptual learning: Differentiation or enrichment? *Psychological Review, 62,* 32–41. This paper was an important influence in reviving the question raised by Leeper.

Leeper, R. W. (1935). A study of a neglected portion of the field of learning—the development of sensory organization. *Journal of Genetic Psychology, 46,* 41–75. An important paper, without apparent effect for a long time, probably because for a long time S-R learning was all that psychologists were interested in.

Learning Set

Duncan, C. P. (1958). Transfer after training with single versus multiple tasks. *Journal of Experimental Psychology, 55,* 63–72.

Harlow, H. F. (1949). The formation of learning sets. *Psychological Review, 56,* 51–65. This article clearly summarizes the learning set phenomenon. For an example applying learning set ideas to human learning, see Duncan (1958).

Delayed Learning

Rozin, P., & Kalat, J. W. (1971). Specific hungers and poison avoidance as adaptive specializations of learning. *Psychological Review, 78,* 459–486. A good summary of data and theory.

S-S Conditioning

The interesting and powerful conditioning theory developed by R. A. Rescorla and A. R. Wagner is described in

Rescorla, R. A. (1975). Pavlovian excitatory and inhibitory conditioning. In W. K. Estes (Ed.), *Handbook of Learning and Cognitive Processes,* Vol. 2, ch. 1, pp. 7–35. Hillsdale, NJ: Lawrence Erlbaum Associates.

Other References

Brogden, W. J. (1939). Sensory Preconditioning. *Journal of Experimental Psychology, 25,* 323–332.

Morgan, L. C. (1900). *Animal Behavior.* London: Arnold.

Pavlov, I. P. (1928). *Lectures on Conditioned Reflexes,* trans. H. L. Gantt. New York: International Publishers.

Watson, J. B. (1930). *Behaviorism.* Chicago: University of Chicago Press.

3

Pathways in Learning and Perception

In chapter 2 reference was made to the nervous system. It is now time to look at the nervous system more closely. The role of the brain in human behavior has been much clearer in disease than in health. As a result, much of what we know about the function of the brain has been learned while treating patients with damage to or diseases of the brain. In this chapter, the relationship between brain, mind, and behavior will often be illustrated by evidence from people who have undergone brain surgery for the control of epilepsy. From these patients, we now know a great deal about the specialization of different parts of the brain for higher mental processes including learning, the emotions, and self-awareness.

But before the relationship between brain and behavior can be appreciated, you must learn about the structure and function of the nervous system. Neuroscientists spend their lifetime working out the details, from the molecular systems within individual cells (neurons) to the complex subsystems of cells into which the nervous system is divided. Almost all of this work has been done with experimental animals, mainly rats, cats, and monkeys. We, on the other hand, can devote only two chapters to outline the nervous system, time enough to provide the background for our study of mind and behavior.

The nervous system consists of a collection of *neurons*,[1] which are

---

[1]It also contains blood vessels and supporting membranes, as well as *glial cells*, of which there are many more than neurons. Glial cells may have a supporting function, helping to hold the neurons in place but they also probably have something to do with the nutrition and maintenance of neurons.

elongated cells specialized for conducting electrical current from one place to another. Their primary function is to connect receptors with effectors, directly or indirectly, so that sensory stimulation can guide behavior. *Receptors* are cells specialized for sensitivity to environmental stimulation; *effectors* are the cells of muscle and gland whose organized activity produces behavior. Some neurons lead from receptors into the *central nervous system* (CNS) which comprises the brain and the spinal cord; some neurons lead out of the CNS to the effectors, and great numbers of neurons lead to different points within the CNS itself.

Neurons are microscopic in cross section but vary in length from a fraction of a millimeter to a meter or more. There are some ten billion (10^{10}) neurons in the human nervous system. They are packed together to form the macroscopic (easily seen) structures of *nerves*,[2] *spinal cord* and *brain*. The general plan of the nervous system is the same for all vertebrates; and among mammals the designs are very similar. The human brain, weighing on the average about 1350 g, is some 600 times heavier than the brain of the laboratory rat. The two are very different in shape (Fig. 3.1) because some parts of the human brain have developed more than others. The outer layer in particular has increased tremendously and has become wrinkled to be able to fit inside the skull. The same parts, with the same internal relations, are present in both rat and human brains. Accordingly, we will be concerned with the structure of the mammalian brain in general, referring to the human brain in particular only when some question arises about a special ability, such as speech, which is thought to depend on a greater development of one part of the brain (the *speech areas* of the cortex).

Figure 3.2f shows the adult human nervous system. The *cortex*, that is, the large mass of the cerebrum, with its convoluted outer surface, is on top; the *cerebellum* is below and at the back of the head; and the long, narrow *spinal cord* runs down inside the bones of the spinal column. The plan of its construction and the relations among its parts can be better understood by looking at Figs. 3.2a to 3.2f.

As the single-celled fertilized human egg divides and grows through successive cell divisions, the embryo takes the form of an elongated open tube. The inside of the tube develops into the alimentary canal, from mouth through gut to anus. The outside of the tube, in closest contact with the environment, develops into the skin and the sensory

---

[2]Notice the difference between a "neuron" and a "nerve." A neuron is a single cell; a nerve is a bundle of many of the long fibers from individual neurons—that is, a bundle of axons or dendrites or both. Inside the CNS such bundles of connecting fibers form the "white matter," while "gray matter" consists of closely packed cell-bodies. White matter is something like the cables that connect different parts of a computer.

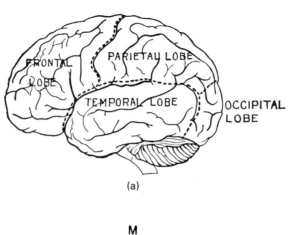

(a)

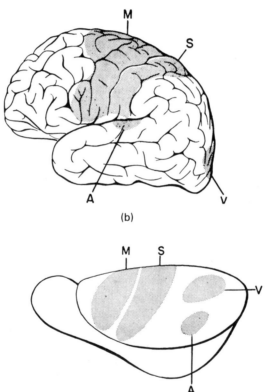

(b)

(c)

FIGURES 3.1a and b illustrate the human brain seen from the left side. In Fig. 3.1a the lobes of the cerebral hemispheres are named. The central fissure separates the frontal from the parietal lobe. The sylvian fissure first runs upwards, then horizontally to the right, separating frontal from temporal lobe and partly separating temporal from parietal lobe. In Fig. 3.1b the approximate locations of the motor (M), somesthetic (S), auditory (A) and visual (V) areas of the human cortex are shown. Figure 3.1c illustrates the same locations on the smooth cortex of the rat brain.

42

and neural apparatus. Repeating the theme of the embryo as a whole, the central nervous system also develops as a hollow tube, but it is closed at both ends and it remains a hollow tube in the adult organism. The only complication at first is that the forward end is larger than the hind end (Fig. 3.2a).

With growth, the connections inside the walls of the neural tube become complex, but the tube remains a hollow structure whose walls are thicker in some places than in others, with bulges here and constrictions there. The hollow of the tube in the spinal cord is so small it can hardly be seen; but in the brain it is enlarged in four places, the *ventricles*. The ventricles are filled with *cerebrospinal fluid*, which also surrounds the brain and cushions it within the bony box of the skull (Figs. 3.2c and 3.2d).

The brain consists of the *brain stem*, which is the front end of the original neural tube located inside the skull, and three main out-growths, the cerebellum and the two cerebral hemispheres.

The *cerebellum* coordinates movements made voluntarily with the automatic movements made while the body is routinely busy: for example, walking, standing, and reaching. In coordinating voluntary movements to the body's routine postures, the cerebellum probably does some motor learning. It is an important integrating center for movement, but it does not seem to be involved in thought or in the direction of behavior. The cerebellum does not participate in setting goals, but once a goal is set the cerebellum helps to reach it.

The *cerebral hemispheres*, on the other hand, are essential to mental processes. Their development accounts for the difference between lower and higher animals, and if they are removed, nothing remains to the animal that can be called thought or consciousness. Thinking does not occur in these hemispheres alone or in the cerebral cortex alone: they are necessary to thinking, but they function as a unit with the forward end of the brain stem, which is also necessary for thinking.

Figures 3.2d, e, and f show that the hemispheres are attached to a very small part of the brain stem.

Each hemisphere is really a sort of ballooning out of the neural tube, like a soft spot in an automobile tire, but flattened to fit into the skull. This is seen clearly in the cross-sectional diagram (Fig. 3.2d).

The "balloon" spreads forward and back and up over the top of the brain stem to which it is attached, hiding the place of attachment. In higher mammals, and especially man, the great growth of the outer cortical layer, the *neocortex*, also results in a folding and wrinkling (Fig. 3.3) so that much of the cortex itself is hidden from sight in the *fissures*. The protruding part, between two fissures, is a *gyrus*. Figure 3.3 shows the neocortex visible from the left side of an exposed human

44

FIGURE 3.2. Stages in the development of the central nervous system. In (a) and (b), the tubular form is still evident. The cross-section (a) illustrates how the nervous system develops as a hollow tube, closed at the rostral (head) end. In cross-section (c), at a later stage, the two swellings are the beginning of the cerebral hemispheres; the spinal cord, of which only the end is shown, remains tubular. In (d) and (e), the main divisions of the CNS of an animal such as the rat are illustrated. Cross-section (d) shows the diencephalon A, the midbrain B, the medulla and pons C, and the cerebral hemispheres H. The view from above in (e) shows how the hemispheres F are crowded together around the front end of the neural tube, over the top and towards the tail (caudal) end, so they hide the central tube (A and B) and the cerebellum (D). Finally in (f), the human CNS seen from the right side. Because humans walk erect, the brain stem bends forward at B, and the cortex is deeply wrinkled. The spinal cord is shown embedded within the vertebrae of the spinal column, with the ends of spinal nerves extending forward.

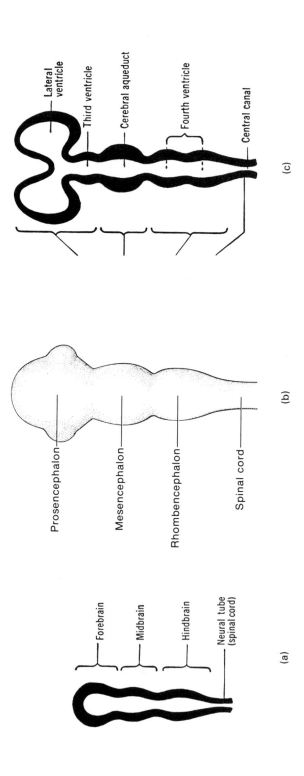

(a)

Forebrain
Midbrain
Hindbrain
Neural tube (spinal cord)

(b)

Prosencephalon
Mesencephalon
Rhombencephalon
Spinal cord

(c)

Lateral ventricle
Third ventricle
Cerebral aqueduct
Fourth ventricle
Central canal

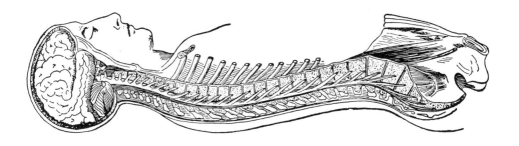

(f)

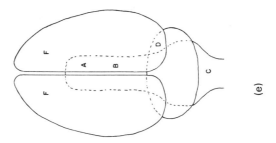

(e)

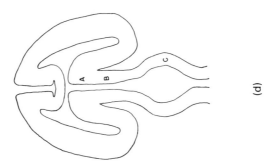

(d)

45

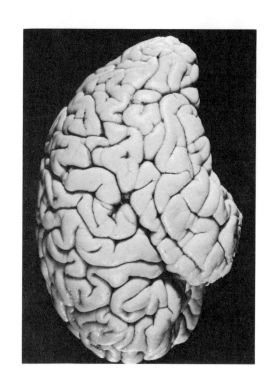

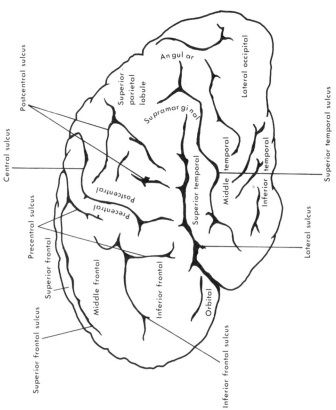

Central sulcus

Postcentral sulcus

Precentral sulcus

Superior frontal sulcus

Superior frontal

Middle frontal

Inferior frontal

Inferior frontal sulcus

Orbital

Precentral

Postcentral

Superior parietal lobule

Supramarginal

Angular

Lateral occipital

Superior temporal

Middle temporal

Inferior temporal

Lateral sulcus

Superior temporal sulcus

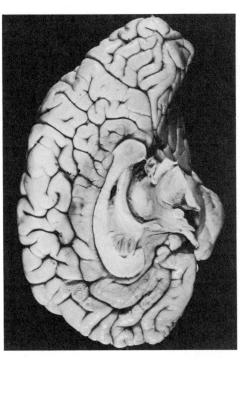

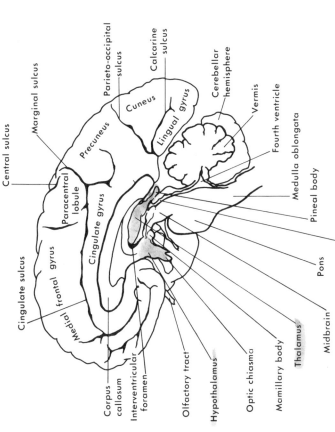

FIGURE 3.3. The top drawing and photograph locate and name the gyrii and sulci on the outer surface of the left hemisphere of a human brain. The bottom drawing and photograph locate and name the gyrii and sulci on the inner (medial) surface of the right hemisphere of the human brain. In both drawings and photographs, the forward direction is to the left. The stippled area in the bottom drawing outlines the brain stem to which the hemispheres are attached, and locates and names the brain stem structures visible in the photograph. (Drawings from Gardner, 1978. Reproduced by permission. Photographs courtesy of Montreal Neurological Institute.)

brain. The front part of the cerebral cortex is the *frontal lobes*, whose known functions include those involved in controlling and motivating organized sequences of behavior. On both sides, the frontal lobes are separated from the rest of the neocortex by the central fissure, a prominent and regular fold in the cortical surface, which runs vertically across both hemispheres.

The rest of the neocortex, dorsal from the central fissure, is divided by anatomists into three separate lobes. The *temporal lobe* is folded forward along the lower edge of the cortex. It is separated by the *sylvian fissure* from the parietal lobe above it. The *parietal lobe* lies behind the frontal lobe, and is separated from it by the central fissure. Both the parietal lobe and the temporal lobe share a common, poorly defined boundary with the *occipital lobe*, which is the most posterior part of the neocortex.

Much of the cortical tissue lies within the large fissures which divide the hemispheres, and within the fissures which separate one lobe from another. The frontal, parietal, and occipital lobes extend deep within the median fissure, and the temporal lobe extends deep within the sylvian fissure, which divides it from the parietal lobe.

The forward end of the brain stem is the *diencephalon*, of which the upper half is the *thalamus*, the lower half the *hypothalamus* (Fig. 3.3).

This is where the cerebral hemispheres are attached to the stem, and all their complex connections with the rest of the brain and spinal cord funnel through this region. The thalamus is a waystation for incoming sensory paths; all sensory input to the cortex (with the single exception of olfactory excitations) is relayed here. The hypothalamus has motor functions rather than sensory ones. It is closely connected to the hemispheres but may be considered as the highest level of reflex organization in the brain stem; the hypothalamus contains control centers for water intake (thirst), temperature regulation, and appetite. The *unconditioned reflex* is subject to some control from thought processes. This does not mean that the hypothalamus is unaffected by the cortex—quite the contrary—but for much of its activity, the cortex does not appear to be necessary.

All parts of the nervous system share in controlling behavior, but the vital contribution to behavior that involves learning and thought is made in mammals by the cerebral cortex and its closely related structures. The brain stem, with its subdivisions, has a complex structure, but it is not necessary to go into this for our purposes. Think of it simply as an elaboration of the front end of the spinal cord. The brain stem and the spinal cord by themselves can regulate many of the bodily functions necessary to life: digestion, circulation, posture, grooming, even some aspects of mating. To do this, they possess very complicated neural interconnections. But the cerebral cortex, its sensory and motor connections, and the closely related underlying parts of the brain are necessary to direct the animal in an adaptive and intelligent way. Although some very simple kinds of learning can occur in an animal without the cerebral cortex, almost all the learning involves neural circuits that include the cortex.

The brain exercises a hierarchical system of control, with the cortex at the highest level. A basic function like walking may be regulated in the brain stem, cerebellum, and spinal cord—that is, the neurons and connections necessary for a person to put one foot ahead of the other, and to stay balanced while doing so, exist in those areas and can function independently there. But the brain stem centers for walking, or eating, or breathing are subject to control from neural circuits involving the cortex—and these circuits can direct, modify, amplify, or inhibit the activity of the lower brain stem or spinal cord centers.

The *unconditioned response* discussed in chapter 2 was the unlearned part of a simple learned behavior called a *conditioned response*. It was illustrated by the example of salivation as an *unconditioned response* produced in the presence of food in the mouth. It is produced as a *conditioned response* following training with the *conditioned stimulus*, which precedes the presentation of food. From this simple example it might be thought that all complicated behavior is built up from separate, small, unconditioned responses linked together by Type-S or Type-R conditioning. Not so. The "stimuli" that precede some responses are complex and are themselves developed through learning. Also, many unlearned behaviors, or "responses," are themselves very lengthy and complicated, involving the successive action of many groups of muscles and glands over long periods of time. Walking is an example, and some aspects of mating behavior is another.

Aimless walking, or mating behavior without a suitable mate, are useless in themselves, but when they are properly directed at the right time they contribute to an animal's well-being. In a sense, these behaviors without learned direction are very complicated unconditioned responses, which can be set off either by the correct unconditioned stimulus or, even without an external stimulus, by direct electrical or chemical stimulation of the nervous system in the brain stem region.

Paths in the nervous system are classified as afferent, efferent, and internuncial. *Afferent* paths conduct from receptors to the CNS, and within the CNS from lower to higher centers; *efferent* paths conduct from higher to lower centers, and from CNS to effectors. *Internuncial* paths connect different points inside the CNS at about the same level.

The terms neuron and synapse are considered in detail in chapter 4.

For the present, suffice it to say that a neuron is a single nerve cell, and a synapse is the place where one neuron makes connection with another; it is the switching point, the place where it is determined what direction a neural "message" will take. You may think of the synapse as a sort of barrier that an excitation must get past. Some barriers are difficult to pass, others easy. There is often a choice: Which of two or more paths will be followed at this point? The difficulty of getting through any one synapse is supposed to change with learning. If neuron A has synapses with B and C, the difficulty of passing them determines whether the neural message traveling along A will follow B or C—or both, or neither. Learning means a change in the direction of messages in the CNS. Because of the all-or-none principle (chapter 4), which means that an excitation, once started in a neuron must sweep down all its branches, switching is not possible halfway along a neural fiber. Therefore, it must occur at the synapse.

Some learning involves the suppression of responses—learning not to do something—or the suppression of a part of a response, changing its pattern. This is done by *inhibitory neurons*, which are found throughout the CNS. Their effect is to block transmission. Inhibition makes the neuron temporarily difficult to excite. Suppression also occurs by strengthening a competing response, for example, learning to turn left, which prevents turning right.

INTO AND OUT OF THE CORTEX

Now let us see how excitations move from the sense organ to the cortex—where we assume that many of the changes take place in the learning of mammals—and out of the cortex to the motor organ. (Lower animals have little cortex or none, so the changes must occur in other structures, but we are concerned with the mammalian brain.)

Except for the sense of smell, each sensory surface (skin, retina, inner ear, etc.) on one side of the body is directly connected with a *cortical sensory area*, specialized for that sense, on the opposite side of the brain. As we will see, there are also connections with the same side, but in general the paths are so laid out that a stimulus event on one side of the body has its main effect on the opposite side of the brain. There are also *motor areas* on each side of the brain, and these too have crossed-over connections, so that the right side of the cortex controls the left side of the body, and vice versa.

To see where these areas lie, consider first Fig. 3.1, which shows the division of the cerebral cortex into *frontal, parietal, temporal* and *occipital* lobes. The division, made by the old anatomists centuries before much was known about how the brain functions, is more or less arbitrary. Some of the dividing lines do not mean much, psychologically or physiologically. However, two of them are important landmarks: the *sylvian fissure* and the *central fissure*. The sylvian fissure is the deep cleft that partly separates the temporal lobe from the rest of the brain. In Fig. 3.4 it can be seen, for example, that the *auditory area* lies on the lower lip of the fissure. Also, the *speech area* can be described roughly as the cortical region surrounding the sylvian fissure on one side of the brain, usually the left side. The central fissure is less easy to see, but equally important. It is the dividing line between the frontal and parietal lobes, and it also separates the motor area, in front, from the somesthetic area, behind (Fig. 3.1).

The *somesthetic* or *somatosensory* area on one side receives sensory messages from all parts of the body on the opposite side (plus some from the same side, but these are fewer and less important). *Somethesis* means "body sensitivity," including sensations of touch, warmth, cold, and itch from the skin; sensations of deep pressure and muscle tension and joint pressure inside the skin; and sensations from the visceral organs. It also includes pain from any of these regions.

Figure 3.1 shows the locus of these specialized areas for rats and for humans. One can see here the kind of structural change that has occurred with the growth and infolding of the cortex in the higher animal. The rat is a smooth-brained animal, and there is no basis for dividing his brain into lobes. His specialized sensory areas are in plain sight. In the human being, with an enlarged and wrinkled cortex, the visual area has practically disappeared into the posterior cleft between the two hemispheres, and the auditory area into the sylvian fissure. The simpler rat's brain shows more clearly than the human brain how these specialized areas relate to one another.

The cortical area specialized for smell lies deep underneath the frontal lobes, in a part of the brain that evolved much earlier than the cerebral cortex. The area specialized for taste is a part of the somesthetic cortex, but less is known about the taste, or gustatory, cortex than is known about the cortex specialized for hearing, touch, and vision. The cortical areas for hearing, touch, and vision are the highly organized end-stations of the afferent paths from the corresponding sense organs. These paths are specialized for rapid conduction to the cortex and for keeping distinct the excitations produced by stimulation of even slightly different points in the sensory surface.

As we have seen, the more highly developed senses are "lateralized," so that the left side of the body is chiefly represented in the right somesthetic area. The right ear, though it conducts to both auditory areas, does so more quickly and strongly to the left; and though both

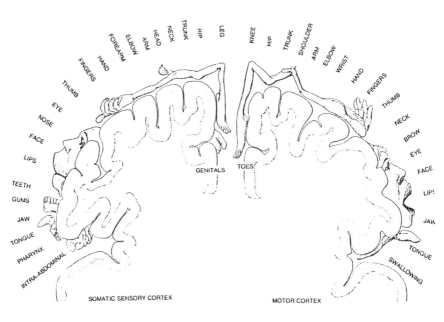

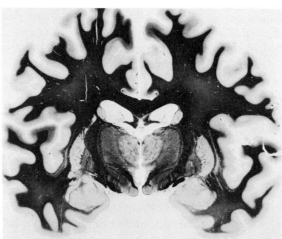

FIGURE 3.4. Drawing and photograph of a cross section through the human cerebral hemispheres near the central sulcus (see Fig. 3.3). The words and illustration on the left side of the drawing indicate the approximate location on the cortex of the main somesthetic projection area from each of the body locations named. The words and illustration on the right side of the drawing indicate the approximate location on the cortex of the main motor cortex for each of the body areas named. (From Nauta, W.J.H. and Fiertag, M., 1979. The Organization of the Brain. *Scientific American, 241*, 88-111, and Geschwind, N. (1979) Specializations of the Human Brain. *Scientific American, 241*, 180-201.)

52

eyes are connected to both visual areas, the connections are such that the left visual field—not the left retina—is represented only in the right visual cortex.

The *retina* is the light-sensitive sensory surface at the back of the eye. In lower vertebrates, the left eye appears to be connected solely with the right hemisphere of the brain, and the right eye, with the left hemisphere; but in mammals there is a peculiar departure from this scheme (Fig. 3.5). The outer (temporal, towards the side of the head) part of each retina is connected with the occipital lobe on the same side (ipsilateral connection); the inner (nasal) part of the retina is connected with the occipital lobe on the opposite side (contralateral connection). In humans, all of the retina to the temporal side of the *fovea* (the central fixation point and the region of clearest vision) is connected to the occipital lobe on the same side, so that nearly half the connections are ipsilateral. Light rays from the left and right visual fields cross as they pass through the lens. All optical events to the left of where the subject is looking, therefore, stimulate the right halves of both retinas and are conducted to the right occipital lobe. Thus, the right side of the brain deals with the left visual field, just as it predominantly deals with the left-sided auditory and somesthetic events, and also controls motor activity on the left side by way of the crossed-over paths from the motor cortex.

Damage to one side of the brain, then, causes both sensory and motor defects on the other side of the body. Left-sided wounds in the motor area of the frontal region produce a right-sided paralysis. An extensive injury is likely to involve also the somesthetic area just behind the motor area (i.e., behind the central fissure; Fig. 3.1), and then the patient will have a *hemianesthesia*, or loss of sensation on the same side of the body as the paralysis. Since a large injury on the left side of the brain is also likely to involve the speech areas surrounding the sylvian fissure, there may also be aphasia—a general disturbance of speech—to a more or less serious degree.

In the auditory system, the connections of one ear with both sides of the brain are good enough so that no deafness may be noticed after brain damage to one of the auditory areas, but the patient will actually have some loss of ability to localize sounds, as well as some other defects that are harder to detect except with special tests. For vision, however, the "lateralization" seems to be complete. Damage to one occipital lobe can produce a *hemianopia*, or half-loss of vision, in which state the patient can see nothing to one side of what he or she is directly looking at. If the wound is on the left side of the head, the patient cannot see things in the right field, and vice versa.

Also of importance is the internal arrangement of the auditory,

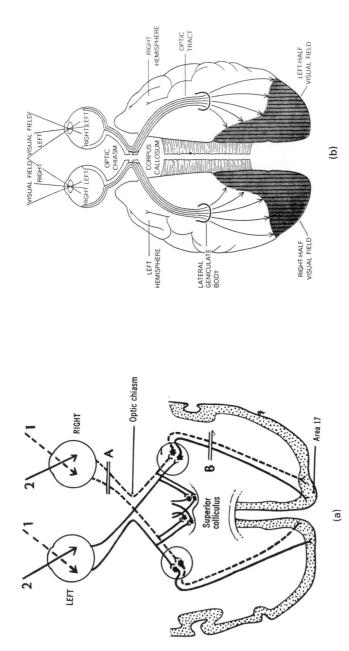

FIGURE 3.5. Visual pathways and the split brain. Figure 3.5a illustrates the normal organization of the visual pathways in the intact human or monkey. The dotted lines trace the visual pathway from right visual field (as seen by the observer) to left visual hemisphere. The solid lines trace the path from left visual field (as seen by the observer) to right visual hemisphere. Some neurons (nerve fibers) in the optic nerves from the eye cross to the opposite (contralateral) side of the brain at the optic chiasm, while other neurons remain on the same (ipsilateral) side. Figure 3.5b illustrates the surgical changes that effectively isolate visual information from the right and left eyes in the right and left hemispheres respectively. The optic chiasm, the corpus callosum and the anterior commissure (not shown) are all cut.

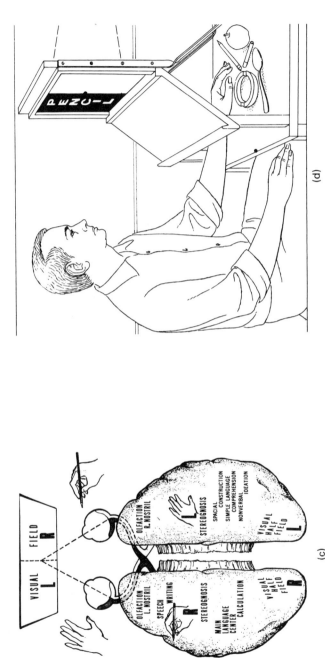

(c)

(d)

Figure 3.5c illustrates the less severe isolation of visual information produced by cutting the corpus callosum (as well as the anterior commissure, not shown), as is done in some cases to relieve severe epilepsy. The result is that information presented in the left visual field is effectively isolated in the right hemisphere, and information presented in the right visual field is effectively isolated in the left hemisphere. Figure 3.5d shows a split-brain patient observing a word flashed briefly to his left visual field (right hemisphere). He will not be able to say the word, because the information conveyed by the word is isolated in his right hemisphere and his speech center is in the left hemisphere. But the limited verbal processing ability of the right hemisphere will enable his left hand (controlled by the right hemisphere) to pick out the correct object—even though the patient cannot explain what object he is selecting, or why! (From Sperry, 1964, 1968. Reproduced by permission.)

55

somethestic, and visual systems. The first principle is "point-to-area" projection of the sensory surface onto the cortex. Each sensory location connects to a particular cortical area, and two adjacent locations on the skin, or on the retina of the eye, or on the basilar membrane of the cochlea (the sensory surface excited in hearing, which is deep inside the skull behind the ear) connect with nearby or with adjacent areas on the cortex.

The second principle is columnar organization by function. In the visual cortex, the neurons that respond to one aspect of the visual environment at one location—horizontal lines, for example—are located together in columns that are perpendicular to the surface of the cortex. These neurons are separated from others that respond to a different aspect at the same location—vertical lines, for example— which are found in another nearby column.

The third principle is duplication of the cortical "point-to-area" maps. In mammals the cortex is organized so that there are between 3 and 5 *different* areas which receive a topographically organized input from the body. At least two different areas organized by pitch and by location of the sound receive input from the ear, and several areas receive spatially organized input from the eyes. The areas from each sense are close together, but each has its own independent organization. These sensory systems are discussed in detail in chapter 12.

Any pattern of sensory excitation is reproduced at least once in the cortex (Figs. 3.1, 3.4, 3.5), although there are changes in orientation and size. In the somesthetic cortex, the legs are at the top, the head at the bottom; "up" in the visual field becomes "down" in the visual cortex. The face and hand areas in the somesthetic cortex are enlarged—which corresponds with the fact that the skin of face and hand is more sensitive, more discriminative than that of upper arms, legs or trunk— and the fovea and the central area of the retina also have an enlarged representation. This makes for some distortion of the cortical patterns as compared with the sensory surfaces. But points that are nearby in the periphery are nearby in the cortex, and the patterns are recognizable despite the distortions.

The motor area similarly has a point-to-point correspondence with the periphery, and the connections are also in parallel. That is, two fibers from the cortex that lead toward a leg muscle lie close together and so can reinforce one another's excitations and produce contraction of the muscle more reliably. The motor cortex is organized in the same way as the somesthetic cortex, with leg movement represented at the top, hand and arm movement below, and face movement (and voice production) at the bottom of the motor strip that lies in front of the central fissure (see Fig. 3.1).

The principal path from the motor cortex to the lower centers is a large bundle of fibers known as the *pyramidal tract.* Not all the motor connections from the cortex are in this tract, and the tract also includes some other connections from the brain stem to the spinal cord, but there are direct connections between the cortex and motor centers of the cord in the pyramidal tract. When the brain of a patient is being operated on under local anesthetic only (so that cutting open the skull does not cause pain and the patient can remain fully conscious), stimulation of the hand area of the motor cortex produces a movement of the hand that the patient cannot prevent. The conduction is highly reliable, and the same effect can be produced repeatedly. The reason seems to be that the connections of the pyramidal tract are in parallel, as noted earlier, and some neurons reach all the way from the cortex to the place where the motor nerve leaves the spinal cord, with no synapse until they near the motor neurons. For example, some neurons run all the way from the cortical leg area at the top of the motor strip down nearly to the end of the spinal cord.

These outgoing, or efferent, connections are made in the *ventral* half of the cord (next to the belly), whereas incoming or afferent connections are made in the *dorsal* half (next to the back), conforming to a general rule that in the spinal cord and brain stem motor functions are ventral and sensory functions are dorsal. You will recall that the predominantly motor hypothalamus is in the ventral part of the diencephalon, the predominantly sensory thalamus in the more dorsal part. The cross section of the spinal cord in Fig. 3.6 shows how the spinal nerve (right) divides near the cord to allow all the afferent fibers to enter the *dorsal root* (top of the diagram) and the efferent fibers to leave by the *ventral root.* The afferent fibers branch inside the cord, making connections with the efferent fibers at this level but also sending branches upward in the cord to connect with higher centers.

LATERAL CONNECTIONS; THE SPLIT-BRAIN EXPERIMENT

We have seen how afferent excitations get to the sensory projection areas of the cortex and how efferent excitations get from the motor cortex to the muscles. Our next question concerns the coordination of the two halves of the cortex. For example, we have separate visual areas, one on each side of the brain: how is it that we do not see the world in two halves but as a single, unified visual field?

The brain has two almost symmetrical sides, and on both sides there are cortical areas mainly responsible for sensory input and motor output. The two sides are closely connected, particularly at the level of

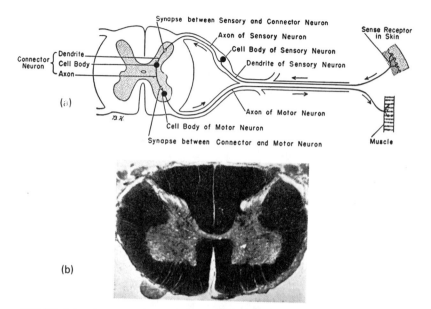

FIGURE 3.6.   Cross sections of the spinal cord. A, diagram of the pathway of an unconditioned reflex; a "connector neuron" is internuncial. (From C. A. Villee, Biology, Saunders.) B, photomicrograph of human cord; the white matter of the cord is stained black so it can be seen under the microscope, the gray matter remains gray, forming the dorsal horns (toward the top) and the ventral horns (bottom). (From Gardner, 1978.)

the cerebral cortex, where the two-sided division is physically most evident. There are large bundles of internuncial neurons that run in paths called *commissures,* connecting many of the corresponding areas on the two sides. The largest of these commissural paths is the *corpus callosum* (Fig. 3.5) which provides a bridge between the two halves of the cortex, connecting visual area with visual area, auditory area with auditory area and so on. The corpus callosum also connects the corresponding parts, so that in the somesthetic cortex the thumb area on one side is connected with the thumb area on the other side, and vice versa. Thus, the left hand *does* know what the right is doing, and the normal subject has one visual world, not two.

This bridge, together with smaller ones in the cortex and at all levels of the brain stem, makes it possible for the organism to have one mind—one set of reaction tendencies, with coordinated perceptions and thought processes—instead of two. Experimentally, however, it is possible to cut the monkey's corpus callosum and enough of the commissures below it so that much of the coordination is lost. This is shown in Figs. 3.5b and 3.5c.

A longitudinal cut can also be made in the *optic chiasm,* the place where the two optic nerves are intertangled, as half the fibers from each eye cross over to the contralateral side. Now the left eye is connected with the left cortex only, and the right eye is connected only with the right cortex. This is the *split-brain preparation* of R. W. Sperry (1964, 1968). The two halves of the brain can now be taught different things without apparent conflict. With the right eye covered, the monkey is trained to choose a square and reject a circle to get food; with the left eye covered, to reject the square and to choose the circle. The second task is learned as easily as if the first—opposite—task had not been learned, and both tasks are remembered as if two different animals had been taught these two things.

It is not too much to say that the split-brain monkey has two separate minds. They are very similar minds, having been connected during growth; they learned the same things and so must be used to reacting in the same way. But it is possible by another brain operation to make one of the minds quite different from the other. Removing the temporal lobe from one hemisphere makes for calmness and a lack of hostility at the approach of the caretaker. When the eye that is connected only with that hemisphere is open and the other eye closed, the monkey appears to be tame; but when the eye connected with the normal hemisphere is open the monkey becomes his normal, unlovely, mean-spirited self (unlovely and mean-spirited toward human jailers, at least). The two monkey minds are now different personalities.

These results are dramatic enough, but even more dramatic results have been obtained by Sperry (1968) and Gazzaniga and Joseph (1978) with patients in whom the corpus callosum had been cut for the relief of epilepsy. As we will see in the next section, the right and left halves of the human brain have different functions; and the result of cutting the corpus callosum is not only two human minds in the same body, but two minds that are different. One mind can talk, for example, and the other cannot, though it has some comprehension of speech. When Sperry *talked* to the patient he was giving information to both minds, but by using the senses of vision or touch he was able to give information to only one of the two minds.

Sperry's experiment demonstrated that an object shown briefly in the left visual field while the patient looks straight ahead can be seen and recognized by the right hemisphere only (Fig. 3.5c). Similarly if a hidden object is put into the left hand, it is only the right hemisphere that receives the information. If the experimenter sets out a number of objects and asks the subject to select a specific one (Fig. 3.5d) the right hand, under control of the (ignorant) left hemisphere, starts to make a wrong choice but the left hand pulls the right hand away and makes the correct choice.

In a further experiment, the patient was instructed to look at the midpoint of a screen onto which two diagrams were flashed briefly: a dollar sign on the left and a question mark on the right. The patient was asked to draw what he saw, using the left hand which was kept out of his sight. The left hand drew a dollar sign. Then, asked what he drew, the patient answered that it was a question mark! The left hemisphere did not know what was drawn, but thought it did; the right hemisphere, which did know, was unable to say so.

In the normal brain, information flows between the two hemispheres through the corpus callosum[3] and the other commissures and unites the separate hemispheric experiences into one which the normal individual can describe to himself and to others by using language. There is some evidence that in the rare case where a human being is born *without* a corpus callosum the right hemisphere adopts the functions normally divided between both hemispheres (Lassonde, Ptito, & Laurencelle, 1984). But when the corpus callosum and other commissures are cut later in life, the two halves of the brain have separate thoughts, separate knowledge, and separate intentions—two minds in one head. The left hemisphere "mind," which talks to the world and to itself, knows its own right-hemisphere mind only by watching and feeling what the right-hemisphere mind *does*. It is hardly better informed about its own right-hemisphere mind than we are.

LATERALIZATION AND DOMINANCE

The human brain has in the course of evolution developed a unique feature: the two halves of the brain are specialized in some of their activities. In most people, the left half of the brain is dominant, controlling speech and the activity of the more skilled right hand. The right half of the brain, however, is specialized for form perception and perception of spatial relations. These differences are not absolute: the right hemisphere has some speech comprehension (Sperry's split-brain patients showed this), and the left hemisphere has some space and form perception, particularly for the recognition of small, complex stimuli (Sergent, 1984). But large injury to the left temporal lobe in most persons produces a severe *aphasia*, a disturbance of speech, with loss of comprehension as well as of speech production, and injury to the right temporal lobe disturbs visual pattern perception and other nonverbal abilities.

---

[3]And the *anterior commissure*, a small but important pathway joining cortical areas concerned with emotions and vision.

Handedness—using one hand more easily for skilled movements and preferring it when a choice is possible—is the most familiar sign of the lateralization of brain function. It is not known in any animal but man. Monkey or chimpanzee, or cat or dog, may have a preferred hand or paw, but this appears to be a matter of learning. Human handedness is familial; that is, it runs in families.

Some 5% to 7% of human beings are left-handed, and 15% to 20% are more or less ambidextrous. It is uncertain how many people have the speech center on the right (perhaps 5% to 10%) or how many have a mixture of left and right localization (like ambidexterity in handedness). But it is definite that speech localization and handedness do not always go together: a left-handed person may have speech localization on the other side—that is, although the preferred hand is controlled from the right side, speech is nevertheless controlled from the left.

Speech that is controlled from the right side may be a result of heredity—just as handedness is hereditary—but it may more often be due to brain injury on the left side at or about the time of birth. In that case, the right half of the brain may take over part or all of the control of speech.

SUMMARY

The nervous system is made up of a very large number of neurons, cells that are tiny in diameter but vary in length from a millimeter or so to, in large animals, a meter or more. A nerve is a bundle of hundreds or thousands of neurons. These connect directly with the spinal cord and brain stem, providing a basis for unconditioned reflexes. Conditioned reflexes involve higher brain centers (especially the cortex, in mammals). The structure of the brain is developed from a hollow tube, and the large hollows that remain are the ventricles. The highest centers are in the two cerebral hemispheres, one on each side of the original tube, with first and second ventricles inside and the cortex like the bark of a tree on the outside.

In human beings, unlike any other animal, there is a specialization of function in the two hemispheres: one, usually the left, containing centers for speech production and control of the preferred hand (on the opposite side); the other specialized for form and space perception and control of the less preferred hand. The two hemispheres are normally coordinated by the corpus callosum, a bridge consisting of fibers that connect corresponding points on the two sides. It is possible, however, to cut this bridge, in which case the functioning of the two sides of the brain may be so independent of one another that there are, in effect, two minds in one head.

GUIDE TO STUDY

Subdividing the brain into different parts is partly arbitrary, because the parts work so closely together, but names for the different parts are necessary so that we can talk about them.

You should be able to name and locate: the four lobes of the cerebrum in a sketch that includes the location of the central and sylvian fissures and the sensory and motor areas.

You should be able to sketch the anatomical relations of the spinal cord, brain stem, cerebellum, diencephalon, and cerebrum, and the relationships of thalamus and hypothalamus.

You should be able to illustrate how the two halves of the two retinas connect with the visual cortex, and how the body is represented in the somesthetic and motor areas.

Be able to explain the split-brain study with monkeys, and the evidence from human patients with a severed corpus callosum, which led Sperry to speak of the patient as having two minds.

NOTES AND GENERAL REFERENCES

Anatomy

Gardner, E. (1978). *Fundamentals of Neurology*. Philadelphia: Saunders. A very good briefer guide to neural anatomy.

Werner, Joan K. (1980). *Neuroscience: A Clinical Perspective*. Philadelphia: Saunders. A well-organized elementary text with a clinical orientation.

The Brain. (1979, December). *Scientific American*. A single-topic issue containing excellent review articles. Of particular relevance to this chapter: "The Neuron," C. F. Stevens (pp. 54–66), "The Development of the Brain," W. M. Cowan (pp. 112–133), and "Brain Mechanisms of Vision," D. H. Hubel & T. N. Wiesel (pp. 150–163).

Speech, Handedness and Cortical Function

Milner, B., Branch, C., & Rasmussen, T. (1964). Observations on cerebral dominance. In A.V.S. de Reuck & M. O'Connor (Eds.), *Ciba Symposium on Disorders of Language*. London: Churchill.

Milner, P. (1970). *Physiological Psychology*. New York: Holt, Rinehart & Winston.

Penfield, W., & Roberts, L. (1959). *Speech and Brain Mechanisms*. Princeton, NJ: Princeton University Press. Classic account of the results of clinical investigations on human patients.

Stuss, D. T., & Benson, D. F. (1984). Neuropsychological studies of the frontal lobes. *Psychological Bulletin, 95*, 3–28.

Split-Brain Preparations and Lateral Dominance

Gazzaniga, M. S., & LeDoux, J. E. (1978). *The Integrated Mind*. New York: Plenum. Reviews experimental studies of language and thought in human split-brain patients.

Lassonde, M., Ptito, M., & Laurencelle, L. (1984). Etude tachistoscopique de la specialisation hemispherique chez l'agenesique du corps calleux. *Canadian Journal of Psychology, 38*, 527–536.

Sergent, J. (1984). Inferences from unilateral brain damage about normal hemispheric functions in visual pattern recognition. *Psychological Bulletin, 96*, 99–115.

Sperry, R. W. (1966). The great cerebral commissure. In J. L. McGaugh, N. M. Weinberger, & R. E. Whalen (Eds.), *Psychobiology* (pp. 240–250). San Francisco: W. H. Freeman. A report of the original split-brain experiments with monkeys.

Sperry, R. W. (1968). Hemispheric deconnection and unity in conscious awareness. *American Psychologist, 23*, 723–733.

CHAPTER 4

The Nervous System in Development and Learning

In chapter 2 we saw that learning takes a number of forms. Some forms, like Type-S or Type-R conditioning, seem easy to describe. These simple forms of learning, in simple animals, are also probably easy to explain. In the invertebrate mollusc *Aplysia*, which has a nervous system containing only about twenty thousand neurons, direct connections between sensory and motor neurons are responsible for both unlearned and learned behavior (Fig. 4.1). However, even a simple learned response in mammals—for example, a CR in which a dog lifts a paw to avoid shock—becomes complicated when we try to understand how it is produced by the dog's larger nervous system. Human perceptual learning and the acquisition of knowledge are even more complicated.

Learning is not the same at all stages of development. Adult learning capacities are so familiar to us that we do not realize how remarkable they are. But these capacities depend on learning in infancy and childhood. We have to learn in order to learn. For example, learning people's names requires having first learned to see their faces as distinct. Learning to use words requires having first learned to hear and to make the distinctive sounds of the language. Childhood learning establishes fundamental motor skills that lay the foundation for adult motor skills. Childhood learning also includes the latent learning from which mental development proceeds. This is why a child who has already learned a good deal before entering school is in the best position to learn schoolwork easily.

In this chapter we study three aspects of the central nervous system that are important for learning. The first is individual neurons and their synapses. The second is neural circuits. The third is neural circuits modified by learning, or *cell assemblies*.

NEURONS

Neurons do not act in isolation, but are organized into circuits. In a circuit, the activity of one neuron or group of neurons influences the activity of another neuron or group of neurons, or even feeds back upon itself to influence its own activity. The circuit properties of *feedback* and *feed-forward* permit sustained and controlled neural activity as a result of brief sensory stimulation. For psychology, the fundamental process in the nervous system is the communication between one neuron and another that occurs at their junction, or *synapse*. Changing the efficiency of communication at the synapse is what produces learning. As a result of repeated sensory stimulation and motor activity, specific neural circuits become established through changes at the synapses between many pairs of neurons. Neural circuits established through repeated experience are called *cell assemblies*, which form the neural basis of learned behavior, perception, and thought. A well-established cell assembly may consist of simple circuits that can excite one another but are not necessarily all active at the same time.

Neuron and Synapse

Many interesting things happen inside a neuron. But as students of psychology, we have time to pay attention only to what happens at the surface of the neuron, the *membrane*, and at the places where one neuron communicates with another: the synapses. Our main interests are (a) how the neuron is stimulated by other neurons to conduct electrical impulses, (b) how electrical impulses are conducted along the neuron, and (c) how the impulses conducted along the neuron stimulate other neurons to conduct impulses. The electrical nerve impulses conducted along neurons eventually stimulate the body's glands to secrete, and the muscles to contract or relax, and so they control behavior.

The synapse is the area where one neuron transmits information to a second (Fig. 4.2). At each synapse, chemical or electrical signals are generated by a neuron. Then they are received by a second neuron,

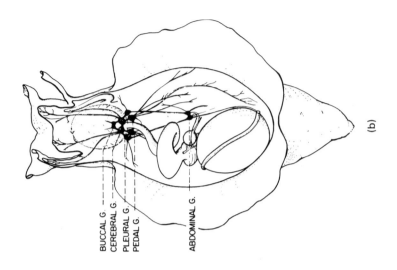

(b)

BUCCAL G.
CEREBRAL G.
PLEURAL G.
PEDAL G.

ABDOMINAL G.

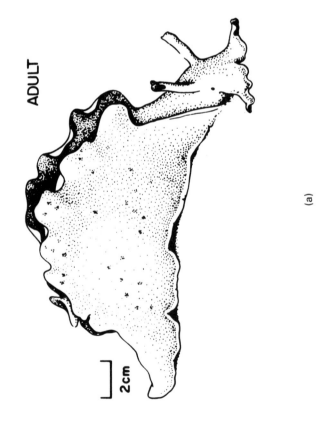

ADULT

2cm

(a)

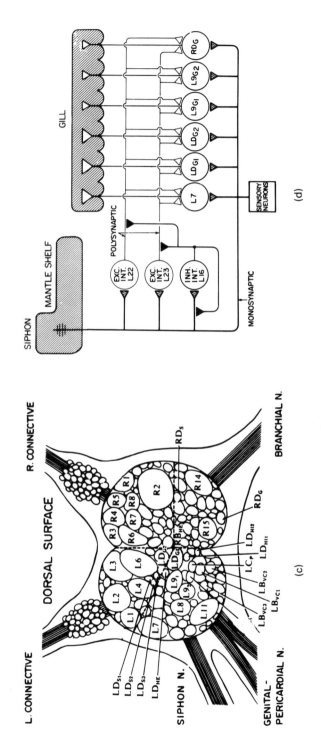

FIGURE 4.1. The nervous system of *aplysia californica*, a marine snail. Figure 4.1a shows *aplysia* opened from the top (dorsal) side to reveal the simple nervous system—a set of ganglia (G), which are collections of nerve cell (neuron) bodies, and nerves which interconnect the ganglia as well as send signals to and receive signals from the organs and muscles. There are about 20,000 neurons in *aplysia*. Figure 4.1c shows the cell bodies within the abdominal ganglion. The size, location and connections of these cells are genetically determined and are the same in every *aplysia*. In (d) is shown the results of an analysis of one function of the abdominal ganglion. The gill withdraws when the siphon mantle shelf is touched. This reaction habituates (stops after repeated exercise). Habituation is the result of changes at the junctions (synapses) between the sensory neurons and the abdominal motor cells L22 and LDg1 through RDg. (From Kandel, E. R. (1979). Cellular insights into behavior and learning. *Harvey Lectures, Series 73.* New York: Academic Press.)

67

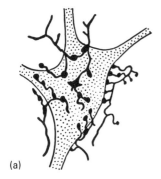

(a)

FIGURE 4.2.   Drawing (a) and electron micrograph (b) of the synapses that functionally connect the axon terminals of one neuron to the cell body or dendrites of another. The axon terminals are the swellings at the ends of the black lines (axons) which impinge on the gray cell body in the drawing (a). A synapse in the electron micrograph (b) is the shaded area in the upper center of the picture between an axon terminal (lower right) and a dendritic process (upper left). (Drawing from Gardner, (1978) *Fundamentals of Neurology.* Philadelphia: Saunders. Micrograph courtesy Prof. A. Beaudet, Montreal Neurological Institute.)

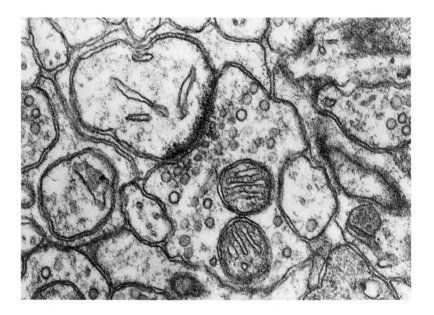

(b)

where they modify its chemical and electrical activity and eventually affect the generation of further chemical or electrical signals in both the second neuron and the original neuron.

Some of the forms taken by neurons are shown in Fig. 4.3 (see also Fig. 4.7). Most neurons, like these, can be thought of as one-way streets. Synapses at the street entrance respond to messages sent from other neurons. Synapses at the street exit transmit chemical or electrical messages to other neurons. The messages from the synapses entering the neuron affect its production of electrical nerve impulses. These impulses then carry information about the messages received from the entrance to the exit, where the impulses modify the production and release chemical or electrical messengers in synapses at the exit.

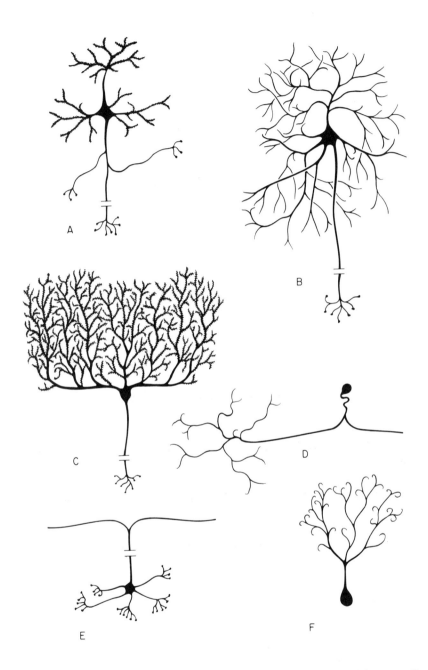

FIGURE 4.3. Examples of the varying morphology of different types of nerve cells. The interrupted processes indicate axons. A, pyramidal cell; B, stellate cell; C, Purkinje cell, D, bipolar dorsal root ganglion cell; E, granule cell; F, amacrine cell. (From Werner, J. C. (1980) *Neuroscience: A Clinical Perspective.* Philadelphia: Saunders. Reprinted by permission.)

In Fig. 4.3, the *dendrites* are the fibrils at the entrance: a neuron may have one, a few, or many dendrites. The *axon* is the fibril that conducts nerve impulses to the exit, away from the *cell body* and towards the *axon terminals*. At synapses on the axon terminal (exits), the nerve impulses stimulate the release of chemicals called *neurotransmitters*. These neurotransmitters are released into the space between adjacent neurons and are absorbed by the directly adjacent dendrites, cell body, or axon terminals of another neuron. The absorbed messengers then influence the transmission of impulses in the other neurons.

Both axon and dendrite are electrical conductors, but they conduct in different ways. The axon works on the *all-or-none principle*. This means that every electrical nerve impulse that is generated at one end of the axon and travels along the axon is equally large and equally fast; the individual impulses are exactly alike. A record of some of these impulses recorded on an oscillograph is shown in Fig. 4.4. Notice the variation in the *rate* of impulses, which is the number of impulses per second recorded at a point on the axon. This variation is the way

FIGURE 4.4. Records of nerve impulses triggered by light falling on part of the eye of an invertebrate animal, *limulus* (horseshoe crab). Relative light intensity is indicated to the left of each record, with the highest relative intensity (1) at the top. The frequency of nerve impulses (the number per second-see the time scale at the bottom) decreases as the intensity of the light decreases. Thus the physical intensity of the light is transduced into the frequency of nerve impulses generated at the sense receptor. (From Miller, W. H., Ratliff, F., & Hartline, H. K. (1979). How cells receive stimuli. In R. Held and W. Richards (Eds.) *Perception, Mechanisms and Models*. San Francisco: W. H. Freeman. Reprinted by permission.)

information is carried along the axon by the nerve impulses. A high rate stimulates the neuron to release a lot of neurotransmitter at its axon terminals, while a lower rate means that less transmitter is released, other things being equal. The nerve impulses are able to carry information effectively for long distances.

In the dendrites and the cell body, unlike the axon, the size of the electrical signal at any point can vary. An electrical signal is first generated at the synapse on the dendrite or cell body, where neurotransmitters are absorbed from an adjacent neuron. The strength of this signal varies with the amount of neurotransmitter absorbed from the other neuron. The strength may also vary with the history of activity at that synapse, which is a mechanism for learning. The strength of the signal also varies with distance from the place where the neurotransmitter was absorbed. This means that a strong signal at the far end of the dendrite (see Fig. 4.3) may be reduced to a weak signal by the time it reaches the cell body. But signals produced in a dendrite or cell body can be cumulative. If several other neurons release transmitter to the synapses at different locations on the dendrite but at about the same time, then the effects of each separate signal generated by the absorbed neurotransmitters will add together, and the combined signal reaching the axon may be large enough to start up a sequence of identical all-or-none impulses that move along the axon towards the axon terminals.

In some neurons, the dendrites both receive and send messages. The signal in the dendrite may thus be strong enough to activate these synapses, resulting in back-and-forth communication between one neuron and another. Synapses in a dendrite can transmit messages to either the axons or the dendrites of another neuron.

The *nerve impulse* is the fundamental process of neural transmission. The important facts for our purposes are summarized as follows:

1. It is a change, both electrical and chemical, that moves across the neuron at a fast but limited speed,[1] the rate varying with the diameter of the fiber (up to 120 meters per second in large fibers, less than 1 msec in the smallest).

---

[1]Students sometimes think that an "electrical" nerve impulse must travel at the same rate as an electrical current. This is not so. In order to understand why not, think of the nerve impulse as an electrical (and chemical) *disturbance* which travels much more slowly. It is something like a thunderstorm that moves across the countryside; electrical currents, in the form of lightning flashes, may travel very fast, but the storm itself moves at a rate of perhaps only 10 to 15 miles per hour, just as a hurricane does, though it consists of 100-mile-per-hour winds. The current flow in and around the nerve impulse may be fast, but the locus of disturbance, the impulse, moves in a relatively slow way along the nerve fiber.

2. This disturbance can set off a similar one in a second neuron, across the synapse, or when it reaches a gland or muscle cell can cause it to secrete or contract.

3. The neuron needs a definite time to "recharge" itself after firing in this way.

4. Immediately after firing, nothing can fire the neuron again; but a little later, before recharging is complete, the neuron can be fired by a strong stimulation.

5. When the neuron fires, its cell body and axon fire completely—the all-or-none principle.

The *absolute refractory period* is the first stage of recharging, about a millisecond in duration (0.5–2.0 msec), when the cell is incapable of firing, no matter how strong the stimulation. The *relative refractory period* follows, in which a strong stimulation can fire the cell; this is about a tenth of a second (100 msec) or longer. The term *limen*, or *threshold*, refers to the strength of stimulation necessary to produce a reaction, so we can say that in the absolute refractory period the limen (or threshold) is infinitely high and that it is higher in the relative refractory phase than when the cell is resting. For large cells the refractory period is shorter and the resting limen is lower—that is, large cells can be re-excited sooner, and are more easily excited, than small ones.

What are some of the elementary consequences of these facts? Any nerve or bundle of neurons is made up of fibers varying in size, and hence in speed of conduction. If, therefore, a strong stimulus fires all the neurons in a given bundle, the "volley" of impulses starts out at the same time but is dispersed, in time of arrival, at the other end. A short, sharp stimulation of the foot, for example, does not produce an equally brief excitation at the level of the spinal cord, but a scattering of impulses extending over an appreciable part of a second. (The dispersion in time is still greater at the level of the cerebrum.) Next, the refractory period means that the fastest frequency of firing in a single fiber is of the order of 1000 per second, since it takes about a thousandth of a second (1 msec) for the fiber to recover each time.

The logical consequences of the all-or-none principle are quite clear. A strong stimulation does not produce stronger impulses in a fiber. It can, however, fire the cell more frequently, by catching it earlier in the relative refractory period. Thus, *intensity* of stimulation is translated into *frequency* in the CNS. Furthermore, because different afferent cells have different limens, a stronger stimulation excites more cells, which again means an increased frequency of firing. Hence, the all-or-none principle applies to a single impulse in a single fiber, but not to the repetitive firing of the fiber nor to a bundle of fibers.

The diagrams of Fig. 4.5 illustrate the nerve impulse. One new term must be introduced: ions. *Ions* are either atoms, molecules, or parts of molecules that have an *electric charge*. The electric charge results from the ion's having an unequal number of electrons—each carrying one unit of negative electric charge—and protons, each carrying one unit of positive electric charge. When there are more electrons than protons in the ion, the ion has a negative charge; when there are more protons than electrons in the ion, the ion has a positive charge.

The neuron, and the fluid between the neurons, both contain ions. In the resting state there are relatively more negative ions inside and positive ions outside the neuron. The ions are separated by the cell membrane, which allows some ions to pass through, but not others. This is an unstable equilibrium: a very slight electrical disturbance in the neighborhood of the membrane can upset the balance and allow the positive ions on the outside to pass through the membrane. When this happens, the outer surface of that part of the neuron becomes negative, an electrical effect referred to as the "action potential." The polarization (i.e., the separation of positive and negative ions by the membrane) has disappeared, and depolarization spreads by disturbing the equilibrium of the region next to it, so that it travels along the axon. No sooner is the equilibrium upset, however, than the cell begins to restore it by moving the positive ions outward, a process that takes altogether about 1 msec; that is, the nerve impulse lasts about 1 msec at any one point in the cell (0.5 msec in large fibers, 2.0 in small, Fig. 4.6).

The entire process is actually more complex than we have described. The positive ions moving inward are sodium ions, but other positive potassium ions are moving outwards, to restore the resting potential, while the sodium ions are moving inward. The all-or-none action of the axon makes possible a rapid conduction to distant points. A further contribution to this end is made by the *myelin sheath*, a fatty covering surrounding many nerve fibers (this is what makes the white matter white). At intervals of a millimeter or so there are gaps in the sheath (the "nodes"); the electrical potential at one gap produces an excitation at the next gap, starting what is really a second nerve impulse at that point. The myelin sheath over the intervening part of the fiber appears also to prevent the impulse from occurring in the internodal region. Thus, the impulse does not travel continuously along the fiber, but jumps from node to node at a faster rate perhaps than continuous travel would permit.

When Are Neurons Active?

The neuron is a living cell and, being alive, must be active. If it is not excited from outside, it tends nonetheless to fire *spontaneously*. That

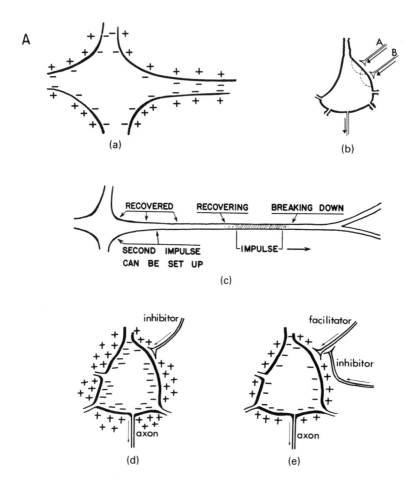

FIGURE 4.5. Simplified outline of the electrical activity in neural impulse transmission. Figure 4.5a indicates the usual resting state of the neuron cell body: the cell body has a negative potential relative to the extracellular fluid outside. In (b), two excitatory axons impinge on the cell body. Each axon secretes chemical neurotransmitters that reduce the potential difference between the cell body and the extracellular fluid. They *depolarize* the cell membrane. If enough depolarizing neurotransmitter is released in batches close enough together in space and time, then a sudden spatially localized reversal of the cell membrane potential will begin in the cell body and be transmitted down the axon (c). More than one impulse can occur at the same time in the same neuron, because a second impulse can be started in the "recovered" region as soon as the first impulse has moved along the axon fiber and the cell-body has returned to its normal negative polarity. Some axons prevent, rather than produce, neural transmission in other neurons. The neurons that prevent transmission are called inhibitory neurons. They work in either one of two ways: by directly increasing the negative polarity of the cell body (d), or by preventing a facilitatory axon from having its excitatory effect (e).

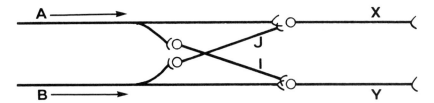

FIGURE 4.6. A neural circuit illustrating *feed-forward* and *inhibitory rebound*. Neurons A and B directly excite neurons X and Y, respectively. A inhibits Y through inhibitory interneuron I, and B inhibits X through inhibitory interneuron J. As a result of these feed-forward connections and as a result of changes over time in the effectiveness of neural transmission at the various synapses, changes in the firing rates of A and B can amplify changes in the firing rates of X and Y.

is, the cell stores up energy received from the blood stream until a point is reached at which the membrane polarization breaks down—so the cell fires. Some neurons will eventually die if not excited from outside (see chapter 7, Fig. 7.3). It is true, however, that in normal circumstances the cells of the brain are always active, as shown by the EEG or by recording electrodes inserted in the brain. The activity continues even in sleep, although in sleep the pattern of activity changes (see chapter 10, Fig. 10.2).

Communication Among Neurons

When nerve impulses travel down on the axon to the region of the axon terminals, they trigger the release of messengers at the synapses. Some of these messengers are ions, which move through synaptic *gap junctions* from the axon terminal of one neuron into the adjacent neuron, where they produce an electrical signal.

Most of the synaptic messengers are chemical *neurotransmitters*, which are produced in the axon terminals of the neuron, and are stored in tiny sacs called *synaptic vesicles*. When a train of nerve impulses reaches the axon terminal, some of the vesicles are emptied into the synaptic cleft between the axon terminal and the dendrite or cell-body of an adjacent neuron. The neurotransmitter then passes through the synapse into the adjacent neuron, where it changes the membrane potential. Depending on the type of synapse, the neurotransmitter either decreases the membrane potential (at an excitatory synapse) or increases the membrane potential (at an inhibitory synapse).

The effect of the neurotransmitter on the adjacent neuron accumulates over a short period of time. If enough excitatory synapses are activated, the membrane potential will be reduced enough to generate a nerve impulse. But if inhibitory synapses are activated, the membrane potential is increased, or the membrane is *hyperpolarized*, which prevents generation of a nerve impulse. Since a neuron can be contacted by both excitatory and inhibitory synapses (as many as 80,000 different synapses on the dendrites and cell-body of a cortical neuron), the net effect depends on the balance between the activity at the excitatory and inhibitory synapses over a short period of time.

The neurons produce a variety of different neurotransmitters, but the axon terminals of most individual neurons produce only one kind of neurotransmitter. Depending on the particular synapse (and the other neuron beyond it) the effect of the neurotransmitter may be excitatory or inhibitory. Each individual neuron is responsive to only a few of the many excitatory or inhibitory neurotransmitters which are produced by other neurons. In this way, the nervous system is divided by the neurotransmitters into separate systems. Adjacent groups of neurons are separate if they do not interact either anatomically or chemically. Different systems of neurons, responding to different neurotransmitters, have been related to different aspects of behavior. Some differences among neural systems with different neurotransmitters are discussed in chapter 10.

Summation

One nerve impulse delivered to a synapse is not enough to fire the adjacent postsynaptic neuron. For reliable activation of a neuron it is necessary that the impulses sum over time, or over more than one of the many synapses on the average neuron. *Summation* in behavior is the reinforcement of the action of one stimulus by that of another. If one touch on the skin or one slight sound or one glimmer of light is not enough to affect behavior, two together may sum their effects and be able to do so. As we have seen, the strong stimulus cannot produce bigger nerve impulses, but it can excite more impulses per second, which sum and are more likely to reach the limen of behavioral response.

At the synapse, a single axon, delivering an impulse to another neuron, produces a slight depolarization that is not usually extensive enough to result in firing. Two such axons side by side, however, will produce a greater area of depolarization (Figs. 4.6, 4.7) which is more likely to be effective. Especially with continued rapid firing, the postsynaptic neuron must be relatively refractory, and the summation of impulses from a number of presynaptic axons will be necessary if the firing is to be maintained. Since the impulses must arrive close together in time in order to sum, perhaps within a millisecond or so, timing becomes very important in neural functioning.

Fatigue and Inhibition

Fatigue in the neuron is, first, the refractory period. The absolute refractory period lasts only for the duration of the impulse at one point, about 1 msec. During the relative refractory period, the cell can be fired again, but full recovery takes from 80 msec (in large fibers) to a second or so (in small ones). Second, a cell that fires at a rapid rate begins to have a supply problem. The sodium ions that move inward when the cell fires are not excreted completely for some time, and so accumulate when the cell is continuously active. Full recovery may take an hour or more.

Inhibition occurs in two ways. In one way, the postsynaptic neuron is made harder to fire; in the other way, the presynaptic impulse is made less effective. In the first mechanism, an inhibitory neuron produces *hyperpolarization*—the opposite of depolarization—in the postsynaptic neuron, which makes it harder to fire. In the second, an excitatory neuron delivers a weak excitation to the presynaptic axonal ending. This produces a partial depolarization of the ending, so that when a normal impulse arrives its effect is diminished and the postsynaptic neuron does not fire.

Many neurons in the spinal cord (Renshaw cells) are specialized for inhibition, and many of the short-axon cells found in the brain have the same function. They are of the highest importance in learning, for learning is the elimination of wrong or irrelevant activity as well as the establishment of the right activity. Learning must be both the formation of new associations and the elimination or suppression of previously existing ones that interfere.

Feed-Forward

Central nervous system activity varies over time because of the interaction of excitatory and inhibitory neurons. The simple set of neurons pictured in Fig. 4.6 can produce a complex pattern of neural activity. The pattern is called *inhibitory rebound*. If neuron A is firing faster than neuron B, then neuron X will be active and neuron Y will be inhibited. A excites X directly, and inhibits Y indirectly because A excites the inhibitory interneuron I. Because the rate of activity is higher, neurotransmitter is used up faster in neurons X and I than in neurons B and J.

Let us suppose that because the stimulation to each neuron has equalized, the firing rates of neurons A and B also equalize. The neurotransmitters in A and I have been used up, while the neurotransmitters in B and J have not. Thus, the firing rate in B will now produce a

FIGURE 4.7. The organization of the cerebral cortex. Figure 4.7a is a photomicrograph of a section of cat cortex, giving an idea of the complexity of interconnections— even though about only one neuron in sixty is visible using the tissue staining technique that produced this slide. (From D. A. Sholl. *Organization of the Cerebral Cortex.* London: Methuen.) Figure 4.7b is a drawing of the interconnections among an even smaller proportion of human cortical cells—perhaps one in 1,000. Re-entrant (feedback) paths are visible in this drawing and are schematized in B' (From Lorente de No. In J. F. Fulton, *Physiology of the Nervous System.* New York: Oxford University Press.) Figure 4.7c is a schematic diagram of feedback relations among neurons actually observed by Lorente de No. The entering axon excites the dendrites of four neurons, A, B, C, and D. Of these, B and C send impulses out of the system to excite other systems, but impulses from A and D are delivered only within the system itself. A-B, B-E and B-E-E' form closed circuits that can hold excitations and cause B to continue delivering impulses outside the system. (After Beach, Hebb, Morgan, & Nissen, 1960; see p. 467. Adapted by permission.)

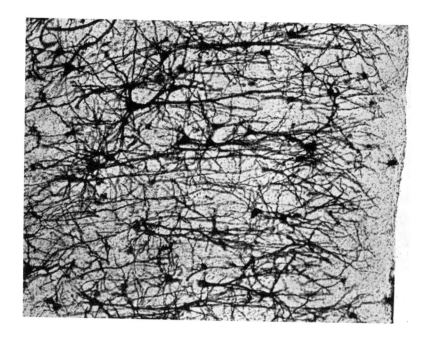

(a)

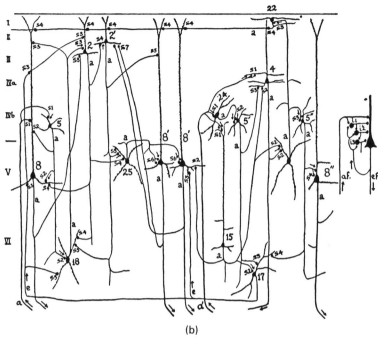

(b)

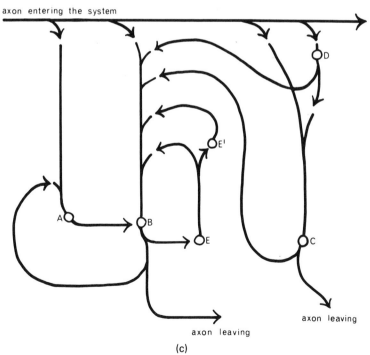

axon entering the system

axon leaving

axon leaving

(c)

79

stronger excitatory effect on J and Y than will the same firing rate in A. As a result, neuron B will fire neuron Y and inhibit neuron X, even though input to A and B is the same. The conclusion is that when the rate of firing in A has been greater than the rate in B for some time, a return to balance between the firing rate of A and B will lead to a rebound in favor of the neural pathway producing excitation of Y by B. This is an example of a *feed-forward circuit*, where the actions of neurons at one point in a neural circuit feed forward to influence the activity of neurons at a later point in the circuit. The psychological consequences of neurotransmitter exhaustion and rebound are seen in the *perceptual aftereffects*—about which more will be said in chapter 12.

Feedback

In chapter 3, it was said that adjacent small areas of the brain's cortex represent adjacent sensory areas or adjacent motor areas of the body. Also, larger cortical areas are organized into units having some common function, like responding to input from one eye or to movement of the hairs on the skin.

Studies of patients undergoing brain surgery to cure epilepsy show that brief electrical stimulation of an area of the sensory or motor cortex leads to either a localized movement of some part of the body, or to an apparently isolated sensory experience, whether visual, auditory, or tactile. However, stimulation of the exposed *temporal cortex* in humans leads to longer sequences of multiple sensory experiences and which last for a few seconds at least. Thus, there is a contrast between two effects of electrical stimulation of the exposed cortex; in one case, a momentary sensation or movement, in the other, sustained multisensory experience. What neural mechanism organizes individual neurons into systems which can maintain activity long enough to correspond to this sustained experience? The mechanism is feedback.

Feedback means that the present output of a system has an effect on its output at a later time. In the case of a single neuron (Fig. 4.7), the neuron's output activity, passing through a series of other cells, feeds back upon the neuron to facilitate the neuron's input, to inhibit a cell that might itself otherwise inhibit the neuron, and so to insure the continuity of activity for longer than would have happened if the output of the cell had not entered a feedback loop. This is called *positive feedback* because it increases the output of the system; in this case, the output of the single cell. When the microphone of a public address system picks up the amplified voice from its loudspeaker and recycles it through the amplifying system, there is uncontrolled positive feedback, and the system responds for a longer time, and more loudly, than it would have without the feedback. Positive feedback sustains or increases the activity in a circuit of cells.

If the output of a single neuron is fed back in another way, the activity of the system will be reduced rather than enhanced. For example, in Fig. 4.7c, if the neural output activates an inhibitory cell, then the system will tend to return rapidly to its resting state in response to an input which is above the resting level. This is called *negative feedback*. Negative feedback inhibits, or limits, neural activity in a circuit.[2]

NEURAL CIRCUITS

Much of the CNS is filled with neural paths that lead back into themselves. Figure 4.7b shows this in schematic form. It is a drawing by R. Lorente de No, the distinguished neuroanatomist and physiologist to whom we owe most of our original knowledge of these matters. Figure 4.7 is a schematization of another such drawing, allowing the closed paths to be seen more clearly. Figure 4.7a shows the kind of photomicrograph from which such drawings were made; it gives some idea of the complexity of the structures we are discussing. Remember that Figs. 4.7b and c are only sketches of circuits that are actually much more complex.

Many of these closed paths are completed in the cortex, but others are corticothalamic, running from cortex to thalamus and back to cortex; and some of them must similarly involve other subcortical structures, such as the hippocampus, which, in the human being lies inside the tip of the temporal lobe and, as we will see (chapter 6), appears to play an important part in memory.

Well-defined neural feedback circuits have been found in the olfactory bulb. The sensory cells for smell are located in the olfactory mucosa of the nose. When these cells are stimulated by the appropriate chemical in the air, they fire; and because the neurons in the olfactory bulb are arranged in a recurrent circuit that provides a positive feedback loop, the firing of the sensory neurons is sustained, provided the

---

[2]Feedback is really a comparison process. The output level of a system is compared with a preset goal; if the output deviates from the goal, positive feedback increases the deviation, negative feedback decreases the deviation. Another way to describe feedback is to say that the feedback regulates the input; if the input deviates from a goal, the system output acts to reduce the deviation (negative feedback) or to increase it (positive feedback). See Powers (1978) for a good explanation of the role of feedback in psychological systems.

smell is one the animal has been conditioned to expect. But if the same smell is unexpected, the stimulus to the olfactory sense cells will not set off a positive neural feedback loop. Instead, the firing is inhibited. The activity in the local loop is thus under the control of the activity of other brain centers, which are responsive to whether or not the smell being recorded in the neural circuit was expected.

This example illustrates not only the sustaining effect of positive feedback on the activity produced by a sensory stimulation, but also the interaction of the local neural loop with influences from the rest of the central nervous system, which carry information about the effect this sensory stimulation has previously had on the animal.

The cortex and its main subcortical sensory connection, the thalamus, are well organized to provide neural circuits. A good example is the *visual occipital cortex*. Through the approximately 2 mm depth of the cortex there are six cell layers, each with a different function. The inputs to the cortex from the thalamus arrive in the middle layer. Other layers contain small cells that interconnect with each other in recurrent patterns like those in Fig. 4.7. Some cells leave the cortex and return to the thalamus. The top layer of cells is mainly a network of dendrites allowing cells of adjacent layers to interact. A section through the thickness of the cortex shows inputs from and outputs to subcortical centers as well as vertical layers of cells that can interact with one another through their axons and dendrites and between which the synaptic changes associated with learning can occur.

What each visual cortex cell does is explained in detail in chapter 12. For the moment let us say simply that the visual cortex is highly specialized to analyze the visual environment and much of this organization depends on the inherited patterns of interconnections among cells. The potential anatomy for neural circuits is established at birth. Given normal development, the efficiency of particular circuits can change as a result of the learned changes in efficiency of conduction at the synapse.

Throughout this book, reference is made to systems of cells that, through experience, have come to provide feed-forward or feedback. These systems are called *cell assemblies*,[3] efficient circuits that develop from repeated use, but they depend at first on the fixed neural connections that in a normal animal are largely dependent on the evolutionary development of the species.

SYNAPTIC CHANGES IN LEARNING

Now we come to the crucial question: What happens in the brain when something is learned? The answer is that we do not know for certain.

We know a great deal about the end results of learning and the conditions under which it occurs, but the fine details of the process in the brain are still unclear. Let us see if, from our knowledge of neuron and synapse, we can arrive at a theory to account for the phenomena we do understand.

There is a long-standing theory (James, 1961) that when two brain processes are active at the same time, they tend to make permanent connections with each other. This idea has been used to explain the association of ideas and to explain sensory associations, and there is good reason to think that something of the kind does happen. Figure 4.8 shows what is implied about individual neurons at the synapse. Two brain circuits, A and B, are excited at the same time. These may be primitive, unlearned neural circuits, or they may have been previously formed as cell assemblies by a neural process like the following. As an example of the observable conditions that might stimulate these circuits, remember the sensory preconditioning experiment (Fig. 2.8) in which a light is paired with the presentation of a sound. A is the neural circuit activated by the sound; B the circuit activated by the light. A neuron, A, happens to be one whose axon ends at B, a neuron that is part of circuit B. The impulses in A then release neurotransmitter from A to B while B is being fired, as a part of circuit B. Our theory states that when this happens, a learned connection is formed between A and B. We can express this theory in general terms:

When an axon of excitatory neuron X releases neurotransmitter to neuron Y while neuron Y is firing, some change takes place at the synapse between X and Y, which makes future activity in X more effective at firing Y.

We have no conclusive explanation for the nature of this change. When transmission at the synapse becomes more effective for learning, it may be because more neurotransmitter is accumulated in presynaptic axon X, or because the neurotransmitter released by X becomes more effective in stimulating Y to fire when it is absorbed by Y, or both.

The mechanism in Fig. 4.8 has been diagrammed for only one pair of neurons, A and B. But when we talk about an association between two perceptions (e.g., between sound and light in the sensory preconditioning experiment) we know that many contacts are required—a single pair of neuron contacts between circuits A and B could not reliably excite the entire B circuit. The highly organized anatomy of the sensory cortex means that a stimulus like light or sound does activate many neurons, and the extensive interconnections between axons and cell bodies of cells that extend through both the cortex and the subcortex insure that the circuit overlap required for one circuit to excite another is present.

For excitation, our theory says: if excitatory neuron X, in contact

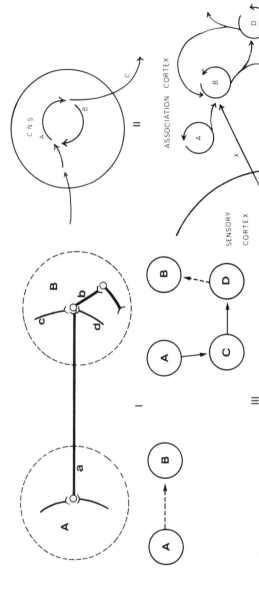

FIGURE 4.8. Schematic illustrations of some of the principles of cell assembly activity. I shows a mechanism for establishing synaptic connections. A is a group of active neurons, of which only one (a) is shown completely. B is a second group of neurons active at the same time, of which only two are shown completely. Since a and b are active together and an axon of a is close to b, a will become connected with (better able to facilitate) b. II illustrates a re-entrant, closed or reverberatory pathway. When incoming neural impulses excite A, A excites B, which again excites A, and so on. The continuing excitation may then be transmitted to other CNS systems, or to motor organs, via C. III illustrates direct and indirect cell assembly associations. On the left, some axons from neurons in group A end close enough to neurons in group B so that a direct A-B connection can be established when the two are active together. On the left, no axons from A approach B, but among A's many connections (associations from common experience) is one with C, which is connected with D, whose axons do reach B and thus make a connection A-C-D-B possible. IV illustrates selective transmission from the sensory cortex. X, Y and Z are sensory transmissions; A, B and C are closed systems (cell assemblies). A is active before the sensory input occurs; B, C and D become active after the input occurs; E and F are inactive. In these circumstances, excitation X would have its effect, and then Y, but Z would not have an effect.

84

with Y, is active and Y fires, X becomes more likely to excite Y. The learned effects of inhibition are just as important for our theory as the effects of excitation. For inhibition we propose a similar principle. When an axon of inhibitory neuron X releases neurotransmitter to neuron Y while Y is inactive, some change takes place at the synapse between X and Y that makes future activity of X more likely to inhibit Y. In other words, the learning has strengthened the inhibitory effect of X on Y.

To complete our account of what happens at the synapse during the course of learning, some mention of reinforcement and consolidation is necessary. These terms are defined and discussed at length when we deal with memory in chapter 6. Now we will say only that the synaptic changes of learning are temporary until they have had a chance to become consolidated. Consolidation takes time (up to an hour) and reinforcement may promote consolidation.

Early Learning

The preceding sections suggest why mental growth depends on stimulation from the environment. The stimulation has two effects. One is to produce perceptual learning, which enables the young animal to perceive better and develops the capacity for images and ideas. The development of cell assemblies then provides the basis for making new associations among cell assemblies once they are formed.

Perceptual learning occurs when common events in a baby's experience—the sight of a face or a hand or the milk bottle, the sound of a mother's footsteps, the taste of milk, the touch of a finger on cloth—repeatedly excite groups of neurons in the cortex. The neurons that are excited when one of these things happens are not the same every time, but a common core of neurons is excited every time. The core neurons therefore tend to become connected with one another in a single system, the cell assembly. These neurons are in feedback circuits (Figs. 4.7, 4.8); therefore, the system can continue to be active after outside stimulation has ceased. Also, the system may be excited by another system, instead of by the sensory event that originally formed it. While it is being excited by its own proper sensory stimulation, the activity of the cell assembly is perception; if it is active after the sensory stimulation has ceased, or if it is excited by another cell assembly rather than an external stimulus, the activity is a mediating process. Mediating processes include the experiences of thought, imagery, and memory.

As the cell assembly continues to be activated, its organization becomes more precise and well-defined. This improvement in organization means increased clarity and distinctiveness of perception; but since it is also laying a basis for ideation, we can think of this as *conceptual* learning too.

A word should be said about the increase in the distinctiveness of perception. At an early stage in learning, many of the cortical neurons that are excited by, say, seeing a face must be different from one time to another, so it would make little difference to the baby's behavior if he sees the same face a second time, or a different face. But the common core of neurons excited by one face is different from the core excited by the second face, and if both faces are seen often, the two core groups will be organized in two assemblies, becoming more distinct as organization goes on. For behavior, the existence of two distinctive cortical processes—two different assemblies—means that two different responses become possible. Inhibition presumably plays a part in this process, tending to suppress firing by neurons that are not part of the assembly and thus making the perception more clear-cut and distinctive.

The infant's world of ideas and objects is very different from ours. We take for granted that things exist in one place at a time, remain in place when they are hidden, and can be moved from one place to another. But these properties of the world of objects develop gradually in the infant's experience.

Studying infants' perceptions and ideas is challenging work. It requires careful observation and recording of such behavior as reaching, grasping, sucking, head turning, eye movements, breathing, heart rate, and signs of happiness or discomfort. These are the infant's reactions to the world. We can learn something of the infant's world by varying the environment and recording the resultant changes, or lack of change, in the infant's behavior.

Two-week-old infants react with pleasure to the sound of mother's voice coming from an image of mother's face. But they are upset when they experience an artificial combination of mother's face and a stranger's voice. Clearly, 2-week-old infants have learned to expect a familiar voice from a familiar face. On the other hand, they are not upset by three simultaneous images of mother! Although they have come to associate a familiar voice with a familiar face, 2-week-old infants have not yet learned to associate only one place with a familiar face. Five-month-old babies are upset by three simultaneous images of their mother, but they are not upset by three simultaneous images of two strangers and one mother. Five-month-old infants expect both only one place and a familiar voice to be associated with a familiar face.

The Swiss psychologist Jean Piaget (1953) observed that infants younger than 4 or 5 months stop reaching for an attractive object once it is hidden under something else, even though the hiding was done in the infant's full view. But infants older than 5 months continue to look for the missing object; they now demonstrate that they have the idea of the object without the stimulus of the object itself. Their idea is imperfect, however; a 5-month-old infant who earlier found an object hidden under a cloth will look for the object under the cloth again, even after watching the object being hidden under a newly introduced pillow! Consistent expectations about what actually happens in the world of visible objects develop slowly in the infant: the details of this development are still being worked out.

T.G.R. Bower (1982) has extended this type of experiment to show that infants younger than 4 months old do not respond to the visual characteristics of an object. They identify an object by its movement. Hence, an object can change its appearance in mid-trajectory without exciting an emotional reaction. At about 4 months, babies recognize object qualities, and object visual transformations elicit interest or surprise.

The variety of CRs that can be established in a baby's first weeks of life is limited, and in part the reason may be the absence of a network to provide for direct associations (Fig. 4.8). (We know that indirect association is important at least for adult learning, in everyday life as in the laboratory. In the laboratory, for example, a subject with the task of associating "rock" and "run" in a long list of paired associates tied this particular pair together in memory by thinking, "Throw rocks at a dog and he runs.") The characteristics of learning change greatly as a child grows—there is, for example, no immediate one-trial learning in early infancy. This must be due partly to the fact that the brain is not fully developed, but part of the reason also seems to be that learning takes place increasingly against a broad background of common associations.

CELL ASSEMBLIES: THE BASIS OF THOUGHT

Another way of putting what has just been said is that the development of cell assemblies, and the resulting thought processes, are what transforms infant-style learning into adult-style learning. Though we do not know exactly how cell assemblies work, there is a good deal of empirical evidence to indicate that they exist and that they are the basis of thought (Hebb, 1968).

Cell assemblies can be excited by other cell assemblies, in the total absence of the sensory events that originally established the systems. Cell assemblies thus meet the requirements of brain processes corresponding to ideas. The very essence of an "idea" is that the experience occurs in the absence of the environmental event it corresponds to. You need not have an elephant present to think about elephants, and the discomfort of wet clothes in the rain can be imagined long after your clothes and skin are warm and dry.

Cell assemblies also explain latent learning. Latent learning occurs when learned associations are formed among cell assemblies, although no motor behavior occurs in relation to either assembly. For example, successive presentations of sound and light activate the cell assemblies for sound and light, even though the animal experiencing the two stimuli presented together is not actively responding to either. Not all learning involving cell assemblies leads to immediate action; behaving and learning can be separated. Motivation, the study of what transforms learning into behavior, is considered in chapters 10 and 11.

ATTENTION AND CONCENTRATION

The selectivity of brain response is, from a psychological point of view, *attention* or *set*, to which we will return in the following chapter. Before we conclude the present account of the development of perception and thought, there is one further point that is suggested by what we know of the anatomy and physiology of the brain.

The human brain is as large as it is so that human beings can learn so many different things. Its size also means that there are many more neurons in the brain than are needed for learning any one thing. As we have already seen, neurons fire spontaneously if they are not being kept active. The many neurons that are not necessary for a learning task may, when the task is prolonged, become active anyway, producing other thoughts besides the ones that concern the present task. This is the student's problem of attention and "concentration": to respond to, and think about, only the subject matter at hand. How is it possible?

First, the cell assemblies that are active presumably tend to inhibit random activity by other neurons, and this inhibitory action may become more and more effective as mental growth goes on and assemblies become better and better organized. Young children have a notoriously short attention span, which does increase as they grow older. Second, the span of attention is longer for the more intelligent subjects at any particular age, provided the topics they attend to have many facets to think about. We may suppose that the more intelligent person has developed more cell assemblies, which would provide more inhibition to control the random extra activity in the brain. What the full story is here we do not know, but it seems that the "interesting" task— the one that is easy to concentrate on—involves both complexity and some level of arousal (chapter 10). The complexity makes it possible to find different ways of thinking about the material, making more assemblies active. Another way to add to the interest of a dull learning task, as we will see in the discussion of study method in chapter 6, is to make the learning active, though it is not clear theoretically why this should contribute to the inhibition of the random extra activity of the brain cells that are for the moment unused.

SUMMARY

This chapter provides a short account of what is known about the functioning of the single neuron, what is known about neural circuits, more theoretically, what is known of the changes that occur at the synapse in learning. An important part of the process is inhibition, eliminating irrelevant or conflicting response. It is proposed that in mammals, especially humans, an essential part of learning is the development of cell assemblies—closed systems capable of briefly maintaining their own activity—and a background of interconnections between assemblies corresponding to familiar events. It is also proposed that this development is what happens as the infant's style of learning changes to an adult style. The structure of the cortex appears to rule out direct s-r connections in mammalian learning. Cortical transmission thus appears relatively inefficient from one point of view, but from another it has the advantage that much irrelevant excitation from the sense organs is screened out and not allowed to disturb behavior. Finally, the chapter points to a disadvantage arising from the large size of the human brain, related to the student's problem of concentration.

GUIDE TO STUDY

You should understand clearly the meaning of all the italicized items in this chapter.

Define and identify the following on a sketch: axon, dendrite, synapse.

Explain the all-or-none principle.

Describe and illustrate neural circuits that exhibit feed-forward and feedback.

Explain the rules for strengthening and weakening connections at the synapses.

Explain the theory of how a cell assembly is formed and how it maintains its own excitation.

Explain why a large brain may be a handicap to learning.

NOTES AND REFERENCES

Early Learning

Bower, T.G.R. (1982). *Development in Infancy, 2nd ed.* San Francisco: W. H. Freeman. Reviews experimental and observational studies on space perception, object perception, motor development and cognitive and social development in infants. Brings up to date the observational and experimental tradition established in the next book.

Piaget, J. (1953). *The Origins of Intelligence in Children.* London: Routledge & Kegan Paul. Translation of *La naissance de l'intelligence chez l'enfant* (1963). Neuchatel: Delachaux et Niestle. Classical work by the great Swiss psychologist, which outlines his theories of the development of intelligence.

Neural Mechanisms in Learning

Beach, F. A., Hebb, D. O., Morgan, C. T., & Nissen, H. W. (Eds.) (1960). *The Neuropsychology of Lashley.* New York: McGraw-Hill.

Bindra, D. (1976). *A Theory of Intelligent Behavior.* New York: Wiley.

Grossberg, S. (1982). *Studies of Mind and Brain: Neural Principles of Learning, Perception, Development, Cognition and Motor Control.* Boston, MA: D. Reidel. An ambitious book that outlines a mathematical theory of brain function consistent with the principles outlined in this chapter.

Hawkins, R. D. and Kandel, E. R. (1984). Is there a cell-biological alphabet for simple forms of learning? *Psychological Review, 91,* 375–391. A theory of how S-S and S-R learning take place in a simple organism at the single-cell level.

Hebb, D. O. (1968) Concerning imagery. *Psychological Review, 75,* 466–477.

Powers, W. T. (1978). Quantitative analysis of purposive systems. *Psychological Review, 85,* 417–435. Review of feedback principles in behavior which is consistent with the principles outlined in this chapter.

Neuron and Synapse

Kandel, E. R., & Schwartz, J. H. (1981). *Principles of Neural Science.* New York: Elsevier North Holland. An excellent detailed review of the function of the neuron and the central nervous system. Well written and illustrated.

Milner, P. M. (1970). *Physiological Psychology.* New York: Holt, Rinehart & Winston. A psychologically oriented account of neural function, in considerable detail but intelligible.

Shepherd, G. M. (1979). *The Synaptic Organization of the Brain, 2nd ed.* New York: Oxford University Press. An excellent, readable summary of the organization of synapses and neural circuits for different areas of mammalian brain.

The Human Brain and Mind

Luria, A. R. (1972). *The Working Brain: An Introduction to Neuropsychology,* (B. Haigh, trans.) New York: Penguin. A well-written book describing the functions of different areas of the brain and how they interact in normal thinking and behaving. It is based on human clinical studies, most of them Russian.

Penfield, W., & Roberts, L. (1959). *Speech and Brain Mechanisms.* Princeton, NJ: Princeton University Press. Classic description of experiments with epileptic patients undergoing brain surgery; describes the experiences produced with electrical brain stimulation.

CHAPTER 5

The Control of Behavior: Cognitive and Noncognitive

Ultimately, all behavior is a reaction to the environment. The relationship between behavior and the environment can be direct or indirect, changing within the same animal and varying from one animal species to another. An example of a direct relationship is the unconditioned reflex, in which an environmental stimulus produces its highly predictable effect almost at once. An indirect relationship is the activation of cell assemblies. Activation of these complex cortical circuits means that the behavioral response may be delayed, as in latent learning (see chapter 2).

Behavior in which a response follows reliably and quickly after a stimulus depends on relatively direct connections in the CNS; when behavior does not show this immediate relationship to a stimulus, we must assume that its CNS connections are less direct. The first kind of behavior is reflexive, or sense dominated. The second kind of behavior depends on mediating processes (ideas, thinking), which here are assumed to consist of the activity of cell assemblies (chapter 4). The presence of cell assemblies permits a delay between stimulus and response and introduces other kinds of complications into behavior, for example, the phenomenon of *set*.

That higher animals have mediating processes and therefore are less directly controlled by sensory events does not mean they have less need of sensory information or are less influenced by it. All behavior is affected by sensory information, all the time. Behavior is fundamentally an adaptation to the environment. For a behaving animal, the environment *is* sensory information. Behavior takes an animal away from harmful environments toward favorable ones. A behaving animal can change its immediate environment in ways that make survival more likely. Not all behavior, however, is adaptive in such a narrow sense: neither sexual behavior, nor maternal behavior, nor play is necessary to an animal's immediate survival. But with these forms of behavior also (for example: finding a mate, returning infants to the nest, or engaging in rough-and-tumble with another animal) sensory guidance is always an essential factor. No organized behavior is possible without it.

A one-celled organism such as amoeba does not have the specialization found in higher animals. All of its behavior results from actions within a single microscopic cell. Nevertheless, amoeba behavior can be very complicated. Some species join together to form a visible organism, a slime mold, with specialized parts that help the amoeba species to establish itself in a new area. The behavior is controlled by chemicals secreted and recognized by each amoeba, specifically when food in the environment becomes scarce. But a single cell does all the work of providing for its own survival: it detects food, moves toward it, ingests and digests it, and excretes wastes. The single cell is simultaneously nose, mouth, and alimentary canal. As a result, the amoeba has a limited ability to capture food and to avoid destruction: only events in its immediate vicinity, at the present moment, affect its behavior.

In higher animals, specialization of parts permits an extraordinary sensitivity of some cells (the receptors) to environmental events, so that food or danger is detected at a distance, and an equally extraordinary speed and precision of movement in other cells (the muscles). But specialization means that the receptors and effectors are spatially separated; hence, there must be some means of communication from one to the other. This is the first function of the nervous system: *spatial integration* or coordination of parts. The specialization of effectors also means that they must be active in a definite sequence, or at just the proper time, in order to have their effect: this *temporal integration* is also achieved by the nervous system.

For example: when a mosquito alights on one's forehead and begins operations, the skin of the forehead has no adequate means of self-defense. Nerve fibers in the skin transmit the excitation, originating in the skin, to the central nervous system, whence it is relayed to effectors at a distance, the muscles of a hand and arm. The mosquito is swatted. For successful defense, cells at a distance must be called upon, and they must be called upon in the proper order; the muscular contractions involved in a swift, accurate movement must be timed very precisely or the hand will reach the wrong place. Another example: the nose of a hungry animal smells food but, though it needs nutrition as much as the rest of the body, it cannot obtain the food directly; it must initiate a complex series of activities in other parts of the body, in a definite order. The end effect is that food gets into the stomach, and the blood stream delivers to the olfactory cells of the nose (and of course to other parts) the proteins, salts, sugar, and so forth that they need in order to keep on serving their function.

The role of sensation is clear, not only in initiating the activity but in continuing to guide it throughout. In swatting a mosquito, the muscular contractions to be made depend on the initial position of the hand; they are determined by the sensory processes that, coming from muscle and joint (chapter 12), "tell" us where our limbs are at any moment. Similarly, the predatory animal seeking food must change the course of its movements as the prey changes position. Sensory control is involved in any form of adaptation to the environment, simple or complex, and we must recognize it as a first principle of behavior.

But cell assemblies, and the ideas or thoughts they make possible, allow the nervous system to exercise control very indirectly. Sensory control is necessary to carry out behavior, but cell assemblies in the higher animal guide the sequence and direction of behavior. As a result, the behavior of the higher animal is no longer fully controlled by its immediate sensory input. The higher animal, as a result of the complexity of its central nervous system, has a mind of its own.

Figuratively, a "mind of one's own" means that one does not merely follow sensory instructions but may go counter to, or act without, instructions—the brain of the higher animal does not merely "do what it is told" by the sense organs. But the phrase is applicable literally as well as figuratively. Mind is defined as the complex activities of the brain of a higher animal. These complex activities have developed so that messages run within the brain, as well as into and out of it. Such internal activity, infinitely more complex than words can suggest, is mind. We are not directly aware of the activities of our own brains. Only a small part of this activity is returned to us directly as conscious self-awareness. The internal complexity of central nervous system activity is what distinguishes higher from lower animals, and it is what makes the behavior of higher animals less directly controlled by immediate sensory input. For example: a barefoot boy steps on a sharp stone and pulls back his foot. We may think of this as simple in–out (reflex) transmission: in from the skin of the foot to spinal cord, out to leg muscles. But something else may happen also. The boy stops, stands for a moment, then goes back for his sandals. He has "thought" about it and "decided" that the beach is too rough for barefoot walking. Cell assemblies have been activated and mediating processes ("thoughts") are the result. This is a complicating factor in the relation of sensory events to the concomitant behavior.

Thus, roughly speaking, we have two main classes of behavior, though one overlaps the other. One class is reflexive; the other involves a thought process to some degree. In both, sensory guidance is essential; but in the first the guidance is a full control—sensory events by themselves take charge and elicit the complete pattern of response as long as no other event interferes. The second class involves a much more complex process at the level of the association cortex in the cerebrum.

REFLEXIVE OR COGNITIVE BEHAVIOR?

As far as we know, all behavior of lower organisms, such as ant, bee, housefly, jellyfish, cockroach, and spider, is reflexive and does not justify any reference to mental processes: there is no mind, consciousness, emotion, purpose, or perception. There is also a great deal of reflexive behavior in higher animals, including human, but it can be modified or superseded by mediated behavior. When this reflexive behavior is learned, it can often be described as Type-S (Pavlovian) or Type-R (Thorndikian) conditioning (see chapter 2). To understand the problem of mind, we must separate reflexive from mediated behavior and not make the mistake of seeing mental processes everywhere. It is possible, even probable, that conditioned reflexes in humans involve mediating processes resulting from cell assembly activity, but we will be on firmer ground by working with the assumption that the ordinary CR results from the operation of direct neural pathways, even though part of the pathways go through the cerebral cortex.

We assume that some (lower) behavior is fully reflexive and that other (higher) behavior is not. Since neural conduction is relatively rapid, direct connection of the reflexive behavior means that a reflex response to a stimulus should occur promptly, unless some other process interferes with it. In addition, a reflexive response cannot occur when the appropriate stimulus is not present. When analyzing some new piece of behavior, we ask whether by these standards it is reflexive. If the behavior is not reflexive, even if it seems simple, then cell assemblies are involved and we are dealing with mediated behavior. Given the same sensory input, mediated behavior varies from one occasion to another; the response is not directly determined by the stimulus.

Reflexive and mediated behavior are broad classes; they merge with no clear dividing line. The fundamental principles of neural action are the same in both classes. We know more about the relatively simpler reflexive behavior, and the main problem in psychology is how to apply this knowledge to the more complex mediated behavior.

SENSE-DOMINATED BEHAVIOR: UCR AND CR

In psychology as in other fields of science the simpler explanation is preferred to the more complicated, as long as the facts permit. We prefer reflexes to mediation whenever possible, since reflexes involve fewer steps and thus are simpler. But we must ask what properties of behavior are implied if the reflex explanation is to be satisfactory.

The essential idea is that reflexive behavior is directly controlled by sensory stimulation. This means that the response occurs within a second or two of the stimulus and that the same response follows the stimulus each time, provided there is no interference from background stimulation and learning has not occurred. (If, for example, pain followed a response on the preceding occasion, the response might not be repeated; but this would mean that learning had occurred.) Neural conduction is fast (ranging from about a meter per second in small fibers to 120 m/sec in large ones). With a reflex, there is little delay of response following stimulation.

An unconditioned response (UCR) begins and ends with stimulation and it is highly predictable. If stimulation for two incompatible reflexes is given simultaneously, of course, only one reflex can occur. A pin-prick in the foot of a newborn infant produces a flexion (withdrawal) response of the leg; mild pressure on the sole of the foot produces an extensor thrust—if both stimuli occur at the same time, only one response can be made, usually the flexion. Also, especially in older subjects, mediating processes can interfere with reflex processes. The reflex response to a pain stimulus in the fingers, for example, is to pull back the hand; but if one is holding a valuable teacup that has become too hot, the pain reflex is usually inhibited long enough for one to set the cup down before letting go of it. Similarly, one can often inhibit a cough.

Otherwise, however, the UCR is constant and predictable. There is a long list of separate reflexes: the pupillary response to increased light in the eye, producing contraction of the pupil; salivary reflexes produced by stimulation of the mouth; sucking reflexes in the baby, produced by stimulation of the lips; sneezing, coughing, eye watering, produced by irritations of nose, throat, or eyeball; reflexes of heart and arteries, regulating the flow of blood to different parts of the body; reflexes of the stomach and gut, controlling digestion and the movement of food through the alimentary canal; a large number of postural reflexes, producing maintenance of orientation of the body in space; and so on. All these UCRs are consistent in their action, and there is no doubt that the responses are controlled sensorily.

Now let us see how these considerations apply to the learned reflexive responses, the CRs.

In our first example, the CS is a buzzer; the UCS is an electric shock to the foot delivered two seconds after the buzzer begins. After a few trials, the animal raises his foot off the grid immediately when the buzzer sounds and continues to do so on almost every trial. We may then think of a fairly direct pathway from certain cells in the ear to the muscles of the leg (Fig. 5.1a).

If the connection does not work every time, we need not reject this conclusion; any path through the nervous system must thread its way through a tangle of other paths and is exposed to possible interference from other processes, especially inhibition. We can ask whether a given stimulus connection *tends* always to arouse the same response (any deviations from this response being referable to interference or fatigue); or whether, on the other hand, the same total pattern of stimulation produces systematically different responses on different occasions.

Thinking not of single stimuli but of the total pattern of stimulation, as in the preceding paragraph, helps us deal with another possible difficulty. Having established a CR to the buzzer, we take the animal out of the apparatus and sound the buzzer. The CR does not appear. This does not necessarily mean that the response is not reflexive, but, rather, shows that auditory stimulation is not, by itself, enough to account for the response. But we can assume that auditory stimulation is supported by stimulation from eye, nose, and skin—that is, by sight, smell, and touch of the apparatus. In the apparatus at least, the experimenter can elicit the CR whenever he wishes by manipulating the animal's environment: thus the behavior is controlled by sensory stimulation. The powerful theory of Rescorla and Wagner (Rescorla, 1975) introduced in chapter 2, can be used to explain many examples of reflexive (Type-S) conditioning.

Another problem is this. In Pavlov's procedure, the CS is presented for 15 seconds before the UCS. Early in conditioning the animal secretes saliva as soon as the CS is presented, but then the CR is delayed and eventually is made only in the last 2 or 3 seconds before food appears. The same thing happens in conditioned-avoidance ex-

Schematic diagram of a S-R connection via the mammalian cortex; not a straight-through connection, as Thorndike would perhaps have suggested, because the cortex does not seem to work that way, but still relatively direct.

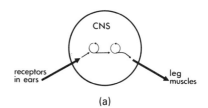

(a)

Diagrammatic representation of a reverberatory pathway; incoming stimulation excites A; which excites B, which re-excites A and so on. It is suggested that this is the mechanism of holding or trace activity, in principle. C represents other paths which may be excited by collateral fibers (branches) from B, and which might be excited each time the excitation travels round the closed pathway.

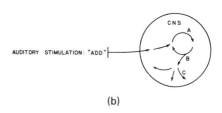

(b)

Diagram of a possible mechanism of a set to add. The excitation from the prior stimulus, "add", is held in a reverberatory loop. The second stimulus (8,2) is connected with two motor paths, and can evoke "ten" or "six"; but the reverberatory activity supports only one of these and the response is "ten". If the prior stimulation had been "subtract", a different reverberatory circuit would have been active and would have determined the response "six". Needless to say this diagram is entirely schematic.

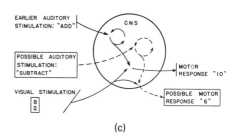

(c)

Schematic diagram of a mechanism of attention in which a central process, C_1, supports one sensory input (from A). C_2 supports another (B). Event A will be responded to if C_1 is active, event B if C_2 is active.

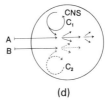

(d)

FIGURE 5.1. Diagrams illustrating (a) a noncognitive central process, and (b, c and d) several different cognitive central processes.

periments. A buzzer is presented for 10 seconds, followed by shock if the rat does not move off the grid that delivers the shock. Early in conditioning the rat jumps as soon as he hears the buzzer, but eventually a time comes when he does not move till 7, 8 or 9 seconds later. Are these delays compatible with reflexive behavior, in which a response should be prompt? They are, perhaps, if the response is being inhibited—as Pavlov's results indicate—and if the inhibition itself is under sensory control. (Sense dominance may be inhibitory as well as excitatory.) A more likely hypothesis, however, is that the inhibition is controlled by a mediating process—a combination of cell assemblies—with limited duration. With these data, no final decision is possible.

Here is a clearer case. Changing the experimental conditions, we get a different kind of conditioning. Instead of presenting the CS for the full delay period of 10 seconds, we present it for 1 second and give the UCS 9 seconds later. Once again we obtain a 7- or 8-second delay in response. What produces the CR? When it does occur—8 seconds after cessation of the CS? In some manner the brain holds the activity aroused by the CS, instead of transmitting it at once to the effectors. Such behavior is not reflexive but involves mediating processes, to which we now turn.

THE MEDIATING PROCESS

The typical problem of mediated behavior arises when there is a delay between stimulus and response. What bridges the S-R gap? In everyday language, "thinking" does it. The stimulus gives rise to thoughts or ideas that continue during the delay period and cause the response. And, in fact, we are now talking about the thought process. But because the words "thought" and "idea" have been around for a long time and have acquired a number of meanings, it is difficult to use them precisely though they are still useful in a general sense.

Mediating process has a more exact and more limited meaning. It may be defined as an activity of the brain that can hold the excitation delivered by a sensory event after the event has ceased and thus permits a stimulus to have its effect at some later time. To mediate means to form a connecting link, and the simplest function of the mediating process is to link sensory stimuli directly with responses. Theoretically, however, the mediating process can be excited by other mediating processes as well as by its own sensory event, and when a number of mediating processes interact in this way—being excited by each other as well as by sensory events—the result is thinking. Theoretically, therefore, a mediating process might also be defined as the unit or elementary component of thought, replacing the term "idea."[1]

We do not know what the physiological nature of a mediating process is. We do know, though, that the only way it can hold an excitation for some short period of time is by means of the circuits discussed in chapter 4 (Figs. 4.7, 4.8). One circuit could not hold an excitation long enough to correspond to an idea, but a number of them combined in a cell assembly might do so. Still longer holding could occur with several cell assemblies, assembly A exciting assembly B, which excites C, which excites A again. In this text, therefore, it is assumed that mediating processes consist of cell assemblies. The cell assembly idea is a hypothesis about how mediating processes work. We know from observations of behavior that mediating processes exist. Consequently, we can speak with confidence about mediating processes; when we speak of cell assemblies we are talking about a specific theory of mediating processes.

Now let us look at the behavioral evidence. Suppose that a friend asks you to add some numbers. Because you haven't been told the numbers, you cannot respond immediately. In a while, your friend says "four, seven" and you immediately respond "eleven." You could not respond adequately to the first stimulation ("Please add") alone, nor to the second stimulus alone ("four, seven"): the response could only be made to both. Hence, the information in the first stimulation must have been *held* until it could be combined with the second. This kind of behavior, familiar to everyone, is the simplest and clearest evidence of the existence of mediating processes. The behavior takes us beyond what can be explained by reflexes. *The capacity for holding an excitation in the central nervous system is the primary mark of the higher animal.*

The simple closed paths of the figure in the present chapter (as well as in Fig. 4.8, if you will recall) are conventional representations,

---

[1]The careful reader may observe that the discussion deals with mediating processes only, not with mediating *responses*. A distinction is maintained in this text between responses, as observable behavior, and unobserved processes in the CNS, on the ground that we must not use a terminology that confuses facts with hypotheses (see chapter 1). Some other writers are not as persnickety, but when they say "mediating responses" they are apt to mean an actual muscular contraction—one that bridges a gap in time between a stimulus and a response. Instead of a closed path in the brain itself, the closed path of a "mediating response" is from brain to muscle (causing contraction) back from muscle to brain (sensations of muscle contraction), and so on. This kind of mediating or bridging certainly occurs and is important in behavior, but "mediating response" is avoided in the present text because of the inevitable risk of confusion with "mediating process" as purely intracranial (i.e. ideational) mechanism.

deliberately schematized so they will not be taken for reality. The closed-loop diagram of one or two arrows is a symbol to represent a self-re-exciting system, just as the chemist has his conventional symbols for the improbable atomic structures he talks about and the physicist has his to represent battery, condenser, or ground in electrical circuits. In other words the loops of Fig. 5.1 (and Fig. 4.8) are not pictures, but a kind of pictorial shorthand.

SET AND DELAYED RESPONSE

Imagine an intelligent student for whom simple arithmetical operations are easy. We seat her before a screen, tell her that pairs of numbers will be flashed on it, and instruct her to give their sums as quickly as possible. We then present a series of combinations such as 8, 2. We always obtain a correct and rapid response. A given stimulus pattern always produces the same response, and the reaction time is short, or about a second. This is a highly practiced form of behavior; no thought appears to be involved, and we might conclude that the behavior meets the criteria for reflex behavior—promptness and reliability.

But the response depends on the student's being *set* to add. The 8, 2 combination produces the response "10" every time—until we say "now subtract" (or divide, or multiply). Now the same stimulus pattern produces, with equal speed and reliability, the same response "6" (or "4" or "16"). It is clear, then, that the response is not determined by the present stimulus pattern (8, 2) alone, and therefore the behavior is not reflexive. *The response is determined by two stimulations, one of which has to be held and has its effect only after an interval.* The highly schematic diagram of Fig. 5.1c illustrates how this might occur, developing further the idea presented in Fig. 5.1b. (It shows also, in the broken lines, what would have happened if the earlier stimulation had been different and had produced a set to subtract.)

The paradigm (the clear representative example) of set is as follows: First stimulus A is presented and then a different stimulus, B; B promptly elicits a response C, but only if A was presented first. A *sets* the organism, or prepares it, so B can have its effect.

The *delayed response* procedure provides us with another example of set, in the behavior of the monkey. (The preceding discussion has referred several times to a delay in responding, but the term "delayed response" technically refers to W. S. Hunter's 1913 method, about to be described.) The monkey is allowed to see food put in one of two containers out of reach. A screen is then put between the monkey and the containers, so that he cannot later find the food simply by keeping his eyes fixed on the correct container. After a delay of 5 seconds, 10 seconds, or more, the screen is removed, the two containers are brought within reach. The monkey is then permitted to choose between them.

The monkey succeeds at this task, in a way that provides some evidence of the presence of mediating processes. In one experiment particularly, the evidence was decisive (O. L. Tinklepaugh, 1928). In it the experimenter sometimes used lettuce, which the monkeys liked, as the food reward, and sometimes banana, which they liked better. When the monkey saw lettuce being put into one of the containers, chose the right one, and found lettuce in it, he took it and ate it. But when he saw banana being put in and then found lettuce—the experimenter having deceitfully made a change during the delay period—the monkey did not take the lettuce, but showed surprise and searched in and around the container (apparently looking for the missing piece of banana). On occasion the animal simply had a temper tantrum instead.

Here is our holding process again. Seeing banana put into the food container had some lasting effect, as shown by the conflict that appeared when lettuce was found instead. We know that when the monkey found lettuce without having an expectancy of banana, he reached for it and ate it. This is consistent with a direct sensory control of response. But the temper tantrum, and failure to take the lettuce, is not: this behavior must be *jointly* determined by a mediating process resulting from the earlier stimulation and the effects of the present stimulation.

The problem of holding does not always arise when there appears to be a delay of response. A lower animal may succeed in delayed-response tests by immediately making a postural adjustment and maintaining it. For example, when the animal sees food put into the right-hand container, he may move over to that side of the cage and wait there until the screen is raised; then he simply chooses the near container. Monkeys and chimpanzees do not solve the problem in this way; they usually move around during the delay period. If we did not have any other data, we might suppose that the monkey would tense the muscles of the hand nearest the food and keep them tensed while he moves around. When the screen is raised and he turns back to face the containers, he could then choose the correct one by using the hand whose muscles were contracted.

However, there is usually no sign at all of the monkey's "remembering" the location of the food in this way, and the lettuce-versus-banana experiment has special importance in ruling out such an explanation as far as the higher animal is concerned.

SELECTIVITY IN BEHAVIOR: ATTENTION RELATED TO SET

It was noted earlier that the distinguishing mark of the higher animal is the capacity to hold an excitation for some time before it has its effect on behavior. The mediating process that does the holding is apt to introduce *selectivity* into the behavior as *attention, set,* or both. Accordingly, these also are marks of higher behavior. Attention is selectivity in what is responded to, or sensory selectivity; set is a selectivity of motor rather than sensory response. Often, attention and set go together.

Selectivity is constant at any one time but is easily changed from one time to another. This has already been illustrated by the set to add. Presented with a visual stimulation of a pair of numbers, the subject *consistently* produces one response to each pair as long as that set lasts; when the set is changed to subtraction, a different response to each pair is made—again consistently. It is characteristic of such sets that they change readily, so that with the same stimulation the response varies systematically from one time to another. With the visual stimulus of 6, 3 we do not get a random variation of "9" and "3," but a response that is highly predictable, provided we know what the subject's set is. Thus, the mark of higher behavior is not mere selectivity of response: the lower animal is also selective, but he is always selective in the same way because he is built to behave in that way only. The higher animal is capable of responding in many different ways at different times but at any one time tends to respond in only one of those ways—a *changeable selectivity* of response.

Attention is closely related to set. Fig. 5.1d illustrates a way in which a mediating process would support one response and not another. A and B are two stimulus events whose effects are transmitted to the higher levels of the CNS. C_1 is a mediating process supporting the input from A—that is, it excites the same central paths that A does—so that the excitation from A is transmitted farther. A is "noticed" by the subject and is likely to affect behavior. C_2 is a mediating process that would similarly support B, but it is not active and it is therefore much less likely that B will have any effect. It is not noticed. This will be true especially if C_1 tends to inhibit C_2 and vice versa: either A or B will be attended to, but not both. *Attention* may, then, be defined as an activity of mediating processes (C_1 or C_2) that supports the central effects of a sensory event, usually with the implication that other sensory events are shut out.

Now compare Figs. 5.1c and 5.1d. You will see that we are talking about a process very similar to that of set. The two terms really have almost identical meanings, but the word set is usually applied (a) when the process is thought of as the selection of one response rather than another and (b) when one can point to a specific preceding experience that excites the mediating process doing the selecting, or "sets" the animal. The similarity between the two is such that we sometimes speak of a "perceptual set," a set to perceive one way rather than another, and this obviously is a form of attention as defined above.

THE TEMPORAL INTEGRATION OF BEHAVIOR

The behavior of higher animals is consistent. This means that an observer can relate an animal's behavior at one time to its behavior at another time, independent of momentary changes in the environment. Mediating processes explain this consistency.

An animal with only unconditioned reflexes (UCRs) depends completely on the stimulus and its own internal state to guide its behavior. For example, the internal state of a thirsty animal (the concentration of solutes in the blood) makes it likely to drink water when water is a stimulus. This probably happens because the physiological variable—the concentration—has a direct effect on the sensitivity of synapses in the unlearned reflex path connecting the stimulus of water with the response of drinking. In the same way, the internal state of a hungry animal makes it likely to eat when food is the stimulus. The same animal, in an environment containing both food and water, will drink when thirsty and eat when hungry. Its behavior is predicted by the changes in internal state that make one or another unconditioned response more likely, and by the sequence of environmental stimulations that trigger one or another of the unconditioned responses.

An animal that can learn either Type-S (Pavlovian) or Type-R (operant) conditioned reflexes shows more consistent behavior than an "unconditioned reflex" animal. Pavlovian, or operant response, learning means that the regularity of an environment in which one event follows another predictably is matched by the animal's behavior as it anticipates a change in the environment over a period measured in seconds. The consistency can be made longer if the environment is arranged so that one conditioned response produces a stimulus for a second conditioned response, and so on. By following one conditioned response by another, a chain of conditioned response behavior can be produced that extends the predictability of behavior over minutes, or even hours, in a sufficiently regular environment.

But this kind of consistent behavior depends on maintaining a carefully controlled sequence of stimuli that produce the successive conditioned responses. If the chain of stimuli is broken, the behavioral consistency disappears. Mediating processes, by contrast, allow animals to produce behavior that is consistent over long periods, from minutes to years, in environments that fluctuate unpredictably. The holding property of a mediating process allows a learned anticipation to be retained, as in the trace CR, without requiring the response chaining or postural rigidity that limits the capacity of a lower animal to delay a particular response. Because the mediating processes can be an anticipation, they allow an animal to anticipate future stimulation and to compare the actual outcome with the outcome anticipated earlier. The result of this comparison guides behavior—witness the disappointed monkey in the delayed-response task who anticipated a banana and got lettuce instead. The monkey's search for the banana was guided by the discrepancy, or mismatch, between anticipation (banana) and outcome (lettuce).

The disappointment of the monkey that, shown a banana, gets lettuce instead is an example of the characteristic behavior of the higher animals, including ourselves. This characteristic behavior depends on the existence of mediating processes that allow an animal to (a) hold the effects of a stimulation, (b) anticipate the occurrence of a future event, and (c) compare the actual event with the anticipated one. Subsequent behavior depends on the comparison.

Mediating processes in human and chimpanzees allow the use of symbols associated with environmental events or with behavior that can communicate wants, intentions, and anticipations. In humans, we call this highly developed, highly abstract behavior, which is dependent on mediating processes, *language*. Chimpanzees have been taught to use a simple symbol system, invented by human experimenters, to communicate with us in a simple way about their environment. By communicating through symbols, one animal's experience can be communicated to another without requiring the other animal to share directly in the experience. The development of language—first spoken, then written—has parallelled the development of human culture.

It is important to remember that behavior at any instant is determined simultaneously by sensory input and by mediating processes that maintain anticipations and intentions. The sensory input directs behavior by immediately releasing learned and unlearned reflexes and is also compared with the anticipated outcome of behavior directed by mediating processes. The results of these comparisons help to determine the direction of future behavior. The role of mediating processes in language and thinking is discussed further in chapter 13.

WILL

The behavior of a higher animal depends on all of its conditioned reflexes and mediating processes—all of its present environment, plus the sum total of all of its past environments, plus its biological capacity to learn and to respond. An observer has no more than a sketchy understanding of an animal's past environments. Biological capacities vary from one animal to another. Thus, practically speaking, an observer never knows enough to predict the animal's behavior, because the behavior depends on past events—conditioned reflexes and mediating processes—that cannot be completely known.

If all of an animal's past and all of its biology could be known, its behavior still could not be predicted. It is not widely realized that for all but the simplest physical systems, such prediction is beyond the capacity of our present logic and mathematics. The limited ability of logicians and mathematicians to predict simple physical systems cannot by any stretch of the imagination be extended to the complexity of a higher animal.

Logical machines like computers are predictable—that is, what comes out can theoretically be determined by what goes in. Although computers have been widely used in psychology to *simulate* certain aspects of behavior, especially in the interesting areas of problem solving, no one has yet proven that the behavior of a living organism can be completely imitated by logical computation. And there is at present no reason to think that this is possible.

Statistical prediction has replaced strict prediction in many problems—both physical and biological. Statistical prediction means: "If I place a dog in a restraining harness, ring a bell, and follow the sound of the bell with the sight of food, after 20 pairings of bell and food the dog will, in nine experiments out of ten, salivate to the sound of the bell on the 21st pairing." This kind of prediction is commonly used by both applied and theoretical psychologists. But even statistical prediction has its limits. It works best with reflexive behavior, when the appropriate stimulus is known. But remember our example of set: the stimulus 8, 3 when preceded by the stimulus "add," leads to a response of "11," when preceded by the stimulus "subtract," leads to a response of "5." The same stimulus, preceded by a different mediating process, may lead to a radically different response, which can be predicted with a certainty only if one knows the previous mediating processes. We are, then, back to the difficulties mentioned previously: both the incompleteness of knowledge, and the ultimate inability to predict from even a full history of past events. Nevertheless, useful information has been obtained—on a probability basis—about even fairly complex behavior of higher animals, including humans. The factual content of this book includes some of the more important predictions, especially for humans. Of course, there is both a practical and a theoretical limit to the accuracy of behavior prediction: even "perfect knowledge," if such were possible, would not mean perfect prediction. Will, or volition, or choice, are words which mean that to an observer the behavior of another higher animal is not perfectly predictable. When the animal behaves in an unpredictable way, the animal is said to be willing, or choosing. Will is the practically and theoretically unpredictable component of observed behavior.

As we observe others, so we observe ourselves. We are consciously aware of only a small part of our own brain activity and definitely are not consciously aware of all of our past sensory environments. As a result, we are not consciously aware of our own complete history of conditioned reflexes and mediating processes. Thus, to ourselves, our own behavior is to some degree unpredictable. And we say that we "will" to do something because we could not predict in advance that we would choose to do it!

SUMMARY

All behavior is guided by the sensory environment through control exercised by the central nervous system. Reflexive, or sense-dominated behavior, is controlled by more or less direct connections between neurons conveying sensory information and those which organize the performance of responses. Much of the behavior of higher animals involves mediating processes roughly corresponding to ideas or images. Mediating processes can hold a sensory input for a considerable time and can be activated by other mediating processes. According to the theory presented in chapter 4, mediating processes are the activity of cell assemblies, which are neural networks developed through experience.

Set is a kind of behavior which demonstrates that mediating processes can modify the response to a stimulus. Under identical stimulus situations, one or another response may occur, depending on the particular mediating process active at the time. Attention is the sensory equivalent of set: Active mediating process may make an animal more likely to respond to one stimulus than to another. Will refers to the unpredictable behavior of any higher animal, including oneself. There is a limit to self-knowledge, which means that we cannot perfectly predict the behavior we ourselves will choose.

GUIDE TO STUDY

For review, be able to produce schematic diagrams representing what happens in holding, set, and attention. Note that the delayed-response procedure, involving holding followed by a later stimulation (when the screen is raised so the animal can make his choice between the two containers), calls for the same diagram as that of set. Explain why the delayed response is a special case of set.

Be able to explain how the holding process frees the subject from immediate sensory dominance, and how "will" essentially means the absence of such dominance.

Be able to explain the significance of a CR that occurs only after the CS has lasted for 5 seconds, as distinct from a CR that appears at once; and how a delayed CR (5 sec after the CS has stopped) relates to the existence of a mediating process.

Be able to explain what is meant by anticipation and how anticipation contributes to organized sequences of behavior.

NOTES AND REFERENCES

The goal of this chapter is to develop the idea that unlearned reflexes, learned reflexes, and mediating processes are complementary means by which behavior is controlled in response to the sensory environment. A secondary goal is to discuss the limits on the predictability of behavior—limits set in theory and in practice. Not all psychologists agree on these limits. Both learned reflexes and computer simulation models have their advocates as candidates for a satisfactory description of the behavior of higher organisms. Some of these points of view, as well as fundamental work on set and mediated behavior, are represented in the following selection of books and articles.

Set and Delayed Response

Gibson, J. J. (1941). A critical review of the concept of set in contemporary experimental psychology. *Psychological Bulletin, 38,* 781–817. A good review of the phenomenon, but treats it as a mystery (which it was in 1940); no explanation attempted.

Hunter, W. S. (1913). The delayed reaction in animals and children. *Behavior Monographs, 2.* (Part 6). Report of the original delayed reaction experiments.

Hunter, W. S. (1917). The delayed reaction in a child. *Psychological Review, 24,* 75–87. Report of an improved procedure still in use.

Leeper, R. W. (1951) Cognitive Processes. In S. S. Stevens (Ed.), *Handbook of Experimental Psychology.* New York: Wiley. Still a valuable review despite its date. Includes a report of Hunter's and Tinklepaugh's experiments.

Skanes, G., & Donderi, D. C. (1973). Stimulus set, response set, and word identification.

Journal of Experimental Psychology, 99, 413–423. Illustrates the difference between stimulus set (attentional set) and response set and shows how they interact in experiments with words as stimuli.

Mechanics of Thought

Hebb, D. O. (1960). The American Revolution. *American Psychologist, 15,* 735–745.

Hebb, D. O. (1963). The semiautonomous process: its nature and nurture. *American Psychologist, 18,* 16–27.

Meehl, P. E., & MacCorquodale, K. (1951). Some methodological comments concerning expectancy theory. *Psychological Review, 58,* 230–233.

Miller, G. A., Galanter, E., & Pribram, K. (1960). *Plans and the Structure of Behavior.* New York: Holt. A readable, interesting and stimulating account of thought in terms of the functioning of a computer, with due respect paid to feedback principles.

Rescorla, R. A. (1975). Pavlovian excitatory and inhibitory conditioning. In Estes, W. K. (Ed.) *Handbook of Learning and Cognitive Processes, Vol. 2.* ch. 1. pp. 7–35. Hillsdale, NJ: Lawrence Erlbaum Associates.

CHAPTER 6

Learning, Memory, and Forgetting

Every student knows that learning a formula or a definition is only part of the job: it must also be remembered correctly until the examination. In this chapter we will consider memory and forgetting: what makes the results of learning persist or not persist and how error may be introduced into memories.

Some learning is used at once and not again. You ask "What time is it?" and need remember the answer only long enough to set your watch. This is known as *short-term memory*. If, instead, you are a character in a detective story and need to establish an alibi, you will have to remember the answer until after you have been cross-examined in court and set free: this we call *long-term memory*. In these two situations, the *acquisition* of the learning is about the same—a momentary stimulation and one-trial learning—but the *retention* differs. A question to be discussed, then, is what determines retention.

"Memory" is a slippery term. Primarily, it means the retention of the effects of learning of any kind (which is what it means in the title of this chapter), and this is the way it is generally used in psychological discussions. But it has a popular meaning too. The popular meaning includes only what you can recall. The two meanings are very different. Let us say that 2 years ago you took a course on Patagonia and learned the names of all the principal villages, but today you cannot recall one. By the popular meaning, you remember nothing from your course on

Patagonia. Have you forgotten completely? It would be easy to show that forgetting is not complete—that your memory for Patagonia is not zero. There might be perhaps 50% retention, as you would see if when you relearned the names you needed only half as many trials to learn as you needed the first time (the savings method of measuring retention). Or, for another example, ask an experienced typist what finger is used to type the letter s. There is a fairly good chance that he cannot tell you, especially if you make him keep his fingers still. Does this mean that he has no "memory" of where s is on the keyboard? Of course not. If you sit him down at the typewriter and ask him to type "Mississippi" without looking, he does so at once without a mistake. It is easy to deal with memory in terms of "acquisition" and "retention"; in the first or Patagonian case, we can speak of 50% retention; in the second (Mississippi) we say that the typist's early training established two modes of response, verbal and manual, that there is some loss of the verbal response, but that the retention of the manual response is perfect.

SHORT-TERM AND LONG-TERM MEMORY

Much learning is transient and unstable. During waking hours, human beings are continuously engaged in perceiving, and the result is a continuous acquisition of knowledge. But most of this turns out to be of no significance and is rapidly forgotten. Some, however, does last. What makes the difference between short-term and long-term memory? It seems that *short-term* memory may be a *reverberation* in the closed loops of the cell assembly and between cell assemblies, whereas *long-term* memory is more structural, a *lasting* change of synaptic connections. Synaptic change presumably would take time and might be possible only if the reverberation of short-term memory lasted long enough to give it a good start. All this is theory, but it suggests that the two kinds of memory work together. The longer the reverberation of short-term memory lasts, the more likely it is that a long-term memory will be established. Thus, exciting events, which cause the arousal that is discussed in chapter 10, would be remembered because arousal makes for longer-lasting reverberation.

A simple experiment illustrates the two kinds of memory. College students were asked to repeat several series of nine digits (the same nine digits, for example, 951437826, each time presented in a different order) read aloud at the rate one digit per second. Nine digits is too many to be repeated reliably after being heard only once, so few subjects remembered the first series. But the experiment had a special feature: Unknown to the subjects, every third series was the same. The question was, would this series be learned because it was repeated? Would hearing it on the third trial have some residual effect that would be added to when the same series was repeated on the sixth trial, and so on. Or would the intervening series prevent this? The experiment showed a steady improvement in memory for the repeated series, but not with the others.

The short-term memory for nine digits is very brief. There is no hope of succeeding with the task unless one listens carefully to the series as it is read and then repeats it at once. This experiment shows that listening to a set of digits does more than set up a short-term memory. There is also some beginning of a long-term structural change that is left behind. The memory of one series seems to be completely erased by hearing the following one, and there is no interference by one series on the next (that is, there seems to be no tendency to repeat some of the digits in the order given in the preceding series). But it is only the short-term memory that is erased completely. It leaves behind it a trace that is added to on every third trial and forms the basis of a long-term memory. The two mechanisms seem different in kind, but they collaborate closely with each other.

SYNAPTIC CHANGE AND CONSOLIDATION IN LONG-TERM MEMORY

In long-term memory there is another factor. Once begun, presumably by the short-term mechanism just described, the long-term memory trace needs to be left relatively undisturbed for some time if it is to become firmly established. The necessary synaptic changes must be allowed to mature, as it were, much as raw whiskey must be left to sit a while in its oaken barrels if it is to become fit to drink. Whiskey takes a year or more; learning needs something between 15 minutes and an hour. The maturing process is known as *consolidation*, and its duration is the *consolidation period*.

The need for consolidation is demonstrated by failure of retention when brain function is disrupted soon after learning has taken place. *Retrograde amnesia* is the failure of retention that occurs when a blow on the head has caused partial or complete loss of consciousness. Suppose a car driver on his own side of the highway is hit by a car from the other direction, one that has gone out of control and has crossed into his lane. He is knocked out briefly, then gradually comes back to full consciousness. It is not surprising that his memory is impaired for events following the accident, his brain being more or less addled for the time being; but it is very significant that he cannot remember what happened just before the accident, when his brain was functioning normally. If he had not been hit on the head—if at the last instant the other car had managed to avoid him—he certainly would have remembered seeing the car headed straight for him: The learning would have been retained. Such a concussion wipes out learning that we know must have occurred. But it does not wipe out all learning, only recent learning. Old, well-established memories are unimpaired, and the longer the interval between acquisition and concussion, the less the impairment. In that interval, something is happening to make memory less vulnerable to disruption. The something is what is known as consolidation.

Electroconvulsive shock (or electroconvulsive therapy: ECS or ECT in abbreviation) has the same effect on consolidation and can be used experimentally with man or animal. Human experiments are possible because the shock—a current passed through the head—is sometimes used in the treatment of serious depression, for which it is very effective. A patient scheduled to have the treatment at 11:00 a.m. can be asked to learn something just before then. For example, at 10:30 he can be given 10 nonsense syllables to memorize. The next day at 10:30 a.m., when he has fully recovered from the immediate state of confusion following the shock, he is tested to see how many of the syllables he can repeat. If the shock was given right after the learning, we can expect that he cannot repeat any of them. Even the savings method shows no retention in such experiments, the patient usually taking as many trials to learn the list of syllables the second time as the first.

To be certain that the forgetting is not due merely to the passage of time, we can do a control test (chapter 8) on another day, when the patient is not having shock treatment. Using another list of 10 syllables of about the same difficulty, we might now find that the patient is able to repeat three, four, or five syllables after 24 hours, a considerable saving on relearning the list. The loss following shock, therefore, is more than can be accounted for by normal forgetting or by the emotional disturbance caused by the ECT.

This is how consolidation has been studied formally. It shows that the longer the shock is delayed following learning, the less the disruptive effect on retention. But informally the effect of electroshock on retention is even clearer; for the patient not only forgets nonsense syllables, he also forgets entering the treatment room, having the electrodes placed on his temples, and receiving the shock itself.

There is a small number of patients from whom we can learn more about consolidation. Inside the tip of the temporal lobe is a structure called the *hippocampus*. For the treatment of severe cases of epilepsy, it has sometimes been necessary to remove part of the hippocampus on both sides, together with some of the overlying cortex. The patient then loses the power of consolidating learning (Milner, 1970). Things learned before the operation are not forgotten, and short-term or immediate memory, lasting 1 or 2 minutes but not much longer, is not impaired; but there is an almost complete loss of new long-term memories. It seems therefore that the hippocampus, by itself or with neighboring cortex, plays a large part in the consolidation process. It probably does not control the whole process by itself; if it did, we would expect to find a comparable failure of retention in lower mammals with injury to the hippocampus, and this is not observed although there are some defects.

What consolidation is we do not know, nor how the hippocampus affects it. Results of experiments with lower animals, however, suggest a relation to reinforcement. The animal experiments used primary reinforcement, whereas the human (clinical) observations concerned cognitive learning with no primary reward. One possibility therefore is that the hippocampus is needed for unreinforced cognitive learning, to supply some sort of substitute for primary reinforcement.

Both consolidation and reinforcement act *after* the response being learned has been made. Might reinforcement have its effect by promoting consolidation? There has been much argument in the past about reinforcement and how it produces its effects. One view, called *reinforcement theory*, is that reinforcement is needed for all learning and that it has its effect by somehow strengthening S-R connections. This was Thorndike's early proposal. Pavlov, on the other hand, thought the food he gave his dog served only to make CS and UCR occur at the same time, in temporal contiguity. Occurring together was enough to form the association. This is *contiguity theory*. Both views may contain some truth. We have seen how readily latent learning takes place, even without apparent reinforcement. Reinforcement, in Thorndike's sense at least, is not necessary. On the other hand, there is learning that is hard to understand except in terms of reinforcement and a strengthening of connections. Skinner's shaping (chapter 2) is an example. How might the strengthening result?

One possibility is that the medulla of the adrenal gland secretes a hormone—epinephrine—into the bloodstream after a reinforced learning experience (McGaugh, 1983). Then in some unknown way this hormone, which does not enter the brain easily from the bloodstream, may increase the chemical and electrical activity at synapses that have just been active, thus strengthening the responses that have just been made, the ones which were followed by reinforcement.

The adrenal glands are active in stressful conditions and may reasonably be suspected of such a role. Cognitive learning, without stress or primary reinforcement, may need help from the hippocampus to make the gland secrete the same hormone. When a mediating process causes a response whose feedback corresponds to that mediating process—when expectation is confirmed, when the intention to make a skilled movement is followed by just that movement—it may be the hippocampus that throws the adrenal gland into action to cement the synapses that did it. This, of course, is all gross speculation. Nevertheless, the parallel between reinforcement and consolidation seems important and should be noted.

THE CHEMISTRY OF CONSOLIDATION

It is still not clear how a synapse is modified to consolidate memory. Because neural transmission at a chemical synapse depends on the release of neurotransmitter chemicals, anything that permanently changes the amount of or the effectiveness of neurotransmitter released when a neuron fires might help to consolidate memory. The metabolism of neurotransmitter production and release is quite complicated; there may be several different consolidation mechanisms. In the simple animal *aplysia* (discussed in chapter 4), the amount of neurotransmitter released can be changed by (a) making it easier for calcium ions $(CA++)$ to flow into the neuron whenever the neuron generates an action potential that is transmitted along an axon to the synaptic terminal. The flow of $CA++$ ions depends, in turn, on (b) the amount of chemical called adenosine monophosphate (AMP) present in the cell. The amount of AMP is increased (c) when another neuron releases the neurotransmitter serotonin to the synapse of the first cell. Thus one way to produce relatively long-lasting changes in the strength of a synapse is to stimulate the synapse with a second serotonin-releasing neuron (Kandel, 1977, 1979). Other influences on the strength of the synapse—on its effectiveness in releasing neurotransmitter and so influencing the firing of other neurons—remain to be discovered.

FORGETTING: INTERFERENCE AND DISUSE

"Forgetting" here refers to normal forgetting by a subject whose hippocampus is intact and whose brain is otherwise in a normal state. It also means that no special training has been given to cause a failure of response. When special training is used, we speak of the *extinction* of response, which is dealt with later in this chapter.

Spontaneous forgetting, then, or failure of retention in the ordinary course of living, is what we are now concerned with. It may be due to *interference* from other learning, or to *disuse*, or to both. Interference may be *proactive* or *retroactive*. Proactive interference (also called proactive inhibition) is an impairment of retention of one thing, B, because something else, A, was learned earlier. Retroactive interference (also, and classically, known as *retroactive inhibition*) is an impairment of retention of A because of learning B subsequently. Figure 6.1 shows how the two are demonstrated experimentally. The impairment is greatest when A and B contain similar but not identical material.

Disuse refers to the tendency of synaptic changes of learning to regress and become less effective as time passes, even though consolidation has occurred, if the synaptic connections are not activated. Disuse results in forgetting: If you don't practice your basketball shots or your French verbs, you will forget them because of lack of practice. But there is also much forgetting in which disuse plays little part and that must be attributed to retroactive interference instead.

It seems likely that proactive interference and retroactive interference must have their effects in different ways. Proactive interference seems to make later learning (Fig. 6.2b) less stable, whereas retroactive interference exerts a positive suppression. Also, retroactive interference may be an impairment of consolidation, for the second learning has the greatest effect on the prior learning when it occurs immediately afterward.

Retroactive interference appears also to be the most powerful of the three mechanisms discussed here (i.e., more powerful than proactive interference or disuse). Its existence has been thoroughly established in

Experiment	Group	Stages		
		1	2	3
Proactive interference	Experimental	Learn A	Learn B	Tested on B
	Control	Do nothing	Learn B	Tested on B
Retroactive interference	Experimental	Learn A	Learn B	Tested on A
	Control	Learn A	Do nothing	Tested on A

FIGURE 6.1. Experiments demonstrating proactive and retroactive interference. Each experiment has two groups of subjects: an experimental group, whose performance demonstrates the interference effect, and a control group, whose performance does not demonstrate interference. Each experiment has three phases. On phase three, experimental group performance is worse than control group performance for both the proactive and retroactive interference experiments.

subjects as different as cockroach and man. The evidence indicates that any activity interposed between learning and testing must itself cause some learning and hence interfere with the retention of the prior learning. It is impossible for a normal waking subject to perceive and remember nothing of what is happening around him just because he is told to do so. Therefore, a control group would also have some retroactive interference from such incidental learning. In an effort to obtain a control group that learns nothing during the waiting interval, experiments have been done in which the subject sleeps during the interval. With the same subject, the retention of nonsense syllables can be measured when the syllables were learned just before going to bed and before a normal day's activity. The results of one such experiment are shown in Fig. 6.2. In the first hour the subject lost as much in the sleeping condition as in the normal-activity condition, but of course one cannot go to sleep instantly, so there would be retroactive interference at first. After the first hour in the sleeping condition, when the subject actually was asleep, there was practically no forgetting. The existence of retroactive interference is firmly established. However, there is some evidence to show that disuse must have its effect also. For example, goldfish that were active during the period between learning a simple maze and being retested, retained more of the original learning than goldfish that were less active (French, 1942); if the forgetting was due to retroactive interference the result should have been the other way round.

Another example, with cockroaches, demonstrated forgetting that seems to require both retroactive interference and disuse (Minami & Dallenbach, 1946). Cockroaches were trained to avoid the dark end of an alley. Each of the control animals was then allowed to enter a small hole, where the animal immediately became inactive, in a possibly sleep-like state. Each experimental animal was kept in a small cage and was moderately active for the same length of time. All were then tested. From Fig. 6.2d it can be seen that the active animals lost more (i.e., took more trials on relearning: the savings method) than the inactive ones, which clearly indicates retroactive interference. But the inactive ones also lost a good deal in the first 2 hours, a loss that cannot be explained away by supposing that it takes a cockroach 2 hours to go to sleep in these conditions. The results are best understood by supposing that the loss by the inactive animals was due mostly to disuse, and the greater loss by the active animals due both to disuse and to retroactive interference.

There is clinical evidence to support the conclusion that some forgetting is due to disuse. The human child who has normal vision for the first 2 years of life and then becomes blind will have lost, by the time he has grown up, all his visual learning and will be indistinguishable from one who has been blind from birth.[1] It might be suggested that the loss is due also to retroactive interference, the effect of all the other learning the blind child must do. But if he does not become blind until the age of 5, he does not lose all the effects of visual learning, although retroactive interference should have its effect here as well as with the child who becomes blind earlier. Retroactive interference undoubtedly has some effect, but it does not explain the whole loss in the child who becomes blind at the younger age.

EXTINCTION AND THE ELIMINATION OF ERROR

The clinical data just referred to show us that there is some memory that is permanent. Indeed, common experience tells us the same thing, though psychology is hard put, in some cases, to explain why some information is retained and other information is not. Frequency of repetition is one factor that makes for longer retention. Another is the degree of emotional excitement aroused in the learning situation. Some learning persists, however, that may have resulted from a single exposure to a not-very-exciting situation; and sometimes the persistence of a habit or a cognitive memory may be undesirable.

Extinction is the process of abolishing a learned response by withholding reinforcement. Obviously, it applies only where there is a known reinforcer. There are two forms of extinction, temporary and lasting.

The phenomenon of temporary extinction was discovered by Pavlov. When a salivary CR has been established, the repeated presentation of the CS with the UCS in one training session (lasting about an hour) makes the CR first diminish and then disappear. When the dog is brought back the next day, however, the CS again elicits the CR. Pavlov showed that the temporary disappearance of the CR is due to some sort of inhibitory process that is generalized and affects all other CRs while it is present. This is extinction with massed trials.

With spaced trials, one or two a day for a number of days, or with massed trials repeated daily (still without reinforcement), the result is a lasting disappearance of the CR (though it can be reestablished with training and shows savings in the number of trials necessary). Just what

---

[1]There are definite defects in space perception in the congenitally blind. Compared with those who became blind later in life, the congenitally blind make amorphous clay models, are poorer at estimating size or identifying shapes (thus doing badly in form-board tests in which blocks are fitted into receptacles which they fit exactly), and make lower scores than blindfolded normal subjects in maze learning.

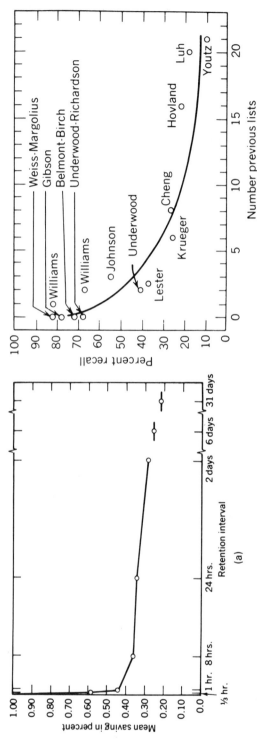

(a) This graph illustrates the savings method for measuring memory. The subject was Herman Ebbinghaus, the inventor of the nonsense syllable. The ordinate, percentage saved, records the time spent to relearn eight lists of nonsense syllables after a given length of time (recorded on the abscissa) following the original learning. One hundred percent savings means that no mistakes were made on relearning. 0% means that it took as long to relearn the lists as it originally took to learn them. (From Kintsch, W., 1970, *Learning, Memory and Conceptual Processes*. New York: Wiley [after Ebbinghaus]. Reprinted by permission.)

(b) This graph illustrates proactive inhibition. It is harder to learn new nonsense syllable lists as the number of previously learned lists increases. The ordinate is the percentage recalled after 24 hours, and the abscissa is the number of lists previously learned. Data are from a series of different experiments (from Kintsch, 1970).

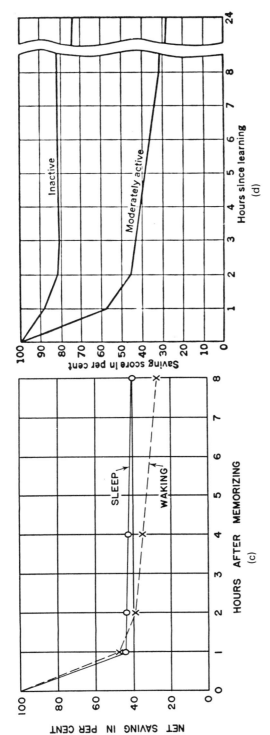

(c) This graph illustrates retroactive inhibition, which may be caused by the failure of consolidation. The ordinate is percentage saved. One case is for an interval filled with sleep, the other for a waking interval filled with other activities, including other learning. (Adapted by permission from Woodworth, R. S. and Schlosberg, H., 1954, *Experimental Psychology.* New York: Holt).

(d) This graph illustrates retroactive interference in the cockroach. Animals that were inactive between learning and testing make better retention scores during the test than animals that were active in the interval and presumably learning other things. Note however the loss by the inactive group during the first two hours, which suggests an effect of disuse. (Data of H. Minami and K. Dallenbach, 1946, from Woodworth and Scholsberg, 1970.)

FIGURE 6.2.

119

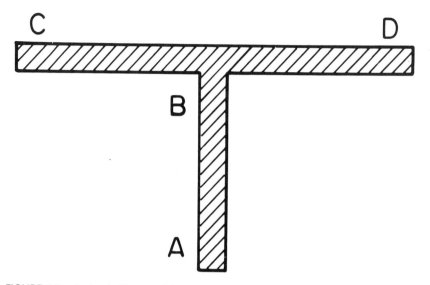

FIGURE 6.3.   A simple T-maze. A is the starting point, and B is the choice point. The goal box, where food is put, may be at either C or D.

happens—the nature of the basic mechanism—is not clear. The response that is extinguished may be a well-established one for which consolidation has long been complete, so the process is not a reversal of the synaptic changes of learning. It seems therefore that the extinction trials must add some further learning that modifies or inhibits the earlier learning.

The elimination of error—that is, the extinction of a wrong response—in the acquisition period is somewhat easier to understand. Figure 6.3 represents a simple T-maze for the study of learning in the rat. The animal is started at A, and food is put at D. Suppose he turns left when he reaches the choice point, B, then goes to C, then turns back and reaches the food at D. And suppose that because of some accident of past learning, he does this repeatedly. At first one might think that the more often the left-turning response follows the stimuli of the choice point, the stronger the S-R connections would be and the more likely the rat would be to turn left. But we know, of course, that this does not happen—the more often he turns left, the less likely he is to do so the next time. We can understand this from the principles of reinforcement. The response of going toward C is not reinforced,[2] whereas a turn toward D is positively reinforced whenever it occurs.

---

[2]Besides being unreinforced, entry into the blind alley may cause frustration, an emotional disturbance that, if it is strong, is disruptive of the behavior it accompanies (see chapter 10).

Once the right-turning response at B is well established, eliminating it may be more difficult. We place the food at C instead of D, but it may take considerably more trials to extinguish the right-turning response than it took to establish it. What is happening, however, is easily understood as the addition of further learning that interferes with the earlier learning. Turning left at B prevents turning right.

We can regard this as the normal mechanism of eliminating error: the establishment of a correct response that prevents the occurrence of a wrong one by rewarding the correct response and not rewarding the other. But there are certain situations, especially some human learning situations, in which this method of dealing with error encounters difficulties. For example: Every amateur typist knows that typewriters spell badly, much worse than a good pencil and that the errors may be extraordinarily persistent. A common "typo" is "hte" for "the." How can one eliminate these repetitive errors? One logical procedure is to practice the troublesome word, typing it correctly by itself hundreds of times. Another way is to type the error, also hundreds of times. In one experiment comparing these two methods, practicing the wrong behavior was more effective than practicing the right one. In a later test of this result, no difference was found, a result that itself is remarkable: to perfect a certain behavior, A, it is just as effective to practice a different one, B, as it is to practice A itself. Returning to the rat in the T-maze, we see that the cases are quite parallel, for the more often the rat "practiced" entering the blind alley, the less likely that response was to be made. Perhaps, then, typing the wrong word is a form of extinction, although here, as in other forms of extinction, exactly what happens is not too clear.

DISTORTIONS OF MEMORY: TESTIMONY

There is a classic experiment that has been reported many times. About 1902, Professor von Liszt, criminologist at the University of Berlin, was lecturing about a book when a student suddenly shouted, "I want to throw light on the matter from the standpoint of Christianity!" Another shouted, "I cannot stand that!" The first jumped up, shouting "You have insulted me!" The second replied in kind. The first drew a revolver. The second ran at him, and, as Professor Liszt stepped between them, the revolver went off. After he had gotten control of the situation, Liszt asked the other students to write reports of the incident. He of course had planned the incident and could compare the eyewitness accounts with what had actually happened. In the accounts were alterations as well as omissions and additions—clear evidence that even intelligent witnesses, with nothing to gain from false reports, can make gross errors in testimony concerning a relatively simple incident.

The testimony of witnesses can also easily be influenced by the examiner's questions. As an experimental demonstration, Professor Elizabeth Loftus (1979) showed college students a film of a traffic accident. The students then answered questions about the accident. Some were asked, "About how fast were the cars going when they smashed into each other?" Others were asked, "About how fast were the cars going *when they hit each other?*" Students who heard the first question, with the phrase "smashed into," gave a higher average estimate of speed than the students who heard the second question, with the word "hit." Students who heard "smashed into" were also more likely later to report having seen broken glass, although there was no broken glass visible in the accident film (Fig. 6.4 and Table 6.1).

FIGURE 6.4. Adding information later can alter memory. The original information was a film of an auto accident. Later, observers were asked "About how fast were the cars going when they smashed into each other?" Other observers were asked a similar question, but with the phrase "smashed into each other" replaced by "hit each other?" Then all the observers were asked "Did you see any broken glass?" The table shows that more of the observers who heard the question with the phrase "smashed into each other" remembered seeing broken glass. There was actually no broken glass visible in the original accident film. (From Loftus, 1979. Reproduced by permission.)

TABLE 6.1
The Loftus Memory Experiment: How Observers Recalled an Auto
Accident with No Visible Broken Glass.

Question asked: "How fast were the cars going when they . . .	Recall Memory for Broken Glass?	
	Yes	No
. . . smashed into each other?"	16	34
. . . hit each other?"	7	43

Loftus' demonstration shows that "consistent" memories of an event may mix information from different and sometimes unreliable sources. The mixing is not deliberate, and the witness is not aware of it. Loftus also showed that the misleading information had the greatest effect when it was presented well after the original event, because the original memory weakens over time through forgetting caused by disuse or retroactive interference. When the misleading information about the event is delayed, it combines with a weaker original memory to produce a greater distortion. When the misleading information is presented shortly after the event in competition with a stronger original memory, it produces less distortion in the memory. This is why a lawyer's "leading question," asked months after the event, stands a good chance of eliciting a biased answer from an honest witness with a weak memory for the event.

MEMORY TECHNIQUES

H.M. was the patient who could remember nothing new after the tips of the hippocampus on both sides of his brain had been removed. Another person with an unusual memory was S., who had the opposite problem—instead of remembering nothing new, S. could forget nothing old. He was studied by the Russian psychologist, A. R. Luria (1968). S. had a remarkable untrained ability to create clear and unusual mental images and then to associate these images with arbitrary lists of words and numbers. These associations between images and lists persisted in memory and allowed S to retrieve the lists almost perfectly, often in any order, years after they had been presented. This was a mixed blessing. When S wanted to express a thought in words, the previous images associated with each word interfered with the development of the thought, and S was often left with a confused set of sensory images. S was able to turn his unusual ability to profit as a stage performer, but he lived all his life with an almost automatic attachment of sensory images to every word he heard. The association to a sensory experience of another sensory memory, often in a different modality—for instance, the association of colors with sounds—is called synesthesia.

Associating words with visual images has been recognized since antiquity as a way to remember words. Although details vary, the basic idea depends on the fact that a series of visual images is usually easier to recall than a series of words. A list of words—for example, the outline of a speech—is associated with an ordered set of visual images, for example, the successive corners, from left to right, of the hall in which the speech is to be given. Then as the speaker views each of the corners of the hall, the word associated with that location is remembered (Fig. 6.5). Associating a word with a place can be made easier by finding an unusual visual image relating the word and the place. For example, if the first theme of a speech on psychology is "The Contribution of Aristotle," the speaker may visualize a statue of Aristotle standing in the leftmost corner of the room. Deliberate practice of this kind of associative learning is one method used by performers who have trained themselves to remember well (mnemonists), but who do not necessarily possess superior unaided recall ability as an accompaniment to their superior memory (Ericsson, 1985; Ericsson & Chase, 1982).

Some words are easier to remember than others. As the previous examples suggest, the easiest words to remember are associated with the clearest visual images. According to one theory, permanent memory takes two forms: sensorimotor images or symbols. The images originate from any sensory or response system; the symbols originate from the auditory and verbal motor system most of us use to hear and produce words. All else being equal, images are easier to remember than words. Words that are closely associated with images are easier to remember than words without closely associated images. For most people, "house" evokes an image more rapidly and more clearly than "theory," and "house" is an easier word to learn in a simple memory task (Paivio, 1971).

Although it is interesting to know that high-imagery words are easier to remember, we seldom have to remember a string of unrelated high-imagery words. Without employing memory tricks, even with the clearest imagery and the closest attention, the capacity to attend to and then to recall a series of unrelated things is limited. For normal adults the limit for immediate recall of unrelated things is about seven items (Miller, 1954).

But everyday life requires that we remember related things so that they can be recalled and used correctly. Not only that, but there are often more than seven items in the lists of related things to remember. How are these items remembered? Although there is uncertainty about the details, there is general agreement that memory for related materials depends on a process called *chunking*, or recoding.

Chunking is the ability to relate new memories to old, so that the new memories can be organized in ways that are easier to remember. For example, a string of binary digits (0s and 1s) much longer than seven items can be remembered if the digits are chunked by a simple arithmetic rule into decimal digits (0 through 9). The binary string 101000100111001110 can be chunked as 101 00010 01110 01110, and then into the successive decimal digits 5, 2, 14, 14, well within the memory span (example after Miller, 1955). The new memory—a string

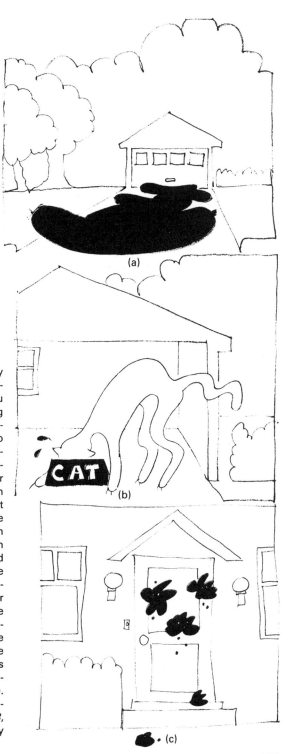

FIGURE 6.5. The memory method of locations is illustrated here. Suppose you must remember a shopping list; for purposes of illustration we shorten the list to three items. First you establish locations in a visually familiar place: your house, for example. Then you place an image of each shopping list item in association with one of the places: sausages on the driveway (a); cat food in a dish in the garage (b), and tomatoes splashed on the front door (c). As you mentally "walk through" your house while in the store, the vivid images are easy to remember. The trick is to make good images that combine the familiar home locations with the items to be remembered. (After Bower, (1970). Analysis of a mnemonic device. (*American Scientist, 58*, pp. 496–510. Adapted by permission.)

125

of binary digits—was transformed through previous learning into a shorter series of familiar items well within the memory span.

A more complicated example can be drawn from your experience at a lecture. The lecturer usually makes some effort to relate the new thing to be remembered by analogy or by similarity to something already known. The lecturer should relate the series of new points to each other by the same means. If the lecturer fails to make the connection between the new and the old, then you must make it for yourself or risk forgetting what was said. To be remembered, new information must be chunked or recoded, in association with previously well-established knowledge. Chunking means that short-term memories are associated with each other through connections with established knowledge. Once they are chunked and the chunks have been consolidated from short-term into long-term memory, the new information in turn becomes a part of the permanent store around which other new information can be chunked. The chunking process repeats itself as permanent memory grows in size and complexity.

STUDY METHOD

At the beginning of this chapter it was observed that the problem is not merely to learn but to learn *and remember*, for example, long enough to pass examinations. You may even want to remember longer than that. It is easy to read a paragraph in a textbook and, for the moment, know what it contains, but then comes retroactive interference due to learning the next paragraph and the one after that. The net result is that after reading through a whole chapter, you may find you can recall only the last page or so. How is this to be avoided? How is the learning to be retained?

Good study methods provide an answer. Almost any student can benefit from a book on study methods. However, the ones who need it least often benefit the most; others, with bad habits, find it difficult to change. Nonetheless, this must be said: *if you have trouble getting down to study, find it hard to concentrate, or cannot recall what you have read, buy a book on study methods and use it. Study it; it will* repay the time invested. The following brief survey is made with the hope that it will induce you to go further.

A good study method makes study easier and more tolerable as well as more efficient. A bad study method is inefficient and makes the task unpleasant and hard to face. Many students, including some very intelligent ones, do not realize that there is more than one way of attacking, say, a chapter of history. They sit down to read the chapter through, trying to retain detail at the same time—trying almost to memorize. No technical book is meant to be read that way, still less to be memorized. Retroactive interference has full opportunity to take effect, and the concentration on details keeps the student from attending to the large picture, the organization of the chapter as a whole. His attention wanders; he realizes that he is not concentrating as he meant to. He knits his brow, stares harder at the page, resolves to stop thinking about other things, and tries again to read and remember. It is an impossible task with technical material of more than a few paragraphs. Attempting it is unpleasant as well as inefficient.

A good student doesn't go at the task in such a way; students who know how to study do not begin by reading the chapter. Instead they set out to see first what it is about: by reading the summary if there is one, looking at the headings, sampling and skimming and relating what they find to what they think the author's views are—all with the objective of knowing, before even reading the chapter, what it says and what its general meaning is. This method allows them to recall relevant information and provides the means of chunking, or recoding, the material to be remembered. There is only minimal risk of retroactive interference. Instead of learning a series of details, meaningless in themselves until related to the main theme, the details are fitted into and become part of a single larger picture. No interference is involved. The larger picture is what is remembered, not the details, although in fact the large picture also has the effect of making detail easier to recall. Also, no heavy effort at concentrating is called for, either in the preliminary scanning of the chapter or in the later mastery in detail.

A further step toward the avoidance of that strain of concentration made necessary by bad study habits comes with the extensive use of notetaking. Merely making a note on a difficult passage has the effect of attending to it; and if there is something that you particularly want to fix in memory, make a note—write it out on a piece of paper, even if you throw the paper away later. *Do not underline if you want to recall; write it out.* The student's aim should be that of the lazy person—to get the most for the least work—but a lazy person with intelligence. Take the trouble to make notes. It more than repays the extra time and effort.

Your notes should not merely summarize. You should be asking questions, commenting and criticizing, looking for evidence to support ideas of your own, and in general taking an active attitude toward your task. It is not true that we learn only by doing. As we have seen, latent learning is an outstanding characteristic of the human species, but even latent learning is supported and maintained by a critical and active mental attitude.

For the student with good study habits, study is not the nightmare it sometimes is for others—it may almost be fun. If it is a nightmare for you, or if you have difficulty persuading yourself to get down to work, or if you have trouble recalling what you have studied or trouble getting it down on paper in the examination, consider: it may not be your intelligence, but your study method that is at fault. Get hold of a good book on studying and use it. What has been said here is only a beginning.

SUMMARY AND GUIDE TO STUDY

Before going further, you might use this chapter as material for a *practical exercise in study method*. First look through the chapter and make a list of the headings. Under each heading, make a list of the technical terms found in that section (mainly the italicized terms, but look also for technical terms you are already familiar with). Then make a list of the principal problems that are discussed. Prepare a summary and a brief study guide as if for another student, along the lines of the suggestions for review in the previous chapter summaries in this text. When you have organized the chapter for someone else to study, you may be surprised to find that you do not need much more study yourself—all that remains for mastery of the material may be to fill in the details.

Now for a summary, which you may compare with your own: If learning is to last, a period of consolidation is necessary. We do not know what happens in this period, but it may be when primary reinforcement has its effect. The need for consolidation is shown by the disturbing effects of shock following learning. The hippocampus appears to be essential for consolidation of human learning, less necessary in lower mammals (but this may be because the human learning studied was cognitive, without primary reinforcement, whereas the animal experiments used primary reinforcement).

Normal forgetting seems mainly due to retroactive interference, a disturbing effect of later learning on the retention of earlier learning, but there is proactive interference as well and some evidence of an effect also of disuse. We speak of "forgetting" when no active steps are taken to change the response. When one deliberately sets out to suppress a habit, this is called "extinction," which takes two forms: a temporary extinction with massed trials, due to inhibition, and a lasting extinction with spaced trials (probably a form of new learning that prevents the old learning from having its behavioral effect).

Distortions of memory are of great practical importance, as, for example, in legal testimony. Distortion may occur because some items in a complex memory have dropped out; and thought processes (recalling and thinking about the events in question) may have the effect of rearranging and adding to the retained items ("It must have happened that way").

Our knowledge about memory does add something to the practical advice one can give about studying. Every student should become familiar with a good book on how to study.

NOTES AND GENERAL REFERENCES

Short- and Long-Term Memory

Deutsch, D., & Deutsch, J. A. (Eds). (1975). *Short-term Memory*. New York: Academic Press. An interesting set of papers emphasizing the biological foundations of short-term memory.

Hebb, D. O. (1961). Distinctive features of learning in the higher animal. In J. F. Delafresnay (Ed.), *Brain Mechanisms and Learning*. Oxford: Blackwell. Reports the repetition of digits experiment.

John, E. R. (1967). *Mechanisms of Memory*. New York: Academic Press. An integrated theory of memory that stresses the statistical nature of the neuronal activity which constitutes memory.

Miller, G. A. (1954). The magical number seven, plus or minus two: Some limits on our capacity for processing information. *Psychological Review, 63,* 81–97.

Milner, B. (1970). Memory and the medial temporal regions of the brain. In K. H. Pribram & D. E. Broadbent, Eds., *Biology of Memory*. New York: Academic Press.

Minami, H. & Dallenbach, K. M. (1946). The effect of activity upon learning and retention in the cockroach. *American Journal of Psychology, 59,* 1–58.

Unusual Memory

Ericsson, K. A. (1985). Memory skill. *Canadian Journal of Psychology, 39,* 188–231.

Ericsson, K. A., & Chase, W. G. (1982). Exceptional memory. *American Scientist, 70,* 607–615. Argues that exceptionally good memory is simply a skill that combines ordinary memory processes—primarily "chunking"—with an extraordinary level of practice.

Luria, A. A. (1968). *The Mind of a Mnemonist*. (L. Solotaroff, trans.) New York: Basic Books. Description of the talents of the Russian mnemonist S.

Other References

French, J. W. (1942). The effect of temperature on the retention of a maze habit in fish. *Journal of Experimental Psychology, 31,* 79–87.

Grossberg, S., & Stone, G. (1986). Neural dynamics of word recognition and recall: Attentional priming, learning and resonance. *Psychological Review, 93,* 46–74. A memory theory based on an elaboration of principles consistent with the cell assembly ideas developed in chapters 4 and 5.

Loftus, E. (1979). *Eyewitness Testimony*. Cambridge, MA: Harvard University Press. An interesting account of both experiments and legal cases involving eyewitness testimony, including evidence that memory for events can be modified by "leading questions" long after the event took place.

McGaugh, J. L. (1983). Hormonal influences on memory storage. *American Psychologist, 38*, 161–174. Reviews the evidence that body hormones like epinephrine have an effect on the consolidation of learning in the brain.

Paivio, A. (1971). *Imagery and Verbal Processes*. New York: Holt, Rinehart & Winston. Develops the dual coding theory of memory: memory is both imagery and verbal.

CHAPTER 7

Heredity, Maturation, and Early Learning

The preceding chapters have raised the question of the relation between heredity and environment and the effect of early experience on the development of behavior. We now look more closely at these issues and at a related one: the age-old but still confusing question of instinct.

You have already been cautioned against placing heredity in opposition to environment. It is common to talk as if a perception, for example, might be entirely inherited or entirely learned, as if maternal behavior must be either inherited or learned, and so on. This kind of either/or choice creates confusion, due (1) to thinking of only two variables (there are more) and (2) to forgetting the role of early experience.

A central issue in psychology is the nature of learning and the part it plays in the development of adult characteristics. But equally important—the same issue in reverse, the other side of the coin—is the role of maturation, or growth, in determining the structures in which the learning must occur. Growth occurs in all parts of an animal, including the central and the peripheral nervous system. Theoretically, we can distinguish between learning and growth, but practically they are inseparable: there is no behavior that is independent of the animal's heredity, or its growth to maturity, or the supporting environment; and no higher behavior that is uninfluenced by learning.

INSTINCTIVE BEHAVIOR AND MATURATION

"Instinct" is a term of doubtful scientific value, for reasons that we will come to later. "Instinctive", however, is more useful as a rough term to designate certain kinds of behavior. Instinctive behavior may be defined as complex species-predictable behavior: at a higher level than reflex behavior, not requiring special conditions of learning for its appearance, but predictable simply because we know that we are dealing with a particular species in its ordinary habitat.

The distinction between instinctive behavior and reflex behavior (which, of course, is also species-predictable) is clear in principle, although in practice the two classes overlap one another and a sharp dichotomy is probably impossible. A reflex response occurs in a specific group of effectors and is evoked by stimulation of a specific sensory surface. Light falling on the retina results in pupillary contraction; acid in the mouth results in salivary secretion; stimulation of the newborn infant's palm produces clasping by that hand, and stimulation of the infant's lips produces sucking movements. The pupillary reflex is not possible without the retina, the clasp reflex is not possible without the receptors of the palm, and so on. Instinctive behavior, on the other hand, is usually not dependent on any specific receptors, and it characteristically involves a large proportion of the effectors of the whole body, rather than being limited to one gland or muscle group. Also, it commonly includes elements of learning.

All instinctive behavior involves reflex elements[1]: Part of the pattern can be eliminated by loss of a sense organ or muscle group, but the overall pattern remains fully identifiable. The instinctive maternal behavior of the female rat is only slightly affected by the loss of any one of the senses of vision, smell, or tactile sensitivity in the snout. Loss of two of these senses does affect the behavior significantly, showing that they are all involved in the behavior, but no one of them is essential (Beach, 1939, 1955).

Instinctive sexual behavior by the male rat shows the same picture.

---

[1]Like any other complex behavior, any response must affect the animal's posture, which is reflexively controlled though higher centers can impose changes on these reflexes and thus produce what we classify as a nonreflexive action. Thus if a male animal has a leg amputated there will be a recognizable change in his approach to the female, but the overall picture of male sex behavior will also be recognizable. In the second place, instinctive behavior in general includes two phases, *preparatory* and *consummatory*, and the consummatory phase is essentially reflexive. In food-getting behavior, the search for food and seizing it are preparatory, whereas mastication, salivation and swallowing are consummatory. Damage to throat muscles would prevent completion of the consummatory activity, but the instinctive pattern would still be identifiable.

Even if the genitalia are removed, the pattern of mating behavior can be obtained, right up to the point of intromission and ejaculation. Although an essential reflex element of the total pattern is missing, the pattern is recognizable and complete as far as it is mechanically possible. Reflex behavior is primarily a local process; instinctive behavior primarily involves the whole animal (Fig. 7.1).

The special attribute of instinctive behavior is that it does not have to be taught or acquired by practice. For example, a female rat can be brought up in isolation, without ever having an opportunity to observe another female caring for her young. At maturity the female is mated and put in a cage outfitted with strips of paper. A day or two before

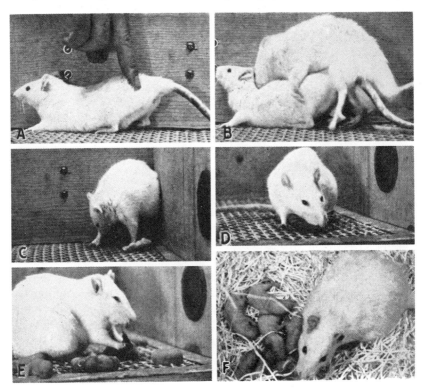

FIGURE 7.1. Instinctive behavior in the female rat. (a) tactual stimulation elicits the receptive posture reflexively. (b) mounting by the male. (c) delivery of the young. (d), cleaning a pup and removing the amniotic membrane. (e) eating the placenta (the mother seldom pays attention to the young until the placenta has been eaten). (f) the litter has been gathered together in the nest; in a cold environment the nesting material would be pulled up over mother and young so that they could hardly be seen. (Photographs taken in The Wistar Institute by Dr. Edmond J. Farris and William Sykes. From E. J. Farris & J. Q. Griffith, (19) *The Rat in Laboratory Investigation.* New York: Lippincott. Reproduced by permission.)

giving birth, she begins gathering paper together to form a primitive kind of nest. When the young are born she promptly cleans them, collects them into the nest, and crouches over them in a way that makes suckling possible. In short, even with no opportunity for practice, she performs a complex task quite competently.

A virgin female rat, with no previous experience, can be made to exhibit maternal behavior, including nest building, when she is given a transfusion of blood from a female rat who is about to give birth! Not only is the basic behavior unlearned (although it may improve with experience), but it is induced by hormones that circulate in the blood of the pregnant female. The exact sequence of hormone activity responsible for stimulating maternal behavior is still being studied. Many examples could be given: the web-building of spiders, each making a web characteristic of its particular species; the complex courting and mating behavior of birds; the migration of some fish for great distances to spawn in a particular stream, and the nest-building and fighting patterns of others.

The farther down the animal scale we look, the more rigid and unvarying is the predictable pattern of behavior. But it is quite evident that there is much that is "species-predictable" about the behavior of the higher mammals, including human beings. Is species-specific human behavior instinctive too?

Two kinds of Behavior, Learned and Inherited

Much of our difficulty with this question comes from thinking of behavior as being of two different kinds: learned and unlearned, with the idea that the learned behavior is more or less independent of heredity and that unlearned behavior is determined by heredity alone. But now consider this case. Neither a human baby nor a chimpanzee baby needs to learn how to have a temper tantrum. The behavior is complex but quite characteristic in form, so that no experienced observer has any difficulty in identifying it. The baby does not have to practice it (nor to see how others do it) in order to produce, on the first try, a first-class sample. It is therefore "unlearned." But it is not independent of learning, for the baby must have learned, for example, to want something outside his reach and to see that it is being withheld from him. The tantrum itself, then, is not learned but is dependent on the existence of other learning (Dennis, 1940).

Shall we then conclude that there are three kinds of behavior: (1) learned, (2) unlearned but dependent on learning, and (3) unlearned, determined by heredity alone? We might ask instead whether this kind of classification is justified at all. It may not be. Let us now consider two sets of facts: the first concerns maturation, the second, the effects of early experience. We will then be in a position to take a different approach to the whole heredity–environment question.

Maturation

It is obvious that some of the changes in behavior following birth are due to physical growth, especially the increase of the infant's muscular strength. It is not so obvious that growth is also going on in the nervous system and that learning is not the whole explanation for other changes that are observed. The human brain at birth has all the neurons it will ever have, but many connecting fibers are still incomplete.[2] Learning processes cannot strengthen synaptic connections between two neurons until parts of the neurons are in close proximity. That is, learning cannot occur until physical maturation has reached the proper stage.

We think of the infant as learning to walk once his muscles are strong enough to hold him. But throughout this period, apparently one of practice, what is going on is at least partly the completion of a certain level of growth in the nervous system. When this stage has been reached, a comparatively short practice period is enough to achieve walking.

There are several classical demonstrations that the slow process of maturation limits the advantages of practice. For instance, one of a pair of monozygotic (genetically identical) twins was given extensive and early practice at stair climbing. He was helped up the stairs and given many opportunities to practice. The other twin, raised in the same environment, was kept away from stairs until he was a year old, when he was introduced to stairs without formal training: he promptly began to climb them (Dennis, 1940).

Another example is the feeding behavior of young chicks. Shortly after hatching, as the chick begins to peck at things about it, it will succeed in hitting kernels of grain, holding them in the beak and swallowing them. But errors (failing to hit the kernel, but more often failing to hold it until it can be swallowed) are frequent. Accuracy improves rapidly in the first 5 to 10 days, as the chick practices; this looks like learning. Figure 7.2 illustrates the results of an experiment that shows that, instead, much of the change is due to maturation.

---

[2]Many of the axons also lack the myelin sheath (chapter 3), the growth of which continues long after birth. The brain at birth weighs about 425 gm (250–600 gm): at maturity, about 1350 gm (1000–2000 gm). The great increase is partly due to outgrowth of axon and dendrite, but must be due more to the addition of myelin and the proliferation of capillaries and larger blood vessels. There may also be an increase in the number of glia.

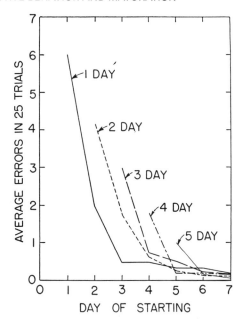

FIGURE 7.2. Maturation of pecking skill in chicks: the number of misses ("errors") made by chicks allowed to begin practice at different intervals after hatching. (After Cruze, Reproduced by permission.)

Some chicks began their pecking 1 day after hatching; others were kept in darkness and fed by hand for 1 to 5 days before they began to practice pecking. The figure shows two things: the older the chick, the more accurate it is without any practice (e.g., the curve for the 3-day group begins at a lower level of errors than that for the 2-day group). But the practice has its effect also, for the 3-day group does not begin at the level that the 1-day or 2-day group has reached by the third day.

This example is particularly instructive. First, it shows clearly how physical growth and learning processes can collaborate in the development of behavior. They are not opposed but instead work together, and only by ingenious experimentation can they be distinguished for theoretical purposes. Another important point is that the learning must occur at the right time: if the chick is kept in darkness very long, grossly abnormal feeding behavior is the eventual result. We must note also that learning is not essential for all aspects of the behavior: the tendency to peck at small objects is present in the newly hatched chick, and it has been reported that no prior experience is needed to make the chick peck at rounded objects in preference to sharp-cornered ones.

This innately established pecking may be classed as reflexive. Unconditioned reflex paths are in general laid down by heredity and growth processes; no learning is involved. Some are functional at birth, like the chick's pecking tendency or the sucking reflex of the newborn mammal, but others apparently have to wait until the neural fibers involved have made connection with each other.

THE EFFECTS OF EARLY EXPERIENCE

In demonstrating the phenomena of maturation, the experimental problem is to find a way of showing that the behavior is not due to learning alone. Now we turn to another situation in which the problem is to show that any learning is occurring at all. The very young infant seems to be doing nothing much but eating, defecating, and growing—vegetating in the intervals between feedings, with some random movement of the limbs and eyes, and some random noise making, but not being affected by what is going on around him. But this is a period of latent learning that lays the basis for all future mental development.

Even before birth, the mammal is exposed to complex tactual stimulation from the various pressures exerted by the uterine wall and by contacts of one part of the fetal body with another (Birnholz & Farrell, 1984). After birth, the complexity of this stimulation is enormously increased. The human baby lying in the crib is exposed to a continuously changing pattern of stimulation. Even in a quiet room in which nothing else is happening, the movement of eyes and limbs changes the visual and tactual input, and there is auditory stimulation from breathing and vocalization. The baby seems mostly unaffected by the stimulation, and it used to be thought that this was a period of physical growth during which the environment was unimportant, except for a supply of food and maintenance of an adequate temperature.

The situation, in fact, is quite different. The sensory stimulations of the early environment are necessary to maintain some neural structures that would otherwise degenerate and for the occurrence of learning, which is essential for normal adult behavior.

Maintenance of Neural Structures

In a normal adult cat or monkey, some cells in the visual cortex receive direct input from the left eye, and some cells receive direct input from the right eye, but most cells receive some input from both eyes. Figure 7.3b illustrates the distribution of visual cortex cells that can normally be stimulated by either eye or by both eyes. The cortical cells, which are primarily connected to one eye or the other, are organized into interlocking rows that can be shown on the surface of the cortex (Fig. 7.3a). The photographic technique that reveals these rows uses a

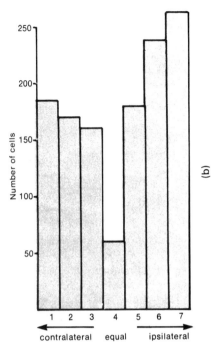

(b)

(b) The relative frequency of cells in 7 categories—ranging from cells influenced only by the contralateral eye, through those influenced equally by both eyes, to those influenced only by the ipsilateral eye—shows that the two eyes are about equally represented in the cortex (the small difference seen between contralateral and ipsilateral eyes on the histogram is not significant). Monocular, or predominantly monocular, cells (groups 1, 2, 6 and 7) are very numerous.

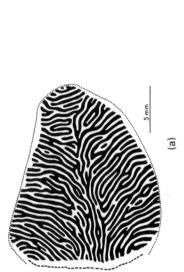

5 mm

(a)

(a) The striate cortex is reconstructed here to emphasize ocular dominance columns. Every other column is blackened to exhibit the twofold nature of the subdivisions: dark stripes represent one eye, and light stripes the other. Shown here is layer IVc of the exposed part of the right striate cortex. Note the relative constancy of column widths.

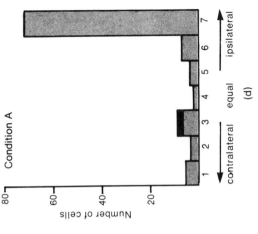

Condition A

Number of cells

80 — 60 — 40 — 20 —

1 2 3 4 5 6 7

contralateral ⟵ equal ⟶ ipsilateral

(d)

(c) Cortical diagram like (a), above, but produced photographi-
cally from the cortex of a monkey, like the one described in (d)
below, whose right eye was closed shortly after birth. The
ocular dominance columns from the open eye are wider, and
the columns from the closed eye are narrower, than in the
diagram of normal cortex shown in (a).

FIGURE 7.3.

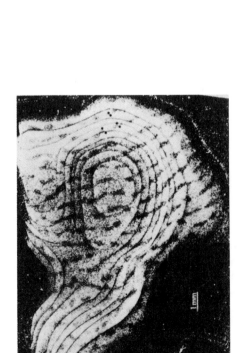

(c)

(d) The right eye of a macaque monkey was sutured closed at 2
weeks of age, and recordings were made from 101 cells in the
left striate cortex 18 months later. The great majority of cells
were in group 7—i.e. they were influenced only from the ipsilateral eye, in this case the left, or normal, eye. The darker colored
area represents a few cells that could have been influenced from
the right eye, but in which responses were abnormal. (From
Hubel, 1979. Reproduced by permission.)

139

radioactive chemical which is diffused only to cells receiving input from one of the two eyes.

If one eye of a young cat or monkey is temporarily covered by patching or the equivalent, the number of visual cortex cells that receive inputs from both eyes is reduced, and the structure of the cortical rows changes. For instance, after 72 weeks when the right eye was temporarily shut, with no patterns but only diffuse light allowed to reach the retina, very few of the cortical cells responded to stimulation from the right eye (Fig. 7.3d). Most of the cells had become attached to the left eye. This was reflected in the size of the rows connected to input from either eye; the left-eye rows were enlarged at the expense of the right-eye rows (Fig. 7.3c). It did not matter that later visual experience was equal for the two eyes: the deprivation, for 72 weeks beginning at only 2 weeks of age, permanently changed the arrangement of synapses in the visual cortex.

Individual neurons in the visual cortex are connected with cells in the retina in such a way that they are specialized for response to lines or edges of a particular slope in the visual field. Thus, a line with one slope excites one set of neurons in the cortex; a line with another slope excites a different set of neurons, even though the line falls in the same retinal area (chapter 12). In the normal animal, these connections are present at birth as well as at maturity. However, if a young kitten's visual experience is altered by goggles restricting one eye to viewing horizontal stripes, then fewer of the cortical cells that receive input from that eye will respond to vertical stripes. Conversely, if the eye is restricted to viewing vertical stripes, many fewer of the visual cortex cells receiving input from that eye will respond to horizontal stripes. These effects endure beyond the termination of the reduced stimulation. Permanent connections that are established at birth can be modified by the unusual experience of the animal shortly after birth.

Early Learning

The sensory events of infancy also determine adult patterns of behavior in invertebrates, fish, birds, and mammals. For example, ants discriminate members of their own colony by odor and attack others, even members of the same colony that have been given the wrong odor. But early experience determines the behavior, for normally antagonistic species will live amicably together if the two are mixed within 12 hours of hatching, and the effect is apparently permanent. Similarly, the sexual behavior of certain fish at maturity is changed by rearing in isolation, the males attempting to mate with both males and females. Many species of birds show imprinting, a lasting social attachment to members of the species to which they are first exposed—normally, of course, their own species, as the parent cares for them. Infrahuman mammals, abnormally reared, show striking effects of deprivation of normal early experience. These are changes of social behavior, of somesthetic perception (including pain reactions; see chapter 12), and of intelligence and learning capacity. As for human beings, several references have already been made to the effects of different environments on mental development. The effect of early environment on intelligence, both animal and human, is discussed in chapter 9.

Imprinting of Birds

When a bird emerges from the egg, the first moving object it sees is normally one of the parent birds. What the chick is exposed to in the first 24 hours or thereabouts of life has a lasting effect, very important in many species as a determinant of the bird's behavior at maturity. This is true at least of "precocial" species, in which the newly hatched chick can walk and follow an adult bird. An early learning occurs that, in part, produces the proper species-predictable behavior. For if instead of an adult of the same species, it is some other species to which the chick is exposed, the bird responds later to that other species as it normally would to its own. The degree of this effect varies from one kind of bird to another, but greylag geese, for example, hatched in an incubator and exposed only to a human being (who feeds and cares for them) will at maturity consort with people, and the ganders will tend to make their sexual advances to people and not to females of their own species. The birds are then said to be imprinted on human beings (K. Lorenz). In the ordinary course of events, such learning would be directed toward the parent bird and would produce normal social behavior at maturity.

An amusing example of imprinting occurred recently in a residential neighborhood of Montreal. A newly fledged crow fell out of its nest. Human neighbors acted as crow foster parents to protect it from cats and cars, against which it had no natural defenses. The crow lived for 3 weeks in the house and garden of a family with a large, friendly black dog. The crow "imprinted" on the dog, following it around the garden and opening its beak in the begging posture which is normally effective in soliciting food from its own large, black, but winged parents. When the crow had matured enough to fly well, it was released in a bird sanctuary far from the neighborhood and—it is hoped—far from any large black dog it might mistake for a parent.

Imprinting has been extensively studied in the laboratory. One form of experiment is shown in Fig. 7.4. A duckling is exposed to a wooden

FIGURE 7.4.   The apparatus used for the study of imprinting. The large decoy moves on a circular track under the experimenter's control; the duckling follows and is thereby imprinted. (From Hess, 1959. Reproduced by permission.)

model that moves in a circular track; the duckling follows and becomes imprinted (Hess, 1959). Such experiments show that there is a critical period after which imprinting will not occur, usually the first 12 to 24 hours of life, depending on the species. Experiments also show that this is a very special kind of learning in other respects. The learning does not require primary reinforcement (a wooden model provides neither food nor warmth), but it appears to depend on the amount of effort expended in *following*. Mere visual exposure is not enough, although it is obviously important when the bird discriminates visually between the imprinted-on object and others; and imprinting has also been obtained in chicks of a domestic breed of hen merely by allowing them to approach a motionless object close to a flickering light at one end of a long runway (James, 1960).

Early Learning in Mammals

In its clearest and most dramatic form, imprinting is a phenomenon that characterizes birds (though there are great differences from one species to another). However, the same kind of effect may appear in mammals, although the learning period needed may be much longer. It is reported that guinea pigs, sheep, goats, and deer brought up by man tend to act like pets and do not respond normally to their own kind. The sheep that has been reared by hand and kept away from other sheep during growth does not join the flock when turned out in the field and will, if given a choice, approach the human caretaker instead. Pet dogs are perhaps showing the same thing when they attempt to mount (make a sexual approach to) the leg of a human being. Female chimpanzees reared in a nursery by human caretakers and ones reared normally by their mothers differ markedly in their preference for human company at maturity; and some of the nursery-reared females are less sexually responsive to male chimpanzees than the others. These observations in general seem to show that some kind of lasting social identification results from the early experience of mammals, even though it is less dramatic than the imprinting of birds.

The experimental study of early learning in mammals, as distinct from the incidental or naturalistic observations of the preceding paragraph, includes the previously described work on chimpanzees reared in darkness and a number of investigations of the development of learning and problem solving that are discussed in chapter 9 under the heading of the growth of intelligence.

Here we will consider some of the drastic changes in the behavior of the dog reared in isolation: changes in social behavior and in the reaction to pain stimuli, and more generally, changes that can only be summed up as changes of personality.

In one experiment (Melzack & Thompson, 1950), Scottish terriers were reared in isolation, from early weaning onward. They could hear and smell other dogs and the human caretakers in the same room but otherwise were cut off from all social contacts. They were kept in small cages just large enough to allow them to stand and turn round comfortably. They grew well and stayed in excellent health until they were removed for testing when they were between 9 and 12 months old (Fig. 7.5a). There was no sign that they were unhappy. A dog that is reared normally and then put in isolation is obviously miserable, but these dogs had known no other existence. They were "happy as larks" and physically "as strong as bulls," in the words of the Scottie expert who supervised their rearing and who won a number of first class ribbons with them at dog shows. Such prizes are awarded only for physical form and posture; in obedience tests the dogs reared in isolation would have gotten nowhere, for they turned out to be almost untrainable. Their social behavior was aberrant in a way that is difficult to describe: they were dominated by normal dogs, would permit another dog to eat simultaneously from the same food dish (the normal Scottie reared outside the laboratory will not permit this), and reacted to familiar or

(a) Littermate Scotties, one reared normally, one in restriction. Visitors were sometimes invited to tell which was which when the two groups were put in a pen together, and usually made the wrong choice. The normal dog is at the left, rather bored with the photographic process; the restricted dog "didn't have brains enough to be bored," in the perceptive comment of the handler—i.e., boredom is a function of intellectual capacity.

(b) Rob at 30 months of age, as reared in conditions of somesthetic restriction. The cylinders permitted fairly free joint movement but radically limited his tactual experience. Note the abnormal sitting posture (see Fig. 7.5c). From Nissen, Chow, & Semmes, 1951. Reproduced by permission.

FIGURE 7.5.

(c) Jed, a nursery-reared chimpanzee infant at four months, the age at which fear of strangers appears. The leg posture is the normal one for the sitting animal: an abnormal posture appears in Fig. 7.5b. (Courtesy of H. W. Nissen and R. K. Helmle, the Yerkes Laboratories of Primate Biology.) Reproduced by permission.

unfamiliar people with a strange combination of approach and avoidance—a sort of diffuse or disorganized emotional behavior that is never seen in normally reared dogs. The peculiarities diminished with time but did not disappear, and the personalities remained grossly abnormal.

The response to noxious stimuli (ones that cause pain in normal animals) was at least as unusual. At such a stimulus, the restricted dog pulled back reflexively as a normal dog would but made no attempt to avoid a repetition of the stimulus and appeared not to be upset by it. One dog, when a lighted cigar fell on the floor, smelled it, burned his nose, and pulled back—but then thrust his nose into the live coal twice more. Another time, when an experimenter stuck a dissecting needle into the dog's skin repeatedly, the dog squirmed each time but made no attempt to escape or to pull out the needle, although its wooden handle was sticking out from his flank. He gave no sign of feeling pain.

These results with pain are paralleled by those obtained with a chimpanzee reared not in isolation but in conditions that restricted mobility (Fig. 7.5b). The chimp had cardboard "cuffs" over forearms and lower legs, loose enough to allow joint movements but preventing the ordinary tactual exploration of the young animal's own body and his surroundings (Nissen, Chow, & Semmes, 1951). Of interest is the unusual posture, different from that of a normally reared chimpanzee of about the same age (Fig. 7.5c). The most important difference, however, is in the experimental animal's response to somesthetic stimulation in tests made when the cuffs were removed at the age of 30 months (corresponding roughly to a human child's age of 3 or 4 years). A normally reared animal pinched at some point on his body that he couldn't see would reach directly and accurately to the spot, to stop the pinching. The experimental animal made inaccurate movements, apparently needing to explore before reaching the right spot. To make sure the animal was doing his best to find the spot as quickly as possible, pin prick was used. The normal control animal objected vociferously and wasted no movements in removing the painful object. The experimental animal, on the other hand, showed no sign that the pin prick was disturbing and even acted as if it was as much pleasant as unpleasant.

A situation was also set up to test simple somesthetic learning. The chimp was placed with a shelf under his chin so that he could not see his hands; the food reward (milk in a nursing bottle) was presented sometimes from the right, sometimes from the left, and the hand on the same side was touched first. In 200 trials, the normal control animal learned reliably to turn his head to the left when his left hand was touched, and to the right when the right hand was touched; but the experimental animal had not fully learned in 2,000 trials.

Behavior and Maternal Separation in Primates

Previous examples in this chapter have emphasized the importance of sensory experience in developing both a normal nervous system and normal behavior. Melzack and Thompson's Scotties were an example of another effect of deprivation: they were docile and disorganized, emotionally unlike the normal adult Scotty, who is an affectionate but scrappy and basically irascible dog. In primates there are even more striking long-term changes caused by even temporary deprivation of the normal sensory and social environment in infancy.

Infant monkeys are dependent on their mother. They normally cling to her and are nursed by her until they are about 4 months old. After weaning, juveniles remain in a flexible but mother-centered group with other juveniles and adult animals until they assume an adult status in the troop. If an infant monkey is taken away from its mother, the effects are immediate and the consequences are longlasting. The infant typically has a "protest-despair" reaction, at first screeching and crying, and then, if several hours have not produced a reunion, becoming abnormally quiet and withdrawn and remaining so for the remainder of the separation. Other unusual behaviors—rhythmic rocking and clasping, and self-mutilation, biting, or head-banging—may also occur. One early separation potentiates the reaction to another, later separation; the protests become sharper but shorter on the second separation, while the despair withdrawal becomes longer lasting and deeper.

The long-term effects of separation are evident when observers rate the sociability and social behavior of a colony of monkeys, including some juveniles or young adults that were separated in infancy. The monkeys that were separated are rated as less socially active. They are more isolated and more submissive, and engage in less social behavior, such as mutual grooming. They may continue to engage in the self-damaging behavior described earlier, and their sexual behavior may be less successful.

There are, however, conditions that minimize the effects of early maternal deprivation. If the mother instead of the infant is removed from the colony, leaving the infant with the other monkeys in the colony, the effects are less extreme. If the infant is older at the time of first separation, the effects are also less extreme. And an artificial mother-substitute with the right tactile qualities—a bottle feeder "surrogate-mother"—will also reduce (although not eliminate) the long-term effects on social behavior. A juvenile that has been separated from its mother and raised with a cloth surrogate will cling to the cloth surrogate for support, as it would to its mother, if it is surprised or threatened; but a wire surrogate with a milk bottle but none of the tactile softness and warmth of the cloth, is not used by the infant as a refuge or reassurance in the presence of a surprise or a threat (Fig. 7.6).

The most noticeable kind of behavior resulting from early separation is "anxious attachment" during adolescence. The juvenile monkey who was separated early wanders less freely from its mother or its peers later on and shows more vocalizing or emotion when a later separation occurs. The degree of despair, the withdrawal characteristic of separation, that will occur on later separation can be predicted from the amount of anxious attachment demonstrated by monkeys who were separated early. Monkeys separated and left with a wire mother-surrogate show much more despair than monkeys separated but raised by a cloth surrogate.

All these effects demonstrate the strong influences that early social experiences can have on the later social behavior of a higher primate. The effects seem to be related to the amount of unrelieved anxiety experienced by the monkey during early separation. If this anxiety is reduced—either because the infant monkey is less susceptible to it or

FIGURE 7.6. Cloth and wire mother-surrogates were used to test the preferences of infant monkeys. The infants spent most of their time clinging to the soft cloth "mother," (right) even when nursing bottles were attached to the wire mother (left). (Courtesy Harlow Primate Laboratory)

because other circumstances have combined to reduce it, such as the presence of other monkeys or of a cloth surrogate-mother—then the effects of later separations will be less extreme, as will the effects of the separation on general social behavior.

It is clear that the higher behavior of the adult, in mammals as in birds, is fundamentally dependent on the experience of infancy. There is some evidence indicating that this need not be true, or that it is only minimally true, of reflex behavior. But normal motivation, perception, and intelligence do require a normal early experience.

At first, this may sound like a denial of the importance of heredity, but nothing could be more erroneous. Both higher behavior and the innate reflex are fundamentally a function of heredity. True, higher behavior depends on early experience, but it also depends on heredity and the growth processes that give us eyes and ears and skin receptors and a nervous system in which learning can occur. Instead of asking whether a given action is hereditary or learned—placing these two influences in opposition to one another—we need to ask how the two have collaborated in producing the action.

Of course, heredity, by itself, can produce no behavior: the fertilized ovum must have a nutritive, supporting environment for its growth before behavior is possible. Similarly, learning can produce no behavior by itself, without the heredity and the prenatal environment that produce the structures in which learning can occur. The two collaborate. Further, it seems highly probable that heredity makes some kinds of learning easy or inevitable and makes other kinds difficult. Thus, it guides learning. Some behaviors that are considered to be unlearned, for example in the insects, may in fact be the result of a very rapid learning made inevitable by the insect's sensory and neural structure.

In the higher animal too some learning is inevitable, in ordinary circumstances, but now there is a larger mass of neural tissue involved. If we assume (see chapter 5) that cell assemblies must be developed before effective transmission can occur at higher levels, the first course of learning may be slow. Theoretically, therefore, we may consider that the function of early experience in the mammal is to build up the mediating processes that, once established, make possible the very rapid learning of which the mature animal is capable.

CODIFYING THE FACTORS IN DEVELOPMENT

In all matters touching on the heredity–environment or maturation–learning question, long experience shows that it is extremely difficult to think or speak with logical consistency or without omitting some obviously important factor. A codification of the factors in development is presented in Table 7.1, which may oversimplify the question but nevertheless helps to avoid the worse oversimplifications that abound in the literature, not only of psychology, but also of medicine, zoology, genetics—in short, the whole field of biological investigation, as far as it touches on the determinants of physical or behavioral growth.

Table 7.1 provides a working classification only, one that at least reminds that there are more than two kinds of factors in development and allows us to talk about them less ambiguously. The scheme is really a sort of mnemonic device, not an exhaustive analysis; if it is carried too far shortcomings will appear. Factor I is classed as genetic, for example, as if the ovum consisted of genetic structures alone. Many ova consist of genetic structures plus nutritive matter (as birds' eggs clearly do). This means that they comprise both Factor I as defined and part of Factor II, the nutritive environment of the developing embryo. This applies in some degree to mammalian ova as well. Factor II should include also temperature, which is physical rather than chemical, and so on.

But if we regard the table as a working approximation, it will help us to avoid certain common fallacies. Much of the discussion of instinct is based implicitly on this kind of argument: Such-and-such behavior needs no special experience, that is, it does not require practice, or observation of others' performance. Hence, it must depend on heredity

TABLE 7.1
Factors in Behavioral Development

No.	Factor	Source, Mode of Action, etc.
I	genetic	physiological properties of the fertilized ovum
II	chemical, prenatal	nutritive or toxic influence in the uterine environment
III	chemical, postnatal	nutritive or toxic influence: food, water, oxygen, drugs, etc.
IV	sensory, constant	pre- and postnatal experience normally inevitable for all members of the species
V	sensory, variable	experience that varies from one member of the species to another
VI	traumatic	physical events tending to destroy cells: an "abnormal" class of events to which an animal might conceivably never be exposed, unlike Factors I to V

alone. Table 7.1 permits us to restate this: Factor V is not involved; therefore Factor I alone is the cause. But this omits Factors II, III and IV (assuming that VI is not involved). In other words, the roles of the nutritive and constant sensory environments, as causal factors in behavior, have been overlooked—and there is plenty of evidence to show that they must not be overlooked.

The schematizing of Table 7.1 helps one to remember that no behavior can be caused by one of these factors alone. No "learned behavior" is possible without Factors I, II, and III, which together make possible the existence of the sense organs, nervous system, and so forth. No "innate behavior" can be produced by Factor I alone; the nutritive environment must act on the fertilized ovum to produce something that can manifest behavior at all.

Factor I, evidently, is the hereditary variable in behavior. Factors II–VI are the environmental variables. Factors II and III are the same in principle, but in practice II is liable to be forgotten: for example, a deficient diet for the mother may impair the infant's brain, and this impairment may be mistaken for a genetically determined lack of intelligence (as it frequently is in the case of slum children). It is not genetic, it is environmental. Also, Factor II is harder to control experimentally; Factor III is easier. It is worthwhile, then, (especially for mnemonic purposes) to separate them.

The interactions of Factors II and III with Factor V are complex. For example, suppose a pregnant rat is experimentally undernourished. Factor II is involved because the rat pups' uterine environment is changed. Factor III is involved because the pups' postnatal environment is changed: the mother's milk is nutritionally deficient. And Factor I is involved because the mother's behavior towards her pups is altered by her own undernourishment (Crinc, 1976). The pups are likely to be more excitable (as measured by defecation and "freezing") in a novel situation and less capable of carrying out skilled movements. Factors IV and V are the same in principle—though IV is predominantly a cause of early learning and V of later learning, and in higher species these have rather different properties. But Factor IV, again, is difficult to control experimentally and is very often overlooked, so these two may also be kept separate in our codification.

Taken together, Factors I to III and Factor VI comprise the constitutional variables in behavior; Factors IV and V the experiential variables. How do these Factors relate to the change in behavior with age? We may define *maturation* in either of two ways: the influence of Factors I to III, which we may refer to as physical maturation (effects of heredity plus growth, only); or the influence of Factors I to IV, referred to as psychological maturation (heredity), growth, and early experience).

The student will find that these two definitions are confused in the literature. For example, in the case of children learning to walk, let us say between 12 and 15 months, we arrange it so that the children in one group are not allowed to practice—that is, assume an independent vertical position with feet on the floor—until they are 12 months old. We see how long it then takes for walking to occur. Ten percent, let us say, are walking after three days' practice. In another group, not allowed to practice until the age of 15 months, we find that perhaps 75% can walk after three days' practice. We can say, then, that the difference between the two groups must be due to the "maturation" that occurs between the 12th and the 15th month. But is this physical maturation solely the result of the operation of Factors I to III? During this time we have not controlled all the aspects of somesthetic experience that come under the heading of Factor IV, and their effects cannot be excluded. We have seen that some sort of somesthetic learning, or development of perception of tactual locus and of the position of the limbs with respect to the body, is going on in this period. No doubt physical maturation is also going on, but such experiments as this do not show that physical maturation alone produces the greater walking readiness of the 15-month-old child than of the 12-month-old. On the other hand, inasmuch as the change is not due to practice in the specific skill of walking, we can regard it as psychological maturation: the operation of Factors I to IV, apart from the ad hoc learning of Factor V.

FURTHER ON FACTOR IV AND INSTINCT

The general conclusion to which all this leads us is that apart from the unconditioned reflex, all behavior depends on the generalized learning resulting from Factor IV stimulation. This does not say that all higher behavior is "learned," in the usual sense of that word: much of it is unlearned but dependent on previous learning. The first temper tantrum; the spontaneous avoidance of strangers that appears at about 6 months of age in the human being, at 4 months in the chimpanzee; the first new sentence constructed by the child, or the first imaginative response: none of these can be called learned behavior but all require other learning that has resulted from exposure to the normal environment of the species.

Instinctive behavior also requires prior learning, and all our evidence indicates that it is wrong to think of instinctive behavior as a separate class, distinct from another class of learned behavior. Instead, the two classes overlap one another, with no clear line of demarcation. As for the term "instinct," it must be, by definition, that process within the nervous system that produces instinctive behavior, and we can see now why it is a misleading term. It implies that instinctive behavior is produced by a special activity or part of the brain, separate from the brain processes that control learned behavior and separate from those that make up what we call intelligence. But this is not so.

In addition to the facts already discussed, Beach (1959, 1955) has provided evidence to show that instinct is not separate from learning or intelligence. He has shown that learning ability in the male rat, as measured by maze performance, is correlated with the level of sexual activity. The better learner copulates more efficiently and frequently. Sexual behavior in the female at this phyletic level is largely reflexive and does not correlate with learning ability. But maternal behavior does—the female that is best at maze learning is the best mother.

There is no ground, therefore, for thinking of instinctive behavior as having a special kind of neural control, of being immune to the effects of learning and distinct from the operations of intelligence. Instinctive behavior does not depend on practice (or imitation) and thus is not learned in the usual sense of the term. Yet, as we have seen, the learning induced by Factor IV may play a significant part in it. We conclude that instinct is the neural organization, over and above reflexive organization, which is common to a whole species: determined by a common heredity and the common features of the environment. The learning that is part of it is learning that inevitably occurs in the whole species (except when an individual animal's environment differs significantly from the usual environment of the species and produces aberrant behavior). Growth processes and early experience between them determine the neural organizations that impel the animal faced for the first time with a particular class of situation to respond in a particular way. These processes are complex, and we have hardly begun to understand them, but in principle there is nothing any more mysterious about instinct than about other aspects of behavior.

Instinctive behavior does not imply advance knowledge of its end effects, inherited from the animal's ancestors. It is performed for its own sake, not for what it will achieve in the future. The pregnant rat builds a nest before her first litter is born because she somehow wants to build a nest, not because she knows why her belly is swollen and that the pups will need shelter. The primary reason that human beings engage in sex is not to produce another generation of troublemakers in this troubled world but because human beings like sex.

Human Instinct?

It has already been said that it is confusing to apply the term "instinctive" to human behavior, because of the connotations attached to the word. It is almost an article of faith for many psychologists that humans have no instinctive behavior, no matter how the term might be defined. Human behavior is, however, species-predictable in many of its aspects.

People everywhere have a fondness for the sound of their own voice. They sing and listen to songs, tell elaborate tales for their own sake (some of them true), or talk when there is no need of communication. People everywhere use tools, organize social groups, avoid darkness in strange places. All cultures are said to have developed string games similar to the childhood game of cat's cradle. The taboos of incest or food use, the belief in spirits good or evil, the tendency to ornament the body in particular ways and to impose strong sanctions against ornamenting it in other ways—all these are behaviors that, in their details, are subject to the influence of special learning, but which in one form or another spring up in every society of which we have knowledge. In detail, therefore, they are not species-predictable; but in a larger sense they are. The fact that the specific way in which the hair may be worn varies from culture to culture, or from one time to another in the same culture, does not change the fact that all cultures at all times have such rules and that they play an important part in the behavior of people in the presence of their fellows. We cannot predict the content of folk tales in a culture encountered for the first time; but we can safely predict that there will be folk tales, learned and passed on from generation to generation. The false opposition of the "instinctive" to the "learned" has tended in the past to prevent us from seeing these common features of human behavior and from recognizing that they must result, much as the instinctive behavior of rodent and carnivore does, from (a) the way we are made and (b) the universal features of the human environment.

HEREDITY AND MENTAL ILLNESS

The confusion characteristic of discussions of heredity and environment is very marked when it comes to mental illness. The issues here are so serious that one can understand a lack of judicial calm in thinking about them, but their seriousness also makes it important to be as clear about them as we can.

Implicitly or explicitly, the question has been approached as the old dichotomy: Is mental illness caused by an abnormal heredity, some weakness of the germ plasm of the patient's parents, or by bad experiences and the special learning produced by such experiences? This is a false dichotomy, an either-or approach that nearly always leads one astray. Translate the question into the terms of Table 7.1, and it becomes, Is Factor I or Factor V the cause of mental illness? First, this leaves out Factors II, III, and IV, and second, it rules out the important possibility of an interaction between factors. A certain heredity may predispose to mental illness in one set of environmental conditions but may produce a highly stable, well-adjusted person in another; or a given set of environmental conditions may bring out the best in people of one heredity and cause breakdown in others.

Attitudes toward these questions are greatly affected by the results of a study of the incidence of schizophrenia among close relatives of schizophrenics (Kallman, cited in Roth, 1957; Faraone & Tsuang, 1985). The study shows that the closer the genetic relationship, the more likely it is that the relative will be schizophrenic. Thirteen percent of the brothers and sisters of schizophrenics (excluding twins) are also schizophrenic. Twelve to 13% of ordinary (fraternal) twins also have the disease, a figure that rises to 91 to 92% for identical twins. Identical twins, of course, have identical genetic constitutions because they grow from a single fertilized ovum: fraternal twins result from the chance fertilization of two ova at about the same time and are no more closely related, genetically, than are other brothers and sisters.

These results have sometimes been taken to mean that heredity is the whole cause of mental illness, or nearly the whole cause. That this is not so is clear from data provided by M. Roth (1957), using further data from Kallman (Table 7.2). Tuberculosis shows a similar picture, and in tuberculosis we know that the environment plays the decisive part. An environmental action—exposure to infection by the tubercle bacillus—is essential, and we cannot possibly conclude that heredity is the sole cause of tuberculosis. The similar figures for schizophrenia mean that one may inherit susceptibility to the disease, but inherited susceptibility does not make heredity the whole cause.

Table 7.2 makes the same point as Fig. 7.2, which showed that

TABLE 7.2
Incidence of Tuberculosis and of Schizophrenia Among Relatives of
Patients Having Those Diseases
(in Percent)*

Degree of Relation	Frequency of TB in the Relatives	Frequency of Schizophrenia in the Relatives
Half-brothers or sisters	11.9	7.3
Brothers or sisters	25.5	12.9
Ordinary twins	25.6	12.5
Identical twins	87.3	91.5

*After Roth (1951) from Kallman. Reproduced by permission.

improvement in pecking by the newly hatched chick is a joint product of physical maturation and experience or learning. The table shows that heredity and environment can interact similarly in disease. It makes clear that the heredity of the person exposed to tuberculosis plays a large part in determining susceptibility to the infection. Otherwise we cannot account for the difference in frequency for fraternal twins and identical twins. Both kinds of twins are usually brought up in the same environment and if one is exposed, the other is very likely to be exposed also. The great difference in the incidence of the disease can only be explained by the fact that the identical twins have the same hereditary susceptibilities.

The figures for schizophrenia demonstrate this differential even more clearly. The difference between 13% for fraternal twins and 92% for identical twins can only be understood by concluding that there is a hereditary susceptibility to schizophrenia. This does not, however, diminish the importance of stresses from the environment—just as tuberculosis occurs only by an environmental action on a susceptible constitution, so schizophrenia may occur only with social stress.

There are in fact cases that demonstrate this connection. One of a pair of identical twin girls, very strictly brought up, had an unhappy affair and developed schizophrenia (but recovered later). Her twin stayed on an even keel, psychiatrically speaking, throughout the episode. Of course, the stresses involved in schizophrenia are not usually so specific. More likely they are probably the prolonged and general stresses of the home and social environment. Such influences would affect both of a pair of twins equally, and this helps to account for the very high frequency with which both have the disease.

SUMMARY

The development of behavior and the characteristics of behavior at maturity depend on a number of influences that are classified here as Factors I to VI. Heredity by itself (Factor I) cannot produce behavior, nor can learning by itself, without heredity and the nutritive environment necessary to produce an organism in which learning can occur. The unconditioned reflex does not require learning, but all other behavior, including instinctive behavior in mammals and much instinctive behavior in other animals, involves learning determined by the experience of infancy (Factor IV). An essential point is that much behavior is not learned but still is dependent on the existence of other, prior, learning.

GUIDE TO STUDY

Be able to define, describe, or explain

(1) instinctive behavior as distinguished from instinct and from reflexes;

(2) physical versus psychological maturation;

(3) the phrase "maintenance of neural structures by experience," and the term "experience";

(4) imprinting;

(5) the six "factors" or classes of influences on behavior.

Be able to explain the evidence that learning and growth interact in chickens' pecking.

Be able to explain

(1) how early experience affects important aspects of behavior in species as different as ants, geese, dogs and apes;

(2) how it is shown that instinct is closely related to learning and intelligence in the rat;

(3) what evidence, comparing schizophrenia and tuberculosis, shows that mental illness is determined by both heredity and environment.

What other species-predictable aspects of human behavior can be listed, in addition to those mentioned in the text?

NOTES AND GENERAL REFERENCES

The general point of view of this chapter derives from Frank Beach's paper of 1955, a culmination of a series of studies of instinctive behavior in mammals. One important early study appeared in 1939:

Beach, F. A. (1939). The neural basis of innate behavior: III. Comparison of learning ability and instinctive behavior in the rat. *Journal of Comparative Psychology, 28,* 225–262.

Beach, F. A. (1955). The descent of instinct. *Psychological Review, 62,* 401–410. The first real clarification of the heredity-environment problem with respect to behavior.

Emphasis on the Innate

Carmichael, L. (1927). A further study of the development of behavior in vertebrates experimentally removed from the influence of external stimulation. *Psychological Review, 34,* 34–47. Experiments on the maturation of reflexive responses.

Cruze, W. W. (1935). Maturation and learning in chicks. *Journal of Comparative Psychology, 19,* 371–409.

Dennis, W. (1940). Infant reaction to restraint: an evaluation of Watson's theory. *Transactions of the New York Academy of Science, Series 2,* 202–218.

Faraone, S. V. & Tsuang, M. T. (1985). Quantitative models of the genetic transmission of schizophrenia. *Psychological Bulletin, 98*, 41–66.

Gottesman, I., & Shields, J. *Schizophrenia and Genetics: A Twin Study Vantage Point.* New York: Academic Press.

Iacono, W. G. (1985). Psychophysiologic markers of psychopathology: a review. *Canadian Psychology, 26*, 96–112. Evidence for other genetic abnormalities associated with schizophrenia.

Lamb, M. E. (1975). Physiological mechanisms in the control of maternal behavior in the rat: a review. *Psychological Bulletin, 82*, 104–119.

Roth, M. (1957). Interaction of genetic and environmental factors in the causation of schizophrenia. In D. Richter (Ed.), *Schizophrenia: Somatic Aspects.* New York: Macmillan.

Effects of Early Experience

Birnholz, J. C., & Farrell, E. E. (1984). Ultrasound images of human fetal development. *American Scientist, 72*, 608–613.

Chow, K. L., Riesen, A. H. & Newell, F. W. (1957). Degeneration of retinal ganglion cells in infant chimpanzees reared in darkness. *Journal of Comparative Neurology, 107*, 27–42.

Crnic, L. S. (1976). Effects of infantile undernutrition on adult learning in rats: methodological and design problems. *Psychological Bulletin, 83*, 715–728.

Hess, E. H. (1959). Imprinting. *Science, 130*, 133–141.

Hubel, D. H. (1979). The visual cortex of normal and deprived monkeys. *American Scientist, 67*, 532–543.

James, H. (1960). Imprinting with visual flicker. *Canadian Journal of Psychology, 14*, 13–20.

Lorenz, K. Z. (1952). *King Solomon's Ring.* New York: Thomas Y. Crowell. Cited in chapter 1, but very relevant here also.

Melzack, R., & Thompson, W. R. (1956). Effects of early experience on social behavior. *Canadian Journal of Psychology, 10*, 82–90.

Mitchell, G. D., Harlow, H. F., Griffin, G. A., & Moller, G. W. (1967). Repeated maternal separation in the monkey. *Psychonomic Science, 8*, 197–198.

Mineka, S., & Suomi, S. J. (1978). Social separation in monkeys. *Psychological Bulletin, 85*, 1376–1400.

Nissen, H. W., Chow, K. L., & Semmes, J. (1951). Effects of restricted tactual experience on the behavior of a chimpanzee. *American Journal of Psychology, 64*, 485–507.

Rajecki, D. M. (1973). Imprinting in precocial birds: interpretation, evidence and evaluation. *Psychological Bulletin, 79*, 48–58.

Riesen, A. H. (1964). Arrested vision. In S. Coopersmith, Ed., *Frontiers of Psychological Research.* San Francisco: W. H. Freeman.

Senden, M. V. (1960). *Space and Sight* (P. Heath, Trans.). London: Methuen.

CHAPTER 8

Statistics and the Control Group

It is time to learn something about statistics. You do not yet need to learn how to calculate standard deviations and correlation coefficients, but you should know what they are and how they are used. Otherwise much of psychology must be taken on faith, which is no way to become a scientist. We have already referred to *control groups*, whose use requires statistics, and the chapter about intelligence that follows this one will require even more statistics. So now is a good time to explain the nature of statistical thought.

All measurement is subject to error, and it is as important to know the size of the error as it is to know the value of the measurement. When a specific future event is predicted on the basis of past observations, or when a general conclusion is drawn from a small set of examples, the prediction of the conclusion is based on probabilities, not on certainties. To evaluate probabilities, we use statistics, which are, therefore, an essential part of the scientific method.

Statistical methods are usually presented in mathematical terms, but statistics is essentially a way of thinking, one that often involves no computations and no use of formulas. It has two functions: (1) to describe data in a way that permits us to see the pattern in a mass of facts and (2) to provide rules for inferring general principles from a limited set of observations.

It is sometimes said that science is not interested in the unique event. This is certainly not true. If, just once, the sun turned a mottled green for 30 seconds and then recovered its usual disposition, we can imagine what a commotion would be stirred up in astronomical circles.[1] But it is true that a scientist usually studies classes of events that are regular over repeated observations, and the unique event may be considered of interest because it implies the existence of a new class of possibly repeated events.

The scientist generalizes from the known to the unknown. The conclusion from an experiment always concerns more than the specific objects or events that were a part of the experiment. For example, 43 specific chicks fed nutritional supplements grow faster on the average than 43 other specific chicks raised identically but not fed the supplements. This is an observed fact. The conclusion is an inference that all chicks would grow faster if fed supplements. The statistical conclusion is "The difference between the means is statistically significant," a statement that distinguishes between the fact of a faster average growth for these particular chicks, about which there is no doubt, and the inference about the growth of all chicks in such conditions. When a difference is found to be "significant," it implies a general conclusion.

Inference from the particular to the general is not peculiar to science; it is a fundamental feature of human thought, and so too is the descriptive function of statistics. Statistical thinking is of interest to psychology students for two reasons: principally to explain how research is made more precise and controlled, and also as an interesting aspect of human thought.

For example, if you have concluded that men are taller than women, by not restricting your conclusion to the specific men and women you have personally seen, you have made a statistical inference. If you have ever calculated an average, you have created a statistical description. If you have decided that the average day in July is warmer than the average day in March—without adding daily temperatures and dividing by the number of days—then you have made a statistical summary from your own, necessarily limited, past experience, and you have also made a statistical generalization, predicting what will happen next year and the year after that.

---

[1] A young Russian had such a phenomenal visual memory that he never forgot anything, and so could never free himself from a flood of involuntary visual images which came to mind every time he thought of the simplest thing he had previously experienced. This scientifically interesting single case study was described by the neuropsychologist, Alexander Luria, in *The Mind of a Mnemonist* (Basic Books, 1968; see also chapter 6, this volume). Unique cases have been very important in psychology: Sigmund Freud developed his theory of personality by analyzing unique cases.

STATISTICAL CONCLUSIONS WITHOUT COMPUTATION

If the present chapter is not "statistics without tears," it may be that at least fewer tears will be shed than usual. Our object is to help you learn to think statistically. A good deal can be learned from data by simply arranging them in an orderly way, especially in graphic form. If you understand the terms used and the relationships explained in the graphic examples, you will have the background necessary to understand statistical calculations when you need to learn them.

Two basic concepts, *sample* and *population,* are very important. The scientist works from a *sample* in order to draw conclusions about a *population* or *universe.* The sample is one set of some of the items making up the population. It is the available collection of facts or observations, their number being finite and usually rather small. The population is not necessarily a real population of people or animals. Instead, the population consists of *events* or *properties* of objects or events. In an experimental science, a population is characteristically hypothetical and infinitely large. The sample is a set of properties or events that have actually been observed, whereas the population or universe includes all the properties or events in this class (i.e., of the same kind) that could have been observed in the past or that may conceivably be observed in the future.

To illustrate: An astrophysicist who wants to know what shooting stars are made of manages to find fifty meteorites and measures their composition. This is the sample. The population, however, includes future meteorites as well as past ones that were not recovered. Using his sample, the astrophysicist may go on to draw conclusions about objects that hit other planets, thus going even further beyond the observations in the sample. But going beyond immediate observations is the essence of science.

Another example: A psychologist bred rats selectively for maze-learning ability, mating males who learned well with females who learned well, and males who learned poorly with females who learned poorly. After several generations of such selection, the descendants of the good learners always learned faster than the descendants of the poor learners. Twenty good and 20 poor learners of the sixth generation were tested. There was one sample of 20 animals from each of two theoretically infinitely large populations: namely, rats bred selectively from good and from poor maze-learners. Apart from the two samples, these populations do not exist in reality, for no one else has bred animals this way. But the conclusion was that future samples would show the same differences. The statistical inference is about learning ability in two infinitely large, hypothetical populations of all rats that will be, or might be, obtained by the breeding operations that were carried out. No one really cares, scientifically speaking, about the maze-learning ability of a specific rat. The important question concerns the relation of heredity to the learning ability, or intelligence, of rats in general or even of mammals, including humans, in general. Drawing such conclusions about hypothetical populations and making such generalizations is certainly subject to error. But we must generalize, and statistical methods allow us to measure the error.

The difference between the physical sciences and the biological sciences, including psychology, is not that physical sciences are exact and biological sciences inexact. The difference is in the degree of exactness, which is related to the number of variables that must be considered simultaneously and the extent to which each of them can be controlled. The biological sciences generally deal with larger errors than the physical sciences, although this is not always true. Consider the limited accuracy of weather prediction. The statistical principles used to make predictions and to measure error are the same whether the errors are large or small. Statistics is not a substitute for obtaining clear answers but a means of checking and controlling hasty conclusions by providing an estimate of the errors to which any conclusion is inevitably subject.

AN EXAMPLE

The first step in statistics is to describe the sample. Consider, for example, the error scores obtained by each of 31 rats in a simple maze problem. Each number represents the total errors for an individual rat: 27 9 13 32 23 26 18 21 15 24 23 19 19 4 29 22 23 7 30 17 26 17 10 22 17 16 36 27 22 12 26. The properties of the sample become easier to see by merely rearranging the scores in order from lowest to highest: 4 7 9 10 12 13 15 16 16 17 17 17 18 19 19 21 22 22 22 23 23 24 26 26 27 27 29 30 32 33 36. The highest and lowest values, and the *range* of values, which is the difference between the highest and lowest values, are evident at a glance. The *median* value, 21, is found by counting to the mid-point in the series from either end. When there is an even number of scores the median is halfway between the two middle scores. The *average* in elementary arithmetic is the sum of the scores divided by the number of scores. In this sample it is 20.4. A shorter word often used by statisticians in place of average is *mean*.

The list of scores, now ordered, still contains all of the information in the sample, but because the list contains 31 numbers it is difficult to read and understand. The next step is to describe the sample in a simpler way. Whenever a sample description is simplified, some detail is lost, but something else is gained—ease of understanding. To simplify the description, we count the number of scores that fall within a specified *range* of scores and then substitute this count for the original list of scores. This can be done in another list, or table, as in Fig. 8.1a. Instead of 31 sample scores, there are eight successive *ranges* of scores, and eight *counts* of the number of scores falling within each range of scores. A clear way to summarize these counts is to draw a picture called a *frequency histogram,* in which the ranges of scores appear in order across the bottom of the picture, and the number of scores falling within each range is shown by the height of a bar drawn above the range. Some detail is lost: the lowest error score could be any number from 0 to 4, but the frequency table (Fig. 8.1a) and the frequency histogram (Fig. 8.1b) bring out characteristics of the sample data that were not seen in the list of 31 scores. Figure 8.1 show us that most of the scores occur at the middle of the distribution and that few scores fall within either the extreme high or low ranges. The mean of the scores—20.4 errors—falls near the center of this almost symmetrical frequency distribution.

Compare Fig. 8.1b, the frequency histogram of 31 error scores, with Fig. 8.1c, the frequency histogram of the heights of 8,585 men. They have something in common: most scores are at the center of the distribution, few are at the extremes. As the number of items in the sample increases from 31 to 8,589, the frequency distribution tends to become smoother and more symmetrical, with many scores in the center of the range, falling off rapidly to a very few in the extremes, or "tails" of the distribution. This is common in collecting samples from many populations. The larger the sample, the more the scores tend to be concentrated uniformly and symmetrically in the center of the range.

Figure 8.1d looks like Fig. 8.1b and 8.1c carried to an extreme of smoothness and symmetry. It is a mathematically ideal distribution of scores, which tends to be most frequent in the mid-range and to be symmetrically distributed. The ideal frequency distribution of Fig. 8.1d is called a *normal probability distribution.*

Two aspects of a normal probability distribution are most important: the *central tendency* and the *dispersion.* The central tendency is the single most representative value of the distribution. It is the average value, or *mean.*[2] The dispersion is a measure of the degree to which the

---

[2]The reason this value is most representative is because the standard deviation of scores measured from the mean, rather than from any other value, is smallest. Thus in choosing the mean as the representative value, we minimize the amount of measured deviation from the most representative value.

FREQUENCY DISTRIBUTION OF ERROR SCORES BY
31 RATS IN A MAZE TEST

Interval	Frequency
0–4	1
5–9	2
10–14	3
15–19	9
20–24	7
25–29	5
30–34	3
35–39	1

(a)

FIGURE 8.1a. Distribution of error scores for 31 rats in a maze test. These data are in the form of a table, which summarizes the scores by grouping them into intervals of five and reporting only the number of rats which obtained scores within each interval.

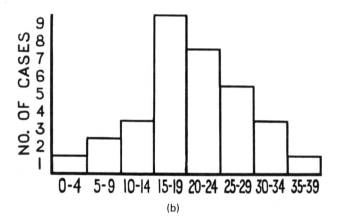

(b)

FIGURE 8.1b. Frequency histogram showing the errors made by 31 rats in a maze test. The data are from (a). Each range of scores is placed in increasing order from left to right across the bottom. The number of cases within each range is indicated by the height of the vertical bar over the range: the scale for these bars is on the left.

frequency distribution spreads symmetrically on either side of the mean. It is the *standard deviation*, abbreviated SD. The larger the value of the standard deviation, the wider the distribution of scores around the mean.

The standard deviation is, as its name suggests, a widely used (standard) measure of how much the scores in a sample deviate from the average, or mean, of the sample. It is calculated in three steps. First, find the difference between every score in the sample and the mean of the sample scores. Next, square each of these differences—which automatically assures that all of the squared differences are positive. Then average the squared differences. Add them up and divide by one less than the number of squared differences, which is the same as one

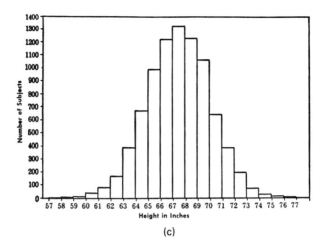

(c)

FIGURE 8.1c. Frequency histogram for heights of 8585 men. The principle is the same as in (b). Successive ranges in increasing order are marked off from left to right across the bottom. The number of cases in each range is indicated by the height of the vertical bar over each range. The scale is on the left.

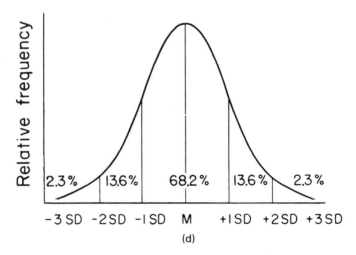

(d)

FIGURE 8.1d. A normal probability distribution: the mathematical ideal of the preceding frequency distributions. Along the scale at the bottom, each score is expressed as a positive or negative deviation from the mean of the distribution, and the unit of the deviation scale is the standard deviation. The height of the curve above each point on the scale indicates the relative frequency of scores which deviate the indicated distance from the mean. The vertical bars mark off portions of the curve which fall within 1 SD on either side of the mean, between 1 and 2 SDs on either side of the mean, and between 2 and 3 SDs on either side of the mean. Sixty-eight percent of all scores fall within 1 SD of the mean, 95% fall within 2 SDs of the mean, and 99% within 3 SDs of the mean.

less than the number of scores.[3] Finally, calculate the square root of the averaged squared differences.

There is an important mathematical relationship between the size of the standard deviation and the scores in the ideal normal probability distribution. About two-thirds (68%) of all the scores fall within the central range of the distribution, which extends from 1 SD below the mean to 1 SD above the mean. This is mathematically true for the ideal distribution, and it is approximately right for the distribution of 8,569 scores in Fig. 8.1d. Similarly, about 95% of all the scores in an ideal normal probability distribution fall within the range that extends 2 SDs on either side of the mean, and 99% within the range extending 3 SDs on either side of the mean. This is again approximately true for the distributions of Figs. 8.1b and 8.1c.

Let us look more closely at the relationship between sample and population. Suppose that we want to know how tall the average male college student is. Having searched out and measured 20 of these creatures, we find their mean height to be 177 centimeters. Is this the value we are looking for? We know that men differ in height, so we cannot measure only one, or two, or three. We need a large group. Is 20 large enough? We track down 20 more and measure them, and this time we get a mean of 178.5 cm. Three more groups of 20 give means of 178.05, 171.9, and 181.9 cm. *The means of the samples are variable too.* We pool the five groups and get a mean for the 100 men: 177.5 cm. But another group of 100 would give us still another mean. The larger the samples, the less variable their means will be, but the variability will not disappear. We cannot get a final, precise answer, and we must try another approach.

Because the sample means themselves are variable, we do not know which mean is closest to the true, or population, mean. But the frequency distribution of sample means, like the frequency distribution of individual sample scores, approaches the ideal normal probability distribution as more and more sample means are included. We can calculate the standard deviation of the distribution of sample means (called the *standard error of the mean*, abbreviated SE), and then we can specify the range of means within which 68% ($\pm$ 1 SE), 95% ($\pm$ 2 SE) or 99% ($\pm$ 3 SE) of the sample means are likely to fall. Thus, while we cannot state exactly the value of the population mean, we can state the range within which 95% or 99% of the sample mean estimates will fall. The *mean of this distribution of sample means is the best estimate of the population mean.* The standard error of the distribution of

---

[3]For technical reasons the divisor for the standard deviation is one less than the number of scores averaged.

sample means allows us to calculate the range within which 95%–99% of the sample means will fall. This range is called the 95% or 99% *confidence interval* for the population mean.

Suppose we then find another sample of men (from a small college) with a mean height of 120 centimeters. This mean height falls outside the 95% confidence interval established from our original sample of means. Thus, the probability is less than 5% that the new mean of 120 centimeters is a sample from the same population as the earlier samples, with a mean of 177.5 centimeters.

It is customary to emphasize two levels of probability: the 5% and 1% levels. In the example just used, we may say that the mean obtained differs significantly from 177.5 cm at the 5% level. In other words: the difference can be given some weight, since a chance difference as great as this would be found less than 5% of the time. However, the chance difference at this level of significance *can* occur—once in 20 comparisons.

For a higher degree of confidence, the 1% level is adopted, with a 1-in-100 chance of being wrong. When one encounters the statement that a difference is "significant" it signifies, by common convention, that the probability is at least 19 to 1 against this being due to the operation of chance in obtaining our sample; "highly significant" may be considered to mean that the probability is 99 to 1 against. Alternatively, one may say that a difference is "significant at the 5% level" or at the 1% level.

Summarizing: we can never say what, precisely, is the true value of the mean of the universe from which a sample is drawn. But we can, with the proper computations, determine the probability that it differs from our estimate by more than any given amount. Also, we can state limits within which it must lie, with a probability of 85%, or 99%—or if we wish, 99.9%.

No one can do more. Improved methods of measurement and larger samples cut down the size of probable error but do not abolish it. They decrease the uncertainty range within which the true value lies, but do not decrease it to zero.

RESTATING MATTERS, WITH SOME FURTHER (IMPROBABLE) EXAMPLES ABOUT THE MEANING OF AVERAGES

Statistics requires thinking in a new way about the meaning of averages and related matters. We cannot know the exact value for the height of the average man, or the income of the average family. But is this not the sort of thing the census does for us? Even though it is impractical to measure all men, considering some of the out-of-way places in the world, why should it be impossible to obtain a precise value for the mean height of all adult male Americans, or Indonesians, or Greeks? But as we will see in a moment, precision in this sense is chimerical. The scientific use of statistics really does ask for a new way of thinking, which though inherently simple is at first hard to achieve.

Let us see why it is chimerical to ask for an exact figure for the mean height of American male adults. First, there is the fact that every measurement has its error. Next, any biological population is not static but changing. A number of American males die daily, and a number reach the birthday that marks adult status. If we are really to have a precise figure for the whole population and not a sample (however large), we must fix on some date and hour—say 12:00 noon, July 1, in the year following the decision to undertake the project—and with the aid of 10 or 12 million assistants get everyone measured within a few minutes of the hour, including all those on their sickbeds, aloft in airplanes, at sea or abroad.

Now, assuming that we could succeed in this improbable undertaking, the mean we obtain will be out of date by July 2, well before the necessary computations could be completed. The net result of all this labor would therefore be, at best, a precise value for the population at a particular time in the past, not the present. To apply it to the present at once involves an element of estimation. We cannot treat census figures as precise, factual values, independent of inference. They are estimates—from very large samples, it is true, and with correspondingly small deviations from the "true" value—but still estimates that are subject to error. For most purposes we will be better off if we recognize this fact in the first place.

THE SIZE OF ELEPHANTS

Now another improbable example, which may help us in understanding the logic of this method: Let us suppose that an explorer who has penetrated a wilderness in the mountains of Mexico, where no one has been before, discovers and traps an elephant 1 meter high at the shoulder. He has seen no others, nor heard of any. What information has he about the species, the population from which his sample of one has been drawn? His best estimate of the mean height of the species is 1 meter; but having only one elephant in his sample he has no basis for estimating variability and thus no basis for saying how far off his guess about the average height might be.

Even with a single specimen, however, he is bound to have formed some idea of the size of other members of the species, and there are some conclusions that can quite logically be drawn. He can rule out the hypothesis, for example, that the mean of the population is 1.5 m, the standard deviation 200 cm. This situation is shown roughly by the curve with the largest mean, Fig. 8.2a. He can also rule out the hypothesis that the mean is 1.25 m, SD 10 cm (smaller curve, Fig. 8.2a). Both hypothesis imply that the first animal he happened to encounter

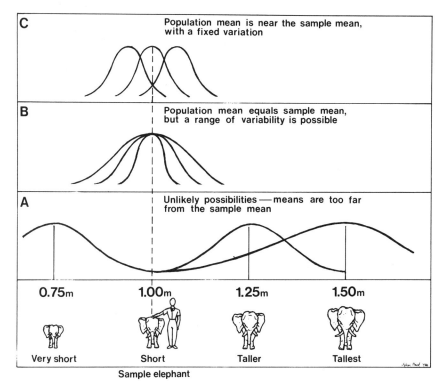

AVERAGE HEIGHT OF THE ELEPHANT HERD
BASED ON A VERY SMALL SAMPLE OF ONE VERY SMALL ELEPHANT

FIGURE 8.2 The height of elephants. One small elephant—1 meter high—was captured. What are the likely values of the mean and standard deviation of the height of the elephant population of which the one captured animal is a sample? The possibilities on line A can be rejected: the sample height is too distant from the hypothesized means, given the hypothesized standard deviations. The distributions on line B are all possible, given the one-elephant example. The height of the single elephant is the best estimate of the population mean, while the standard deviation is undetermined. Line C shows the situation after three more animals have been captured. The mean of the sample—still 1 meter—is the best estimate, but now the standard deviation of the sample has been determined, and the standard deviation of the population can be estimated from it. The two adjoining distributions show that other mean values, differing slightly from the obtained sample mean, are also possible.

is one of the very smallest—2½ SDs away from the mean of the distribution. The probability that this would happen is well outside the 95% confidence interval around the mean. Similarly, he can rule out the hypothesis that the mean height is 0.75 m, standard deviation 5 cm (Fig. 8.2a). Many hypothesis cannot be ruled out, but some can be.

His most likely hypothesis is represented by one of the curves of Fig. 8.2b: some distribution centered about a mean of 1 meter. The different curves in Fig. 8.2b are meant to show that with a single specimen nothing is known about the variability and so the SD may be large (considerable spread in the curve) or small (little spread). As Fig. 8.2c shows, these curves may be shifted somewhat to left or right and still represent tenable hypotheses, as long as the given sample value, 1 meter, remains in the central part of the curve.

When four more animals are captured, giving values of 97, 98, 100, 102 and 103 cm, an estimate of variability can be made (it is small) and now the distance becomes smaller by which the curve can be shifted to left or right and still represent a tenable hypothesis. The point of this example is that we can quite freely form hypotheses about the population, after seeing a sample from it, but must then proceed to test them rigorously. The elaborate machinery of statistics, the formulas and computations omitted from this book, make it possible to state precisely what the probability would be of obtaining a known sample from any given hypothetical population. If the probability is low, we disregard that hypothesis (but cannot rule out absolutely and finally, for the very improbable sometimes happens).

This process, however, cannot select from among those hypothetical populations that might reasonably have produced our sample, the one correct hypothesis. The larger the sample, the more we can narrow the zone within which probable answers lie, but we are always left with an uncertainty range, even if small. This is represented in principle by Fig. 8.2c.

To be epigrammatic, science works not with absolute truth but with a probable error. Its hope is to reduce error to a minimum. The scientist *thinks* in terms of truth when he sets up a hypothesis for testing, for what he says in effect is: Let us suppose that the true mean has such-and-such a value; if so, what would be found in a sample? But the result, the only conclusion that can be justified, is that the "true" value has a certain probability of lying within a range of possible values.

COMPARING TWO VALUES

Now a different but related case: the comparison of values and the determination of significant differences between samples.

Take first a familiar case, the comparison of the heights of men and women. Suppose that we have two samples, 100 in each, of the heights of college men and women. The two means are 177.5 cm and 166.1 cm. Are men taller than women? That is, if we had the mean of all men's heights would it differ from the mean of all women's?

We attack the question by assuming that the heights of men and women are not different. This is the null hypothesis. It amounts to assuming that the two samples of heights come from the same population. Now we can ask: What is the probability that we would draw from the same population two samples like these, with means that differ as much as these? We know that any two samples from the same population will give different means, just by chance. Is that what has happened here? But the answer here might well be that two such different samples could come from the same population less than one in a thousand times; it is thus very unlikely that the null hypothesis is true. We therefore reject it and conclude that men and women differ in height. The usual way of reporting such a result is to say that "the difference between the means is significant" (or in this case, of course, very highly significant).

This method of analysis might be applied to an experiment in the following way. We want to know whether the frontal part of the brain is more important for maze learning than the occipital part. We remove approximately equal amounts of brain tissue from two groups of rats. Those with frontal damage make, let us say, a mean of 42.1 errors; those with occipital damage, 55.7 errors. Our two samples are certainly different, but is the difference significant? We apply the null hypothesis, assuming that there is no difference in the means of all rats with such frontal lesions and with such occipital lesions, and see how often two such samples would be drawn from a single population. The variability in our two groups is great, indicating a wide "spread" in the curve representing the parent population (as in Fig. 8.2a), and this implies that the uncertainty range is large. As a result, computation shows that our two samples might be obtained from a single population about 20 times in 100. The difference is far from the 5% level of significance, so we cannot reject the null hypothesis. We have not yet established the proposition that occipital damage is worse than frontal damage in its effect on maze running. Keep in mind, however, that the odds still favor the proposition. By increasing the size of the samples, and thus decreasing the uncertainty range—the amount by which the means may vary—a further experiment may find a significant difference after all.

In the preceding examples, we have dealt with measurements and normally distributed values. One is not limited to measurements and normal distributions in statistical thinking. Suppose we are interested in the relation of ferocity to heredity in rats. We bring up 20 rats from an albino laboratory strain and 20 from a wild gray strain, all separated from the mother at weaning and brought up singly in identical cages. Heroically, the experimenter reaches into each cage when the occupant has reached 100 days of age and picks up the animal once. He counts the bites received: 1 bite from the albinos, 13 from the grays. There are methods of computation (e.g., Chi square, which need not be described here) that make it possible to determine that this result is highly improbable on the assumption that biting rats are equally likely to occur with either heredity. The result is therefore highly significant. We reject the null hypothesis (that there is no difference in the frequency of biters in the two universes, all hypothetical albinos and all hypothetical grays, brought up in this particular way). Rejecting the null hypothesis is equivalent to concluding that there is a relation between heredity and ferocity. Here we treat biting as an index of ferocity, but the procedure does not measure ferocity in the individual animal, and we have no idea whether it is normally distributed (Fig. 8.3).

THE CONTROL GROUP

The experiment just considered brings us to the use of the control group. In the physical sciences, it may often be possible to hold constant all but one of the factors that might affect the outcome of an experiment. The remaining factor, the *independent variable*, is changed systematically, and the experimenter observes the effects in the *dependent variable*. In a study of the pressure of the atmosphere, for example, the independent variable may be height above sea level; the dependent variable is the height of a column of mercury in a barometric tube. Other influences that might affect the outcome are eliminated or kept constant: temperature, contaminating substances in the mercury, movement of the surrounding air, and so forth.

In the biological sciences, one can only approach this ideal procedure. In psychological research, there are two difficulties that frequently demand the use of control groups as a substitute for the ideal procedure. One is that taking a psychological test usually changes the subject; a later test does not give the same result because of *practice effect*—the subject remembers the first test. The second difficulty is that animals are extraordinarily complex. After we have used up our first sample (the first subject or group of subjects), we cannot get a second identical with the first, because human beings and other animals differ in many ways that we cannot identify before beginning an experiment.

Suppose, for example, that we want to find out whether removing

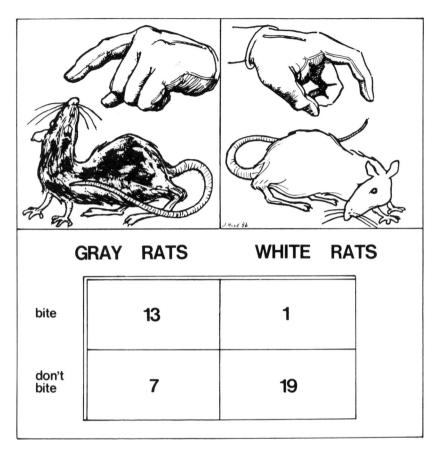

FIGURE 8.3   An exciting experiment that rejects a null hypothesis based on counting. The null hypothesis is that gray rats and white rats are equally aggressive: The experimental test is to extend a safely gloved finger into the rat's cage and observe whether the rat attacks the finger. If the null hypothesis is correct, each strain of rats will attack about equally often. The figures illustrate the outcome: 13 of 20 gray rats attacked, whereas only one of 20 white rats did. A technique called Chi-square analysis enables us to determine that the frequencies are "significantly different." Thus, the null hypothesis is rejected and the alternative conclusion—that gray rats are more aggressive—is accepted.

the frontal lobes of a monkey's brain affects his ability to learn a visual discrimination. In an ideal procedure, we would measure the monkey's learning ability, remove the frontal lobes, and measure learning ability again. But in reality the second measurement is disturbed by memory of the first. We must measure learning ability by the number of trials, or the number of errors made, in achieving the discrimination. In the second measurement there will almost certainly be a practice effect, and we do not know how great it will be. Next best, in a slightly less ideal world, we would obtain two monkeys identical in all respects; we would remove the frontal lobes from one, have both learn the task under identical conditions, and see how much faster the normal monkey learned, compared with the one operated on. But in practice we cannot find two identical subjects, animal or human. (Identical twins are identical with respect to heredity, but it is impossible that everything that has happened since birth that might affect them psychologically is exactly the same. Also, of course, there are not many of them.) Thus we are driven to the comparison of two groups, an *experimental* group and a *control* group, large enough to make individual differences average out. If the original learning capacity of two subjects is not identical, the average for two groups is likely to differ much less and the probable degree of difference can be dealt with statistically.

The ideal cases referred to, however, should be kept in mind, for they tell us what we are trying to achieve by the use of the control group. In the frontal lobe question referred to, we would like to measure the learning ability of the same monkey with and without frontal lobes, with the second measurement not being affected by the first. This is impractical. So is the hope of finding two identical monkeys. But it is not impractical to find two groups that, if they are large enough, will be much more similar, as groups, than two individual monkeys. Our choice of a control group, then, is a matter of choosing animals as much like the animals in the experimental group as possible, in every way that affects visual discrimination.

The experiment may then proceed in one of two ways. First, we can operate on one group and test both. We compare the mean scores of the operated animals and of the normal control subjects and see whether they differ significantly. Statistics at this point enables us to evaluate the probability that the difference we have found is due simply to accidental differences in our two groups, treating them as two samples in the way already described. The second procedure would be to test both groups, operate on one, test both groups again, and see whether the increases in score by the normals (due to practice effect) are significantly greater than the increases by the operated animals (though the experiment might come out with a still clearer result, the normals all showing increases and the operates all showing losses).

The principle is clear: Make your control group like the experimental group in every way that would affect the outcome of the experiment, except for the one variable in which you are interested. The pitfalls consist mainly of not recognizing a variable that affects the results. If one is picking rats out of a colony cage, and puts the first 10 into the experimental group and the second 10 into the control group, one overlooks the possibility that the most easily caught animals, or the ones that come to the front of the cage and allow themselves to be picked up, are tamer than the others; and this difference is likely to affect any experimental result. The easiest solution is to put No. 1 into the first group, No. 2 into the second, No. 3 into the first, and so on. (There are more sophisticated ways of doing this by the use of random numbers assigned to the animals, but we need not go into this.)

Again, in clinical investigations one does not have the choice of one's "experimental" group, and one perforce must try to find a similar control group. This is usually difficult. The clinical group (corresponding to the experimental group of the laboratory) generally includes people of all sorts of occupations, rural and urban, educated and uneducated, old and young. It is difficult indeed to persuade a group of similar persons who are not ill and have no reason to take tests to give up the time to act as subjects—especially since they are apt to view any psychological test with suspicion. But if one wants to know whether removal of the human frontal lobe affects intelligence, and if the clinical group with frontal lobe operation has, say, a mean age of 40 and a mean of 8 years' schooling, one must make one's comparisons with a group that is similar in these respects, as intelligence test scores vary with amount of schooling and with advancing age.

CORRELATIONS

Correlation is the degree of relation between two variables. A *coefficient of correlation* measures this relationship. Correlation coefficients range from plus 1 to minus 1. Plus 1 represents a perfect relationship between the two variables, high values accompanying high values, intermediate values accompanying intermediate values, and so on. Minus 1 *also* represents a perfect relationship, though it is reversed; the highest score on variable I goes with the lowest score on variable II, next highest on I, with next lowest on II, and so on. The relation is perfect in this sense. Once you know someone's score on test I, you also know his or her score on II. Finally, a correlation of zero means no relation at all; here a high score on the first test might go with a high, a medium, or a low score on the second.

To see better what is meant, consider Fig. 8.4. In Fig. 8.4a, tests I and II have a zero correlation. Knowing a score on test I tells us nothing about test II. Now consider Fig. 8.4b. Tests I and II are perfectly and positively related (such perfection rarely occurs in psychology). If we know a child's score on test I we do not have to give test II; the two tests

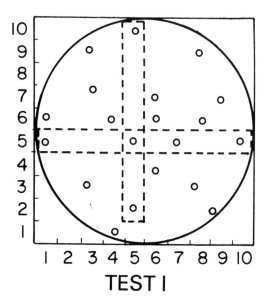

(a) Data with a correlation coefficient of −0.05. The scores on the two tests are unrelated. For any one score, the range of scores obtained on the other test is very large. The envelope is circular.

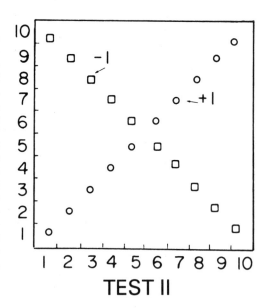

(b) Data with correlation coefficients of +1 (circles) and −1 (squares). Two different populations, each with twenty pairs of test scores, are illustrated here. For the positive correlation (+1), a score of +1 on one test predicts a score of +1 on the other. For the negative correlation, a score of +1 on one test predicts a score of −1 on the other. For any score on either test, the range of scores obtained on the other test is limited to one value, and the successive scores on one test are associated with successive scores on the other. The envelope containing the data points is a single line.

FIGURE 8.4 Correlations. Each panel illustrates a characteristic of the correlation coefficient. Each point represents the pair of test scores obtained by one person on two occasions. Data from 20 people (20 points) are plotted in each graph. The dotted lines

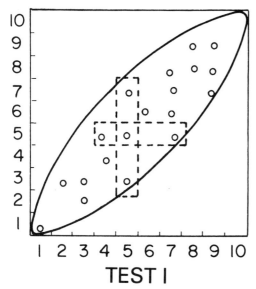

(c) Data with a correlation of .90. A high score on test I is most likely associated with a high score on test II, and vice versa. For any one score, the range of scores obtained on the other test is greater than with a perfect correlation of plus or minus one, but less than with a correlation of zero or practically zero. The envelope containing all the data points is elliptical.

TEST I

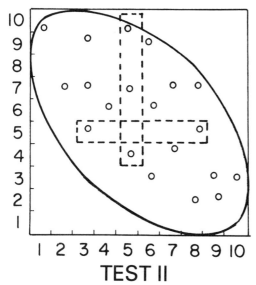

(d) Data with a correlation of −.66. A high score on one test is most likely associated with a low score on the other, and vice versa. For any score on one test, the range of scores obtained on the other test is greater than with a perfect correlation of plus or minus one, but less than with a correlation of zero or practically zero. The envelope is elliptical.

TEST II

illustrate the range of scores obtained on either test by people who obtained a score of five on the other test. The solid lines outline an envelope which contains all of the scores.

correlate 1.00, so the second score can be determined as soon as the first is known. Similarly, when the relation is perfect and negative, if a subject makes a poor score on test I we can predict, without further testing, a good score on test II.

These, however, are only the extreme cases. It is important to know the degree of relation, roughly, that is represented by such correlation coefficients as 0.30, 0.50, −0.70, and 0.90. In general, one may say that the relation is not nearly as close as one of these figures makes it sound. The first, 0.30, represents a barely discernable relation. A correlation of 0.70 is not a 70% correspondence, or agreement 7 times out of 10, but 49%; a correlation of 0.90 represents a 81% correspondence.[4] In psychology, because we must often deal with coefficients below 0.60, it is common to speak of one above this value as representing "a high correlation." But this is misleading, suggesting as it does a close relation between the two variables. It would be better to reserve the term "high correlation" for coefficients above 0.90.

All this has more meaning if expressed graphically. Figure 8.4c shows a plot of two sets of scores where the correlation is 0.90. It is reasonable to speak of this as a high correlation, but let us see how close the correspondence really is. The vertical lines in the third diagram, on each side of the value 5 on the abscissa (horizontal axis) (for test I) contain the entries of all subjects who made 5 on the first form of the test. On the second test, these subjects made scores ranging from 3 to 7. Evidently no very close prediction of the second score is possible, despite the correlation of 0.90.

Figure 8.4d shows a somewhat lower negative correlation, −0.66. A comparison of Figs. 8.4c and 8.4d shows clearly that the thickness of the envelope enclosing the entries on such a correlation plot is the essential factor in predicting the second score from the first. With a high correlation, we have a thin envelope; when the vertical lines are drawn, as in Fig. 8.4c, only a short segment is enclosed, which means that the amount of variation in the second test is small—and prediction is good. When the correlation is lower, the envelope is broader and prediction is poor. In the perfect case, the correlations in Fig. 8.4b, the band has no width whatever (all the points plotted fall on a single straight line) and prediction is perfect.

This graphical analysis is of course rough, and there are much more exact ways of dealing with the predictions that can be made and with

---

[4]In a manner of speaking. These values are obtained by squaring the coefficient of correlation ($0.70 \times 0.70 = 0.49$, $0.90 \times 0.90 = 0.81$), and what they represent more exactly is the proportion of the variance (SD^2) in one test that is predictable from or determined by variance in the other.

their degree of error. But it is still true here, as elsewhere, that a good deal can be learned about complex data by simple inspection, and there is no other way that is as good for conveying the fundamental meaning of a correlation coefficient, high or low.

With a correlation, it is clear that we are always dealing with a causal connection. The connection may be very indirect, however, and a correlation, in and of itself, does not tell us what causes what. If variables I and II are correlated, I may cause II, II may cause I, both may be caused by an outside factor III, or there may be a mixture of these relations. It is known, for example, that intelligence test scores are correlated with years of schooling—but we cannot leap to the conclusion that one's IQ is determined by one's education. The relation may be just the opposite—those who have not the intelligence to do well in school tend to leave earlier than others, which means that intelligence affects amount of schooling. A more important factor may be that intelligent parents tend (a) to have intelligent children and (b) to encourage their children to continue their schooling. In this case, the parent is the outside factor, III, which determines the level both of II (intelligence) and I (schooling); I and II could thus be correlated without one's causing the other.

Mental age in the growing child is known, for example, to be correlated with length of the big toe. This old joke might well be remembered by the student: The statement is quite true, for as a child grows, his capacity for solving problems increases at the same time that his bones are growing in length, and the two therefore show a significant correlation. This may help the student to see that, though a correlation shows a causal relation *somewhere*, it does not necessarily mean that one of the two things correlated causes the other.

SUMMARY

Statistics is concerned with evaluating the errors that must occur in any set of measurements or in generalizing from known data (a sample) to the larger class of values or events to which the data belong (a population or universe). It is a fundamental part of the scientific method. Mathematical methods of statistics increase the exactness with which the estimate of error is made, but they are not the essence of statistics; graphical methods, and simple inspection, are often sufficient for a particular problem where the results are relatively clear cut. Some scientists say they make no use of statistics; what they really mean is that inspection is sufficient for their purposes, without formal computations.

The first step of statistical analysis is a description of the available data, the sample. Two values are of primary importance: a measure of central tendency and a measure of dispersion. The central tendency is a single representative value, or average. There are several kinds of averages, of which the most important is the (arithmetic) mean. Dispersion is the extent to which individual cases deviate from the average; one index of deviation is the range, but a more useful index is the standard deviation, or SD. This is particularly so when we are dealing with samples that approximate the "normal probability distribution," the symmetrical, bell-shaped curve frequently found with biological data.

Given the mean and the SD, we can then ask how probable it is that our sample has come from any given hypothetical population. If the probability is low, we reject the conclusion that the sample has come from that population. For scientific purposes, it is customary to work with two levels of "significance" (i.e., of probability) in drawing such conclusions: the 5% level (when it is reasonably sure that the sample has not come from that population) and the 1% level (still surer).

We use essentially the same method to determine whether an experimental treatment of some sort has had an effect on a group of subjects. We have an experimental group and a control group, the latter treated in exactly the same way as the experimental group except for the one treatment in whose effects we are interested. What we ask is whether the two samples, the data from the two groups, could come from the same population. That is, we make the *null hypothesis*: we assume that the treatment did not have an effect. Any difference between our two groups may have occurred by chance, since any two samples from the same population are likely to differ. Statistics allows us to determine just how probable such a result would be—how often we would get, from the same population, two samples as different as these two. If the probability is below 5%, we reject the null hypothesis, that is, we conclude that the treatment *did* have an effect. The chance of being wrong in this conclusion, of course, is 1 in 20; if we wish to be more certain to avoid a wrong conclusion, we may use the 1% level instead.

Correlation is the degree of relationship between two variables. A coefficient of correlation is a quantitative measure of the relation, ranging from plus 1 to minus 1. Graphical analysis is very useful here as well, since the strength of the relationship can be visualized easily.

When two variables are correlated, there is a causal relationship, but from the correlation alone one cannot determine what causes what: I may cause II, II may cause I, or they may share common causes, III, IV, and so on.

GUIDE TO STUDY

Be able to define and give examples of each of the following terms:
1) sample;
2) population;
3) mean;
4) null hypothesis.

What can a scientist do with a single case? Consider both examples (from the text) of a single small elephant, and the observation that the sun turned a mottled green for 30 seconds.

Explain how the use of statistics differs from an exhaustive description of a complete population.

Give examples of interesting populations that cannot be completely described. Can you think of any interesting populations that can be completely described?

Describe two ways, one graphical and one computational, in which the relationship between two variables can be described in a sample.

Give two examples of measures of central tendency and two examples of measures of variation. Be able to explain how each is computed.

NOTES AND REFERENCES

Obviously this chapter does not deal with all aspects of statistical thought, and offers no help to one who wants to make active use of statistics himself. The intention here is only to enable the student to comprehend the meaning of certain commonly made statistical statements. A number of books are available in this field and you should consult your instructor when you want to go further, for these texts vary in the extent to which they involve the reader in details and thus vary in difficulty. However, an authoritative and effective treatment will be found in either of the following books:

Ferguson, G. A. (1980). *Statistical Analysis in Psychology and Education*, 5th ed. New York: McGraw-Hill.

Hays, W. L. (1963). *Statistics for Psychologists*. New York: Holt, Rinehart and Winston.

CHAPTER 9

Intelligence

Among such great pioneers of psychology as Freud, Pavlov, Thorndike, and Watson, two are great because they learned how to measure something that could not be measured before. As mentioned earlier, Hermann Ebbinghaus invented nonsense syllables and then measured memory by counting the number of syllables a subject could remember some time after having learned a list of them. Alfred Binet, with whom we are now concerned, invented a set of simple questions and problems to put to children and, by counting the number of satisfactory answers and comparing them with those of other children, both defined and measured a child's intelligence. The questions and problems were simple indeed, related to common everyday experience, and it was a stroke of genius to realize how revealing they could be of a child's mental development. Binet made the great discovery, and all later work on intelligence is really a development of his original idea. Test items (the individual questions or problems) have been extended and improved, tests suitable for older persons and for measuring different aspects or kinds of intelligence[1] have been developed, but it was Binet who showed in principle how all this could be done.

---

[1]Verbal and nonverbal intelligence. There are sex differences; girls do better with verbal tests; boys with mechanical, spatial and quantitative tests. Males may be reminded that language is the distinguishing characteristic of the human species. Lower animals also do better on nonverbal tasks.

Binet's goal was practical: to classify pupils in a large city school system (Paris, France), and intelligence testing remains a practical activity today. Naturally, the practice was inspired by theory. In the 19th century, Charles Darwin argued in the *Origin of Species* that humans were an outcome of natural selection, and later he argued that humans share a distant ancestor with modern apes and monkeys. Differences between species were the result of natural selection, described by Darwin as "survival of the fittest." The individual differences that helped animals to survive and reproduce were continued in their offspring. Individuals whose characteristics were unfavorable either did not live long enough to mate or were unsuccessful in mating; hence, their characteristics did not continue. Species differences arose when mating populations with different characteristics were segregated, and evolution within one species continued as the adaptive characteristics of certain individuals were favored by natural selection.

Sir Francis Galton was an English scientist and statistician. He invented the concept of correlation, discussed in chapter 8. Following publication of Darwin's theory, he tried to measure people and to relate his measurements to their achievement of fame and riches. He hoped to discover key abilities that led some people to be successful in the Darwinian sense. He measured mostly physical aspects, like height and strength of grip, and did not succeed in relating his measurements to success. Binet, however, succeeded where Galton failed. He found that he could predict fairly well how children would succeed in school. From success in school some, but by no means all, of success in modern life can be predicted.

It is now of little practical importance whether or not differences in ability among people are due to heredity in the Darwinian sense. As we shall see later on in this chapter, it is very difficult to measure the degree to which any measurable ability is the result of simple heredity. Differences among people do exist, and some means of assessing their potential for benefiting from education is needed. Experience has shown that the best predictor of educational achievement tomorrow is yesterday's educational achievement: To predict how well someone will do in school next year, observe how well he or she did last year. Why, then, are intelligence tests needed? Because in certain cases, yesterday's achievement may not be a good predictor of tomorrow's achievement. Children with emotional difficulties, children whose education has been interrupted for some reason or another, or children whose health has limited their educational opportunities, can be assessed better by giving them an intelligence test than by reviewing their perhaps limited or unusually interrupted progress in school.

Intelligence test results depend less on specific schooling than do other measures of academic achievement. As a result, intelligence tests are better than school results for comparing children who have been raised within the same culture, but who have not gone to the same schools. This is how Goldfarb (1943) used intelligence tests when he discovered the developmental differences between some children who were raised in an orphanage during infancy, and a group of other children raised in the homes of foster parents. It is for these reasons, as well as for the theoretical interest in the nature and origin of the abilities measured by intelligence tests, that intelligence testing continues to be an important educational and psychological tool.

The kind of material that is used for the measurement of intelligence might include asking a child what a match is used for, what time of day it is when the sun is in the west, the meaning of the proverb "Once bitten, twice shy"; or what holds airplanes up, or in what respect an airplane is like a balloon. The subject may be asked to complete an analogy like "Boy is to girl as man is to _____," or the more difficult "Raindrop is to air as bubble is to _____." One can ask who Einstein was, or Hitler. One can put a picture pattern before the subject and have it copied with blocks. Some of the "problems" are suitable only for very young children, some only for older ones, but a list of items, running from easy to difficult, can be prepared and used to find out the level of difficulty an individual can deal with. A total score can be determined by giving one point for each item successfully completed, and this score can be used to compare the subject with others.

Having made up such a list—the first intelligence test—Binet determined the average score made by 3 year old children, 4 year olds, 5 year olds, and so on. A child of 6 years who made a score that was average for children of 5 was said to be retarded in intellectual development and to have a *mental age* of 5. Or if the score was halfway between the averages for 7 and 8 years, the child was said to be ahead of the 5 year old group with a mental age of 7.5.

The next development was to define an *intelligence quotient*[2] or IQ. With MA being mental age, and CA being chronological age, IQ is defined as follows:

$$IQ = \frac{MA}{CA} \times 100.$$

Thus an 8 year old with a mental age of 6 has an IQ of 75; if instead he has a mental age of 10, his IQ is 125. The IQ is therefore an index of the *rate of intellectual development.* An IQ of 100 means an average rate of development, 95 a slightly slow rate, 90 a slower rate, and so on.

---

[2]This important step was taken by Wilhelm Stern.

For adults, the situation is somewhat different. The intelligence that is measured by such tests does not continue to rise much after the age of 15 or thereabouts (no exact figure can be given, since the cessation of development is not abrupt). But we know that those with low IQs during childhood continue to make low scores at maturity, and high childhood IQs lead to high scores at maturity. What we can do therefore is to work out IQs for adults that correspond to their probable IQs in childhood. The mean IQ for the whole population is considered to be 100, and the standard deviation of IQs is 15 (see chapter 8). Taking the mean score of the adult population on an IQ test, we say that those who make that score have an IQ of 100—by definition. A score that is made or exceeded by only 15.9% of the population is 1 SD above the mean (see chapter 8, Fig. 8.1) and equals an IQ of 115; one made or exceeded by only 2.3%, 2 SDs above the mean, equals an IQ of 130; and so on, with in-between scores treated accordingly. The IQ makes possible a direct comparison of the child's rate of development with that of others; at maturity IQ compares an adult's ultimate attainment with that of others and refers only by inference to the rate of development.

RELIABILITY AND VALIDITY

There are two questions one must ask about any mental test: How accurate or reliable is the measurement it makes? and, Is it measuring what it is supposed to measure? The first is technically the question of *reliability*; the second, the question of *validity*. Ideally, to answer the second question one must have a perfect, or practically perfect, measurable standard against which to compare the test. We have no perfect measurements (see chapter 8), so we must approach the matter indirectly.

Reliability is fairly straightforward. It is defined quantitatively as the correlation between the scores on a test made by the same subjects on two different occasions—preferably using different forms of the test. With repetition of the same form the subject is likely to remember and repeat the answers given to questions at the first time of testing. Figure 8.4c is an example in which the correlation between the two forms of a pictorial test of intelligence in adults was 0.90. Here we say that the reliability of the test was 0.90. Reliabilities for the well-established intelligence tests run at or over 0.90; the resulting error of measurement is small and reliability, on the whole, is very good.

For validity, there is no simple answer, especially where the intelligence of older people is concerned. Existing tests are mostly tests of *academic* and *clerical aptitude*: that is, what they measure is related to success at school or at college or at desk-work occupations. They do not measure the abilities needed for chess, for understanding and getting on with people, for interior decorating, or for being an inventor. Even in academic matters they may predict who will do well in advanced examinations but tell us nothing about who will be leaders in research; in officer's training school they may tell us who will receive good marks but nothing about which cadets will become leaders.

A particular problem concerns the evaluation of adult intelligence. The widely used tests are all developments of material designed originally for school children: to test adults, the same kinds of questions are used, but more difficult and more bookish. For a good evaluation (unless one is simply trying to predict academic performance) something closer to adult interests is needed. One example is provided in Fig. 9.1a, which was designed as part of a nonverbal test. (The subject has only to point to "what is funny or out of place.")

For their primary purpose—the prediction of school performance—the existing tests are good, though far from perfect. The real validation comes from the experience of several generations of testers. But these "intelligence tests" are not tests of general intelligence—at least not after the age of 6, 7, or 8—for there are important aspects of human intelligence that they do not touch at all.

(a)   (b)

Figure 9.1. Two examples of nonverbal adult intelligence test items. In (a), the task is to point to the part of the picture which is "funny" or "out of place". Not what is impossible: rather, what is possible but inappropriate. In (b), the task is to assemble the pattern shown (blue and yellow in the original) from colored wooden blocks. (From the Kohs Block Design Test © Stoelting Company, Chicago, IL. Reproduced by permission.)

THE HEREDITY–ENVIRONMENT QUESTION

The classical view in psychology was that intelligence is determined essentially by heredity. This view seemed to be supported by such experiments as the following:

Learning ability was tested in a large number of laboratory rats. The brightest males and females, those with the fewest errors, were then bred with each other, and the dullest males and females of the dull group were bred with each other. This was continued until by the seventh generation it was found that there was little or no overlap in the scores of the bright and dull groups: practically all the bright strain made better scores in maze learning than any of the dull strain (Tryon, 1940).

This experiment appears to show that intelligence is dependent on heredity alone. However, there are other experiments that contradict the conclusion. Rats have been divided into two groups, one group reared in a restricted environment (each animal alone in a small cage he cannot see out of, containing no objects and presenting no opportunity for problem solving), the other reared in a "free environment" (a large cage containing the whole group and laid out like a sort of amusement park for rats with a variety of barriers to give experience with varied paths from point to point) (Forgays & Forgays, 1952; Hymovitch, 1952). Or, as described in chapter 7, some dogs have been reared in restricted cages, others as pets in normal homes (another form of free environment). When such experiments have been done, the animals reared in restriction show marked deficiencies in maze learning and the solution of simple problems. These experiments appear to show that intelligence is determined by environment, not by heredity.

But is it? Look again at the two kinds of experiments in the light of chapter 7, especially Table 7.1. In the breeding experiment, all the animals were reared in identical small cages, thus keeping environmental differences from affecting the results. In the study of restricted versus free environment, heredity is prevented from having any systematic effect by splitting litters. The two groups have the same heredity, just as in the other experiment the two groups had the same environment. What the experiments show, therefore, is that both heredity and environment determine adult intelligence. If one source of variability in adult performance is held constant, all the variability (the difference between individuals or groups) comes from the other source, as one might expect.

With this point in mind, we can examine the result of a related investigation of human intelligence. Identical twins are twins that originate from a single fertilized ovum and thus, according to genetics, have the same hereditary characteristics. If they are brought up in different environments, we should be able to see what kind of effect variations of environment have upon intelligence. Psychologists have therefore been very interested in identical twin orphans adopted by different families. It has been found that their IQs are very similar, and this finding has sometimes been used as an argument that adult intelligence is determined by heredity, not by environment.

But when we look at the evidence, we find that most of these pairs of children were brought up in very similar environments. When a pair of twins is orphaned, they may be adopted by the neighbors, which implies similar environments—the same community, plus the fact that all the families in one neighborhood are apt to have about the same economic and social status. Or the twins may be taken charge of by a social agency, and this again means that they will get into foster care or adoption, environments that have much in common, social workers having strong ideas about who is fit to bring up children. In this kind of "experiment," differential effects of environment are minimized, and it is hardly surprising to find similar IQs in identical twins with similar environments. The fact that the IQs of identical twins are more alike than those of fraternal twins shows that heredity is important, just as the rat breeding experiment did; but it does not show that heredity is the only variable (Farber, 1981).

Sometimes it is recognized that heredity and environment both affect intelligence, but each is assigned a percentage related to its importance—for example, 80% of intelligence is determined by heredity and 20% by environment. This division is nonsensical. If taken literally, it would mean that one person would have 80% of the problem-solving ability of another person despite never having the opportunity to learn a language, to learn how people behave, and so forth. Conversely, it would mean that a seriously brain-damaged or genetically deficient newborn human infant, if reared in a favorable environment, could develop 20% of normal human problem-solving ability. Instead, both heredity and environment are 100% important. Asking how much heredity and environment each contribute to intelligence is like asking how much the width or the length of a field each contribute to its area. Neither contributes anything by itself.

Though we cannot experiment with the effect of environment on the intelligence of the growing child, there are cases in which its importance has been unequivocally demonstrated. Goldfarb (1943), as we saw earlier, showed that an orphanage environment may be sufficiently unstimulating to account for a deficiency of 23 points in the IQ scores of children reared in orphanages compared with the scores of children raised in foster homes. Also, children who grew up on canal boats in England, removed from many of the normal experiences of other children, showed a sharp decline in intelligence scores. Their mean IQ was 90 at the age of 6; 77 at age 7½; 60 at age 12. An IQ of below 70 is ordinarily considered to mean mental deficiency, whereas 90 is within the range of normal ability. Again, a very similar picture (mean IQ for 7 year olds, 84; for 15 year olds, 60) was found for children growing up in isolated mountain communities in the United States. The higher IQs for the youngest children show that the low IQs at later ages do not mean deficient heredities—if they did, all the scores would be low. Instead, it appears that the social and cultural environment was sufficiently stimulating for normal development of intelligence in the first 4 or 5 years of life, but progressively inadequate from then on. (A poor social and cultural environment has somewhat the same effect as the childhood hyperactivity discussed in chapter 1).

INTELLIGENCE AND FAMILY SIZE

About the simplest description of a child's environment is the size of the child's family along with the child's birth order (first, second, etc.). Family size changes as more children are born, whereas a child's birth order is, of course, fixed. A remarkable regularity is seen (Fig. 9.2) when the results of a nonverbal intelligence test (the Raven Progressive Matrices) are plotted as a function of birth order and family size. The figure shows averages from a sample of about 400,000 Dutch men who reached the age of 19 between 1963 and 1966. In this sample, measured IQ decreases as birth order and family size increase. There are exceptions: an only child scores lower than the first child from a family of two children. Also, the scores of children born late into large families are higher than predicted from the general trend. It should be pointed out first that these differences in test scores are actually very small. Second, differences among individual people or particular families are completely eliminated in these average figures. But in a population of 400,000 people, the effects of family size and birth order are clear. Similar results have been obtained from other large samples (Zajonc et al, 1983).

The explanation of these results is that birth order and family size influence two factors: the child's intellectual environment and the child's opportunity to teach. Adults are fully developed intellectually: they talk about the world with better information, in general, than do children. The intellectual level of the child's family is the average of the levels of all of the family members: the parents, any other children,

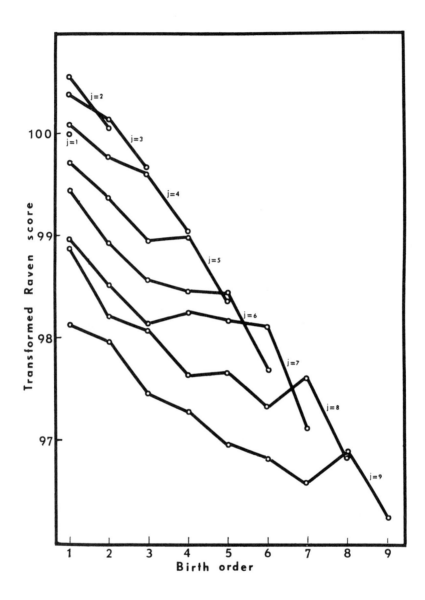

Figure 9.2. Intelligence, birth order and family size. Intelligence, as measured by the Raven Progressive Matrices (a nonverbal intelligence test), declines as family size increases from two to nine children; and (with a few exceptions) within a family of a given size, intelligence declines from the first- to the last-born. Data are from 400,000 Dutch males tested at 19 years of age. (From Zajonc & Markus, 1975. Reproduced by permission.)

190

and the child himself. As the number of children in a family increases, the average intellectual level of the family decreases, but the intellectual level increases again as the earlier born children grow older and complete their intellectual development.

An only child cannot teach anything to anyone: the parents know more than the child, and there are no younger children who know less. The last child in a family cannot teach, because both its parents and the older children all know more then the child does. Teaching, as any teacher knows, is a very effective way to learn. The environment of both an only child and a last child deprives that child of the chance to teach. This is why the measured IQ of an only child is lower than that of the first child in a family of two or three children and why the last-born child of a large family does not show the improvement shown by the later born children in large families as the older children grow up and provide more mental stimulation to the younger ones.

Intelligence A and Intelligence B

Implied by these facts is that the child at birth has a certain capacity or potential for intellectual development, but a stimulating environment is needed if the potential is to be realized. The extent to which intelligence can be developed may be small, in which case no environment can produce a high IQ; then heredity sets a limit on the development. On the other hand, the child may have inherited a good brain, capable of developing a high IQ, and yet in a poor environment the IQ remains low—just as with a child that inherited a poorer brain.

In much of the literature, the term *intelligence* is used to refer both to the original potential (A) and the ultimate level of development (B). This ambiguity has produced confusion since, as we saw in the preceding paragraph, A might be high and B low. They are not the same thing. "Intelligence," at best, is not a very precise term, but things will be less confused if we recognize two quite different meanings, as follows.

The term *intelligence A* refers to an innate potential for the development of intellectual capacities, and *intelligence B* refers to the level of that development at a later time, when intellectual functioning can be observed. Intelligence A cannot be measured, for intellectual functioning is not observed in the newborn; the IQ, therefore, is a measure of intelligence B only. Note that A and B are not wholly separate; on the contrary, intelligence A enters into and is a necessary factor in intelligence B. These terms distinguish two different ways in which the more general term, intelligence, is used.

Another point: The constancy of the IQ is an important concept, but it must be interpreted with caution. In general, the IQ is stable, changing only very slowly (here it is important to remember the difference between IQ and MA). The IQ is "constant" to about age 20 or 30 and then declines slowly with age. In the child, however, constancy of the IQ depends on an adequate environment, as the canal boat children referred to in the preceding section showed clearly. Their IQs were not constant at all but fell steadily, their environment providing inadequate intellectual stimulation for the older child.

It appears that the effects of the environment during childhood tend to be permanent, for good or ill, and that the IQ tends to change less and less as the child grows older, stabilizing at about the age of 15. A child may have a good intelligence A and be reared in a stimulating environment, producing a good intelligence B. Thereafter the adult will always have that level of intelligence (unless disease, malnutrition, or injury affects brain function). But the same child, if reared in an inadequate environment, will have a low intelligence B, and manipulation of the environment after the age of 15 will not significantly raise it.

From these considerations it is clear that the level of intelligence B, which we can measure, does not necessarily reflect the level of intelligence A, hence, we cannot really measure intelligence A. B reflects A if we assume an adequate environment for the full development of A's potential. If the environment is good and B is low, A must have been low also; but a low IQ obtained by a child reared in an inadequate (or doubtfully adequate) environment leaves a question as to whether or not the result is due to a low intelligence A.

It is a well-established principle in psychology that no valid comparison of native ability (i.e., intelligence A) can be based on a comparison of IQs obtained by persons brought up in different cultures. The principle was established during World War I, when mass testing was first used to screen recruits for the U.S. Army. Blacks in general were found to have lower IQs than the white population in general; but it was easily shown that the blacks had, as a group, less exposure to the intelligence test materials by which the IQs were determined. It was also shown that blacks living in the North had a higher mean IQ than the rural white population of some states in the South—a clear indication, if not proof, of the importance of environment in determining the level of the IQ.

As soon as it is realized that any intelligence test assumes an adequate knowledge of or exposure to the test materials, it becomes obvious the the IQ provides no basis for comparing intelligence A in persons from different cultures. We cannot compare the native abilities of Swede and Italian, or of American and Russian. Apart from the language problem, even assuming that one's test has been adequately translated, different patterns of living and thinking and talking would still exist and the same score of, say, 20 items correct in a test of 50 items, would have a different value in the two social environments.

This conclusion must hold also for different social strata in the same culture. If we cannot legitimately compare blacks and whites in the United States because they have not had the same exposure to the test material, neither can we compare two whites when one has grown up in a well-to-do home and the other in the slums of a big city. Such comparisons within one culture can effectively be made with respect to intelligence B at the age of 15 years or later, because the intelligence test does have this kind of validity. If the IQ is low because of a poor environment, intelligence B will be low also—the poor environment will have had its effect on the subject's general ability in the culture. But once again, the low IQ in a person from a poor environment does not permit the conclusion that intelligence A is low and that the person would still have been unintelligent if he or she had grown up in a better environment.

INTELLIGENCE AND ABILITIES

Binet and his successors learned how to measure the growth of skills especially related to success in school by what we now call IQ tests. But the intelligence quotient—a single number—is too simple to describe competence in the many skills on which people differ. Intelligence is related to rate of learning (see chapter 2). But transfer from one learned skill to another helps to determine the direction and variety of learning. For example, learning to read transfers to many other abilities, since it makes other knowledge accessible. Learning mathematics transfers to scientific and technical skills, because mathematics is the language of scientific and technical knowledge. Learning to play the violin transfers to a somewhat narrower set of other skills, while learning to repair automobile engines transfers mainly to the other types of engine repair. An adult has a range of acquired skills, transferred from those which were learned in childhood and adolescence. Unless specific skills are learned during childhood and adolescence, many adult abilities cannot be acquired: for example, scientific work requires the necessary mathematics, and skilled musicianship, which requires both theoretical knowledge and great manual dexterity, is usually acquired only after years of practice.

IQ tests supply a single number describing a person's ability. Clearly, this is unsatisfactory and an oversimplification. On the other hand, if we just acknowledge that everyone is different and leave it at that, we ignore any knowledge about what abilities people have, and we lose the opportunity to measure the skills that prepare people for one or another kind of work.

A solution to this problem lies in the correlations among scores on tests of mental abilities (see chapter 8). Suppose a large population of people (over 500) is given a vocabulary test: twenty items of the sort, "What does 'impediment' mean?". Each person's score is the number of words successfully defined. The same population is then given a test of verbal information, where they are required to give basic facts like "What country has the largest land area?" The score is the number of items correctly identified. The same population is then given a block design test, in which the score is the number of patterns correctly matched by a set of colored blocks in 3 minutes, and finally an object assembly test, in which the task is to look at the picture of an irregular flat object (Fig. 9.1b) and assemble it out of a set of wooden parts. The score is the number of objects correctly assembled in 5 minutes.

A correlation coefficient (see chapter 8) can be calculated between the scores on every pair of tests. The correlation coefficient (r) describes the relationship between the test scores for the entire population: an r of 1 means that the tests are in perfect agreement; an r of -1 means that they give perfectly opposite scores (high on one means low on the other); and an r of zero means that over the entire population, the score on one test is unrelated to the score on the other.

Table 9.1 shows a set of imaginary correlations between each pair of the four hypothetical tests we have described: vocabulary (V), information (I), block design (B), and objects (O). There are four important points about the correlations in Table 9.1: (1) The correlations are all positive; (2) the correlation between vocabulary (V) and information (I) is high; (3) the correlation between block design (B) and objects (O) is high; and (4) the correlations between vocabulary and information, on the one hand, and block design and objects, on the other, are low.

TABLE 9.1
Correlations Among Ability Tests
Imaginary Data

Tests	Correlations		
	I	*B*	*O*
Vocabulary (V)	.523	.054	.061
Information (I)		.116	.128
Block Design (B)			.556

Factors of Intelligence

Each of these observations illustrates one aspect of the relationships among tests of ability. First, all of the tests are usually positively correlated: a person who does well on some tests tends to do well on all of the tests. This is equivalent to saying that there is a *common factor*—general intellectual ability, or intelligence—that characterizes each person's test performance. One measure of this general ability is a single IQ number.

Second, vocabulary and information are more highly correlated with each other than either test is with block design and objects. At the same time, block design and objects are more highly correlated with each other than either test is with vocabulary and information. This means that independent of the general tendency of people to be more or less capable (as described by IQ, which is the general positive correlation among tests), there are separate sets of abilities, usually called factors, on which people differ above and beyond their tendency to be either more or less generally capable. In other words, you may say of someone, "He is pretty smart, but he is especially good at arguments," indicating both a general factor of ability or intelligence and a specific factor of verbal ability. Another example: "She is bright in school and very good at mechanical things," indicating one level of general and a second level of specific performance factor.

These examples illustrate a general principle. Many different kinds of abilities can be evaluated by giving tests to a large number of people. The correlations among all of these tests can be calculated. These correlations can be used to place the tests into groups with common properties: those tests that correlate highly with each other define such a group. These groups, called *factors*, provide a useful description of abilities that falls somewhere between the oversimplification of a single IQ number and the truism that everyone is different. Instead of describing a person by one specific number, or giving up altogether, we can assign a person a score based on several ability factors, thus establishing a profile, rather than a single number, to describe each person's abilities.

There is little agreement on the most useful number of factors with which to describe human abilities nor on the specific tasks that should be used to measure those abilities and define the factors. It is generally recognized that verbal abilities and certain spatial abilities—as in our example—form separate factors, but there is less agreement on other primary factors. However, these techniques—imperfect as they are— are widely used in situations where some differential measurement of individual abilities is needed. And finding the best description of the structure of human abilities, as determined by correlations among ability tests, is an unresolved problem of great theoretical interest.

THE DEVELOPMENT OF INTELLIGENCE

The development of intelligence is a complex phenomenon, and we are far from understanding it. Studying infants and young children is one of the most difficult tasks in psychology. Unlike college students, children (and their parents) must be coaxed and persuaded to cooperate. Long experiments must be avoided. The art of the researcher is to arrange short tasks that show how intelligence develops and how adult intelligence differs from that of the infant. The developmental psychologist must have patience and ingenuity.

Much of what we do know is the result of the work of the great Swiss psychologist, Jean Piaget. Beginning as Binet did with the observation of his own children in their home environment, Piaget traced the way an infant's apparently uncomplicated reflex activity develops into adult intelligence.

The Concept of an Object

The behavior of adults towards objects is consistent; the behavior of infants towards objects is not. Piaget observed the following inconsistency: an infant between 4 and 6 months old, shown an interesting object, reaches over and picks it up. When the object is partially covered by a cloth, the infant still reaches and picks it up. But when the object, in full view of the child, is completely covered by the cloth, the infant ignores the cloth-covered object. "Out of sight, out of mind" accurately describes the impermanence of objects for the 4–6-month-old infant. Despite the infant's evident motivation to hold and inspect something of interest, as soon as that something is no longer visible, it is no longer available as a stimulus to behavior. Unlike the mental representation you keep of your coffee cup when you put it in the cupboard, a mental representation of the object does not persist in an infant after the object disappears from view.

Infants also respond to motion differently than do adults. They show a lack of the object constancy that characterizes adult behavior. For an adult watching an object move from one place to another, the object at rest in the first location and the final location is clearly the same object that moved from the one place to the other. T. G. R. Bower (1982) produced an ingenious demonstration to show that 3–4-month-old infants do not relate the experience of a moving object to the experience of an object at rest. A toy railroad car with flashing lights was centered before a seated infant (Fig. 9.3). The car rested on the track for 10 seconds, then moved slowly to the infant's right, then stopped for 10 seconds, and then moved back to the center again, stopping directly in front of the infant. This pattern was repeated several times. The infant looked at the car where it was stopped and followed it with his eyes as it moved slowly from place to place. Assuming that you were as interested in the toy railroad car with flashing lights as was the infant, and assuming that you now saw the toy car move in the other direction (to the infant's left), where would you look? You would follow the

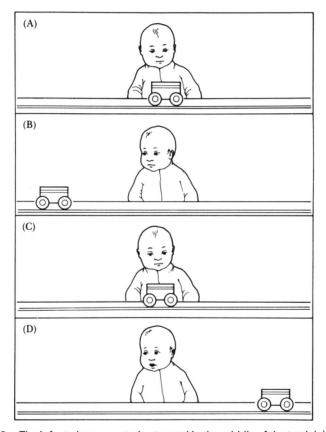

Figure 9.3.   The infant observes a train stopped in the middle of the track (a). The train moves to the infant's right and stops again (b). The infant follows the train, and observes it while it is stopped. It then returns to the middle and stops (c). The infant follows it back to the center and observes it stopped. After several repetitions of this routine (a, b, c) the train departs from the middle to the infant's left (d). Instead of following the moving train to the left, the infant looks for the stopped train on the right! (From Bower, 1982. Reproduced by permission.)

moving car to its new location. Not the infants. They continued to look to their own right and were visibly surprised when they did not see the car there, despite the fact that the car had been moving in front of them in the opposite direction. Bower suggests that the infants saw the moving and the stationary cars as different. The stationary cars appeared in a pattern: center, right, center, which the infants soon learned to predict. The moving car was something else again; it was not related to this regular pattern and did not predict the stationary pattern. The infant, in other words, did not track one object as it moved from center to right. Instead, he looked at a pattern of stationary objects and the unrelated experience of a moving object. The mental representations of stationary and moving objects were not united in a single object concept.

Children's Magical Thinking

If we as adults were able to view ourselves and our society objectively and in perspective (as some being with greater intelligence or from another universe might see us), the thinking of the child might seem more akin to that of the adult than it does at present. Piaget has shown that there are magical and animistic stages in the child's thoughts. Intelligent people in civilized society have outgrown such things, or so we claim. But have we? Magic is the action of symbols—ideas expressed in words, gesture, or ritual—upon things at a distance and in the future. We disavow some of its cruder forms, but a superstitious belief in lucky and unlucky actions affects the behavior of most of us, at least to some mild degree. Animism is the idea that an object, inert by itself, is active because it is inhabited by some nonphysical agent. We have seen that an animistic theory of behavior is intellectually respectable and an important feature of society (chapter 1). Also, one's thinking is tinged with animism whenever one attributes any sort of consciousness or intention or personality to a physical thing such as a sailing vessel, car, light plane, or computer. It may be difficult indeed not to think at times of an angry sea, a threatening sky, a hurricane as powerful entities to which names such as Louise or Hector are suitable. The child's thinking is less different from ours than at first it seems.

This does not invalidate Piaget's delineation of distinct stages in development. Qualitatively different patterns of thought at different ages must still contain threads of continuity. From one point of view, it may be suggested that the child's magic and animism is simply spread over a wider segment of the environment than the adult's; but at the same time it is true that a predominance of such ideas must give thought a qualitatively distinct character.

At an early stage in development, the child's understanding of events in the world is at a level of simple association. Things that are connected in thought are connected in the environment. Thus, a kind of magical thinking occurs, as for example when the child concludes, because sleepiness occurs in the evening, that his sleepiness brings on the night (magical, because feelings determine events outside). Or the child has seen a difference between the color of things that sink and the color of things that float and thinks of color as determining the buoyancy. For one child, live things are ones that move—therefore clouds are alive but trees are not. For another, live things are warm things—the sun is warm, so it is alive.

Great caution is needed in all this. We must be careful not to put words into a child's mouth, or ideas into a child's head, when trying to find out how the child's world appears. But with care it is possible to find out, for example, that the child's sun would belong with nonliving things if it were cold instead of warm.

As thought develops with experience, the idea of usefulness or apparent purpose enters. Why do boats float? Because they are needed to carry people. Clouds move because rain is needed somewhere else. Rivers and lakes have been made (Paul Bunyan!) so boats can travel on them. Things in general exist because they have a use, are needed. As Moliere put it, noses are shaped so that spectacles can rest on them. Still later, the child begins to think of how such things happen, of the means involved, and introduces an agent of some kind (one might say a supernatural agent, except that the thinking has not reached a stage at which natural and supernatural are differentiated; such conceptions have not yet developed). The clouds must be moved by someone. Primitive as this notion may be, it is at a more rational level than the earlier "magical" ideas. The someone may be God, whom the child thinks of as a very powerful human being. (For the very young child, parents and other adults have infinitely great powers—an almost unlimited capacity for making things happen.)

A Child's Understanding of Dreams

These points have been discussed by Laurendeau and Pinard, who have also provided us with extensive quantitative information about causal thinking in the child, taking as an example a peculiarly psychological phenomenon that has long fascinated mankind: the dream. They have defined four stages of development, as follows:

Stage 0. The child does not know what a dream is or does not understand the questions.

Stage 1. The dream is "real" and exists apart from the dreamer. It is in the bedroom and others can see it; or, if they cannot, it is because the dream disappears when the lights are turned on, or because the dream is under the bedclothes, and so on.

Stage 2. Intermediate: The dream is in the child's eyes or head, and if one could look inside the head one could see the dream, which is like a little show.

Stage 3. Real understanding: The child may say that the dream is in the eyes or in the head, but it is from one's memory, in one's thoughts or imagination. Now the child may have a harder time finding words to describe the dream, since understanding may have outstripped vocabulary.

The rate of development is shown in Fig. 9.4, which will have more meaning if it is illustrated by repeating some of the questions asked, and the answers.

Age 4: When your mother is in your bedroom, can she see your dream too? *Yes.* And if I were in your room, could I see it too? *Sure!* Why do you say that I could see your dream? *Because I think it is still there.*

Age 4½: Is the dream in your room really, or do we just say that? *Really there.* When you dream, are your eyes closed or open? *Closed.* Then where is your dream? *In my room.* How can you see it with eyes closed? *I don't know.* (A 5-year-old, asked the same questions replies that the dream is under the bedclothes [Stage 1].)

Age 6: When you dream are your eyes closed or open? *Closed.* Then where is your dream? *In front of me.* There is something in front of you when you dream? *Yes.* When your mother is in the room, can she see your dream? *No.* And I . . . ? *No.* Why do you say I could not see your dream? *Because it is inside me, but in front of me. I don't understand, I'm mixed up!* (Stage 2).

Age 8: When you dream, where is the dream? *In my eyes. Not near my eyes, in my eyes.*

Age 9: When you dream, where is the dream? *In my head.* In you or in your room? *In me* (Stage 3).

The moral of these demonstrations is that the ability to think about objects and causes develops slowly during infancy and childhood. The evidence does not yet allow a full description of the course of this development. However, it is clear that mental representations (cell assemblies) corresponding to the world as experienced by adults are gradually developed to enable the perception of constant physical

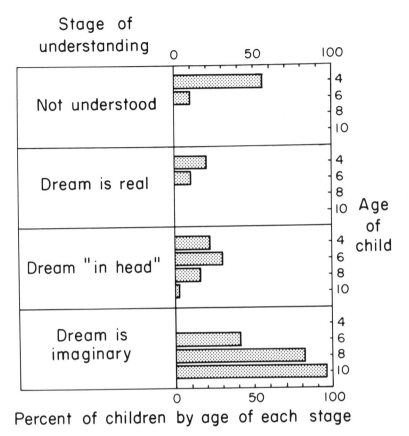

Figure 9.4 Children's understanding of dreams. Dreams are not understood (Stage 0) by about half of 4-year-olds, and a few older children. Some 4- and 6-year-olds think dreams are real (Stage 1). Slightly less than half of 6-year-olds think that a dream is somewhere "in the head" (Stage 2). Almost all 8 and 10-year-olds understand that a dream is imaginary (Stage 3). (Data from Laurendeau & Pinard, 1963. Adapted by permission.)

objects and to enable the separation of an external world of reality from an imagined world of dreams.

The foregoing provides but the barest example of the work done on the development of intelligence by Piaget and others who have followed his lead. A separate problem is to determine the conditions that maximize the development of intelligence, a tremendously important social problem but one about which, unfortunately, we know too little.

Technological development and automation are steadily increasing the levels of education and intelligence required to hold a job, and decreasing the demand for unskilled labor. The level of intellectual functioning of large numbers of people must be raised. How to do it?

More and better schools are only part of the answer, for educability depends on the IQ—on intelligence B—and this in turn depends largely on the intellectural stimulation the child has received in the home and in the wider social environment outside the school. It also depends, of course, on heredity, but even if something can be done to reduce the number of children born with poor intelligence A, it remains essential that children already born realize their full potential intelligence B. It appears certain that large segments of the present population in every country are far from having done so, although there are some grounds for optimism in North America (Flynn, 1984).

The difficulty in raising intelligence for the next generation (remember that the IQ appears to be fixed by about age 15, for all practical purposes) is that the intellectual climate for the growing child is determined mostly by the intellectual level of the child's family (Zajonc, 1984). By the time the child reaches kindergarten or first grade, the effects of a deficient intellectual environment are already in evidence. Various attempts to counteract the deficiency have been made, for example, using television (Sesame Street) or putting the child in a special nursery school for a summer. Valuable as these efforts are, they are nevertheless limited. All our information about the development of intelligence says that no program beginning at 3 or 4 years of age can make up fully for the preceding lack of an intellectually sufficient environment. An hour or two a day may be all that is needed, but it must begin early and continue. It has been asserted that such attempts at "compansatory education" have failed. To this claim it must be replied that a real try to correct the deficiency completely has never been made. The striking results that have been achieved show how much more could be done.

SUMMARY

This chapter is concerned first with the measurement of intelligence, and second with the conditions and course of its development. Binet solved the essential problem of measurement when he abandoned a priori definitions of intelligence and asked instead what differences of response could be found between a more intelligent child and a less intelligent one. No question was included in his test to which intelligent children *should* know the answer; the only questions included were those to which intelligent children *did* know the answers. Intelligence test items are valid if academically and intellectually successful adults and children score high on them and unsuccessful adults and children score low. A test is reliable to the extent that it gives the same result on repeated testing, preferably with different forms of the test so that the earlier answers are not simply remembered and repeated.

The heredity-environment problem reappears as we turn to the topic of intelligence, and the student should keep chapter 7 in mind while working through this one. The adult's level of preformance is fixed by hereditary potential and by environmental conditions that determine the extent to which that potential will be realized. Thus heredity may be thought of as setting limits to intellectual development. Animal experiments have demonstrated the importance of both heredity and environment, and naturalistic observation of identical twins, and of children reared in isolated communities, show that these conclusions apply to human beings as well.

GUIDE TO STUDY

Be able to define:
1) IQ, MA and CA;
2) Reliability and validity.
3) Intelligence A and intelligence B.

Be able to explain the term "constancy of the IQ" and what limitations this concept has for the growing child.

Say why a low IQ does not necessarily mean a poor brain.

Describe the interaction between heredity and experience in determining IQ.

Discuss both the advantages and the disadvantages of IQ as a description of human intelligence.

Give examples of differences between infant and adult object concepts.

Give examples of the evolution of causal explanations in the thought of the child.

Be able to explain the meaning of an ability factor, and how ability factors modify the concept of IQ.

NOTES AND GENERAL REFERENCES

Bower, T. G. R. (1982). *Development in Infancy, 2nd ed.* San Francisco: W. H. Freeman. A review of interesting studies on the development of infant perception, thought and intelligence.

Farber, S. L. (1981). *Identical Twins Reared Apart: A Reanalysis.* New York: Basic Books. Scholarly and readable review of all of the published literature on identical twins to 1979.

Flynn, J. R. (1984). The mean IQ of Americans: Massive gains 1932 to 1978. *Psychological*

Bulletin, 95, 29–51. Evidence that American IQ scores (Intelligence B) have increased since regular testing began.

Forgays, D. G. & Forgays, J. (1952). The nature of the effect of free-environment experience in the rat. *Journal of Comparative and Physiological Psychology, 45,* 322–328.

Ginsburgh, H., & Opper, S. (1969). *Piaget's Theory of Intellectual Development: An Introduction.* New York: Prentice-Hall.

Goldfarb, W. (1943). Effects of early institutional care on adolescent personality. *Journal of Experimental Education, 12,* 106–129.

Guilford, J. P. (1967). *The Nature of Human Intelligence.* New York: McGraw-Hill. Shows how complex a multifactor theory of intelligence can be.

Hunt, J. McV. (1961). *Intelligence and Experience.* New York: Ronald. An important review and synthesis, especially of the human data.

Hymovitch, B. (1952). The effects of experiential variations on problem-solving in the rat. *Journal of Comparative and Physiological Psychology, 45,* 313–321.

Laurendeau, M., & Pinard, A. (1963). *Causal Thinking in the Child.* Madison, CT: International Universities Press.

Marjoribanks, K. (1972). Environment, social class and mental abilities. *Journal of Educational Psychology, 63,* 103–109. Demonstrates the correlation between family environmental variables and measured IQ.

Neff, W. S. (1938). Socioeconomic status and intelligence: a critical survey. *Psychological Bulletin, 35,* 727–757. Included is a summary of the study of intelligence in canal-boat children.

Phillips, J. L. (1969). *The Origins of Intellect: Piaget's Theory.* San Francisco: W. H. Freeman.

Piaget, J. (1950). *The Psychology of Intelligence.* New York: Harcourt Brace. Piaget is a difficult writer, and the student would be well advised to start with Phillips, or with Ginsburgh and Opper.

Thompson, W. R., & Heron, W. (1954). The effects of restricting early experience on the problem-solving capacity of dogs. *Canadian Journal of Psychology, 8,* 17–31.

Tyron, R. C. (1940). Genetic differences in maze-learning in rats. *Yearbook, National Society for the Study of Education.* The classical demonstration of genetic differences in learning ability and intelligence.

Zajonc, R. B. (1983). Validating the confluence model. *Psychological Bulletin, 93,* 457–480.

Zajonc, R. B., & Markus, G. B. (1975). Birth order and intellectual development. *Psychological Review, 82,* 74–88.

CHAPTER 10

Motivational Mechanisms

The function of behavior in evolution is to keep an animal alive and well long enough to mate and in other ways to get the next generation established, the process then repeating itself and leading to still another generation.

Obviously, Darwin's "natural selection" must operate to shape behavior accordingly. Food-seeking and mating behaviors must be present in every generation, for if they are absent the species will cease to exist. A species may emerge with a large brain, capable of speech, and given to abstract problem solving and artistic creation, but it can continue to exist only if, along with these great intellectual endowments, it also has a biologically fundamental capacity to reproduce. Similarly, hunger and pain experiences aid the survival of the species; pain, by diminishing the probability of repeated damage to the body and so of early death; hunger, by ensuring that the animal will expend enough effort to obtain the substances necessary to maintain life. Also, to "get the next generation established" requires some parental assistance to the offspring of many species; thus in all mammals and most birds (with rare exceptions such as the cuckoo), natural selection has produced strongly marked maternal or parental behavior.

Motivation may be defined as the tendency of a whole animal[1] to

---

[1]Component parts of the organism being made up of living cells that must be active or die, are more or less active all the time, but "motivation" does not refer to these activities. It is an organizing principle that accounts for *fluctuations* in the level or form of the behavior of the whole animal. Heart rate and breathing rate are affected by certain changes of motivation, for example, but we do not consider that there is a special motivation necessary 24 hours a day to maintain pulse and breathing.

produce organized activity. This varies from the low level of deep sleep to a high level in the waking, alert, excited animal. The kind of behavior that results, or the kind of stimulation to which the organism is responding, also varies with changes in motivation. Thus, we speak of a person as being strongly (or weakly) motivated, meaning that he or she is active (or lethargic); or we may speak of special motivations such as hunger, sex, and so on. These special motivations are intermittent, they vary in strength, and more than one motivation may be present at the same time. The four types of biologically primitive behaviors referred to in the preceding paragraph are commonly referred to as the hunger, pain, sex, and parental motivations. To these we can add a fifth, exploratory motivation. Although it is not as strictly necessary for survival, it is as widespread as the others, and exploratory behavior must favor species survival by installing the species over a wider territory and making it less vulnerable to local catastrophe.

This terminology is convenient, but not precise. "Hunger" used in this way includes the need for oxygen and water as well as solid foods; "pain" includes various discomforts, such as those produced by low or high temperatures, and so on.

This is not the whole story. As the brain has increased in size during the evolution of mammals, other important motivational characteristics have appeared. The sleep-waking difference assumes more importance. It covers a much wider variation in readiness for response than it does in lower animals and makes it necessary to consider the level of *general arousal* (to be discussed later on in this chapter) in describing the behavior of the mammal. Also, the *emotions* are motivational states that seem to be peculiar to the larger brained animal, and these too must be taken account of.

In this chapter and the next we are concerned with the whole problem of motivation. The present chapter deals with its neural basis and the more fundamental motivations. The following chapter deals primarily with the "higher" motivations—not all of them admirable, by any means—which are characteristic of the higher animal.

THE AUTONOMIC NERVOUS SYSTEM

A basic role in motivation and emotion is played by the *autonomic nervous system*. This is a set of motor pathways to smooth muscles and glands. Smooth muscle lines the walls of the arteries and regulates the blood pressure of different parts of the body; it controls the size of the pupil of the eye, movements of stomach and gut, and erection of hair. In human beings, smooth muscle produces goose pimples, which are caused by the contraction of a small muscle in the skin that makes one's hair "stand on end."

The rest of the body is moved by *striate* (striped), or skeletal, muscle. Striate muscle moves the limbs, the chest (in breathing), the jaws, tongue, and eyeballs. It has a striped appearance under the microscope, hence the name striate. The neurons controlling striate muscle come directly from the brain and spinal cord.

The autonomic nervous system is made up of two subsystems, the *sympathetic* and the *parasympathetic*, which also has two parts, one at each end of the neural tube (Fig. 10.1). Thus the autonomic nervous system has a total of three segments: the sympathetic, in the middle regions of the spinal cord; the upper section of the parasympathetic, emerging from the brain stem; and the lower section of the parasympathetic, emerging from the tail end of the spinal cord. As Fig. 10.1 shows, most organs are controlled by both the sympathetic and the parasympathetic motor systems. The afferent, or sensory, neurons from smooth muscle are simply thought of as sensory fibers, mixed in with those from other bodily structures, which control nonautonomic responses as well as autonomic ones.

The sympathetic and parasympathetic motor systems are in general opposed to each other. What one excites, the other inhibits. Sympathetic fibers, for example, increase the heart rate and slow down the digestive processes of the stomach; parasympathetic fibers slow the heart and promote digestion. The sympathetic system is designed for action in emergency situations. It mobilizes the resources of the body for maximal use in emergencies. It has important connections with what we call the "arousal system" (and will define later). The parasympathetic system is a conservative system that builds up resources. The sympathetic and parasympathetic systems, however, are not completely opposed in their actions; they do collaborate to some degree. But it is useful to think of the parasympathetic as dominant in quiet periods and of the sympathetic nervous system as preparing the animal for "fight or flight."

The sympathetic system increases the heart rate and flow of blood to the muscles for violent emergency action, causing the sweating that controls the resultant heat production, and making the hair stand erect in the emotionally aroused animal. The sympathetic system, then, is directly concerned in the production of emotionally aroused behavior. But this is only part of the total picture: emotional behavior also involves the striate (striped) musculature. The action of the autonomic nervous system is diffuse rather than specific, and it is not easily controlled by cortical processes. The sympathetic system, especially, tends to go into action as a unit. As a result, in "emotional situations"

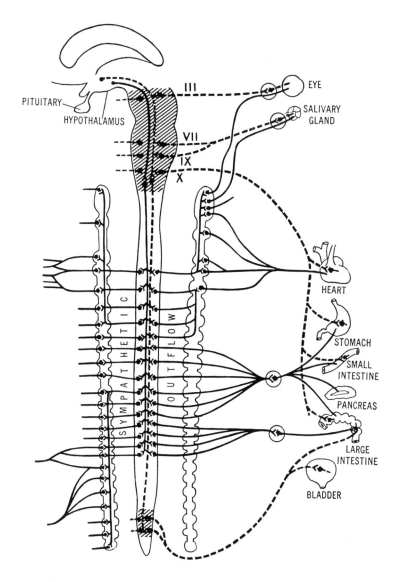

FIGURE 10.1 The autonomic nervous system. The sympathetic segment is in the middle region, its connections shown in solid lines; the parasympathetic has two divisions, the cranial (above) and the sacral (below). Its connections are shown in broken lines (Gardner, Fundamentals of Neurology. Saunders.)

208

in which there is a high level of neural activity ideational or mediating-process activity may be able to control skeletal muscles completely and at the same time may have little or no control over smooth muscle and glands. The person who is angry or frightened may not attack anyone or run away, but the heartbeat increases, the blood pressure rises, and there is sweating and pallor or flushing, because these things are not as strictly under voluntary control as is motor behavior.

Most studies of human emotion are done in the laboratory, where subjects restrain themselves from striking the experimenter when they are made angry. If they become afraid, they do not show it by running away. Although ideational processes can inhibit the action of the subjects' arms or legs, the subjects cannot inhibit their autonomic activity in the same way. Thus, the effect of emotional situations seems autonomic only, and psychologists have talked mostly as if emotion and autonomic activity were the same thing. But this is a misleading conclusion. The normal—uninhibited—expression of anger is attack, and attacking is done with striate (striped) muscles. It is the same with fear and running away. *Striate muscle is as closely related to emotion as smooth muscle is.* The autonomic nervous system more or less reflects the level of excitement in the CNS, but this includes activity that is not primarily emotional (as in a sudden dash for the bus), and when emotional disturbance does occur it excites skeletal muscle as readily as that of the viscera. Trembling of the limbs, disturbance of breathing, and lack of coordination of the fingers—all produced by skeletal muscle—are signs of emotion just as much as sweating and increased heart rate.

An important link in the action of the sympathetic nervous system is the adrenal gland, whose inner portion secretes a hormone, *adrenalin*, into the blood stream. Adrenalin acts directly on smooth muscle, and on the sweat and salivary glands, in about the same way as sympathetic fibers do. Also, it excites the arousal system directly; and since the arousal system excites the sympathetic nervous system (which excites the adrenals), there is a closed positive feedback circuit (Fig. 10.2). The arousal system and the cortex form a closed circuit, each exciting the other, so the arousal system is the focal point where two such feedback systems meet, as Fig. 10.2 shows. The arousal-sympathetic-adrenal circuit in particular must be part of the reason a generalized excitation, or strong emotional disturbance, takes so long to die down, instead of stopping at once when the cause of excitation is removed.

The autonomic nervous system has a special relation to emotion, as part of a more extensive system whose activity is not readily damped once it has been excited. This system is readily aroused by strong or

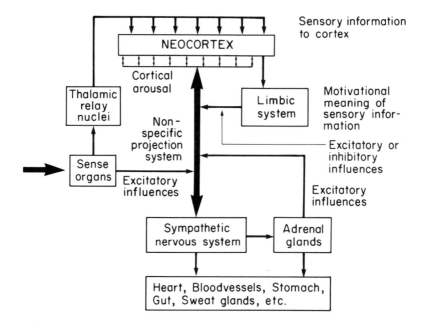

FIGURE 10.2   Diagram showing the relation of the non-specific projection system, or arousal system, to the neocortex, to the limbic system, and to the sympathetic nervous system. Sensory information reaches the central nervous system through the sense organs. Each sensory system has its own specific thalamic relay nucleus, through which sensory information is relayed to specified areas of neocortex. Sensory information also reaches the non-specific projection system, which acts to arouse the cortex and thus to sustain cell assembly activity. If the motivational meaning of the sensory information, which is stored in the limbic system, is consistent with the animals' motivational needs, arousal is facilitated. If the motivational meaning is currently irrelevant, the limbic system inhibits arousal and the cortex is not activated to continue cell assembly activity related to that sensory input. In other words, the animal does not pay attention to the input. The nonspecific projection system also acts on the sympathetic nervous system, which acts on various glands including the adrenals, whose secretions in turn affect the activity of the nonspecific projection system.

unusual stimulation (i.e., events such as pain to which the arousal system does not habituate, and the strange event to which it has not yet habituated).

Homeostatic Mechanisms

Homeostasis is a process that maintains a constant internal environment. Inside the skin of a healthy, uninjured human being the temperature stays the same within a degree or so, and the circulating fluids maintain a remarkably constant chemical composition. A slight deviation from normal sets off activity in a homeostatic mechanism, tending to restore the normal condition.

For example, breathing is part of the homeostatic mechanism that tends to maintain a constant level of oxygen and carbon dioxide in the blood stream. If the CO_2 level falls, or if the O_2 level rises, breathing slows down and reverses the trend. A rise of CO_2 and a fall of O_2 cause faster breathing. Certain receptors in the brain stem (for CO_2) and in the carotid artery and aorta (for O_2) act like the home thermostat that turns on the furnace when the temperature falls and cuts it off when the temperature rises. The body, of course, has its temperature-regulating mechanism also. When body temperature rises above normal limits, sweating and panting occur to dissipate heat. When it falls, shivering occurs to produce heat.

The oxygen–carbon dioxide mechanisms, and those regulating temperature, function reflexively. As long as a reflexive mechanism is adequate, so that the rest of the nervous system is not called into play, we do not consider the homeostatic process to be motivational (i.e., it does not produce arousal, nor affect the course of other behavior). But when the reflex process is inadequate, motivation is affected at once. If breathing, for example, is interfered with, there is a prompt and vigorous reaction from higher neural centers that dominates all other activity.[2] Ordinarily, the need for oxygen remains at a reflexive level and does not involve motivation. Temperature needs, however, differ. Because the temperatures to which people are exposed daily go well beyond the capacity of the sweating–shivering mechanism, maintenance of body temperature within normal limits involves the general course of behavior, rather than being reflexive only. The motivation that is involved in the search for warmth or coolness is the activity of a homeostatic process.

Hunger and thirst are also homeostatic mechanisms: they produce behavior whose direct effect is to maintain the normal concentration of certain substances in the blood stream. The motivation to avoid pain is not so clear a case; it does not directly concern the constancy of the internal environment, although it does act in the long run to do so by preventing injury to the defensive barrier of the skin, for example, or preventing the loss of blood.

Sexual motivation is clearly not homeostatic. Copulation does not raise sex hormones in the blood stream to a normal level or lower them from a higher level. Behavior can be considered homeostatic only if its

---

[2]That is, when choking occurs, not if there is merely too low a level of oxygen in the air.

effect is to regulate the internal environment, minimizing deviations from some zero point or norm. Sex behavior as far as we know does not do this. Therefore, motivation may be biologically primitive, and very powerful, without being homeostatic.

Hunger.   The primary control of eating is located in the hypothalamus. When both ventromedial nuclei of the rat's hypothalamus are destroyed, the rat eats almost continuously if the food is easily available. That is, he can no longer stop eating and becomes as a result enormously obese. If, instead, a more lateral region of the hypothalamus is destroyed on both sides, the rat stops eating and unless fed by hand will die.

The hypothalamus is the rat's food thermostat, so to speak. The lateral region starts the rat eating. The ventromedial region stops it. The two apparently function reflexively in the control of eating. But there is also an important role for learning.

Short-term learning is involved to a different degree in different hungers. Experimentally, we can take a laboratory rat that has always had food available and remove the food from his cage for 24 hours. The food is then put back, and eating time is recorded. We find that in the first 60 seconds the experimental animal eats no more than the control animal, which has had food present continuously; in one experiment with 10 rats, the range of times spent eating was from 0 to 55 seconds. In the next 5 minutes, however, the rate of eating increased. As the experiment continued, with food being made available for a 30-minute period daily, the eating behavior in the first 60 seconds of each day changed, and by the 10th day or so every animal ate voraciously at the first presentation of food.

The same experiment with water deprivation gives a different result: a definite thirst appears quickly. Either learning is not involved in the same way, or it is more rapid.

A sudden acute lack of food does not produce a strong motivation if the subject has not experienced it before. A rat does not run well in the maze for a food reward until he has been put on a 24-hour feeding schedule for some time; only with the repeated experience of hunger, followed by eating, will the rat work energetically for food. In human subjects, similarly, an acute need for food in a previously well-fed subject is far from being as strong a source of motivation as chronic starvation; in the latter case the need may dominate behavior completely.

The homeostasis of hunger is selective for a number of substances— carbohydrates, protein, fats, vitamins and salts—as well as for water. The animal whose food lacks calcium salts, for example, will prefer to drink a weak solution of calcium salt rather than plain tap water. If the diet lacks fat, or thiamine, or another nutrient, a food choice is made that tends to correct the lack.

But learning is again involved in some of these choices, and learning has effects that are not always desirable. Both rat and human being tend to avoid novel foods even though they would correct the deficiency. A most interesting discovery is that when a rat eats a novel food and then becomes sick—even hours later and even if the food was not the cause—any food that tastes like the novel food will be avoided afterward (Garcia et al, 1967). This obviously protects the rat that nibbles at poisoned food and avoids it later, but it keeps the rat from the same food when it is not poisoned. In human beings, also, this may account for the otherwise unexplained food aversions that are so common: a child eats onions, develops a fever that night, and then has a permanent dislike of onions. The mechanism apparently involves the amygdala. (For a review of the experiments on acquired aversion, see Hargrave & Bolles, 1971, and Rozin and Kalat, 1971, cited in chapter 2.)

Artificial Hunger: Addiction. The various human addictions to caffeine, nicotine, and alcohol, as well as to drugs such as morphine or cocaine, are commonly referred to as "habits." They are not merely bad habits, however, like eating with one's knife or mispronouncing some word. "Habit" implies learning, which is certainly involved in addiction, as it is in hunger. But unlike hunger, the addiction has the effect of maintaining the level of a specific substance in the blood even though the presence of the drug in the blood stream was originally neither necessary nor biologically desirable. Once the addiction is well established, the drug becomes necessary to stable neural functioning, and lack of it can be very strongly motivating.

There are two stages in the establishment of morphine addiction and presumably of other addictions as well: an intermediate stage of physiological dependence, and addiction itself. When young chimpanzees were given injections of morphine daily, physiological dependence developed in 5–6 weeks. When the animals were not given their injection, they showed the typical signs of physiological disturbance—restlessness, yawning, scratching; these are called withdrawal symptoms. The chimpanzees were clearly "unhappy" but at this intermediate stage had not yet learned that it was the injection that made them comfortable again. If it was omitted, they did nothing about it.

The experiment required 1–3 months of further injections before addiction itself occurred. Then the animals would try desperately to obtain the injection, dragging the experimenter to where the drug and hypodermic needle were kept, taking the needle out of its case and handing it to the experimenter, and so on (Fig. 10.3b). At this stage, the chimpanzees would do anything they could to get the injection; by now the need for the drug had become powerfully motivating.

In human beings who know they are taking a drug, and that it is the drug that produces the feeling of well-being, the intermediate stage and true addiction may coincide. Essentially, however, the two stages represent different kinds of processes, the first being a physiological modification of bodily tissues, so that the tissues now require the presence of the drug for "normal" (i.e., reasonably stable) functioning. Without the drug, there is irritability, restlessness, and disturbance of work habits and social behavior. The second stage is a learning process. The kind of learning process depends on just how the drug upsets the body's homeostatic balance (Eikelboom and Stewart, 1982).

There is a good deal of evidence indicating that there are considerable individual constitutional differences in susceptibility to addiction. It is often erroneously thought that alcoholism, for example, is simply an attempt to escape from personal troubles or is due to some form of neurosis. Although this may be partly true, there are, of course, some neurotics who fail to solve their problems in this way and despite using alcohol do not become alcoholics, while others with little emotional excuse become addicted at once. Emotional difficulties may be the decisive factor that turns the susceptible person into an alcoholic, but it is very apparent that physiological susceptibility is not the same for everyone. For some people, alcohol produces a homeostatic modification that is, in effect, irreversible and thereafter is likely to dominate behavior, with disastrous consequences.

THE AROUSAL SYSTEM

A sensory excitation affects cortical activity in two main ways. The first is via the specialized sensory pathways (described in chapter 3): the direct routes from eye, ear and skin to the corresponding cortical sensory areas. These pathways are specialized not only to keep each sense distinct from others, but also to keep messages within the same sense distinct. Excitation from the toe, for example, travels by a special subpathway and is not mixed up with excitations from the thumbs or the lips. These are specific afferents, which convey information, guide behavior, determine specific responses.

The second kind of pathway is nonspecific. It does not keep sensory excitations distinct according to their place of origin but pools them and delivers the result to all parts of the cortex. The nonspecific

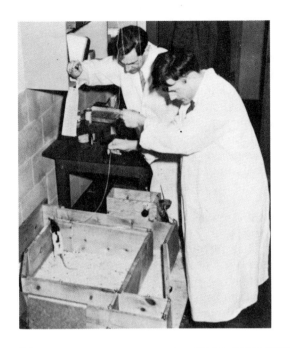

(a)

FIGURE 10.3 Two kinds of artificial motivation. (a) Rat with implanted electrodes, connected with a light flexible wire so he can move about freely. If the experimenters give a brain stimulation in this corner of the maze, the rat will persist in coming back to it, just as if he were hungry and found food there. (b) The chimpanzee Frank voluntarily taking an injection of morphine. (Courtesy of Yerkes Laboratories of Primate Biology.)

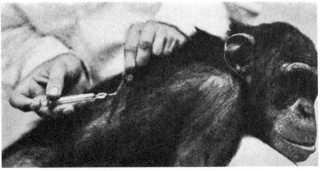

(b)

afferents have the function of "toning up" the cortex, providing a general facilitation to aid cortical transmission, and so make it possible for the messages from the specific pathways to reach the motor system and exert their guiding influence on behavior. The nonspecific pathways are responsible for establishing the level of arousal. Synonyms for arousal are: alertness, responsiveness, wakefulness, vigilance.

Each main afferent path branches as it approaches the thalamus. The main branches go to their own specialized thalamic nuclei,[3] which in turn project—send fibers—to the corresponding sensory areas of the cortex. The other branches go to the *arousal system* (or nonspecific projection system). Though some cells in the system may be fired only by branching fibers from the visual afferent path, others only by auditory or olfactory ones, the level of activity in the whole system is the result of a pooling of the excitatory effects of sensory stimulation from all sources (Fig. 10.2). The general excitation is, in turn, transmitted to the cortex, producing a general level of behavioral excitability, that is, arousal. A low level of activity in the arousal system makes the animal unresponsive; higher levels produce normal alertness or emotional behavior.

The arousal system is not a neat circular structure, but a series of separate nuclei in the midbrain lying parallel to the aqueduct (Fig. 3.2), plus some nuclei in the thalamus. Their physiological role is to activate the cortex, and physiologists generally refer to these structures as the *ascending reticular activating system,* or ARAS. From a behavioral point of view, however, "arousal" is the better term. It is customary to distinguish between the levels of cortical *activation* (the proportion of low-voltage fast waves in the EEG) and the behavioral *arousal* (the level of alertness of the animal).

For our present purposes, the arousal system can be treated as one system with a single mode of action. It has, however, at least two patterns of activity, probably more. All of the patterns produce arousal, but the arousal shows differences. There is strong arousal in both laughter and fear, for example, but recovery from disturbance in one case is quick, in the other slow. Another simplification made here is to talk about the effect of arousal on "cortical transmission." It was observed earlier (chapter 4) that the transmission is really through a series of closed loops or systems of closed loops, many of which join cortex and subcortical structures. The cortex does not function at all as a separate organ; it is an anatomical unit, not a functional one.

The branching of the path from a sense organ, one branch going to the cortex and one to the arousal system, means that a sensory stimulation has two quite different functions. The first can be called a *cue function:* a guiding or steering or informational effect. The second is the *arousal function:* it determines the level of excitement or excitability or wakefulness of the animal, without determining what the animal's

---

[3]A nucleus is a cluster of cell bodies. The sensory nuclei of the thalamus are the final relay points of the specific afferent pathways, receiving axons from below and in turn sending their own axons to the proper cortical sensory area.

behavior will be. The sensory messages that go straight to the cortex guide behavior. They excite specific pathways that tend to produce specific responses or modify connections between cell assemblies so that other messages will produce specific responses (*set*, chapter 5; or *knowledge*, chapter 2). That is, the messages that reach the cortex do this if the arousal system is active, not otherwise.

For higher functions the arousal system is crucial. Without its support cortical processes cease, as far as behavior is concerned. Sensory excitations may still reach the sensory projection areas, but they stop there. The need of summation for synaptic transmission has already been discussed. But the loop circuits or cell assemblies that appear to be the main basis of cortical transmission do not function unless the arousal system is providing a sort of general summation to all cortical synapses. It has been suggested (chapter 5) that assembly A may transmit to or excite assembly B only if assembly C is also active and supports A's action; but this of course cannot happen unless the assemblies themselves are active, and they are not active unless they receive support from the arousal system. Though unconditioned reflexes still function, all conditioned reflexes and mediating processes cease when activity in the arousal system ceases. *All the mammal's learned behavior, and all thought processes or consciousness, depend on the activity of the arousal system deep in the brain stem.*[4]

The level of activity of the system varies normally from a low level in deep dreamless sleep to a high level in the waking, emotionally excited subject. The primary source of excitation of the system is the varied sensory input represented at the left side of Fig. 10.2; monotonous (i.e., unvaried) stimulation from the environment allows the level of excitation to fall and thus facilitates sleep. However, this is not the sole avenue by which excitation is transmitted to the arousal system; Fig. 10.2 shows a "down-flow" from the cortex, which also contributes to arousal. This means that the main source of arousal is sensory stimulation, but that another source lies in the thought process. There can be exciting thoughts as well as exciting sensations. The subject put in a monotonous environment does not necessarily go to sleep.

A repeated sensory event not followed by other events tends rapidly to lose its capacity to produce arousal (though this is not true of some sensations, such as pain). The result is known as *habituation* or

---

[4]As Wilder Penfield first observed in 1938, giving the name *centrencephalic system* to the structures involved and proposing that consciousness is more closely related to the brain stem than to the cortex. It was in 1949 that G. Moruzzi and H. W. Magoun discovered the vital part in consciousness that is played by the midbrain reticular formation ("reticular" simply means that the region looks like a network after being stained for microscopic study).

"negative adaptation." Familiar scenes and familiar events are not exciting. One can "learn" to sleep even in a quite noisy environment if the noises are the usual ones, but the learning appears to be the habituation referred to. A strange environment, on the other hand, is exciting, which appears to make it both frightening and attractive, as we will see in discussing exploratory motivation.

Arousal and the EEG

Behavior is the most important index of the level of arousal, but it does not always provide full information. When the lecturer in the class-room sees a student slumped back in the seat with eyes closed, he cannot tell immediately whether the student is asleep, or daydreaming, or thinking hard about the lecture. More information about arousal level could be obtained by *electroencephalography*, (EEG), though it is hardly practical to use it to detect sleep in the classroom. Under other circumstances, however, EEG is an index of arousal that has a good deal to tell us about what is going on in the brain.

When electronic amplifying devices are applied to the scalp of a human subject, it is found that the brain is broadcasting. Instead of turning the broadcast into sounds, we make it operate an oscilloscope and thus produce a record of the brain's activity. A record of "brain waves" is shown in Fig. 10.4. The broadcasts can be roughly localized to areas beneath and between any pair of recording electrodes, but the EEG record cannot be assigned to a specific cell or to a specific nucleus in the brain. The EEG record is an average of activity recorded between two electrodes. It records both the effects of neural transmission and the slower changes of electric potential that occur in the cell bodies and dendrites of neurons.

Figure 10.4 shows how the EEG changes with different states of arousal. Small, fast waves mean that the arousal system is active; large, slow waves show that it is inactive. The *alpha rhythm* (so named by Hans Berger, because it was the first one to be recognized and studied) represents an intermediate level of arousal; it consists of moderately large, regular potentials, at about 10 cycles per second, and appears when the subject is instructed to close his eyes and relax. If he opens his eyes and attends to his surroundings, or if with eyes closed he is given a problem to solve, the *beta rhythm* appears—small, fast waves characteristic of the actively thinking subject. At times in sleep, on the other hand, and when brain function is impaired by disease or anesthe-sia, there are large, irregular slow waves called the *delta rhythm*, about 2 to 5 cycles per second.

The alpha rhythm is the only clearly distinctive pattern in the EEG. Some subjects do not show it, whereas, in others it is much less regular

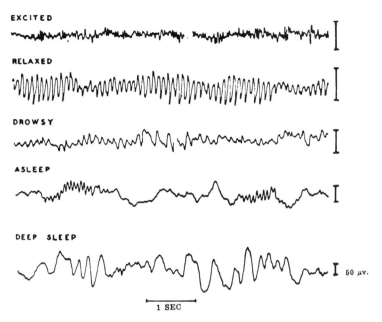

(a) The EEG at five levels of arousal. The second tracing from the top ("relaxed") is the alpha rhythm. In the fourth one ("asleep") the two places where a burst of short, faster waves occurs on top of a slow wave are "sleep spindles." The vertical line at the right of each tracing permits comparison of voltages (e.g., the bottom tracing would have much higher waves if on the same scale as the top tracing). (From H. H. Japser, in W. Penfield and T. C. Erickson, Epilepsy and Cerebral Localization. Charles C. Thomas.)

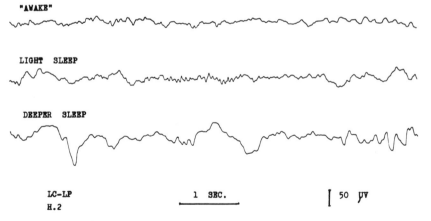

(b) EEG records from a human infant 90 hours old, for comparison with the adult records of A. The waking record of the infant has slow waves, though of much lower amplitude than in the two sleep records, and a marked lack of both alpha and beta frequencies. (Courtesy of A. K. Bartoshuk, Hunter Laboratory, Brown University.)

FIGURE 10.4

219

than the one shown in the second record in Fig. 10.4a. The beta rhythm is a range of irregular frequencies, from 12 cycles per second up. In sleep, there is, as we will see, an activation pattern at times (REM sleep), when slow waves usually appear in combination with faster ones. Also, sleep-deprived subjects may produce slow waves when they are (more or less) awake and responsive to the environment. Finally, the newborn infant shows slow waves as well as faster ones during periods of behavioral wakefulness (Fig. 10.4b), which suggests that the infant's state of consciousness (and that of the sleep-deprived adult) is different from what we know as consciousness in the normal waking adult.

The EEG tells us something important about how the arousal system affects cortical activity. The electrode from which the record is obtained is at some distance from the surface of the cortex, separated from it by scalp and skull, which means that the potentials it records must be averages from cortical neurons. A large potential (a high wave), therefore, means that most of the neurons near the electrode are active at the same time and inactive at the same time; that is, they act synchronously. If they did not, the negative potentials produced by cells that have just been active would cancel out the positive potentials produced by inactive cells, and a flat EEG record would result. Figure 10.4 shows that a low level of arousal means synchronized or simultaneous activity of neighboring neurons in the cortex; a higher state of arousal in the actively thinking or perceiving subject means that neighboring neurons tend to fire independently of each other. This is consistent with the idea that cortical activity in consciousness is the firing of neurons arranged in loops, as in Figs. 4.8 and 5.1. To function effectively, the neurons must fire one after another, not simultaneously. If the cell assemblies are intertwined, as they must be, the neurons would all be in the same cortical region. Thus, if the assemblies A, B, C, and D are active in succession, the individual neurons in this region must not all be active at the same time. The EEG tells us that the neural activity of consciousness is a diffuse firing, a coordination of cells at some distance from each other rather than a local synchrony.

The EEG activity of lowered alertness, drowsiness, or deep sleep tells us that many cortical cells are firing in synchrony, and that these cells are not participating in separate cell assembly activity.

THE LIMBIC SYSTEM

The limbic system is a set of structures, some cortical, some subcortical, that are closely connected with the arousal system. The limbic system plays a significant role in motivation. The system includes the cortex, near the base of the brain, which borders on the corpus callosum (where it dips deep into the midline fissue separating the two hemispheres); the hippocampus; the amygdala (a small group of nuclei in the temporal lobe not far from the hippocampus); and parts of the thalamus and hypothalamus.

The functions of the limbic system are still being explored, but the system is directly involved in motivation and emotion. The hypothalamic centers controlling hunger and satiation are part of the system. There is also a hypothalamic region from which the hunting and attack behavior of cats can be produced; a cat that is usually friendly with a rat in the same cage will stalk and kill it while this region is stimulated, but promptly stops when the stimulation stops. (An electrode is inserted into the brain and cemented to the skull under anesthesia, leaving the upper end protruding through the scalp. This causes no discomfort when the animal has recovered from the operation, and now the part of the hypothalamus reached by the electrode can be stimulated while the animal is moving around, as in Fig. 10.3.) Other regions of the hypothalamus are involved in the control of sexual and maternal behavior.

Fear and pleasure, emotional avoidance and emotional seeking, are at the heart of motivation, and it appears that the limbic system allows the experience of these emotions directly. Delgado, Roberts and Miller (1954) have shown that stimulation of a lateral anterior part of the hypothalamus produces true fear in the rat—not a mere withdrawal, but an emotional state that has the same properties as the state produced, for example, by electric shock to the feet.

At the same time, there are points in the hypothalamus and elsewhere that produce something like pleasure. The procedure is illustrated in Fig. 10.3a, the stimulation being carried out by J. Olds (right) and P. M. Milner, the original discoverers of the effect. The rat is free to move about in the apparatus. If shock is delivered whenever the rat moves to one corner, the rat remains there. If instead he is put in a Skinner box (chapter 2) and the lever is connected with a switch so that each press—or every second or fifth or tenth press—produces a brief stimulation, very high rates of pressing may result, sometimes as high as 2,000 or more per hour.

Damage to the cortex or to sensory and motor structures may diminish intelligence, impair perception, or paralyze while leaving one otherwise the same kind of person. But damage to the limbic system changes personality. Removal of the amygdala will turn a wild animal into a tame one, and small lesions in the ventromedial nuclei of the hypothalamus can have the opposite effect, making a gentle cat permanently vicious. Attacks of spontaneous hyperactivity in a diseased amygdala (such as a tiny localized epileptic process) can turn an otherwise peaceful human being into a ferocious attacker (Mark & Ervin, 1970). The problem of depression, or the schizophrenic's loss of motivation, may well turn out to be a problem of limbic system functioning.

The Limbic System and the Arousal System

The limbic system and the arousal system work together to motivate behavior. It may be oversimple to include all of the brain nuclei and pathways concerned with motivation in either the limbic system or the arousal system. However, the concept of two interacting systems is useful to explain motivated behavior ranging from Pavlovian conditioning to psychopathology, and the relation between the two systems is consistent with what is known about the anatomy and chemistry of the brain.

The best way to explain the interaction of the limbic and the arousal systems is to describe how they respond to an incoming stimulus. Each system has a different role. The arousal system alerts the cortex to a novel stimulus and prepares the brain to learn about it. Remember that the evolutionary goal is survival (and reproduction). Higher animals, especially primates like ourselves, survive not by relying on sharp claws or a thick skin, but by using their capacity to learn. The survival role of the arousal system is to activate the cortex to be ready to form cell assemblies to incorporate new stimuli.

For many stimuli, the learning that incorporates them into cell assemblies has already happened. The motivational part of these existing cell assemblies is recorded in the limbic system, which directs behavior by matching current motivational needs to the motivational outcome predicted by the stimulus. For example, experience has taught that the bell of an ice cream wagon predicts the availability of ice cream. The bell—a conditioned stimulus (CS) in the Pavlovian conditioning paradigm—is now a *conditioned reinforcer* (see chapter 2). As a result of its pairing with a reinforcing US, it too can act as the reinforcing stimulus for new learning. It can also be said to have *incentive* properties. For instance, if you are hot or hungry and hear the bell then your attention and behavior will be directed (on the basis of learning) to the sound. This all happens because the motivational part of the cell assembly group, which includes the sound of the bell, is recorded in the limbic system. If you are not hot or hungry, the bell will have the same motivational meaning but without the same immediate motivational attractiveness or incentive value—and your attention and behavior will not be directed towards it.

On the other hand, if you are hot or hungry, the ice cream—the motivational meaning of the bell—will match a need sensed by the homeostatic centers in the hypothalamus, which are a part of the limbic system. When there is a match, the limbic system will feed back positively into the arousal system, and the arousal system will sustain the cortical activity begun by the sensory stimulus of the bell. This allows the already formed cell assembly established by the bell to continue to direct thought and behavior.

If, on the other hand, the motivational meaning of the stimulus does not match the current motivational needs as sensed by the homeostatic processes, the limbic system "calls off," or inhibits, the cortical activation produced by the arousal system in response to the sensory qualities—the loudness and momentary novelty—of the bell.

How is the arousal system affected by cortical and limbic system activity? Remember that there are two pathways from the sense organs to the cortex. One is fast and direct, through the thalamic sensory nuclei and into the cortex. The other is slow and indirect, through the arousal system into the cortex. The fast pathway carries information quickly to the neocortex. When the stimulus at the neocortical level has activated a group of cell assemblies and its motivational consequences have been evaluated in the limbic system, then the limbic system acts either to help or to hinder the nonspecific arousal activity, which is (relatively) slowly making its way upwards to alert the cortex. Hence, the limbic system, storing and using the learned motivational meaning of familiar·stimuli classified by the cortex, modifies the activation of the cortex according to the match between the motivational meaning of the stimulus and the current motivational needs recorded in the hypothalamus.

It can happen, of course, that a sensory input has not already formed part of a cell assembly group that estalishes its motivational meaning. Then there is no limbic system information available to inhibit the arousal system, and the arousal system activates the cortex. This facilitates the formation of new cell assembly groups. The amount of activation depends on such factors as the sensory intensity of the stimulus or the current level of activity in the arousal system. This level is increased when the homeostatic receptors in the hypothalamus signal a biological need.

The learned consequences of a sensory input may not match the actual events which follow it. Then the animal is caught off guard: the cell assembly previously formed predicts one thing, but something else happens. This is another situation that leads to general cortical arousal. The limbic system, having stored one motivational meaning, feeds back to the arousal system either facilitation or inhibition, depending on whether the anticipated motivational meaning is currently important or unimportant. But if another event occurs instead, the arousal system has no instructions for that event as it arrives over the sensory channels, and it is as effectively novel as if it had never happened before.

The limbic system is essential to establishing and maintaining memory. Damage to the hippocampus or to the lower brain structures reached by it makes new memories impossible (recall H.M. in chapter 6). Severe disruptions of the hippocampus or the structures in the lower brain lead to a loss of awareness of current reality and disorientation in time and space. It is not clear which parts of the limbic system are more directly responsible for the coding of memory and which parts are responsible for the feedback to the arousal system, nor is it yet clear how these two functions are related.

PAIN

Pain in normal people appears to comprise two distinguishable processes: one a sensory event, the other a central reaction with a strong motivational component.

The most striking feature of pain as a sensory process is its tendency to take control of all of behavior. Light or sound, unless very intense, can be disregarded for fairly long periods (i.e., an animal may not respond at all to visual or auditory cues). But even a weak pain stimulus tends to dominate all others in determining the direction of behavior. How this comes about we do not know.

Pain is sometimes spoken of as if it were simply a sensation like other sensations, but it is more than that. There is a sensation to start with, but as Melzack and Wall (1965) have shown, the cortex may suppress the incoming sensory message way down at the level of the spinal cord—or may greatly increase the strength of the reaction to the sensation. When the skin is burned or some other injury happens to the body, there is a fast message to the cortex and also a slow message that travels by separate paths in the spinal cord. When the cortex is deeply involved in some activity—that is, when the subject is strongly motivated—it may act on the fast message and send impulses back to the spinal cord to inhibit further transmission. This explains how one can take the skin off a knuckle in the workshop and not be aware of it if an interesting job is demanding close attention at the time, or how a football player may even break a leg and not know it till he tries to stand up.

There is no specialized cortical area for pain. The sensory information that does reach the cortex arrives at the somesthetic area along with other body sensations. The *reaction* to the information, when there is a reaction, is due to the involvement of other structures, including the arousal system and the limbic system.

At this level, therefore, pain may be more a motivational state, a generalized emotional reaction, than a sensation. Patients suffering from intractable pain are sometimes subjected to "lobotomy," a deep cut made in the frontal lobe at a level anterior to the motor pathways. These patients give a very curious report after the operation: They say that the pain is the same as before the operation—but it no longer bothers them as it did. They are still able to identify the sensory event, that is, to recognize a pain stimulus, as well as before, but the pain has lost much of its dominating control of behavior. In chapter 3 it was said that the frontal lobes are known to control and motivate organized sequences of behavior. Lobotomy severs connections from the limbic system to the frontal lobes, and pain ceases to preoccupy the lobotomized patient.

Animal experiments suggest that some of the motivational aspects of pain are a product of normal experience during growth (Factor IV). It will be recalled that the chimpanzee that had been reared with cardboard tubes over the hands and feet preventing normal somesthetic experience and thus presumably had little or no experience of pain reacted to a pin prick very differently from normal animals. Similarly, dogs reared in extreme isolation, and with no experience of pain except what they may have inflicted on themselves, showed an extraordinary unresponsiveness to noxious stimulation. They made little observable response to pin prick, or to having their tails stepped on. They would investigate a lighted paper match by putting their nose into the flame (thus extinguishing it); when another was lighted, it was investigated in the same way. A normally raised dog, who had not encountered flame before might put his nose into it once, but would not do so again. It was evident that for the experimental animals, pain stimuli had not acquired the same dominance as for the normal animals.

We cannot be certain about the meaning of such data, but it appears that some of the problems concerning pain would be much less puzzling if the following interpretation is sound: that "pain," as the term is ordinarily used, refers both to a discriminable sensory event, which in itself does not have strongly motivating properties, and to a motivational state to which the sensory event gives rise on the basis of past experience with pain. In short, it is suggested that pain in normal subjects is to a large extent an acquired motivation.

Drugs like morphine, administered to control pain, have a greater effect on chronic pain—healing a surgical incision, a broken bone, or cancer—than on acute pain—a cut, prick, or immediate but temporary injury. Morphine and similar drugs directly affect the central nervous system. Throughout the midbrain, and particularly around the cerebral aqueduct (part of the neural tube), there are neurons that are specialized for responding to morphine and similar drugs. The central nervous system produces its own drugs, enkephalins, which act like morphine to control pain. These drugs are blocked by the same chemical agents that interfere with the analgesic (pain-relieving) function of morphine, and their molecular structure is similar to morphine. It is not known how the production of these enkephalins can be controlled; this knowledge would obviously help in controlling pain.

Pain is an extraordinarily changeable experience. There are many ways to control its emotional effect independently of the sensory input causing it. Hypnosis is demonstrably capable of protecting some people against the emotional upset of pain caused by dental or other minor surgery. Acupuncture—an ancient technique developed in China—also prevents emotional disturbance associated with the kind of surgery that ordinarily causes pain. Acupuncture involves inserting needles into the skin at precisely located points and then vibrating the needles. Sometimes a small electrical current is passed through the needle. The effect of these techniques on the sensory component of pain is less clear, but straightforward reports of painless experiencing of normally painful stimuli with either hypnosis or acupuncture indicate that the sensory component of pain is eliminated as well.

No single pain control technique except general anesthesia (which suppresses the activity of the arousal system) works reliably for all people on even a single type of pain. But the potential for controlling pain does exist. The approach taken may be either biochemical through research on the enkephalins, or behavioral through development of hypnotic techniques or acupuncture. Pain in everyday life is a vital stimulus. When pain has already signalled tissue damage or disease, and remedial action is already being taken, then pain may cease to be informative and can be dispensed with. Or if no cure is possible, pain can be eliminated without further endangering the life of the sufferer.

SLEEP

One of the striking characteristics of mammals and birds is the need for sleep. Sleeping is instinctive behavior; it is species-predictable and necessary to survival (G. Moruzzi). It is evidently a form of rest for the nervous system and body, a restorative process, yet it has peculiarities that make it something more than merely a suspension of activity while recovering from fatigue. A fatigued muscle can be rested at once, and the amount of rest that is needed depends on the amount of work done. But if sleep is rest for the nervous system, it has to occur on a more or less fixed schedule. The amount of sleep does not vary greatly with the amount of mental work. Hard thinking does not make one sleepy; it is more likely to make one turn to a different form of mental work, such as some kind of game or reading, until the appointed time for sleep arrives. In fact, what makes one sleepy is not mental activity but a lack of it, what we call boredom.

The brain does not become inactive in sleep. As the EEG shows, cortical neurons are very active during sleep, but in a different pattern. The large potentials of sleep (Fig. 10.4) are not due chiefly to all-or-none firing of cell body and axon, although there is a good deal of such firing during sleep. The potentials are mainly the product of the activity of dendrites, which must have something to do with the recuperation of cortical neurons.

Sleep involves a lowered activity in the arousal system (with some fluctuation), but again there is more involved. We can think of the arousal system as a "waking center," since its activity causes wakefulness. There is also something like a "sleep center" in the brain stem, paralleling the arousal system in the midbrain and continuing forward into the posterior hypothalamus.

The two systems alternate in a 24-hour sleep–waking cycle known as the *circadian rhythm.* "Circadian," from the Latin *circa diem,* means "about a day" but may be used also to refer loosely to other built-in rhythms such as the crab's tidal rhythm (see below) or the bear's annual hibernation. The control mechanism that does the timing is not known, but it is internal—does not depend on external events—and is commonly referred to as a *biological clock.*

F. Brown, whose work first brought the phenomenon to our attention, has shown that certain crabs that forage on the seashore at low tide have both a 24-hour cycle and a 12-hour 25-minute cycle (the period of the tides). A protective color change in the crab is normally coordinated both with the day–night cycle and with the tidal cycle. The change continues thus coordinated even when the crab is kept in a dark room away from the seashore, and the crab in the dark keeps quite good time. The clock can be reset, however, by exposing the crab to a different lighting schedule: turning on the lights in the dark room from 6 p.m. to 6 a.m. for several days reverses the crab's timing—and the new timing will continue if the crab is again left in darkness.

The human 24-hour clock works in much the same way. Travellers in the Arctic night continue to need their sleep at approximately the usual times. Air travellers who suddenly move from their own time zones to zones that are 4 or 5 hours different find that their internal clocks may take several days to reset, and there is some disorganization and discomfort while this is going on.

Our clock can run fast or slow by as much as half an hour a day in extreme cases. This helps to account for some common complaints. If the clock is fast, the person will become very sleepy early in the evening and be unable to sleep in the early morning. Exposure to day–night alternation will help to reset the clock each day (otherwise one would go to bed earlier and earlier and get up earlier and earlier), but the person may remain in a chronic state of maladjustment. A slow clock, on the other hand, means that the person falls asleep half an hour later each night but wakes up at the usual time. The result is increasing sleep deprivation during the week, until the weekend makes it possible to make up the sleep debt—only to start the process over again on Monday (West, 1967).

Being deprived of sleep can have extreme effects. The need for sleep eventually becomes overwhelming—it is reported that soldiers have actually fallen asleep on their feet while marching. In sleep experiments, when a subject is kept awake in the laboratory, hallucinations and mild delusory ideas appear, usually about the third day. R. B. Malmo and W. Surwillo (1960) have described three subjects who were kept awake, with repeated periods of active psychological testing, for 60 hours. One subject had dreamlike hallucinations in which sounds turned into people, arranged in rows and squares. A second subject had no hallucinations but lost the tactual perception of the knobs he was required to handle in the tests and had to look at them to see what their shapes were. The third found that some of his visual imagery became hallucinatory, that is, his visual imaginings changed so as to seem as if he were actually looking at real objects. He also had momentary delusions, believing that the experimenters were controlling his hallucinations.

Dreaming is accompanied by rapid eye movements (REM) and by an activation record in the EEG (small, fast waves) as if the subject were awake and thinking. A human subject, awakened while making such eye movements, will report dream content. If awakened at another time, the subject will report ideas or vague thoughts, but not the rich imaginal contents we describe as dreams.

It seems that dreaming is an important part of the recuperative process of sleep. Experimental subjects were wakened on some nights whenever they started to dream (as shown by their eye movements); as a control procedure, they were wakened on other nights when they were not dreaming, for an equal amount of sleep deprivation. When dreaming was prevented on successive nights, the subjects became irritable and disturbed, but not merely because sleep had been interrupted, for the same disturbance did not occur following the nights when they were awakened between dreams. It was the loss of the special state of sleep that goes with dreams that caused the trouble.

When normal sleep was permitted following several nights of dream deprivation, the proportion of dreaming time went up from a normal 20% to 30%—the subject, so to speak, had to catch up on dreaming.

One other aspect of sleep concerning individual differences must be mentioned. Eight hours is commonly considered the normal sleeping time, but some people need only 6 hours or even less; others, 10 hours or even more. The differences seem to be familial and thus genetic in origin (though no study of this question has been made) and are very deep seated. The 6-hour sleeper cannot believe that the 10-hour sleeper really needs all that time in bed; and the 10-hour sleeper is apt to suspect that the 6-hour sleeper really spends the day catnapping. How else could anyone pretend to get along with only six hours of sleep? On the contrary, W. B. Webb and J. Friel (1971) found no evidence of personality differences between a group of long sleepers and a group of short sleepers. They suggest that the long sleepers are simply less efficient at sleeping and so must put in more time at it.

EXPLORATORY BEHAVIOR: AROUSAL AND AMBIVALENCE

Exploratory motivation is biologically primitive; it occurs far down in the evolutionary scale and must have survival value. In humans and other higher animals, this investigative tendency has broadened to include all that comes under the head of *curiosity*, much more than a matter merely of exploring new regions of space. Here, however, we are concerned only with exploratory motivation in an animal such as the laboratory rat, in order to examine its relation to arousal and the ambivalence that is characteristic of this and other motivations.

Ambivalence is a mixture of opposing motivations. In exploratory behavior, it is a tendency to move toward and simultaneously, to avoid a new territory. Placed in familiar surroundings, but with access to an unfamiliar region, the rat orients towards the unfamiliar region. If he is in his home cage with the door open, in a part of the room he is not used to, he moves towards the exciting outer world, but acts as though he is moving to a point of balance between the exploratory tendency, on the one hand, and fear of the strange on the other. Any sudden noise, even slight, produces a prompt retreat, followed by another advance. The rat's hair is usually erect, showing activity of the sympathetic nervous system. Each advance tends to reduce unfamiliarity, so the "point of balance" becomes farther and farther from home base, and eventually the whole new territory will be explored.

What we know about the arousal system gives some glimmering of what is going on here, even if final explanations are still in the future. Because familiar perceptions lose their power to cause arousal (habituation), arousal is low in the home cage. Looking at strange objects and moving closer, so that they are seen more clearly, increases arousal. As long as this increase stays at a moderate level, it tends to support whatever cortical activity is going on by providing additional summation at cortical synapses. This cortical activity is what is causing the animal to move toward the strange outside world. Hence, looking and moving toward the strange tend to make the animal continue doing so, as long as the resulting arousal is not too high. High levels of arousal, however, tend to produce disorganization in behavior and constitute emotional disturbance. A point will be reached at which the strange object which at first attracted, becomes disturbing instead.

An increase from low to moderate arousal will have an organizing effect on behavior by improving cortical transmission and cell assembly activity. If a high level of arousal facilitates cortical transmission still more, however, it may begin to make possible conflicting cortical processes. The divergent–conduction regions of the cortex will no longer have their important screening function, which allows only sensorimotor transmissions that are supported by facilitation from the cell assemblies already active. A very high level of cortical bombardment from the arousal system of the brain stem provides other facilitation and may make cortical cell assembly support unnecessary. The result is that other messages get through, and new cortical processes are excited. These processes may inhibit the already existing processes, or their motor outflow may excite behavior that conflicts with existing behavior. For example, a limb may simultaneously receive efferent impulses to its extensor and flexor muscles, causing either muscular rigidity or tremor (which is a rapid alternation of extension and flexion). Thus, there may be either a cortical conflict (by inhibition) or overt motor conflict (trembling, paralysis of movement, etc.). If in this state of affairs the animal looks back at the home cage, or if its random movements take it back toward the cage, arousal is decreased; the cortical process that caused the backward movement thus has a chance to continue, since conflicting processes are diminished. The animal will tend in the first place not to continue moving forward to the point at which arousal is too high, or if it does will move back so that arousal can drop to a moderate level.

This is too simple an account of what goes on, of course, particularly because it omits the earlier learning the animal has done in arousal-producing situations. But it does suggest how we may be able in principle to understand ambivalence in the emotion-producing situation.

SEXUAL MOTIVATION

In birds and lower mammals, the most important single factor in sexual behavior is hormonal: estrogen in the female, androgen in the male, both controlled to a considerable extent by the pituitary gland. As we shall see, however, sexual motivation is not completely dependent on this mechanism.

In some mammalian species the male is sexually responsive at only one time of year (the rutting season), but in others, including the primates, the male will respond at any time. The female, on the other hand, always shows cyclical motivation, ranging from a yearly cycle in sheep, for example, to a 4-day cycle in rats. This varying motivation is directly related to the cycle of changes in the ovary. In lower species, the period of estrus, or heat, is clearly distinct; copulatory behavior cannot be elicited except when the blood estrogen level is high. Some chimpanzee females, however, show sexual responsiveness at all times during the ovarian cycle, though it is very weak at the stage of the cycle at which other females are unresponsive. Motivation in the human female is even less controlled by the ovarian cycle than in lower species. Nonetheless, even with great individual differences, the fluctuations of sexual responsiveness still show some relation to the cycle.

The nervous system of the normal animal, male or female, contains the patterns of organization for both male and female behavior. The presence of androgen in the bloodstream of the male sensitizes the neural structures involved in the male behavior pattern, but also sensitizes those of the female pattern. The male pattern is dominant and is always displayed when a receptive female is available, but sexual arousal in the normal male makes it more probable, not less, that the female pattern can be elicited from the same animal if he is mounted by another excited male. The converse is true for the female: one reliable sign of estrus is the occurrence of mounting by the female. These facts are of significance for human homosexuality. It seems probable that humans are constitutionally both heterosexually and homosexually motivatable, with heterosexuality dominant; and that the establishment of one of these modes of behavior as exclusive or predominant depends on a learning process—that is, it is a function of the culture in which a person lives and of the accidents of experience.

The relation of sexuality to cortical function and learning is of considerable interest. In the male rat, copulatory behavior is correlated with learning ability. It is also dependent on the cortex and is impaired by cortical destruction in the same way as maze-learning scores. In the female rat, however, this relation does not hold. Female behavior is much more at the reflexive level, and rather large cortical destructions do not lower the frequency of effective mating (F. A. Beach, 1939). There is also little evidence that the female's copulatory behavior is affected by past experience. At the anthropoid level, however, this changes. The experienced female chimpanzee copulates much more promptly than the inexperienced, although the difference is not nearly as great as with males. In the chimpanzee, and still more among humans, ideas ("attitudes") determined by earlier learning are capable of greatly modifying sexual responsiveness in both male and female; stimuli that have no directly sexual significance can heighten sexual responsiveness or suppress it. In lower mammals, copulation is a compulsive, stimulus-bound form of behavior, especially in the female but essentially in the male also. Strong as the sexual motivation of anthropoid or human may be, behavior at this evolutionary level has come under the control of mediating processes and is far removed from the reflexive behavior to be seen in dog or cat.

SUMMARY

This chapter is concerned with the neural basis of the basic motivations of hunger, pain, sexual behavior, and exploratory behavior. It is also concerned with the neural mechanism of emotion as it relates to the arousal system, the autonomic nervous system, and the limbic system. Arousal determines the level of cortical function from deep sleep to full alertness; this level is recorded in the various wave patterns of the EEG. The autonomic nervous system has two divisions, the sympathetic and the parasympathetic; the latter stores energy, whereas the sympathetic mobilizes the energy for rapid expenditure in emergencies. The limbic system is a fundamental determinent of personality and of such qualities as tameness and friendliness, wildness and ferocity.

Other topics dealt with in the chapter are sleep and dreams, circadian rhythms, the homeostasis of hunger and of the acquired hunger known as addiction, pain, and sexual motivation.

GUIDE TO STUDY

Here as elsewhere, you would do well to devise your own questions—as if you were preparing an examination for another student. But make sure at least that you can answer the following ones yourself:

What are the two routes by which a sensory excitation may affect cortical activity, and what is the meaning of the terms *cue function* and *arousal function*?

How does the brain stem regulate consciousness, and why does thought depend on arousal?

What does the size of an EEG wave tell us about what is going on in someone's head?

Draw a sketch of the three segments of the autonomic nervous system; explain why this ANS has sometimes been thought to be the whole story of emotion, and sketch the dual closed circuit (involving the adrenal gland) which partly accounts for the persistence of an emotional disturbance.

What function has the hypothalamus in hunger?

Where is the amygdala, and what does it do?

What is the evidence for the existence of pleasure centers?

How do the limbic system and the neocortex interact to control cortical activity through the arousal system?

Be sure that you know the meaning of the term "biological clock" and its relation to sleep.

Be able to review the evidence concerning the value of time spent dreaming. What is the meaning of homeostasis? Which primitive motivations are homeostatic and which are not?

What parallel is there between hunger and addiction?

What reason is there to think that "pain" refers to two different things? What does the comparative evidence tell us about the relation of sexual motivation to learning ability in the male, the differences between male and female in this respect, and the tendency of each sex to respond like the other in certain circumstances?

Finally, what has exploratory behavior to tell us about the nature of ambivalence?

NOTES AND GENERAL REFERENCES

Arousal System

Lindsley, D. B. (1951). *Emotion*. In S. S. Stevens, (Ed.), *Handbook of Experimental Psychology*. New York: Wiley. The first application of the discovery of the arousal system to behavioral problems.

Moruzzi, G., & Magoun, H. W. (1949). Brain stem reticular formation and activation of the EEG. *EEG and Clinical Neurophysiology, 1*, 455–473. Truly an epoch-making paper.

Penfield, W. (1938). The cerebral cortex in man: 1. The cerebral cortex and consciousness. *Archives of Neurology and Psychiatry, 40*, 417–442.

Limbic System and Motivation

Delgado, J. M. R., Roberts, W. W., & Miller, N. E. (1954). Learning motivated by electrical stimulation of the brain. *American Journal of Physiology, 179*, 587–593. Describes aversive effects of brain stimulation.

Doty, R. W. (1967). Limbic System. In A. M. Freedman & H. I. Kaplan (Eds.), Comprehensive Textbook of Psychiatry. Baltimore: Williams & Wilkins.

Olds, J., & Milner, P. (1954). Positive reinforcement produced by electrical stimulation of septal area and other regions of rat brain. Journal of Comparative and Physiological Psychology, 47, 419–427. Original account of "pleasure centers" responding to electrical brain stimulation.

Wasman, M., & Flynn, J. P. (1962). Directed attack elicited from hypothalamus. Archives of Neurology, 6, 220–227.

Integration of Arousal and Limbic Systems

Routtenberg, A. (1968). The two-arousal hypothesis: Reticular formation and limbic system. Psychological Review, 75, 51–80.

Biological Clocks and Sleep

Aschoff, J. (1965). Circadian rhythms in man. Science, 148, 1427–1432.

Brown, F. A., Fingerman, M., Sandeen, M. I., & Webb, H. M. (1953). Persistent diurnal and tidal rhythms of color change in the fiddler crab Uca pugnax. Journal of Experimental Zoology, 123, 29–60.

Kleitman, N. (1967). Patterns of Dreaming. In J. L. McGaugh, N. M. Weinberger & R. E. Whalen, (Eds.), Psychobiology. San Francisco: W. H. Freeman. (Originally published in Scientific American, 1960)

Malmo, R. B., & Surwillo, W. (1960). Sleep deprivation: changes in performance and physiological indicants of activation. Psychological Monographs, 74, 1–24.

Moruzzi, G. (1969). Sleep and instinctive behavior. Archives Italiennes de Biologie, 107, 175–216.

Siegel, P. V., Gerathewohl, S. J., & Mohler, S. R. (1969). Time-zone effects. Science, 164, 1249–1255.

Webb, W. B., & Friel, J. (1971). Sleep stage and personality characteristics of "natural" long and short sleepers. Science, 171, 587–588.

West, L. J. (1967). Psychopathology produced by sleep deprivation. Research Publications, Association for Research in Nervous and Mental Disease, 45, 535–558. Chronic sleep deprivation in normal life is dealt with as well as acute deprivation. Note, in the discussion (p. 556) Lubin's report of the man who thought he was being followed by a telephone pole.

Other references

Beach, F. A. (1939). The neural basis of innate behavior: III. Comparison of learning ability and instinctive behavior in the rat. Journal of Comparative Psychology, 28, 225–262.

Eikelboom, R., & Stewart, J. (1982). Conditioning of drug-induced physiological responses. Psychological Review, 89, 483–506.

Garcia, J., Ervin, F. R., & Koelling, R. A. (1967). Bait-shyness: a test for toxicity with N-2. Psychonomic Science, 7, 245–246.

Hargrave, G. E., & Bolles, R. C. (1971). Rat's aversion to flavors following induced illness. Psychonomic Science, 23, 91–92.

Mark, V. H., & Ervin, F. R. (1970). Violence and the Brain. New York: Harper and Row.

Melzack, R. (1967). The perception of pain. In J. L. McGaugh, N. M. Weinberger, & R. E. Whalen (Eds.), Psychobiology. San Francisco: W. H. Freeman.

Melzack, R., & Wall, P. (1965). Pain mechanisms: a new theory. Science, 150, 971–979.

Emotion and Motivation

In the introduction to chapter 10 we said that evolution must build into an animal certain prime directives—to eat, to mate, and to avoid injury. Hunger, sex, and pain are basic motivations essential for survival. In addition, evolution has given mammals a large brain, with a cortex, which has certain other unanticipated consequences.

A large brain has direct evolutionary value, making its owner more capable of learning and of solving problems. The large brain appears to have some indirect motivational ramifications as well. There are motivations that appear to be dependent on intelligence and are characteristic of the higher mammal. They are weaker in lower mammals and wholly absent in most other animals. These characteristics are most marked in humans and are closely related to the structure of human society. The whole of this large area is the concern of this chapter. There is no topic in psychology that is more important and none for which comparative data are more significant. Although ignored by most social psychologists, the behavior of the dog, the porpoise, and the chimpanzee has much to tell us about the nature of our own society.

EMOTIONS, MOTIVATION AND AROUSAL

Emotion is not a term that can be defined precisely, though we know what it means in a common-sense way. It refers to such states as joy, love, pride, and fun, which are pleasurable states (that is, people do not act to terminate them when they occur and at other times act to make them recur). Emotion refers to anger, jealousy, and fear, unpleasant states that people seek to end by attacking or running from their source. Emotion refers to grief, shame, and depression, states of displeasure whose causes cannot be changed by one's behavior. Emotion is both organizing (making behavior more effective) and disorganizing; it is both energizing and debilitating. In other words, emotion refers to very different conditions, which apparently are little related.

However, these conditions do have something in common. They are all special states of motivation and are closely related to arousal. Anger, for example, is a heightening of arousal accompanied by a tendency to attack. Fear is a heightening of arousal accompanied by a tendency to withdraw or flee. When fear is continual or chronic because the threat cannot be escaped, or when there is no external threat and the fear is due to some disorder within the nervous system itself, it is called anxiety. Thus, for some purposes we can discuss emotion as an entity, as a single kind of process; but for others we will be better able to deal with the specific emotions, such as anger or fear.

The Relation Between Arousal and Performance

Let us begin by considering the inverted-U curve of Fig. 11.1, which illustrates the relation of *cue (performing) function* to *arousal function*. The curve shows that the capacity of sensory stimulation to guide behavior is poor when arousal is very low or very high. We saw, in the discussion of exploratory behavior and ambivalence, that cortical function is at its best only in the middle range of arousal. With low arousal, cortical transmission is poor and with high arousal it is too good, permitting the occurrence of irrelevant and conflicting cortical activities. With very low arousal, the sensory message does not get through; with very high arousal too many messages get through and prevent the animal from responding selectively to any one set of stimuli. In other words the animal is unresponsive when arousal is low and too responsive when arousal is high.

Now we can see the relation between emotion and motivation. Emotion in the general sense is closely related to arousal; as arousal increases, so does emotion. The curve of Fig. 11.1 shows, however, that motivation rises at first with arousal but then begins to fall off at some higher level of arousal and may practically disappear at the highest levels.

Though we ordinarily think of emotional excitement as a cause of vigorous, effective response—that is, we think of it as motivating—

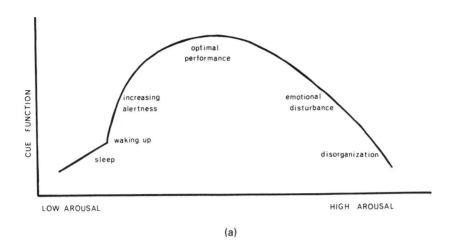

(a)

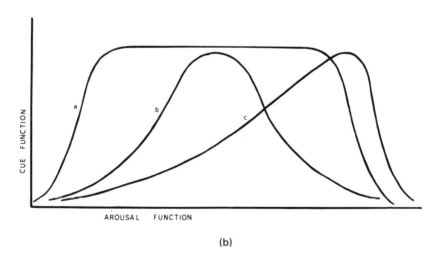

(b)

FIGURE 11.1.

(a) Relationship between the effectiveness with which stimuli guide behavior (cue function) and the level of arousal, varying from deep sleep to disorganizing states of emotion, with maximal behavioral efficiency at an intermediate level of arousal. The shape of the curve must be different for different habits: see (b).

(b) Possible differences in the curve relating arousal to cue function or effectiveness of response, in three habits. In (a), a simple, long practiced habit such as giving one's name when asked, maximal efficiency is reached with low arousal and is maintained over a wide range. In (b), a complex skill, the maximum appears only with a medium degree of arousal. In (c), a performance such as running a race which is relatively uncomplicated but demands full mobilization of effort, the maximum appears with higher arousal.

there is well-authenticated evidence showing not only that it can impair behavior but also that it can reduce the effectiveness of response to near zero. Apparently it does this by abolishing the thought or intention of acting: it produces a loss of motivation. The term "paralysis of terror" is somewhat misleading, but this is what we are talking about. (The term is misleading because there may be no paralysis in the literal sense, the subject usually being capable of movement, and also because in extreme cases the subject's thought may be so impaired that he or she really does not experience what we would ordinarily consider to be fear or terror. These terms refer to a state of mind that includes the *idea* of being injured, of feeling pain, and so on. But there is something that approximates paralysis, either of thought or of bodily movement.)

J. S. Tyhurst (1951) has described the behavior of people caught by a fire in a ship or apartment house or caught by a flash flood. About 15% show really organized and effective behavior; about 70% show varying degrees of disorganizaiton, but are still able to function with some effectiveness; but another 15% (the proportion varied from 10% to 25% in different disasters studied) show completely ineffective behavior: screaming or crying, confusion, inability to move or to get out of bed, or aimless or unsuitable movements. One man, told that the ship was on fire and that he had to get on deck at once, was last seen ineffectually searching for a cuff link. S. L. A. Marshall (1947) has reported similar figures for the stress of battle. Repeated studies in various armies have shown that only about 15% to 25% of infantrymen in the presence of the enemy can be relied on to fire their rifles, with or without careful aiming, and some are incapable of doing so even when prodded by an officer. In a different context, newspapers every now and then report the case of a pedestrian caught in traffic who might have escaped but, making no move, was killed; or a driver whose car stalled on a railroad track before an oncoming train and who sat motionless, apparently unable to stir, and was killed in the ensuing collision.

Such behavior shows that emotion-producing situations can severely impair the processes that control organized behavior, even when the cues are present that should guide the appropriate response. Motivation can be impaired by too high a level of arousal.

There are other phenomena with the same implication—stage fright and "buck fever" (suddenly being given one's great opportunity but being unable to act appropriately). There is a common opinion that the prize fighter's skill may be impaired by anger, and that physicians should not try to deal with serious illness in people to whom they are emotionally attached, the implication being that skill is similarly impaired by worry.

All such examples show that arousal can have a disorganizing effect on behavior. We must not forget, of course, that lower levels of arousal are organizing and that different habits will have different degrees of resistance to disorganization. Logically, a simpler and longer established habit should be less likely to be disrupted than a complex response that depends on the delicate interaction of mediating processes. If anger produces a trembling of the fingers it will disturb a watchmaker's skill but not his ability to swat a fly. Similarly, at a cortical level, worry and concern could impair a physician's skill in diagnosing the illness of a spouse when cancer is in question, but not when the diagnosis is hay fever. In effect, the inverted-U curve has different shapes for different habits, as in Fig. 11.1b. Also, the same degree of arousal may be disorganizing at one point in a series of actions but organizing at a later point. Stage fright, for the experienced actor, is disturbing *before* the performance, but there seems to be general agreement that if there is no stage fright at any time in the proceedings, the performance itself is less likely to be effective.

This discussion can be summarized as follows: The intensity of emotion is directly correlated with arousal. Emotion, or arousal, is motivating up to the point at which conflicting activities in the cortex begin to interfere with one another, preventing the dominance of one activity that would produce *one* set of organized responses to the situation. How high arousal can go, and still be motivating, varies with the kind of behavior. It presumably varies also from one person to another.

Much emotion is correlated with arousal, but emotion cannot be simply identified with it, because the limbic system has a crucial contribution to make and because thought processes are an important feature of any emotion. *Fear* can be defined as arousal accompanied by mediating processes that constitute the idea of being injured and that tend to produce as responses, avoidance and flight. *Anger* can be defined as arousal accompanied by mediating processes that constitute the idea of hurting the person or animal at whom the anger is directed and that tend to produce the corresponding behavior. *Disgust* or *horror* is arousal with no accompanying ideas of being injured, but simply of avoiding the sight, sound, touch, taste, or smell of the thing that disgusts. *Joy* or *love* is arousal accompanied by mediating processes that make for a deeper immersion in, or continued contact with, the activity, person, or thing that gives joy or is loved. The arousal of joy is presumably not the same as the arousal of strong fear. Presumably the pleasure centers are active in one and not in the other (although mild fear may be pleasant, as we will see later). The clearest distinction between the different emotions is in the ideas that go with them, and the behaviors that these ideas (mediating processes) give rise to. No definition of emotion can omit reference to the cortical activity that gives any emotion its identity.

Emotional Disturbance and the Limbic System

As was explained in chapter 10, the arousal system helps to support cortical activity as the cortex receives information from the sense receptors. Direct sensory information comes to the cortex through the thalamus, where the sensory relay nuclei are located. Sensory information reaching the cortex activates circuits (cell assemblies) in which the incoming sensory information is related to past experiences. As a part of the same process, the cell assembly circuits incorporate the motivational meaning of this incoming information. Stimuli like food smells, hormone-produced odors (pheronomes), or the sight and sound of a parent may have an unlearned motivational meaning. But most sensory information—for example, the sight of your old house, your friend, or your dog—are emotionally neutral until an emotional association has been established through learning. The emotional significance of both learned and unlearned sensory information is maintained through cortical connections with the limbic system.

The limbic system, through its close connection with the homeostatic control systems in the hypothalamus (see Fig. 10.2), is responsible for organizing appropriate motivational responses to the incoming flow of sensory information to the cortex. It has a powerful effect on the activity of the arousal system. Suppose, as in the example of chapter 10, that the hypothalamic centers indicate a low glucose level. A stimulus is presented, and the limbic system has recorded that food follows the stimulus. Then the limbic system provides a feedback signal to excite the arousal system, which in turn activates the cortex in response to the incoming food-related conditioned stimulus. (The direct cortical connections, which carry the information necessary to make this limbic system connection, travel faster than the signals through the arousal system.) If, on the other hand, the hypothalamus indicates adequate glucose, the limbic system will inhibit the arousal system in response to this particular sensory input, and the cell assembly activity involving this input will not be facilitated by cortical arousal.

Thus, there are two systems regulating the direction and intensity of cortical activity, and hence the direction and emotional intensity of thought and behavior in higher animals. One system is the arousal system, which determines the general level of activation of the cortex. Although it is not clear how it is done, the arousal system also amplifies particular sensory inputs in response to particular motivational needs. The second system is the limbic system, which relates the perceptual analysis carried out by the cortex to the motivational results. The information available through cell assemblies, which include the limbic system, allows this system to feed back into the arousal system and to control it, amplifying cortical activity for motivationally appropriate stimuli and inhibiting cortical activity for motivationally inappropriate stimuli.

The arousal system and the limbic system are thus related in an important motivational (and emotional) feedback system, which is normally in balance. The cortex is stimulated by the arousal system to organize cell assemblies in response to incoming sensory stimuli; those assemblies which are motivationally important are facilitated, and those that are not important are inhibited. The result is an organized, motivated stream of behavior.

But suppose the limbic-arousal system gets out of balance as a result of an abnormal anatomical or chemical development in one system or the other. If the arousal system is overactive so that the limbic system cannot inhibit it, then the cortex will be activated with a flood of sensory input, and each input will compete to engage cell assembly activity. The cortex is normally activated in this way when previous learning is inappropriate, either because the stimulus is novel or because the situation has changed and the consequences predicted by old cell assemblies did not occur. The result is an alert cortex, ready to develop new cell assembly groups. The new cell assemblies, whose motivational meanings are recorded in the limbic system, will then be able to direct behavior and control further sensory input in an appropriate way. But if the arousal system is highly activated all the time, behavior cannot be organized smoothly on the basis of the match between expectations and motivational needs, and the smooth flow of organized, motivated behavior will be interrupted.

Anatomical or chemical abnormalities in the limbic system can be equally disruptive. If the limbic circuits that incorporate the motivational effect of sensory information are too strong, they may inhibit the arousal systems too completely. Then normal cortical responsiveness to a variety of sensory experience will be reduced. This would be a form of induced sensory deprivation and may lead to hallucinations. Hallucinations and an inability to deal normally with the usual range of sensory experience are characteristics of one type of schizophrenia, and limbic system-arousal system imbalance may be its cause.

This outline of a relationship between the limbic and arousal systems obviously does not explain all emotional disorders. Deeply embedded within both systems, and extending from the midbrain to the forebrain (which, with its clear role in planning or maintaining of directed activity, is involved in anticipating motivational needs) are neural systems that are closely tied to motivation and reinforcement: the neuron tracts from which self-stimulation can be produced. The exact function of these tracts in producing the effects of reward is unclear, although one tract (the dopamine neurotransmitter system, which extends from the substantia nigra nucleus of the midbrain to forebrain structures in the neocortex) is known to be related to schizophrenia. Several independent research techniques have demonstrated that the neurons of this sytem are overactive in schizophrenics. Successful treatment of some schizophrenic symptoms in some people, is obtained by administering drugs whose main effect is to block the transmission of nerve impulses in the dopamine system.

Emotion and Reinforcement

The observed symptoms of depression and grief include a lack of motivated behavior and lethargy, which suggest the low, rather than the high, end of the arousal curve. Depression and grief are probably caused by low activity in reinforcement neurons, which are a part of the limbic system. These systems are composed largely of neurons that use either dopamine or norepinephrine as transmitter substances. In depressed or grief-stricken people, the activity in these reinforcement neurons may not be high enough to sustain behavior that is normally motivated by the expectation of reward. In some cases, the cause of this inactivity may be biological. In other cases, the source of positive reward—the sustaining, motivating influence in life—may have disappeared. In behavioral terms this influence would be called a conditioned reinforcer, but in everyday language it is a husband, wife, lover, favorite uncle, or dog. Cell assembly activity cannot be sustained by the limbic system through positive feedback to the arousal system, because the cell assembly activity previously associated with a positive reinforcer (and many of our daily activities are carried out with associated background reinforcement) no longer leads to the expectation of positive reinforcement. The elimination of the positive motivational meaning of cell assembly activity may lead to a partial shutdown of the arousal system through the failure of the limbic system to communicate positive feedback to it. Under these circumstances, nothing in the ordinary course of life seems "worth doing," and only strong motivating stimuli, including those which normally produce fear or defensive reactions, can stimulate behavior.

Emotion and Intellectual Level

Next we come to the important proposition that an animal's susceptibility to emotional disturbance is directly related to the level of its intelligence. Humans are the most intelligent animals, but also the most emotional; our near neighbors in evolution, the great apes, show their kinship with us more clearly in their emotional characteristics than in their capacity for learning and solving problems. Thus, there is a species correlation between emotionality, in this sense, and level of intelligence.

The correlation is so close that one can hardly avoid the notion that there is a direct causal relation. The facts suggest that emotional disturbance is like a temporary breakdown in a piece of mechanical or electrical equipment; the more complex the equipment, the greater number of things that can disturb its operation, the greater the aberration from normal function may be, and the longer it may take to get it back in working order.

Has this analogy any value? It is consistent with the idea that mediating processes (more complex in higher animals) are a factor in emotion, and it implies that having mediating processes increases the strength and duration of arousal. It does seem that this is so. An important cause of emotional disturbance is a discrepancy between perception and expectation. Why this should cause a sharp rise in arousal is not entirely clear, but cortical events do have a feedback action on the arousal system, so something of the sort must take place. We may note also that the complex perceptions of the more developed brain would allow the more intelligent subject to detect a discrepancy when another subject would not, and that a capacity for thought allows the subject to imagine injuries and insults.

Let us look at the evidence for the claim that emotion is characteristic of the more intelligent animal.

Anger and its close relative *jealousy*[1] are not concepts necessary for classifying the behavior of the laboratory rat. The rat bites to escape capture, or in the course of fighting for food, or to protect its young, but seldom for other reasons. Anger as we know it in higher animals involves a kind of social perception that is beyond the rat's ken, and the dog is definitely capable of jealousy, even, on occasion, of sulking. In the chimpanzee, however, we have the full picture: anger, sulking, and the temper tantrum. The peculiar feature of sulking is refusing to accept what one wanted in the first place. The peculiar feature of the temper tantrum is apparent attempts at self-injury—the child holding his breath, pulling his hair, banging himself against the wall—while watching to see what effect the tantrum is having on the adult who is denying him what he wants. This purposive element is also clear in the year-old chimpanzee infant who takes surreptitious looks at his mother

---

[1] It seems that jealousy differs from anger only in the circumstances in which it appears. In other words, jealousy is anger arising from a particular social situation.

in between his attacks of choking to death or pounding his head on the floor.

The main cause of anger is the perception that someone else is doing something that one does not like. It is common to say that the cause is *frustration*, frustration meaning that one is prevented from getting something one wants. This definition is unsatisfactory: the sight of food out of reach does not produce anger in the hungry chimpanzee. But he does get angry if someone offers the food, then pulls it away, that is, if he is given an expectation of getting it and then perceives the caretaker as deliberately refusing it. Furthermore, anger may occur without frustration. In the chimpanzee world, rain water from the roof that wet Bokar's back did not make him angry, though he did not like it. But he was enraged when Dick spit water at him from the next cage, even if he was not hit. Pan took food from Mona, whom he dominated, in the same cage; her noisy, frustrated rage angered him so that he gave her a beating. The only frustration *he* suffered was of his desire for peace and quiet after he had gotten what he wanted (Hebb, 1945).

The similarity between chimpanzee and human with respect to the forms and causes of anger is clear. The only difference between the two species is the greater variety of things that cause anger in humans, who have greater social perceptiveness and consequently greater capacity for being slighted or insulted and who also have language, to increase still further the range of possible provocations.

THE CAUSES OF FEAR

Fear has the same increasing variety of causes as we go from lower to higher mammals, along with an increase in duration and apparent severity of disturbance. Pain, a sudden loud noise, or sudden loss of support cause fear in any mammal. For the rat, we can add strange surroundings. With the dog, the list becomes longer: strange people, certain strange objects or situations (such as a balloon being blown up before the dog), a large statue of an animal, the dog's owner in different clothing, or a hat being moved across the floor by a thread the dog does not see (Melzack, 1952). Of course, not all dogs are equally affected. Mahut (1958) has shown, for example, that working dogs, bred for intelligence, are more susceptible to fear than bulldogs and terriers, bred for pugnacity. Monkeys and apes are affected by a still wider variety of stimulating situations than dogs, and the degree and duration of disturbance is greater.

Causes of fear in the captive chimpanzee make up an almost endless list: a carrot of an unusual shape, a biscuit with a worm in it, a rope of a particular size, color, and texture (but not other ropes), a doll or a toy animal, a particular piece of apparatus or part of it, and so on. What one animal fears another may not, but as a species chimpanzees are much more susceptible than dogs to fears that do not arise from pain or threat of pain.

Figure 11.2b is a picture of two objects that can produce a remarkable reaction in adult chimpanzees. The "death mask," left, in particular produced screaming, panic-stricken flight in a fifth of the adult animals that were simply shown the object, carried in the experimenter's hand as he walked up to the cage. The response of the remaining adults varied in strength, but most were very frightened, and no animal failed to show erection of hair and avoidance of the test object. The same reaction was produced by a clay model of an adult chimpanzee head about half life-size (this was more frightening than the modeled infant head shown in Fig. 11.2b, a real chimpanzee's head that had been preserved in formalin, a lifelike model of a human head taken from a display dummy, and various related objects, such as a detached human hand from the same dummy). With repeated testing there was some habituation, but no animal approached any of these objects. A doll representing a human infant was placed in the cages of five adult chimpanzees, one after another, but despite the chimpanzee's well-known curiosity and destructiveness with things that can be taken to pieces, the doll remained untouched and intact.

The behavior of younger animals was quite different. One- and two-year-olds (corresponding roughly to human 2- and 3-year-olds) paid no attention at all to the test objects. As the experimenter approached carrying one of the objects, the infants came toward him and, apparently not noticing the object at all, tried to get the experimenter to pick them up. All their attention was focused on his face. Half-grown animals of 5 and 6 years (corresponding to human 8-year-olds) were fascinated by the objects. As the experimenter neared an enclosure containing half a dozen of these youngsters, they approached in a tight cluster as close as they could (quite unlike the adults), clinging to the cage wire and poking their fingers through to prod the model head being shown them. The same objects that terrified the adults—or horrified them—were exciting but not frightening to the half-grown chimps, and were not even noticed by the infant chimpanzees.

There is a clear parallel in the differing reactions of human children and adults to distorted and damaged human bodies. To the limited intelligence of the chimpanzee, a model of a head may be the same as an actual head severed from the body would be for a human being. (In both cases there is a perceived identification of part of a living person, and at the same time a clear discrepancy.) It is not children but their

(a) Monkey solving a problem for its own sake. All the experimenter has to do is to "set" the simple mechanical puzzles (which would offer a 6-year-old child no problem at all), and the monkey will work at them. (Courtesy of H. F. Harlow.)

(b) Objects that caused fear in adult chimpanzees: left, a plaster of paris cast from a death mask of an adult; right, a clay model of an infant's head, nearly life size.

FIGURE 11.2. The effect of sensory stimulation on arousal.

246

elders who are most upset by scenes of violence and broken bodies on TV; a color movie of a major operation may produce nausea and fainting in adults, but not in children; as adults we tolerate the extraordinary brutality of many of the classic fairy stories, presumably only because we were introduced to them at the more bloodthirsty age of 5 or 6 years.

An experiment by H. E. and M. C. Jones provides direct evidence of the increase of emotional susceptibility with age. They recorded the reactions of children and adolescents to a snake, which was torpid and was shown to be quite harmless. The subjects were city dwellers who had not had contact with snakes before. There was little fear in the youngest (about 5 years old), increased interest with only slight signs of caution in those of intermediate ages, and strong avoidance by most of the older subjects. "Fear" is not quite the right word to describe the older subjects' reaction: "horror" is better since they did not expect to be injured (they knew the snake could not hurt them), but it can be said that in general the reaction of most adults to a snake they know is not capable of injuring them is hardly less vigorous than to a dangerous one. It should be emphasized that the "fear" of snakes is not learned. Why it should be so strong is not understood, but it is a product of psychological maturation rather than learning (see chapter 7). The year-old chimpanzee is not disturbed by contact with a snake, but the adult who sees one for the first time is very disturbed, his reaction being about as strong as a human being's.

Emotion and the Social Structure

To ourselves we seem civilized, urbane, not given to senseless fears and outbursts of rage, as the child or the explosive chimpanzee is. The reason, however, may not be that we are less susceptible but rather that we are sheltered by what we call a civilized environment, within which we are not much exposed to the causes of emotional disturbance. It offers physical protection from wild animals or freezing to death and, usually, makes it possible to avoid starving to death. But it also offers psychological protection from emotional disturbance by reducing its causes to near zero. In a "civilized environment" one never has to be in strange places in darkness (thus many adults never discover that they are subject to fear in such circumstances). The adults in a "civilized environment" have learned elaborate rules of courtesy, good manners, and how to behave in public. Their behavior is predictable and usually will not cause embarrassment, shame, anger, or disgust. All this is achieved by prolonged training in childhood and is later enforced by legal penalties (e.g., for slander, indecent exposure, assault, dumping garbage in the street) or by social sanction. In short, in this environment one can usually count on not being suddenly exposed to the causes of strong emotion without warning and without adequate opportunity to avoid them. All this, of course, presumes that we have been trained to suppress strong emotion when it does occur. Emotional outbursts are rare in the civilized adult on his or her own ground, but there is no reason to conclude from this that an adult is less susceptible to attacks of emotion than a five-year-old, who must live in an environment tailored to adult needs rather than those of a five-year-old.

The social problems of race and religious prejudice should show us what we are like as a species. It is common to assume that social prejudice is wholly learned and that if one never let a child hear bad things about other groups, the child would grow up to be without prejudice. We know, however, that more is involved. Such learning does occur and it is important to prevent it whenever possible, for it is learned with extraordinary ease. But prejudice can spring up where there has been no occasion for learning. An essential component of prejudice is the emotional reaction of human beings to the strange, to what is the same and yet different, to what can cause a conflict of ideas.

At first it seems unreasonable to suppose that emotions as strong as those involved in social prejudice could be ignited by such a small spark as a difference in skin color or the knowledge that someone else does not share a religious belief. But the comparative evidence has great weight. The chimpanzee's outright panic at the sight of a model of a chimpanzee head shows how strong the effect of a perceptual discrepancy, as such, can be. Also, if a human is hostile toward a stranger, one might think that this is because he or she has been taught that strangers are dangerous; but the chimpanzee born in captivity and never before exposed to a stranger, chimpanzee or human, shows the same reaction. Clearly the hostility is not something that needs to be learned.

Clearly, strong emotional reactions may be induced by apparently trivial causes in humans as in chimpanzees. Consider that healthy young men, capable of withstanding very serious injury without crying out, are also capable of fainting at the *idea* of a hypodermic injection, even before a needle has even touched them. Or, among trivial differences with large consequences, consider the social use of two words that mean precisely the same thing, one a Latin anatomical term, one coming from Anglo-Saxon and classed as obscene. All that "obscene" can mean in this case is that one word is taboo and the other is not. Society is shot through with taboos, and failure to observe them involves considerable risk. These are taboos in the most primitive sense.[2] The whole structure of society contains a large irrational or emotional factor; failure to recognzie it means failure to understand the social behavior of the human animal.

The attempt to explain racial and religious prejudice as a product of learning arises from the assumption that humans, being intelligent, make their important decisions on the basis of reason. Once we recognize that this is not so and that the possession of intelligence may in fact, through imagination, *increase* the causes of emotional disturbance, we can better understand the nature of our problem in dealing with prejudice, and how dangerous is the assumption that prejudice will disappear if a child is not taught bad things about others.

The child's emotional reaction to the other, to the one who differs, is likely to result in hostility. *But it need not do so.* Learning, which can have negative effects and increase hostility, can instead guide the emotional reaction in the direction of warmth and friendliness. Human motivational characteristics are not all undesirable. The same comparative approach that shows us that unreasoning hostility can arise spontaneously, allows us also to see another and more favorable side of human nature. To this we will turn in a moment.

To sum up the argument of this section: The comparative evidence indicates that the capacity for emotion increases with intelligence. It is the higher animal of whom fear of innocuous objects, or unfounded hostility, is characteristic. At first it may seem that these conclusions cannot be extended to humans, who as adults are less emotional than a fearful wild animal. But looking at the environment in which the traits are manifested, we see that something has been left out of account. The structure of "civilization" is such as to cushion the adult's sensibilities, to protect against the causes of fear, anger, and disgust. The extent and strength of social prejudice (in which reason is used only to reinforce one's unreasoned emotional responses) show how deeply rooted these sensitivities are. Thus, the lack of emotional outbursts in the civilized adult is evidence, not of a lack of susceptibility, but of the effectiveness of the social cocoon in which we live. It does not refute the proposition that emotional susceptibility rises with intellectual capacity.

This susceptibility often has undesirable results, but this, fortunately, is not always so, as we will now see. Humans and apes can feel

---

[2]Consider some of the sexual taboos, for example. A conviction for indecent exposure does not require evidence that the behavior has done anyone any harm, physically or mentally—all that must be shown is that the taboo has been broken. Or consider the taboos attaching to the dead body: there are several legal penalties for "offering indignity" to a corpse, as for example stuffing one into the trunk of your car when taking it to be buried.

fear *for others*, and humans, at least, can be angered by injury or injustice to others.

ALTRUISM IN THE HIGHER ANIMAL

Among the distinctive features of human behavior is the frequency of *altruism*, intrinsically motivated purposive behavior whose function is to help another person or animal. "Intrinsically motivated" means that the behavior does not depend on primary or secondary reinforcement, that the helper receives no benefit except the knowledge that he or she has helped; "purposive" implies that the behavior is under the control of mediating processes, thus excluding the reflexive cooperation of the social insects (ant, bee, termite).

Common experience tells us how frequent such behavior is. Giving money to a beggar, working for the prevention of cruelty to animals, helping a stranger start a car, contributing to disaster funds, helping with the dishes, lending a set of notes to another student—trivial or not, there are endless ways in which human beings do things for others with no expectation of direct return. Often, of course, such acts are performed with the hope of later benefit, but this does not change the fact that truly unselfish acts, great and small, are frequent. Some acts are heroic indeed—consider the number of people who die annually in the attempt to rescue others from drowning or from a burning building.

Nonetheless, there is a long tradition of interpreting *all* of human motivation as selfish. It is thought that generosity is not in the child's nature but is imposed by rewards and punishments and maintained at maturity only by social pressure. It is assumed that when the adult is generous, it is only because of habit or because of reward by social approval and punishment for selfishness by disapproval. It is difficult to refute this proposition directly, because of the multifarious learning of the growing child in society. But there is a disproof in animal behavior.

H. W. Nissen and M. P. Crawford (1936) have shown that begging, for example, is a very powerful stimulus for the chimpanzee. In their experiments, two animals are in adjoining cages and one is given food. If the two are friends, the second may be given as much as half the food as a gift. If they are not friends, the importunate begging of the second animal may still be irresistible, though annoying, and the rich animal may end up by throwing the food violently at the beggar. There is no suggestion in that case that the "rich" animal gets any pleasure from giving to the poor. There is some deeper compulsion, and it is quite clear from the history of the animals, reared in the laboratory, that the gift is not made because the giver was trained as an infant to be kind to beggars.

Chimpanzees and gorillas living free in the wild have been observed giving help to half-grown youngsters in trouble, sometimes even when the helper himself had to venture into the dangerous neighborhood of the human observer. Similar behavior has been observed experimentally. Two adult female chimpanzees, Lia and Mimi, are caged together. A disguised human observer approaches, playing the part of the "bold man," one who is unafraid of chimpanzees. Thanks to the cage wire between him and them, and a stout pair of gloves, he can pretend to answer attacks in a most intimidating manner. Both Lia and Mimi, seeing a stranger approach without the caution usually shown by strangers, attack. Lia is frightened by the vigor of the stranger's responses and runs away, but Mimi is not. Mimi stays close to the wire, trying to catch hold of him; then Lia, though clearly afraid, returns and repeatedly tries to pull the reckless Mimi out of the danger zone. This scene is repeated on subsequent testing.

The porpoise, or dolphin, a marine mammal, must be classed as a higher animal on the grounds of its behavior as well as its large brain, a fifth larger than the human's and with a highly developed cortex. There is well-attested evidence of adult dolphins helping other adults in trouble. J. B. Siebenaler and D. K. Caldwell (1956) report two cases in which a stunned animal was supported at the surface till he could swim again (for porpoises, of course, must breathe). In other cases, females other than the mother have been seen helping newborn porpoises to the surface to breathe for the first time. Finally, W. N. Kellogg (1961) reports two separate instances in which a porpoise helped a human swimmer to reach safety.

In short, the evidence from infrahuman mammals indicates that altruism is a product of evolution and not a value that must forcibly be inculcated into the growing human child because of the needs of society. Here, apparently, we have another motivational consequence of the development of complex mediating processes. It is clear in the chimpanzee and porpoise, at least on occasion, but it is most evident in humans and is obviously an important element in the structure of human society.

PLAY, BOREDOM, AND THE SEARCH FOR EXCITEMENT

Living things must be active, and this is as true of brain as of muscle. Ordinarily both are kept exercised as a result of environmental stimulation and in the satisfaction of biological needs. There are times, however, when an animal has no threat to escape from, no need of food, and no young to care for, no sexual motivation, and no need of sleep. Only one need remains: to be active, physically and mentally.

The play of birds and lower mammals seems largely muscular, though there is evidently a neural component also. The animal does not merely alternately tense and relax the muscles, but indulges in activities that require elaborate neural control, generally those that depend on past learning. Monkeys, apes, and humans, however, engage in a kind of play that is almost entirely mental, with a minimum of muscular activity.

Harlow has shown that monkeys will work for hours at solving simple mechanical puzzles, with no reward other than finding a solution (Fig. 11.2b). Chimpanzees will work for a food reward, but they work much better if the task is interesting and then may work even if they do not want the food. One female solved a series of problems and received a slice of banana for each solution. Instead of eating it, she piled the slices in a neat row on top of the apparatus. Then she repeated the whole series of problems, putting one slice of banana back into the food dish after each trial, apparently for the experimenter.

Such behavior is *play*—when play is defined as work done for the sake of doing it. Obviously it is not primarily physical play, but must exercise the brain more than the muscles. Even the laboratory rat shows something of the same kind. Figure 11.3 shows the plan of an apparatus allowing the rat the choice of a direct route to food, versus an indirect route through a simple maze. Figure 11.3b shows that about 40% of the time the rats preferred to take the longer path, provided the "problems" (so simple that they hardly deserve that name) were changed on each run. Figure 11.3b also shows that an unchanging problem does not have the same attraction. Here only 12% of the runs were through the maze area, the difference showing up even in the first block of five trials. Varying the problems shows that the rat was not merely seeking physical exercise, the unchanged problem had provided as much muscular activity on the average as the changing ones.

It is evident, therefore, that "mental play," involving the brain as much as the muscles, is a characteristic of the mammal and prominent in the higher mammals. Much of our mental play—in bridge, chess, and so on—is competitive, and we tend to think of it as motivated by the secondary reinforcement of the "prestige" or social approval that comes from being better than someone else. But there is also noncompetitive play, such as knitting and singing and birdwatching, and the lower-animal data just discussed show that the need of mental exercise exists in its own right.

Boredom is a state in which the subject seeks a higher level of

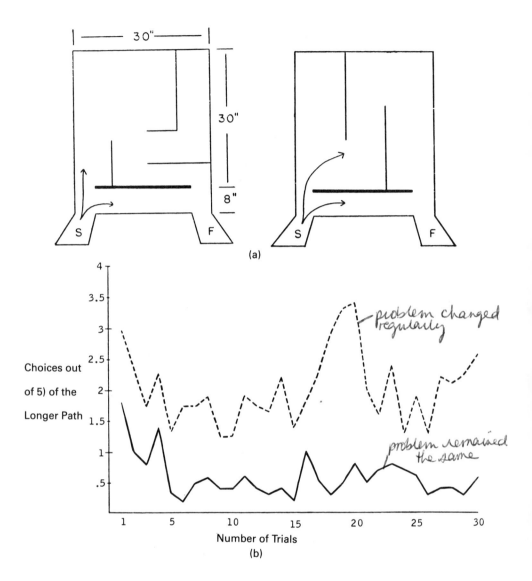

FIGURE 11.3. Rats choose stimulation over speed in solving maze problems.
(a) Two "problems" in a variable-pattern maze, the rat having always the option of going directly from the start (S) to the food (F) instead of going through the problem area. The arrows indicate the two routes from which the animal could choose. (From Hebb & Mahut, 1955. Reproduced by permission.)
(b) Mean number of choices of the longer route in each block of 5 runs by 11 rats, in maze problems of the kind shown in A, above. A mean of 3 thus represents 60 per cent choice of the longer route. The dotted line shows what happened when the problem was changed regularly: the solid line shows what happened when the problem remained the same for many trials.

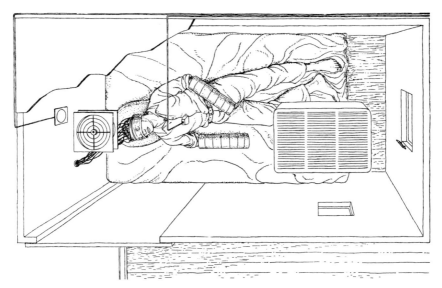

FIGURE 11.4. The subject in the isolation experiment seen from above. Cuffs were worn to prevent somesthetic perception by the hands; the plastic shield over the eyes admitted light but prevented pattern vision. The subject had a foam-rubber U-shaped cushion covering his ears; here it has been removed so that EEG tracings can be taken. An air-conditioner is shown where it would be on the ceiling, upper left, and the microphone by which the subject could report his experiences is seen just above his chest. (From Heron, 1957. Reproduced by permission.)

excitement, usually in some form of play, and the avoidance of boredom is a most important factor in human behavior. The extent to which we are dependent on our normally varied environment and the mental activity it generates is demonstrated in perceptual-isolation experiments (Bexton, Heron and Scott, 1954). College students were paid $20 a day (a high wage at the time) to do nothing—to lie on a comfortable bed with eyes covered by translucent plastic (permitting light to enter, but preventing pattern vision), hands enclosed in tubes (so that the hands could not be used for somesthetic perception, though they could be moved to prevent joint pains), and ears covered with earphones from which there was a constant buzzing except when the subject was being given a test (Fig. 11.4). These conditions were relaxed only to allow the subject to eat or go to the toilet. Few of the subjects could stand the monotony for more than 2 or 3 days, the upper limit being 6 days. The subjects were willing to listen to childish or meaningless talk that otherwise they would have avoided contemptuously—anything to break the monotony. Eventually the need became overwhelming to see, to hear, to be in normal contact with the environment, to be *active*. Nothing like the same pressure develops when people are equally immobilized (with a broken leg, say) but have books and friends to keep them occupied mentally. Clearly, there is a greater need for mental activity than for physical activity.

The experiment showed that humans can be bored, which we knew, but it showed too that boredom is too mild a word for some of the effects of sensory deprivation. The need for the normal stimulation of a varied environment is fundamental. Without it, mental functioning and personality deteriorate. The subjects in isolation complained of being unable to think coherently, they became less able to solve simple problems, and they began to have hallucinations. Some of them saw such things as rows of little men wearing black caps, squirrels marching with sacks over their shoulders, or prehistoric animals in the jungle. These scenes were described as being like animated cartoons. More fundamentally disturbing were somesthetic hallucinations, when a subject perceived two bodies somesthetically or felt as if his head were detached from his body; closely related to this phenomenon was "a feeling of bodily strangeness," for which the subject could give no more adequate description, and several subjects reported that they felt that their minds were detached from their bodies. The subjects' very identity had begun to disintegrate. We saw in chapters 7 and 9 that the development of personality and intelligence depends on exposure to an adequately stimulating environment during infancy. The isolation experiments show that adult human beings continue to be dependent on stimulation in the same way for the maintenance of normality.

AMBIVALENT HUMAN NATURE

We are mammals and a product of evolution, and fundamental to our motivation is the satisfaction of basic biological needs. When these are not met—particularly if the lack is chronic—the attempt to satisfy them generally becomes a dominant motive. (Even here, however, the mediating processes of a large cerebrum have a powerful influence: the starving man may share his food, the woman in danger may invite even greater risk to help her child, and sexual need is characteristically subordinated to the rules and customs of society.)

But when one's biological needs are satisfied we see a very different picture. The ambivalence of the exploratory tendency that is evident in the lower mammal (Fig. 11.3) now extends itself over a much wider field, but apparently still with the same function of reaching a balance between low and high arousal, between boredom and emotional disturbance. We all know that people dislike work; but if they have none, they invent it—though then they call it play. By the same token, fear entails avoidance, and so do horror and offensiveness; yet humans seek situations that produce fear in the guise of "thrill" or "adventure," they are fascinated by newspaper accounts of the mangled human bodies in Monday's report of the weekend highway toll, and they are notoriously charmed by risqué jokes and bawdy songs. Presumably these ambivalent attitudes are to be understood in the same way as the rat's exploratory tendency: as the manifestation of the inclination to increase arousal to the point at which conflicting cortical processes interfere with a closer approach or greater exposure to the source of excitation.

These tendencies penetrate deeply into, and determine, the structure of society. It was suggested earlier that "civilization" is a protective cocoon, an ordering of the physical environment and of human social behavior in such a way as to insulate adult members of society from most of the emotional provocations that they would otherwise be subject to. But the result of such insulation—especially in an economically successful society, such as ancient Rome or the Western world today—is that life may become dull and the need to find excitement pressing, at least for some of the time and for most people. In this light, we can recognize the motivation that underlies mountain climbing, skiing, and auto racing: all activities that depend largely on thrill for their attraction and in which some degree of fear is deliberately courted. We can recognize the motivation behind golf, which might be an old ladies' game if it were not for its constant threat of frustration. It is a notoriously anger-provoking game, as bridge is also. But relatively few people climb mountains or play golf, and above-average intelligence is needed to be really frustrated by bridge. These occupations offer escape for only a minority of the population.

Rome made the discovery that the populace needs circuses as well as bread; our circuses are professional sports. The minor brutalities of hockey and football are a pallid substitute for tossing Christians to the lions, perhaps, but they serve the same function. When we add rock concerts, soap opera, TV, movies, comics, and paperback thrillers, it can be seen that we do fairly well in this respect. For our present purposes, it is important to realize that such activities are not luxuries but necessities, at least at the present stage of development of social institutions.

SUMMARY

The development of a large cortex in mammals increased their capacity to learn and to solve problems, while it also increased their susceptibility to emotional disturbance and their capacity for altruistic behavior.

Human emotional sensibilities have led to organized social patterns that reduce the frequency of emotional stimulation, allowing us to think of ourselves as unexcitable. But apparently trivial stimuli can cause strong reactions. The persistence of racial, religious, and national prejudices—because all people do not look alike, think alike, or talk alike—and the violence that goes with it, show how far we are from being the unemotional and peace-loving creatures we like to think we are.

Two other motivational characteristics are major factors in our social structure. One is the capacity for altruism, which is fundamental to human nature. The other is a need for excitement when the social cocoon becomes too effective and causes boredom. We avoid intense fear but seek mild fear; and so with frustration (in mental or physical work) and disgust (we avoid outright obscenity but enjoy off-color jokes). The stability of society appears to require harmless sources of mild excitement. If harmless sources are not provided, harmful ones may be found.

GUIDE TO STUDY

Review and explain the differences between motivation and emotion in their relation to arousal. Make sure you understand the meaning of the inverted-U curve and why the shape of this curve may be different for a simple habit and a complex one.

Explain the relationship between the limbic system, the arousal system, and emotion, with respect particularly to grief and depression.

What parallel is there between the chimpanzee's fear of a model head and human disturbance at the sight of a badly mutilated human face? What other human sensitivities might be analogous?

Justify in psychological terms the idea that reading an adventure story is a mild form of fear-seeking, by relating this to feedback from cortex to arousal system.

Fear and anger are known to be related; is it possible that arousal is the same in both and that they differ only in the ideas that go with each (expectation of being hurt in one case, of hurting in the other)?

What evidence is there that prejudice need not be learned, though it is dependent on learning (chapter 7)?

How much weight would you give to chimpanzee evidence indicating that altruism is inherent in human nature?

NOTES AND GENERAL REFERENCES

Lindsley, D. B. (1951). *Emotion*. In S. S. Stevens (Ed.)., *Handbook of Experimental Psychology*, New York: Wiley.

Hebb, D. O., & Thompson, W. R. (1958). The social significance of animal studies. In G. Lindzey & E. Aronson (Eds.), *Handbook of Social Psychology*, Vol. 2. New York: Addison-Wesley.

Altruism

Kellogg, W. N. (1951). *Porpoises and Sonar*. Chicago: University of Chicago Press. See pp. 13–15.

Nissen, H. W., & Crawford, M. P. (1936). A preliminary study of foodsharing in young chimpanzees. *Journal of Comparative Psychology, 22*, 383–419.

Siebenthaler, J. B., & Caldwell, D. K. (1956). Cooperation among adult dolphins. *Journal of Mammology, 37*, 126–128.

Fear and Anger

Hebb, D. O. (1945). The forms and conditions of chimpanzee anger. *Bulletin of the Canadian Psychological Association, 5*, 32–35.

Jacobs, W. J., & Nadel, L. (1985). Stress-induced recovery of fears and phobias. *Psychological Review, 92*, 512–531.

Mental Disturbance

Jones, H. E., & Jones, M. C. A study of fear. *Childhood Education, 5*, 136–143.

Lapidus, L. B., & Schmolling, P. (1975). Anxiety, arousal and schizophrenia: A theoretical interpretation. *Psychological Bulletin, 82*, 689–710.

Mahut, H. (1958). Breed differences in the dog's emotional behavior. *Canadian Journal of Psychology, 12*, 35–44.

Marshall, S. L. A. (1947). *Men Against Fire*. New York: Morrow.

Melazck, R. (1952). Irrational fears in the dog. *Canadian Journal of Psychology, 6*, 141–147.

Tyhurst, J. S. (1951). Individual reactions to community disaster. *American Journal of Psychiatry, 107*, 764–769.

Need of Work

Bexton, W. H., Heron, W., & Scott, T. H. (1954). Effects of decreased variation in the sensory environment. *Canadian Journal of Psychology, 8*, 70–76.

Harlow, H. F. (1953). Mice, monkeys, men and motives. *Psychological Review, 60*, 23–32.

Hebb, D. O., & Mahut, H. (1955). Motivation et recherche du changement perceptif chez le rat et chez l'homme. *Journal de Psychologie Normale et Pathologique, 52*, 209–221. The report of rats seeking a more interesting route to food (Fig. 11.3).

Heron, W. (1967). The Pathology of Boredom. In J. L. McGaugh, N. M. Weinberger, & R. E. Whalen (Eds.), *Psychobiology*. San Francisco: W. H. Freeman.

CHAPTER 12

Sensation and Perception

Though they are closely related, sensation and perception are different. Sensory information may determine response in quite different ways. The information may be transmitted directly to muscle and gland, or it may be transmitted instead to the higher centers of the cortex and have its effect only by making changes in the activity that is going on at that cortical level. In the first case, the behavior is sense-dominated and does not depend on perception. In the second, the sensory information affects behavior only in conjunction with the concurrent cortical processes. Very often it has no immediate effect on behavior, but produces latent learning that may or may not have an effect at some later time.

Sensory information that does not reach the cortex does not reach consciousness; but some sensory information that reaches the cortex and influences ongoing cortical processes may also remain outside consciousness. Cortical activity is a necessary condition for consciousness, but it may not be sufficient. Cortical activity can be *conscious* or *unconscious*. Conscious cortical activity generated by sensory input is perception, but we shall see that cortical activity of which we remain unconscious can modify perception.

Sensation means the activity of receptors and the resulting activity of afferent paths to the corresponding sensory cortical area in mammals (or other highest point of afferent conduction in animals without a cortex). *Perception* is the activity of cortical mediating processes to which sensation gives rise (and here we assume that a mediating process is cell assembly activity). Where there are no mediating processes, there is no perception.

Sensation is, in effect, a one-stage process. Perception is characteristically sequential: started by a sensation, there is a preliminary motor reaction with feedback that adds further information, and perhaps a long series of such exploratory reactions, building up to one perception. Visual perception in general depends on complex eye movements; tactual perception, on movement of some part of the body (a hand, paw, snout, or beak is characteristically brought into play). Auditory perception of strange sounds usually involves head movement (and ear movement in lower mammals); also, it often deals with a series of stimuli, extended in time, which is especially evident in the perception of a melody or of speech. Taste, or gustatory perception, uses movements of lips and tongue; smell uses changes of breathing (i.e., sniffing), unless the substance to be identified is very familiar. In short, perceiving involves a sequence of events. Most past discussions of the problem have dealt with the apparently instantaneous identification of events in the environment—usually optical events—but this is a very misleading emphasis. With very familiar objects or events, no overt activity may be needed, and identification is apparently immediate. A single glance, one contact with the hand, is enough; no further investigatory movement is made. But even here, perception may consist of a temporal series of mediating processes instead of a single unitary event.

In summary, perception is a mediating-process activity that normally occurs with some preliminary responses, such as eye movement or touching. Obviously the feedback from them contributes essentially to the end product. With highly familiar things, perception may seem to occur instantaneously, but in some of these cases there may still be a serial order of events within the mediating processes even though it takes only milliseconds to reach completion. Perception is a preparation for response, just as *knowledge* is; in fact, knowledge is perception whose effects last for some period of time (see chapter 2). The response that is made depends on circumstances, and very often the "adequate response" is to do nothing. You see a leaf fall from a tree, or hear the dormitory phone ring, and if you do not collect leaves and are not on answering duty, the perception leads to no further action. But it is a real event and in each case there are many possible responses the perception might prepare you for. There is no one response called for by a perception, so we cannot think of it as an incomplete action. While it lasts, it is knowledge.

SENSORY STIMULATION

We saw in chapters 3 and 4 by what paths sensory information reaches the cortex and how information from different sources is sorted out and delivered to different cortical areas; not only, for example, separating vision from somesthesis, but also keeping one part of the visual field or one part of the skin surface separate from another. To understand sensation better, we need to take the story a bit further. First, the sense organs themselves.

Vision

The eye is both an optical instrument and part of the brain. Figure 12.1a shows the lens system (the cornea, which acts as a lens, and then the lens proper); the iris, which opens or closes to control the amount of light that enters; and the ciliary body, or ciliary muscle, which controls the curvature of the elastic lens and adjusts it to produce a good focus on the retina. (Its connection with the lens is not shown.) The retina is a thin sheet through which light passes easily to the light-sensitive cells at the back, which point away from the *pupil* (the aperture in the iris through which light enters). The light-sensitive cells are *rods* and *cones*. The rods are more sensitive to low light intensities. The three different types of cones respond selectively to different wave lengths (permitting color vision). Both rods and cones are neurons, connecting with an intermediate set of bipolar cells, which in turn connect with the ganglion cells, which send their axons over the surface of the retina to gather at one point as the *optic nerve* connecting with the rest of the brain. Figure 12.1b and c shows why the retina is part of the brain. The cells corresponding to sensory nerves are the rods and cones, which connect with bipolar cells in the same way that afferent neurons from the skin connect with spinal cord cells; thus the optic nerve is really a *tract* in the CNS, though it looks like a nerve.

Two other types of cell found in the retina, the horizontal and the amacrine cells, create a network of interconnections between the rods and cones and the ganglion cells in which preliminary analysis of the incoming sensory information provided by the rods and cones is carried out.

The *fovea* is a small depression in the center of the retina where cones are packed very tightly. It is the point of clearest (or central) vision, the point on the retina where the image of what one is looking at is focused. However, foveal vision is clearest only in normal lighting. The rods are the basis of "twilight vision" (being most sensitive at low

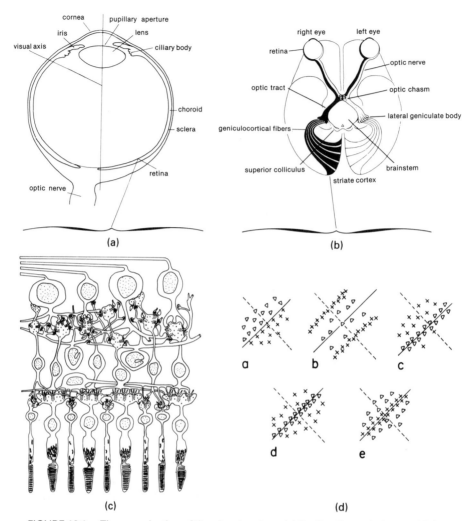

FIGURE 12.1.   The organization of the visual system. (a) Section through the eye. Light
enters the eye from the top, and is focused through the cornea and the lens to form an
image at the retina. The retina in this section is shown detached from the tissues at the
back of the eye to which it is normally firmly attached. (b) The retina is a tissue
consisting of sensory receptor cells (rods, R and cones, C) and other neurons:
amacrine cells, (A), bipolar cells (MB, RB, FB), horizontal cells (H), and ganglion cells
(DG, MG) which send axons through the optic nerve and optic tract to the lateral
geniculate nucleus of the brain. Light reaches the rods and cones, at the back of the
retina, from the top. (c) illustrates the crossed visual pathways in the human visual
system. Neurons (in black) from the left side of both retinas (sensing the right visual
field) project to the left lateral geniculate body, which transmits information to the left
visual cortex. (d) illustrates the receptive fields recorded from some cells in the visual
cortex. The triangles indicate areas from which a cell gives inhibitory "off" responses,
the crosses, areas from which a cell gives excitatory "on" responses. For all of these
cells, the optimum stimulus is an edge or line oriented at 45°. For a, the optimum is a
dark edge to the top; for b, a dark line on a light background; for c, a dark edge to the
bottom; for d, a dark line on a light background; and for e, a light line on a dark
background.

intensities), and they are not found in the fovea. Thus, at night one can see best by looking a little to one side of what one wants to see.

The *blind spot* results from the absence of rods or cones at the point where the fibers from the ganglion cells gather to form the optic nerve, on the nasal side of each retina. Close your right eye, look at some object across the room such as a doorknob, and then move your gaze slowly to the right but at the same level. The knob will disappear when your gaze is about 15° away from it, then reappear as you look still farther to the right. The horizontal and amacrine cells that connect across the retina, from bipolar cell to bipolar cell, may in some cases produce summation and in others inhibition. There is inhibition from each small retinal area to neighboring areas. Some inhibition may be caused by *efferent* fibers in the optic nerve—feedback from higher centers directly to retinal cells.

Our complex visual experience starts at the level of the optic tract, with sensory information from each ganglion cell (approximately six million of them) about a small portion of the visual scene being focused on the retina. Each ganglion cell leaving the retina through the optic tract is sensitive to its part of the visual scene in a complex way. For example, one ganglion cell will be affected by the difference between the light intensity reaching the center (a solid circle) and the surround (a ring surrounding the center) of some small area on the retina. If the center of the area is much brighter than the surround, the ganglion cell will be stimulated into activity; if the center is much less bright than the surround, the cell will be inhibited. To complicate matters even further, not only do the ganglion cells respond to their "own" small area of retina, but their response depends also on the general level of illumination, on the pattern of illumination, and on the different wavelengths of illumination, which are simultaneously reaching the rest of the retina.

It was mentioned earlier (chapter 3) that there are neurons in the visual cortex that are excited only by looking at a line or contour of a particular slope (D. H. Hubel and T. N. Wiesel, 1962). The phenomenon is explained as follows: A cortical neuron receives excitation from a number of retinal cells, arranged in a row. If a line of light falls along this row, the cortical neuron is fired because the light falls on the excitatory centers of all the cells in line. If the light falls across the row, it excites more of the inhibitory surrounds than the excitatory centers, and the cortical neuron does not fire (Fig. 12.1d). Cortical neurons with different connections, of course, will fire instead. There are plenty of retinal cells to permit such a specialization of connections, as the human eye has about a million cones and 37 million rods.

What Hubel and Wiesel (1962) describe is a sensory mechanism, as we use the term sensory here. No mediating processes are involved. Somewhat similar mechanisms account for visual selectivity in frogs without our having to suppose that frogs are perceiving and conscious. The frog will attack—flick out a tongue at—any small moving objects, avoiding larger ones (J. Y. Lettvin et al, 1959). In this way, he catches flies for a living. The frog retina contains receptive areas made up of small groups of *on* cells surrounded by *off* cells. The retina is connected directly with motor centers in the brain stem and can thus control a directed reflex response in the frog. In humans, there is a direct motor connection with the *superior colliculus* as well as with the visual cortex. A baby's eyes shortly after birth tend to follow a bright light reflexively. R. L. Fantz (1961) has shown that the baby will scan visual objects and spend more time looking at some than at others. This "preference" suggests that the newborn may be perceiving, aware of the visual environment, but the behavior can also be explained as a reflex. The method used by P. Salapatek and W. Kessen (1966) is shown in Fig. 12.2, where the baby lying on his back sees a triangle above him.

Hearing

The activity of the ear is less observable than that of the eye, its sensory mechanism being buried deep in the petrous ("rocky") bone of the cranium. It took correspondingly longer to work out the principles of its operation. The outer ear we know; essentially it is a funnel to direct sound waves on to the eardrum. The *middle ear* is a cavity filled with air and connected with the mouth by the eustachian tube, which permits air pressure inside to stay the same as that outside (Fig. 12.3a). Swallowing opens the tube, which is why swallowing relieves ear discomfort when air pressure changes in an airplane. Three small bones, or ossicles, transmit sound vibrations from the eardrum to the "oval window," the entry to the *inner ear.* Here things become more complicated.

The inner ear has two functions: hearing and helping to maintain balance by sensing head movement. It is filled with a fluid throughout its two parts, the *cochlea* (for hearing) and the *vestibule* (for balance). The cochlea is a coiled tube (hence the name, which is Latin for snail shell) as can be seen coiled in Fig. 12.3a; it is schematized, uncoiled, in Fig. 12.3b. The vestibular system on each side contains three semicircular canals lying in three planes at right angles to one another, so that any movement of the head makes the fluid move in at least one of the canals. One canal is shown schematically in Fig. 12.3b, and the relation of the three to the head is shown in Fig. 12.3c.

The three tiny bones (ossicles) of the middle ear (hammer, anvil and

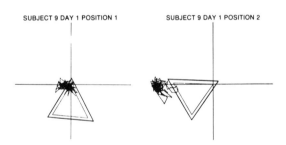

FIGURE 12.2. Recording eye movements in the newborn baby exposed to a large solid black triangle in the "ceiling" above: 25 cm from the baby's eyes. The triangle was 20 cm on the side, and was presented in two orientations, as shown in the two records of eye movements below (for the same baby). (From Salapatek & Kessen, 1966. Reproduced by permission.)

stirrup, or malleus, incus and stapes) transmit vibrations from the eardrum to the fluid of the cochlea, which then produces movement of the *basilar membrane* on which the receptors for hearing are found. Low frequencies of vibration produce deformations (movements) of the upper end of the basilar membrane; high frequencies, deformations of the lower end (Bekesy, 1957). At lower frequencies (less than about 3000 Hz [cycles per second]), some of the receptors on the basilar membrane are stimulated with each cycle of membrane movement. A primary cue to pitch is found in the locus of stimulation on the basilar membrane, which means that different fibers in the auditory nerve are

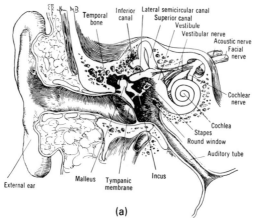

(a)

FIGURE 12.3a. Visualization of the structures of the ear. "Tympanic membrane" equals eardrum. The middle ear is the cavity containing the three ossicles, malleus being attached to the eardrum and transmitting (with magnification) its movements via incus and stapes to the "oval window" (not shown) and the fluid of the inner ear. "Auditory tube" equals eustachian tube. "Superior canal" is one of the three semicircular canals. (E. Gardner, *Fundamentals of Neurology,* Saunders.)

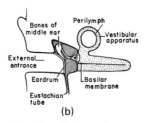

(b)

FIGURE 12.3b. Schematic representation of the ear, showing the bones
that connect the eardrum with the inner ear, the basilar membrane that
carries the auditory receptors, and the
cavity of bone filled with fluid (peri-
lymph) which is continuous with the
fluid of the semicircular canals, one of
these being shown schematically. The
eustachian tube connects with the
mouth, permitting air pressure in the
middle ear to be equalized with external air pressure. The basilar membrane and the tube-like hollow of bone
in which it lies are not straight as
shown in the figure, but coiled like a
snailshell. (After G. v. Békésy, in S. S.
Stevens [Ed.], date, *Handbook of Experimental Psychology,* Wiley.)

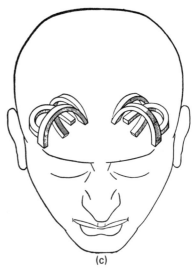

(c)

FIGURE 12.3c. Schematic representation of the three semicircular canals
on each side of the head, showing
how on each side one canal is oriented
in each of three planes: the horizontal
plane and two vertical planes which
intersect at right angles.

266

active in response to tones of different pitches. Another cue is the pulses of nerve impulses from the basilar membrane that follow the frequency of vibrations of the sound waves up to about 3000 Hz.

In each of the six semicircular canals—three on each side—there is a small protuberance, or *cupula*, which is believed to move when the fluid in the canal moves. Disturbing the cupula excites nerve endings contained in it, providing one of the two cues of *proprioception* or *kinesthesis*: the sensation of movement. (The other kind of cue comes from nerve endings in the muscles, tendons, and joints that are stimulated when a muscle contracts and produces a change in the position of one bone with respect to another.) The semicircular canals are stimulated by any movement of the head, but their activity comes particularly to one's attention in the dizziness produced by rapid rotation or rapid irregular movements. The canals are connected directly to the eye muscles. If you roll down a steep grassy bank or rotate rapidly on a piano stool long enough to produce dizziness, you will see the world rotating around you after you stop: the semicircular canals continue to stimulate the eye muscles so that the eyes continue to move, and thus the world seems to be rotating. These eye movements are easily seen by another person. Seasickness, airsickness, and carsickness are due also to overstimulation of the canals.

Skin Senses

The skin is a sense organ, although we do not usually think of it as such. It contains free nerve endings as well as some specialized organs that surround nerve endings and influence the response to vibration and sustained pressure. The skin has four main sensory functions: *touch*, *pain*, *warmth*, and *cold*. The adequate stimulus for touch is not merely contact with the skin, but enough pressure to bend it (if only to a slight degree) or bend a hair. The hairs provide the most sensitive mechanism, each hair having a nerve ending coiled around its base and being stiff enough to act as a lever. The pain referred to is the sensory component of the total process; there is also a component that is emotional rather than sensory (chapter 10). Warmth and cold will be discussed shortly.

Sensory Coding

We have seen that the nervous system can keep different sensory messages distinct from each other by keeping them on separate lines to the cortex. How are the messages kept distinct? Stimulation of the optic nerve always produces visual perception. Sensation from the left foot never gets mixed up with sensation from the right hand. These facts are summarized as the *law of specific energies*. It does not matter how the optic nerve is stimulated. Applying pressure or passing an electric current through it still makes the subject "see" light; the optic nerve is "specific" for visual perception, once it is activated. And, clearly, the specificity is because the nerve leads to the visual cortex. Stimulation of this region is enough, by itself, to produce the effect. A blow on the head that stimulates the visual cortex mechanically makes one "see stars"; the surgeon operating on the brain of a conscious patient applies electrical stimulation to the occipital cortex, and the patient reports seeing a light—though his eyes may be closed and there is in fact no activation of the sense organ. So-called visual awareness, then, consists of the activity of certain paths beginning in the visual cortex; auditory awareness is an activity beginning in the auditory cortex; and so on. The difference between these processes, their distinctivness, is evidently related to the fact that each sense organ connects with a different region in the brain. The routes involved in tactual perception are separate from those of auditory or visual perception. A difference between two perceptions means the possibility of making distinctive responses; this is easy to understand if the sensory excitations reach different parts of the brain, and thus have clearly separate paths from receptor to effector.

The same separation of routes occurs within a single sensory system. We have already seen that each part of the retina is connected with its own part of the visual cortex: the existence of these different pathways within the visual system helps to account for the subject's ability to make different responses to stimuli in different parts of the visual field. A person *knows* what direction a light is coming from, whether he responds to it or not. This means that if further stimulation of various kinds occurs, one can point to it or direct one's gaze toward it or tell you where the light is. Similarly, there are separate paths within the somesthetic system for different parts of the body. The subject knows when he is touched on the hand; if the stimulus is strong enough to produce a response, it is the hand that is likely to move. But specificity in sensation goes further than is accounted for by a complete separation of routes.

Two sensory messages may use the same incoming lines and still be completely sorted out at higher levels in the CNS. This is achieved by *coding* the frequency pattern of the impulses. There are four subjectively different tastes: sweet, sour, salt, and bitter. Other tastes can be described as a blend of these four. Each taste sensation can be produced by a single stimulus substance or class or substances: sugars for sweet, dilute acids for sour, salts for salt, and quinine for bitter. But there is no single nerve fiber reaching the brain from the tongue that responds by firing to only one of these tastes. All fibers respond to each class of substance. Only the rate of firing to each class differs from one fiber to the other. The information that the brain receives about something stimulating the taste buds on the tongue is contained in the rates of firing of many nerve fibers. Since some fibers respond more strongly to salt than to sour, the presence of salt is signalled by the relative rate of firing of one neuron compared to another, not by a single nerve fiber. A comparison process among firing frequencies must be responsible for the final sensation as it is experienced.

The specificity of sensory input is due primarily to the existence of separate routes from different parts of the sensory surfaces. Secondarily it is due to the patterning and timing of impulses. Two different inputs may use, at least in part, the same afferent lines. But if they do, they must be sorted out at a higher level. If the organism can respond differentially to two sensory events, either by giving them different names (i.e., making distinctive verbal responses) or by acting in one case to maintain the stimulation and in the other to discontinue it, then at some point in the nervous system there is a separation of the two processes.

SPACE PERCEPTION

A fundamental function of perception is to inform the perceiver about spatial relations, and in particular about the direction and distance of objects. The classical problem of visual space perception concerns *depth:* how far away is the object that is seen? It seems easy to understand how one can perceive the direction of an object—from the direction in which the eyes must be turned in order to see it clearly. But the retina functions as a two-dimensional surface (even though it is a curved surface), like a photographic plate at the back of a camera. Why does the world not look flat, like a photograph? Why is visual depth so immediate and inescapable? There is also auditory space perception— it is possible in the proper circumstances to *hear* where something is and how far away, even if it makes no noise itself—and this too has been a puzzle.

Visual Space

Accommodation, convergence and *disparity* are cues to visual depth. The least effective is accommodation, the degree of curvature of the crystalline lens that is necessary to produce a good focus on the retina. The necessary curvature increases as objects are brought closer to the eye, within a range of about 2 meters. The lens is elastic, and its curvature is reflexively controlled by the ciliary muscle. The amount of tension in the muscle that is necessary to focus the image, and the resulting proprioceptive sensation (sensory feedback), is one cue to depth. This cue is effective up to about 2 meters from the eye.

Another cue (also for near distances) is the convergence of the two eyes, which is necessary if the image of an object is to be projected on the fovea in both eyes. For far objects the axes of the eyeballs are parallel; for near objects the axes cross, and the sensed position of the eyes in their sockets becomes a cue to the distance of the object looked at. This is effective for distances up to perhaps 7 meters.

Retinal disparity, or *parallax*, refers to the difference in the retinal images that are formed when an object is seen from different angles. Binocular disparity occurs when an object is observed with both eyes open, because the eyes, separated in space, necessarily see the object from different angles. You can demonstrate this for yourself by holding a pencil so that it points directly at your nose, at a distance of 20 to 30 centimeters. By closing first one eye and then the other, you will find that the two eyes have distinctly different views of the pencil, one seeing the point and the right side, the other the point and the left side.

Movement disparity works with either one eye or two: one gets very different views of a three-dimensional object or scene as one moves the head from side to side or up and down.

Both forms of disparity have a strong effect on the perception of the third dimension. The effect of binocular disparity is demonstrated best in the *stereoscope*, a device that presents different photographs simultaneously. One photograph is seen by the right eye; the other, made from a viewpoint slightly to the left, is seen by the left eye. The eyes then deliver to the same parts of the visual area in the brain slightly different patterns of excitation. Instead of two conflicting two-dimensional scenes, a single scene is perceived in depth. The brain integrates the discordant patterns and adds a dimension in so doing.

There are a number of other cues to depth (Fig. 12.4a): the smaller retinal angle of familiar objects farther away; the overlap of near objects over farther ones, partly hiding them; the loss of fine detail in farther objects, their change of color (increasing blueness) when distances become great. But all these cues apply to a single object (or two overlapping objects) without regard to the surrounding environment; and up to this point your reading might suggest that in judging the distance of an object all one takes into account is the appearance of that object. In fact, except when dealing with objects flying or floating in the

(a)

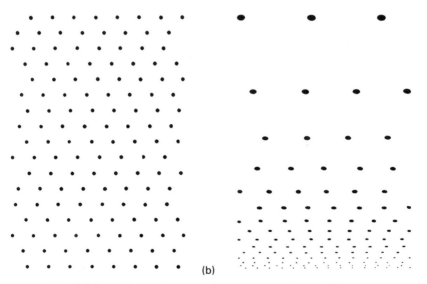

(b)

FIGURE 12.4. (a) Several natural monocular cues to depth are visible in this photograph: aerial perspective, texture gradients, interposition and elevation. (b) Gradients of visual texture—of size and spacing—give the "frontal" (nonreceding) surface. (From Gibson, 1950. Reproduced by permission.)

271

air, all judgments concern objects that are connected with (supported by) extended surfaces, such as the ground, walls of buildings, ceilings, and so on. These background surfaces have a most important influence on perception (Julesz & Bergen, 1983). As they move away from us, they show gradients of *visual texture*, the units into which the surface is divided (Fig. 12.4b; Fig 12.5) and the irregularities within the units (not shown in the figures). These gradients provide cues to the direction of slope of the surface, with respect to the line of vision, and thus provide cues to the size and distance of objects close to or touching the surfaces (Gibson, 1950).

Auditory Space

The design of the auditory system permits discrimination of frequency, intensity, and time differences but nothing else. Just as the visual system uses binocular disparity and other cues to produce depth

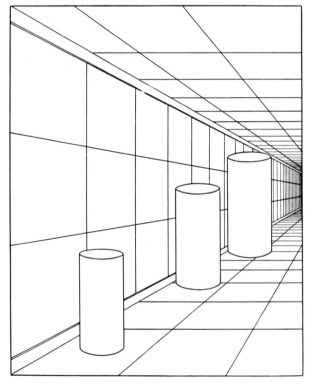

FIGURE 12.5. Perception of size and distance of objects as related to receding surfaces. The three cylinders are drawn to the same size. (From Gibson, 1950. Reproduced by permission.)

discimination, so the auditory system uses the cues of frequency, intensity, and time differences to produce discriminations of direction and distance that in some cases are surprisingly accurate. Sound travels at a low speed (about 335 meters per second, compared with 299,792 km per second for light). The time of transmission from a sound source, then, becomes a factor in discrimination, a slight advantage for the ear over the eye. Another factor is that *sound shadows* (blocking of sound waves by an interposed object) are selective: long waves are not blocked; short waves are. With light the blocking is practically complete. Suppose that a complex sound, made up of high (short-wave) tones and low (long-wave) tones, comes from the subject's left side. His left ear gets both high and low tones, but his right ear is in the sound shadow cast by the head, so the right ear gets the low tones, but little of the high ones. This binaural discrepancy is a cue to which side the sound source is on. With high-pitched sounds, also, the sound shadow cast by the outer ear makes possible a discrimination of front from back.

The most important cues to direction, the ones that tend to dominate, are the relative times of arrival at the two ears and the relative intensity of the sounds at each ear. Ordinarily these two cues work together, but it has been found experimentally that either is effective alone, other cues being held constant, although the time factor is the more important of the two. If a sound reaches both ears simultaneously and with the same intensity, the source must be equally distant from them: that is, it must lie in the median plane, directly in front, above, or behind the head. If it reaches the right ear first, it must be on the right side, but with a low pitched sound (where the shadow of the outer ear is not effective). There is no cue to whether the sound source is higher or lower, front or back. This in fact is the situation with a momentary sound, when echoes (reflections from the ground, walls, or other surfaces) are excluded. But with a continuing sound, or one that is repeated, the subject tilts his head and at once can discriminate up from down; or turns his head to one side and discriminates front from back. (Here is an example of the importance of response for auditory perception, not unlike the importance of eye movement for visual perceptions.)

The discrimination of the times of arrival of a sound at the two ears is astonishingly fine. The time differences involved are of the order of one or two tenths of a millisecond. The same fine discrimination affects the perception of auditory depth. A sound made near one ear produces a binaural difference in time of arrival of something under a millisecond; farther away, the difference is slightly less, yet this difference permits reliable judgments of distance. Echoes are also very important. The subject can judge the distance of a reflecting surface by the time difference between hearing a noise that he makes himself and its echo: about two milliseconds for each 30 cm of distance. Many animals and birds have developed similar auditory skill. The bat is the best known example. When flying it emits very high-pitched sounds and is guided by the echoes, so that it can fly among a number of obstacles without hitting any of them, even when its eyes are completely covered. If the ears are covered, the ability is lost.

The same cue tells us when we are about to bump into something in the dark. This is sometimes a very puzzling experience: Without knowing how, we suddenly realize that some large object is in front of us. The object is detected by means of the echoes of the sound of our footsteps or our breathing. It is easy to show that we are dealing with auditory space perception in this case, because the ability disappears when the ears are plugged. This ability, of course, becomes very important in blindness. When a blind person taps a cane hard on the sidewalk, it is not to feel for obstacles; it is to set up echoes from nearby objects. The echoes locate the blind person with respect to those objects.

We do not of course perceive the echoes as separate events, estimate their time of arrival, and on the basis of the time differences in milliseconds work out the direction and distance of an obstacle, any more than we see visual depth as a result of conscious calculations about retinal disparities. There is instead an automatic transformation of the sensory stimulation into the perception of an object, as a preparation for further response.

DISTINGUISHING PERCEPTION FROM SENSATION

The clearest evidence that perception is more than a complex sensation is the fact that one sensory stimulation can give rise to completely distinct perceptions, and different stimulations can give rise to the same perception. All our knowledge of the sensory process says that the same stimulation produces the same activity in the sensory cortex time after time, but the evidence is quite clear that it need not produce the same perception.

The classical demonstration of variability in perception with the same stimulation may be observed by looking at Fig. 12.6a (also see Fig. 2.7). These are *ambiguous figures*, a conception that we owe to the Danish psychologist E. Rubin (1921). Figure 12.6a may be seen as either a bird bath or a vase, or as two faces. Keep your eyes fixed between the two noses (or in the center of the bird bath). The reversal, the change from one perception to the other, does not require eye movement,

(a) Ambiguous or reversible figure. (After Rubin, 1921. Reproduced by permission.)

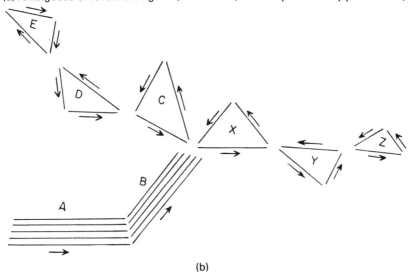

(b)

(b) Schematic representation of an explanation of the reversal of the ambiguous figure. A, B, afferent conduction (in parallel); C, X, alternating assembly actions. It is assumed that C inhibits X and vice versa. C-D-E constitutes one perception; X-Y-Z another (these assemblies must lie intertangled in the same regions of the brain, not spatially separated as above).

FIGURE 12.6.

though the movement definitely permits a clearer perception and affects the rate of reversal. The significance of this observation is that two very different perceptions can occur with the same sensory input.

Nothing in the sensory process itself accounts for this "flip-flop" action. Slow, steady changes might be intelligible, but not the discontinuous alternation of two distinctly different perceptions. But alternation becomes intelligible with the mechanism diagrammed in Fig. 12.6b, which assumes that the two perceptions consist of different sets of cell assembly actions, each preventing activity in the other.

More evidence for the role of mediating processes (cell assemblies) lies in the fact that while a *real* ambiguous stimulus can generate either one of two (or more) ambiguous perceptions, an *imagined* ambiguous stimulus only generates one percept, without the reversals which occur when looking at the real ambiguous stimulus (Chambers and Reisberg, 1985). The real ambiguous stimulus activates alternative cell-assemblies in sequence. The imagined stimulus is perceived when one of the alternative cell-assemblies is activated by another mediating process (cell assembly). Only one of the cell-assembly alternatives corresponding to the ambiguous figure is activated, and there is no sensory input to support activation of the other cell-assembly alternative. As a consequence, only one aspect of the imagined ambiguous figure is perceived.

Figure 12.6 also illustrates the *figure-ground phenomenon*. The *figure* is the region in the total configuration that is perceived at the moment, the rest being *ground* (the alternation that occurs with Fig. 12.6 can thus be described as an alternating figure-ground relation). When the vase is being perceived, the space in the center of the figure appears closer and, in a vague way, more solid. When perception shifts to the two faces, the central space recedes and the two lateral spaces appear closer.

The figure-ground relation is fundamental in the perception of objects and regions of space. The unity of simple, clearly demarcated figures is present in first vision, as far as can be determined from the behavior of the congenitally blind who are given sight at maturity. With such objects, then, the figure-ground relation is independent of experience, but it also seems that with other figures it is much more a function of experience and that the kind of variability in the figure-ground relation that is demonstrated in Fig. 12.6 increases as a result of perceptual learning.

Variability is a general property of perception, not found only with such special stimulus patterns as Fig. 12.6. The ambiguous figure is significant only because it provides an especially clear case. If you fix your eyes on some point of your environment, you will find yourself perceiving sometimes this detail, sometimes that, sometimes the larger scene instead of details; and so on. If you look even at as simple a diagram as Fig. 12.7 you will still find that perception is sometimes of the crookedness of a line, sometimes of the gap at the lower right; sometimes of the whole triangle or perhaps of a badly formed "4." With the dots of Fig. 12.7b you will see sometimes the areas between them, and so on. The sensory input sets limits on what may be perceived—there is no chance that the perception of Fig. 12.7a will be identical with that of Fig. 12.7b—but within these limits variability is pronounced. The constancy of perception with a given sensory stimulation consists of a frequent recurrence of the process that is "the" perception, rather than the maintenance of a single process.

Constancy

Brightness and *size constancy* are two important examples where the stimulus varies while the perception remains the same. Brightness constancy refers to the obvious fact that a white object looks white whether it is in the light or in shadow. In fact, this is rather surprising. On first consideration, "white" means that an object reflects much light; "black," that it reflects little light. A lump of coal lying in the sunlight reflects much more light than a piece of white paper in a deep shadow, yet the coal still looks black and the paper white. What is

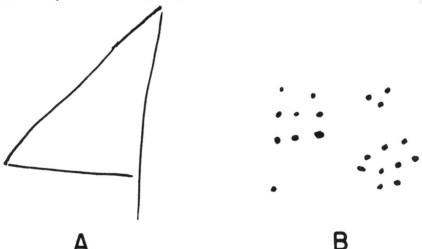

A   **B**

FIGURE 12.7. Variability and structure in perception. The visual stimuli in A and B provide a sensory basis for perception; changes of attention modify the perception from moment to moment.

actually involved here is a phenomenon of *contrast:* though the coal reflects the light, it reflects much less than surrounding objects. When one arranges experimentally to focus intense light on a shiny piece of coal, and *only* on it (e.g., by fastening it with sealing wax to the end of a piece of wire and suspending it in the middle of a room with no other surface near it to be equally illuminated), the coal becomes a brilliant silver in appearance. A piece of white paper in a dark shadow, seen through a reduction screen (which does not permit one to see the surroundings), becomes a dark gray. In ordinary circumstances, where contrast effects are not prevented, white paper moved in and out of a shadow does not appear to change its color but is perceived as white under both conditions: two different conditions of stimulation, but the same perception with respect to the color of the paper.

Size constancy is equally familiar, and equally surprising when one considers what is happening. Visual size is basically dependent on retinal angle of projection; but it is also related to the perception of visual *depth* (i.e., distance from the eye), as shown by the fact that one's hand does not seem to be larger when it is 15 cm from the eye than when it is 30 cm from the eye. (If there is any difference, it is slight.) Yet a hand at the 15 cm distance has a retinal projection approximately twice as great as at the 30 cm distance. A picture on the wall does not appear to expand and contract as one moves closer or farther away; the face of a friend across the table does not appear three or four times as large as that of another friend at the far end of the room. This is size constancy. The constancy is not absolute, and at great distances apparent size is sharply decreased. Also, for some reason, the constancy is much less marked with objects seen in the vertical dimension (up or down). A related phenomenon is the moon illusion, which makes the moon on the horizon seem larger than the same moon at the zenith.

Another instance of the same perception resulting from different stimulations is the *phi-phenomenon,* the perception of motion in moving pictures and illuminated signs. This now commonplace phenomenon involves a really remarkable transformation between what happens on the sensory surface and what happens in perception.

In Fig. 12.8 two light sources are represented. A is lighted for 200 milliseconds; 60 msec after it has been extinguished, B is lighted for 200 msec. Instead of two lights, one after the other, the observer sees a single light that *moves all the way* from A to B. This is the phi-phenomenon. If the interval is too short, two lights are seen simultaneously; if it is too long, two lights are seen one after the other, without movement. The timing that produces the effect varies with the intensity of the lights and the angular distance between them. A number of suggestions have been offered to account for the phenomenon in

FIGURE 12.8.   A demonstration of the phi-phenomenon. Light A goes on, then off; a fraction of a second later B goes on and off. With proper timing, the subject sees, instead of two lights, a single one that moves from one locus to the other.

physiological terms, but as yet there is no satisfactory explanation. It cannot be accounted for by eye movement from A to B because, with two pairs of lights, apparent movement can be perceived simultaneously in opposite directions.

How is all this to be dealt with in objective terms? What does it mean when a subject reports that he sees a light move, under the experimental conditions of Fig. 12.8? It means, simply, that these conditions of stimulation produce, at some level in the brain, the same process that is produced by a light that does move from A to B. There is no reason to conclude that there is any movement of an excitation in the visual cortex from one point to another; indeed, it seems certain there is not. The probability is that events in the sensory cortex follow the course of retinal excitation faithfully, and there is of course no excitation moving across the retina. We can conclude that the same cell assembly activities are aroused either when the retina is stimulated by a light moving from A to B or when the two corresponding points are stimulated with the proper timing. *Sensation* in the two cases differs; *percpetion* is the same. Both are theoretical constructs, events inferred from our knowledge of anatomy and physiology and from the repsonses made by the subject.

What does it mean when with Fig. 12.7b a number of dots appear to be a unified group, a single entity? We can interpret this as signifying that the processes aroused in some part of the brain are the same as would be aroused by a single object occupying the same space.

PERCEPTION AND CONSCIOUSNESS

There are many natural phenomena that we cannot sense directly at all, although other animals sense some of them. Ultraviolet light is one such phenomenon. We do not directly sense electromagnetic waves just shorter than those we experience as blue-violet. Bees are sensitive to ultraviolet light and so can make sensory discriminations on the basis of ultraviolet light which we cannot make. Similarly, pigeons are sensitive to the direction and the inclination of the earth's magnetic field, but we are not. The world we perceive is limited by the phenomena we can sense. These limits are not the same for all animals. We do not have a universal and direct perception of all there is to know about nature. Nor do we have a universal and direct perception of all there is to know about ourselves.

Perception Without Awareness

Perception derives from the activity of mediating processes or cell assemblies. We are not directly aware of cell assembly activity, nor are we directly aware of all of the sensory inputs that stimulate our receptors. Both sensory and perceptual activity can affect behavior without becoming conscious.

The most striking example of a sensory effect without conscious awareness is "blind sight." People who suffer injury to the occipital cortex may develop total blindness or blindness limited to a part of the visual field, depending on the extent of the injury. By blindness we mean the absence of conscious or self-reported visual experience; nothing corresponding to normal vision is experienced from the part of the world projected to the damaged cortical tissue (see chapter 3, Fig. 3.5). A person rendered blind or partially blind by this kind of injury cannot "see" in the affected visual field, cannot read and cannot recognize objects or people.

But damage to the occipital cortex does not destroy all of the neural tracts from the retina to the brain. There are tracts that go from the retina, then to the lateral geniculate body, and then to the brain stem nucleus called the superior colliculus. This is a center where input from the visual system reaches subcortical neurons. Experiments have shown that eye movements can be produced by stimulating cells in this nucleus.

Although patients with occipital damage have no conscious awareness of visual function in the affected area, the following fascinating experiment can be carried out with the cooperation of a blind patient who has suffered occipital damage. A light is presented to the patient within the part of the visual field that used to project the damaged cortical area. The patient, of course, indicates no awareness of the light, asserting that he or she "saw nothing." Nevertheless, the experimenter persists. "Guess," the experimenter asks, "where a flash might have been if you had seen it." Agreeing to the experimenter's bizarre request, the patient points "haphazardly" to some place in the visual field that projects into the damaged area. "If I had seen a light, which I didn't, maybe it was there," the patient responds. The surprise is that the patient's answer is correct far more often than if it had just been a chance guess. In other words, without being aware (conscious) of the visual input, the patient confirms through his or her *behavior* the existence of the sensory input. Thus visual sensory input may have direct control over behavior even when it does not enter consciousness.

In "blind sight," only sensory processes are involved. The retinal pathway to the superior colliculus carries information about where the light was, but not what it was. Responding to a simple sensory cue for position may not require conscious perception in a normal person either—but in someone with an intact occipital cortex, sensory position response occurs along with conscious perception produced by cortical activity.

The following example demonstrates that conscious perception in a normal person can also be influenced by sensory input which does not itself enter consciousness. The experiment is this: A word with a strong emotional meaning, like "cancer" or "failure" or "danger," is presented aurally (to the ear) to an observer at a sound intensity far below what preliminary testing shows is needed to consciously hear it. The subject's job is to detect visually a neutral word presented in a low-level light so that it is hard to see. The result is that it becomes harder to detect the visual neutral word when the emotional word is presented to the ear, even at an intensity where the emotional word cannot be consciously heard. The emotional meaning of the aurally presented word depends on a cortical analysis based on learning. Yet it has an effect on perception at a stimulus intensity far too low to be heard (too low even to make the subject aware that there was anything to be heard). At this low intensity, the cell assemblies that store the word's meaning are activated, and these cell assemblies, acting through the limbic system and the arousal system (see chapter 10 and 11) directly affect the conscious perception of the unrelated neutral word. The same thing can be shown to happen when emotional stimuli are presented visually, at exposures and intensities far too low to produce conscious awareness of the stimuli (Dixon, 1981; Silverman and Weinberger, 1985).

In the "blind sight" example, the intact superior colliculus is a relatively simple sensory system operating without activating the cortex. In the detection threshold example, the mediating processes that changed the detectability of the neutral visual word were certainly cortical, since they concerned a learned skill: identifying the meaning of arbitrary combinations of letters. This means that the observers were not conscious of the sensory input that activated the cell assemblies and modified their behavior.

ORGANIZATION IN PERCEPTION

Now we turn to some further experimental evidence of the complexity of perception, showing that it has an internal structure. Perception was defined as the activity of mediating processes, and we will look first at an experiment in auditory perception (Broadbent, 1954).

Human subjects wore earphones through which were simultaneously delivered two series of three spoken digits, one series to the right ear, one to the left. The digits were separated by intervals of half a second. The right ear might receive 3-7-5, for example, at the same time that the left ear received 8-2-9. The 3 and the 8 would be heard at precisely the same time, and so with 7 and 2, and 5 and 9. The subjects could correctly report all the digits they heard on 62% of the trials, which itself is an interesting result. But more interesting is that in 157 out of 160 trials the subjects of their own accord (i.e., without being instructed to do so) reported the whole series for one ear, in the proper order, before reporting the series for the other ear. In this sort of experiment, subjects report that they hear the digits as two separate sets, one in each ear: they do not hear one set of six digits, which then must be sorted out in thought, but *perceive* them sorted out. The perception is not a loose aggregation of sensory events but is organized to maintain order both in time (the sequence of digits) and space (the ear in which the digits were heard).

A different line of experiment throws light on the organization of visual perception. About 1952, Ditchburn and Riggs discovered independently that stabilizing the image of a line on the retina leads to its rapid disappearance. In normal vision there is always some tremor of the eye muscles. Consequently the retinal image of something looked at, even when one tries to look steadily with no movement of the eyes, is never quite still. There is always some slight variation in the rods and cones that are excited. However, there are several ways of preventing this variation. One way is to use a very small object as target and mount it on a short stalk fastened to a contact lens worn by the subject. Another tiny lens is attached so that the target can be seen and focused on without effort even though it is very close to the eye (Fig. 12.9a). When the eyeball moves, the target—the object looked at—moves with it, and the image is stabilized on the retina. In these circumstances, a straight line will disappear in perhaps 10 to 20 seconds. With more complex figures, part or all may disappear (Pritchard, Heron & Hebb, 1960). This is illustrated in Fig. 12.9b.

The same kind of disappearances are obtained with luminous figures in a dark room (McKinney, 1963) or figures drawn with black lines in a *ganzfeld*—an evenly lighted field extending to the periphery in all directions so that the black lines are the only visual objects. The main difference is that disappearances may not occur as quickly as with the stabilized image. The effect can easily be observed if one draws an outline figure such as a triangle on a sheet of cardboard with luminous paint and then in a dark room looks steadily at one point in the figure. Disappearances do not occur if one moves one's eyes from point to point in the diagram. The disappearances are all-or-none, a whole line or whole figure disappearing at once, though there is some fading first. It seems that the disappearances can be explained as the sudden cessation of the activity in cell asemblies that constitutes perception.

If these disappearances are caused by cell assembly activity, then it should be possible to modify the pattern of disappearances. Cell assemblies are learned, and new learning should change the pattern of disappearance. Learning does have an effect. If two parts of a luminous pattern are associated with a common response word, their disappearances occur simultaneously, whereas the disappearances of parts associated with different response words are uncorrelated. The correlation between parts appearing or disappearing together in time is the result of a new cell assembly linkage brought about by the learning of verbal responses to the visual stimuli. The evidence clearly supports the theory of cell assemblies, which proposed originally that the perception of a triangle, for example, is a composite and that the perception of one side or one angle is the activity of a separate cell assembly. The assembly functions as a system, its reverberatory activity allowing the neurons in the system to support each other's firing. Some neurons in the cell assembly may fatigue and drop out while the reverberation continues, but a point will be reached at which one too many has dropped out and then the reverberation will cease suddenly. The line first fades, then suddenly disappears completely.

However, even if the theory is, as it seems, on the right track, it is not yet completely satisfactory. When a different kind of figure is seen with stabiliization, such as a solid square, the disappearance is not all-or-none but gradual. Cell assembly theory says that perception is a complex of *unitary* processes; it cannot account for the graded disappearance of a solid square. There are other related difficulties from the same set of experiments.

The difficulties may perhaps be handled by assuming that an assembly consists of a number of subassemblies, temporarily functioning as a single system. A subassembly might be as small as one of Lorente de No's closed loops (Fig. 4.7). However, this has not been worked out in detail.

The stabilized-image experiment does show that an object such as a square or triangle, which may seem to the perceiver to be a completely

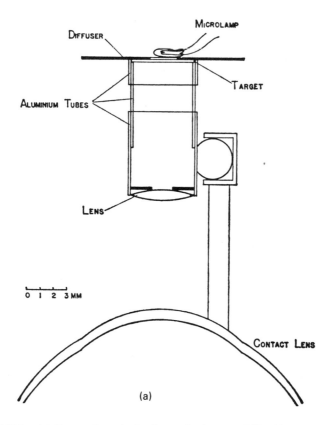

FIGURE 12.9. (a) Contact lens device for projecting a stabilized image on the retina. The target is a photographic negative like (i), (ii), (iii), or (iv) in (b). The image of the target quickly fragments into parts as indicated in the panels in (b) to the right, illustrating typical configurations reported by observers at different times during the observations.

simple unitary event, may actually be a complex that under the right conditions can be broken down into constituent parts. Next we will see that certain evidence from the memory image enables us to carry this analysis a step or two further.

Memory Images

There are several varieties of images: the afterimage referred to in chapter 1; the memory image and the closely related eidetic image; hypnagogic image; and hallucination. The *afterimage* (Fig. 12.10a) is an effect that follows immediately on intense or prolonged stimulation. A

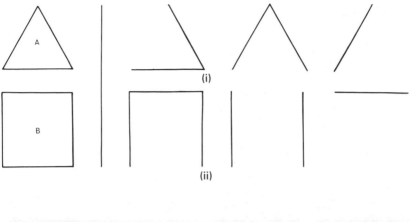

(i)

(ii)

(iii)

(iv)

(b)

memory image is the reinstatement of a perception, as a form of recall; an *eidetic image* is an exceptionally vivid memory image that occurs immediately after the perception (but is not an afterimage). *Hypnagogic imagery*, which usually occurs before one goes to sleep (hence the name hypnagogic), is a prolonged reinstatement of some unusual activity that occurred during the day; it is like a moving afterimage except that it may occur hours after the unusual experience has ceased. *Hallucination* is any strongly convincing imagery of central origin; it is due to spontaneous firing of cortical and subcortical neurons.

—like skiing on roller coaster

Afterimage.   The afterimage is distinct from the others in being under sensory control. When you stare at an image formed from a bright

(a)   (b)

FIGURE 12.10.   (a) For a demonstration of the negative afterimage. Stare at one point
in the picture while counting slowly to 40. A good point to look at is the inner corner of
the person's right eye (on your left as you look at the picture). Then look at a sheet of
white paper. The negative afterimage will appear. It may not at first; if so, stare for 40
seconds at the same point again, not moving your eyes, then try it. Blink your eyes
once or twice. (b) Picture used in an early study of eidetic imagery by Allport (1924).
(Reproduced by permission.) Some of the "eidetikers" (children with eidetic imagery)
could even spell the long German word on the front of the building, in addition to
reporting much other detail, after looking at the picture for 35 seconds only.

surface (Fig. 12.10a) you fatigue the rods and cones of the retina in a
pattern that corresponds to the shape of the bright object. When you
then look away at a plain surface, the fatigued cells can only fire at a
slow rate, as if they were not being stimulated very strongly, whereas
the surrounding cells of the retina fire at a normal rate. The result is a
negative afterimage, a dark object being seen instead of a bright one. If
instead it is a dark object you stare at, as in Fig. 12.10b, the rods and
cones in central vision are being rested while you look at the dark
surface. Thus, when you look away at a lighter surface the same cells
are ready to fire strongly. The afterimage therefore is of a light-colored
object on a dark ground. *Positive afterimages* are produced by a sudden
brief flash of light, very intense if the eyes are adjusted to daylight, less
so if they are dark-adapted. The positive afterimage is easy to observe if
you happen to wake up at night in darkness. Go to the light switch and
flick it on and off as quickly as you can. For some seconds afterward
you will see the scene exactly as you saw it during the brief moment
when the light was on.

Memory Image. The visual memory image has something important to tell us about perception. In visual perception, eye movements occur constantly. But have they any importance apart from enabling us to see the details better in what is perceived? It seems that they enter into and make part of the perception itself. An image of a sports car or a plane or a bicycle is a reinstatement of a perception, with some loss of detail—the perception is happening again, in its main outline. If you will close your eyes and recall the appearance of one of these objects—the sports car, let us say—you will find that it is not possible to have a complete image of the car all at once. Instead, you see now this part, now that part. You move your eyes as, in the image, the point "looked at" changes from the door to the bumper to the steering wheel. It is not possible to have a clear visual image of a complex object without eye movement, or imagining eye movement (which you may be able to do with some practice; but it is easier just to make the actual movements). In the image, in other words, we have a reinstatement of what happened in perception, *including* the eye movement. It appears that the perception is a complex, with its various parts being linked together by motor processes. We may think of it as a series of cell assembly activities. One assembly fires, exciting a motor activity, which excites another assembly, and so on. The memory image includes those motor links.

Eidetic Images. The motor component helps us to understand *eidetic images*. Haber and Haber (1964) have shown convincingly that the eidetic image does occur, in a small proportion of school-age children mainly. There has been some skepticism about this phenomenon, perhaps because the eidetic image acts in some respects like an afterimage (positive), but not in other respects. It is vivid, it occurs only in the period immediately after the stimulation, and it is transient, much like an afterimage; but it does not move as the eyes move, and the child is capable of "looking at" any part of it to see it more clearly, which of course is impossible with an after-image.

In experiments, a child is shown a picture, such as the one in Fig. 12.10b, for 15 to 30 seconds. Then the picture is taken away, leaving behind it a gray surface of about the same size. The child talks as if he can still see the picture on the gray surface. To describe what was at the top, he looks at the corresponding point on the gray surface and then describes it—very accurately and in much greater detail than an adult would. This sounds like mysticism, as if the picture had left something behind it that the child could see. Hence the skepticism.

But if motor movements do make up part of a perception and of a memory image, all this becomes intelligible. If the child's image consists of a number of part-images, and if one of these is excited not directly by another but by the intervening motor link, then when the child wants to "see" a particular feature of the picture again the eye movement he makes toward the corresponding part of the gray surface is a stimulant, helping to re-excite the part-perception that followed such eye movements earlier, when he looked at the real picture. This means that the eidetic image is an exceptionally detailed and vivid memory image and need not be considered mysterious—no more mysterious, at least, than other memory images.

In some unusual adults, eidetic imagery is so strong that it can be used to reproduce three-dimensional images. One part of a pair of stereoscopic pictures is shown to the left eye (with the right eye covered) on Monday. On Tuesday, the other part of the pair is shown to the right eye, with the left eye covered. The subject is asked to remember the picture seen by the left eye and combine it with the picture now being seen by the right eye. The result is a stereoscopic (three-dimensional) image in which the spatial relations are correctly reproduced. The individual images are of an unusual type. The objects in the combined three-dimensional image cannot be seen in either two-dimensional image, but become visible only when the two are correctly superimposed, one to one eye and one to the other. Thus guessing (from either image) is impossible, and the effect depends entirely on the precise combination of a very complex memory image with an equally complex visual image.

The memory image for printed words is also of interest, as a reinstatement of perception. Some people with good memories seem to have a sort of photographic record of what they read. In exceptional cases, they can close their eyes and still see the page they just read. These people tend to explain their memories for verbal material by saying that they just call up an image of a page and read it off. Many people report having memory images of single words that help them with spelling or, in memorizing verse, report having images of whole lines and even of short stanzas.

If you or a friend is such a person, you can make an interesting test. The image in these cases seems just like something that can be looked at as one could look at an actual page. With a real word to look at, one could read the letters backward nearly as fast as forward. Now, think of a long word, such as Louisiana, and form a clear image of it, or have your friend do so. Then look at your image of the word and try to spell it backward, or get your subject to. You, or your friend, will be surprised by the result. The person with a "photographic memory" of a familiar poem cannot repeat the last word of each line, going from bottom to top without first thinking of most of the rest of each stanza. He seems to have a clear picture in his mind, to look at—but he can only look at it in a certain order: the same order in which he saw the actual words on the page, as he read from left to right and top to bottom.

Such an image differs from the image of a car, discussed earlier, in which the parts can be seen in any order. The difference arises from the difference in the way in which perception happened: printed words are ordinarily perceived in a certain order; a car's parts are perceived in any order, and the order differs from one time to another. The image, then, is really a reinstatement of perception, including the motor components. A perception of the whole is unitary, but a complex whole has a structure and in addition to perceiving the whole one may also perceive its parts.

SUMMARY

This chapter makes a distinction between sensation and perception, sensation being the input process, perception the mediating activities to which sensation gives rise. A brief outline of the structure and function of two sensory receptors, the eye and the ear, is given, plus an introduction to some of the principles of sensory coding by which information is transmitted from receptors to sensory cortex.

The perception of space is shown to have both a visual and an auditory basis. Perceptual constancy is described as the phenomenon that maintains the stability of perceived objects despite changes in their sensory characteristics.

Perception is shown to be incomplete. Some animals can respond to sensory input which we cannot, and humans can respond to sensory input of which they remain unaware. Perception is shown to be both sequential and highly organized, and often to involve responses to successive sensory inputs which are smoothly organized into a single percept. An unusually detailed form of perceptual imagery, eidetic imagery, is described.

GUIDE TO STUDY

Here is a list of terms that should be known and understood: afterimage, ambiguous figure, accommodation, basilar membrane, blind spot, constancy, convergence, cochlea, disparity (including movement disparity), eidetic image, fovea, gradient of visual texture, outer, inner, and middle ear, parallax, phi-phenomenon, receptive field of a neuron, rod and cone, semicircular canal.

Be able to list the four skin senses, and the four elementary tastes. Be able to explain how different fibers interact to determine different tastes.

Be able to list the cues to visual depth, explain facial vision, describe a sound shadow.

The text says that perceptions of auditory distance are possible, but does not elaborate. How would auditory distance perception work with echoes of your own footsteps as you approach a wall? Assuming that high-pitched sounds do not travel as far as low-pitched ones, how would auditory distance perception work in telling, by the sound of his voice, how far away another person is?

Why are a baby's eye movements not necessarily an evidence of perception?

How might the ambiguous figure be explained?

What is peculiar about the visual imagery of printed material?

How is movement a factor in visual imagery of nonverbal material?

What is the evidence that not all cell assembly activity is conscious activity?

NOTES AND GENERAL REFERENCES

Good modern accounts of perception are given in texts by W. N. Dember, J. J. and E. J. Gibson, Hochberg, and Neisser. For anatomical and physiological background, the textbook by Milner is recommended.

Dember, W. N. & Warm, J. S. (1979). *Psychology of Perception, 2nd ed.* New York: Holt, Rinehart & Winston.

Gibson, E. J. (1969). *Principles of Perceptual Learning and Development.* New York: Appleton-Century Crofts.

Gibson, J. J. (1950). *The Perception of the Visual World.* Boston: Houghton Mifflin.

Hochberg, J. E. (1964). *Perception.* Englewood Cliffs: Prentice-Hall.

Neisser, U. (1967) *Cognitive Psychology.* New York: Appleton-Century Crofts.

Milner, P. M. (1970). *Physiological Psychology.* New York: Holt, Rinehart and Winston.

Vision

Allport, G. W. (1924). Eidetic imagery. *British Journal of Psychology, 15,* 99–110.

Fantz, R. L. (1967). The origin of form perception. In J. L. McGaugh, N. M. Weinberger, and R. E. Whalen, (Eds.), *Psychobiology.* San Francisco: W. H. Freeman.

Granrund, C. E. (1986). Binocular vision and spatial perception in 4- and 5-month-old infants. *Journal of Experimental Psychology: Human Perception and Performance, 12,* 36–49.

Hubel, D. H. (1967) The visual cortex of the brain. In J. L. McGaugh, N. M. Weinberger, and R. E. Whalen, (Eds.), *Psychobiology.* San Francisco: W. H. Freeman.

Hubel, D. H., & Wiesel, T. N. (1979). Brain Mechanisms of Vision. *Scientific American, 241,* 150–162.

Hubel, D. H., & Wiesel, T. N. (1962). Receptive fields, binocular interaction and functional architecture in the cat's visual cortex. *Journal of Physiology, 160*, 106–154.

Julesz, B., & Bergen, J. R. (1983). Textons, the fundamental elements in preattentive vision and perception of textures. *Bell System Technical Journal, 62*, 1619–1645.

Lettvin, J. Y., Maturana, H. R., McCulloch, W. S., & Pitts, W. H. (1959). What the frog's eye tells the frog's brain. *Proceedings of the Institute of Radio Engineers, 47*, 1940–1951.

McKinney, J. P. (1963). Disappearance of luminous designs. *Science, 140*, 403–404.

Pritchard, R. M., Heron, W., & Hebb, D. O. (1960). Visual perception approached by the method of stabilized images. *Canadian Journal of Psychology, 14*, 67–77.

Rubin, E. (1921). *Visuell Wahrgenommene Figuren*. Copenhagen: Gyldendalska.

Salapatek, P., & Kessen, W. (1966). Visual scanning of triangles by the human newborn. *Journal of Experimental Child Psychology, 3*, 155–167.

Weiskrantz, L., Warrington, E. K., Sanders, M. D., & Marshall, J. (1974). Visual capacity in the hemianoptic field following a restricted cortical lesion. *Brain, 97*, 709–728.

Hearing

Bekesy, G. V. (1967). The ear. In J. L. McGaugh, N. M. Weinberger, and R. E. Whalen, (Eds.), *Psychobiology*. San Francisco: W. H. Freeman.

Broadbent, D. E. (1954). The role of auditory localization in attention and memory span. *Journal of Experimental Psychology, 47*, 191–196.

Licklider, J. C. R. (1951). Basic correlates of the auditory stimulus. In S. S. Stevens (Ed.), *Handbook of Experimental Psychology*. New York: Wiley.

Supa, M., Cotzin, M. & Dallenbach, K. M. (1944). "Facial vision": The perception of obstacles by the blind. *American Journal of Psychology, 57*, 133–183.

Other Senses

Granit, R. (1955). *Receptors and Sensory Perception*. New Haven: Yale University Press. See page 44 onward, and (for warm vs. cold) p. 54 especially.

Pfaffman, C. (1951). Taste and smell. In S. S. Stevens (Ed.), *Handbook of Experimental Psychology*. New York: Wiley.

Imagery

Allport, G. W. (1924). Eidetic Imagery. *British Journal of Psychology, 15*, 99–120.

Chambers, D., & Reisberg, D. (1985). Can mental images be ambiguous? *Journal of Experimental Psychology: Human Perception and Performance, 11*, 317–328.

Haber, R. N., & Haber, R. B. (1964). Eidetic Imagery: I. Frequency. *Perceptual and Motor Skills, 19*, 131–138.

Hebb, D. O. (1968). Concerning Imagery. *Psychological Review, 75*, 466–477.

Kling, J. W., & Riggs, L. A. (1971). *Woodworth and Schlosberg's Experimental Psychology*. New York: Holt, Rinehart & Winston.

Motivation and Perception

Dixon, N. (1981). *Preconscious Processing*. London: Wiley.

Silverman, L. H., & Weinberger, J. (1985). Mommy and I are one: Implications for psychotherapy. *American Psychologist, 40*, 1296–1308.

13

Thought and Language

This chapter is concerned with thought: with consciousness, purpose, insight and creativity, and also with the thought processes that make language possible. Because the perspective of comparative study is as useful here as anywhere in psychology, the discussion does not deal only with human thought. Communication in birds and the solution of problems by chimpanzees help us to see how remarkable our own capacities are. We turn now to the central problem of psychology, the human mind.

A fundamental principle in science is to eliminate unnecessary ideas. Thought and consciousness are two ideas that came under suspicion while the science of behavior was developing. The motivation of early scientists like Thorndike, Watson, and Pavlov was to explain complex behavior by using the simple principles they observed in animal behavior, combining these simple principles in sometimes complex ways. You have already studied classical and operant conditioning, discrimination learning and learning set (chapter 2). Then you were introduced to the theory that the operating principle of the central nervous system—the cell assembly—is more complex than simple conditioned and unconditioned reflexes (chapters 4 and 5).

A question we must now answer is whether there are behaviors that require a more complicated explanation than conditioned reflexes. If so, then the assumption of a more complex nervous system is justified to explain behavior.

INSIGHT

Let us look first at some examples from a classical series of experiments. A chimpanzee is shown food—a banana—suspended above his head, out of reach. Visible at the other side of the experimental room is a box on which he could stand. He jumps repeatedly for the food without success, gives this up, and paces restlessly back and forth. Suddenly he stops in front of the box, then rolls it over under the food, climbs up, and seizes the food. At this point *insight* is said to have occurred (Köhler, 1927).

In a later test, the box is left outside the room, where the chimpanzee sees it as he is being led to work. It is not visible from the experimental room, but the door is left open. At first the animal stays close to where the fruit is suspended, jumping for it and trying one way after another to reach it directly. Suddenly, he stops, stands motionless for a moment, then gallops out into the corridor and returns dragging the box, with which he secures the prize.

This sudden thinking of the answer or "seeing the light" is, of course, well known in human problem solving. But you should not get the impression that insight occurs only in this way, after a delay—it is present also when the subject sees the answer at once—but the sudden solution has a special interest because the sharp break in behavior identifies for us the moment at which a reorganization of thought processes occurs.

Insight can be defined, essentially, as the *functioning of mediating processes in the solution of problems,* and from this point of view it is clear that some mode or degree of insight is present in all problem solving by higher animals. The dog shows superiority to other animals, such as the hen, in the perception of situations that require taking an indirect route to food (*umweg* behavior, Fig. 13.1). The chimpanzee shows superiority to the dog in using objects as stepping stones, as described earlier; there is no reliable report of a dog's ever having pushed a chair or a box into a position from which to climb up to food. This is physically possible; the dog's failure to perform this way shows that the chimpanzee's superiority with "tools" is due to intellectual ability and not solely because chimpanzees have hands, though hands are certainly important in such behavior.

The insightful act is an excellent example of behavior that is not learned but still depends on learning. It is not learned, since it can be adequately performed on its first occurrence. It is not perfected through practice, but appears all at once in recognizable form (further practice, however, may improve it). On the other hand, the situation must not be completely strange: the animal must have had prior experience with

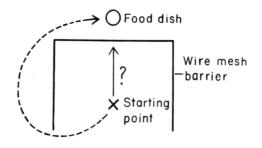

FIGURE 13.1. The umweg (round-about) problem. The animal starts at the point shown, with food in sight through the wire mesh. The insightful solution is to turn away from the food, as shown by the broken line.

the component parts of the situation or with other situations that have some similarity to it.

Chimpanzees, for example, are capable of using a stick to pull in objects that are out of reach; but they do not do so if they have never had experience in manipulating sticks. Six young chimpanzees were tested with food out of reach, and a stick lying in plain view. Only one animal used the stick to get the food; this was a female who had been frequently observed playing with sticks in the past. All six animals were then given sticks as playthings for a 3-day period and at the end of this time were tested again. Never in the intervening 3 days had any of them been observed using a stick to pull anything in. Instead, the stick was used to poke at other chimpanzees, or at the experimenter outside the cage, yet on being retested, three used the stick at once to rake in the food, and the other three did so after one false start. This was a new act and thus insightful, but it also depended on prior experience (Birch, 1945).

Similarly, dogs reared in isolation without the normal opportunity for learning to deal with barriers were markedly inferior to normal dogs in a situation like that of Fig. 13.1, as well as other "insight situations", and we have seen that experience in infancy affects problem solving in the adult rat as well (chapter 7). All our evidence points to the conclusion that a new insight consists of a *recombination of preexistent mediating processes*, not the sudden appearance of a wholly new process.

Such recombinations must be frequent in everyday living, and in a theoretical framework we must consider them to be original and creative. The terms "original" and "creative" as applied to human thought are commonly reserved for great intellectual and artistic achievements. But from the point of view of behavioral mechanisms we see that originality is a matter of degree and that in principle the chef who thinks of a new way of serving potatoes is as creative as the novelist who shows us a new view of human nature. The child who imagines her doll talking to her is being creative—and so is the drunk who has hallucinations.

We speak of insight chiefly in the context of overcoming some obstacle or disposing of a difficulty, but we can recognize that the same kind of process is also involved in suddenly realizing, for example, that a friend is annoyed. Even in one's dreams, when one creates improbable situations, or in daydreams when one imagines how entertaining it would be if the lecturer in a large class fell off the platform, one is recombining ideas to produce what is, to a greater or lesser extent, a new idea. Such products of thought may be bizarre or impractical, but they share a common creativity with insight.

Insight and Purpose

Purpose goes hand in hand with insight in problem solving. Behavior is classed as purposive when it is modifiabile by circumstances so as to produce a constant net effect; it is behavior free of sensory dominance, controlled jointly by the present sensory input and by an expectancy of producing the effect that is its goal. When the situation changes, the behavior changes accordingly.

For example: the chimpanzee that has solved the problem of using a box to climb on to get food is given the same problem, but no box is within reach. He goes over to the experimenter standing nearby and tugs at his clothing to bring him close to the suspended fruit. Then he climbs the experimenter and gets the reward. This is clearly a purposive action. Or when a dog in the umweg problem turns away from food, he is showing a capacity for purposive behavior in his avoidance of the barrier. In each of a number of variations of the situation, the dog immediately modifies his behavior to suit the circumstances and find the shortest route to food.

In principle, a number of examples of a given kind of behavior have to be observed before we can conclude that purpose is involved. It is only in this way that we can learn if the behavior adjusts itself to circumstance. In practice, however, one may know enough about the species—or about a particular animal—to be able to identify purpose in a single trial. Knowing that chimpanzees as a species are capable of complex insightful and purposive behavior, and that a particular chimpanzee has previously used a box to climb on, there can be no doubt about the purposiveness of the whole pattern of behavior when this animal pulls the observer over to the right place and uses *him* as a stepping stone.

In the purposive behavior of human beings, we encounter longer unified chains of action than in any lower animal: "unified" since it is clear that the earlier links in the chain are not formed for their own sake but because they make the later links possible. When a chimpanzee goes to get a stick, returns, and rakes in food, getting the stick does not in itself meet the need for food but rather makes the later part of the whole action possible. In humans, such temporally integrated patterns are much longer. The fisherman in need of food may spend a day or more weaving his net before he even goes near the river. People build shelters before they need them, as winter approaches; and such anticipatory and purposive behavior may involve periods not only of days or weeks but even years.

Human purposive behavior can be studied experimentally as can the purposive behavior of other animals. In an early series of experiments on human problem solving, Maier set the problem; his human subjects volunteered to try to solve it. (This cooperativeness makes research on human problem solving much less frustrating than studying similar behavior in dogs or chimpanzees.) Maier gave his subjects a collection of boards, clamps, and string and required them to construct a device that would place a chalkmark on the floor at two quite distant, previously marked spots. He also asked them to describe what they were doing as they went along.[1] To succeed at this task (see Figs. 13.2 & 13.3), his subjects had to use familiar objects in new ways. As in Köhler's (1927) experiments with chimpanzees, the use of the assembled objects was not immediately obvious. Moreover, much of the subjects' previous experience with these objects was irrelevant to their successful use in the new situation. Since the task had never been performed before, solutions were, by definition, new. The research method in tasks of this type is to record in as much detail what happens and try to interpret it afterwards. The results showed that the typical subject started a few constructions, which, it was clear, were not going to be successful. Those subjects who did succeed first spent some time in thought and then completed the task all at once. The last (and successful) construction was finished quickly and without hesitation; the earlier, unsuccessful attempts had been made hesitantly and with much verbal doubt. Thus, humans demonstrate the temporal pattern of behavior we have characterized in dogs and chimpanzees as insight: a relatively long period of unsuccessful effort, followed by a rapid, final completion of the task.

The Mediating Process

What is insight? Through insight, a large problem finally is solved rapidly, after considerable delay. Unlike conventional learning, which

---

[1]When Maier did these experiments, the observation technique was limited to note taking and still photography; now video tape immensely simplifies the task of recording data but at the price of immensely increasing the amount of data that must later be analyzed.

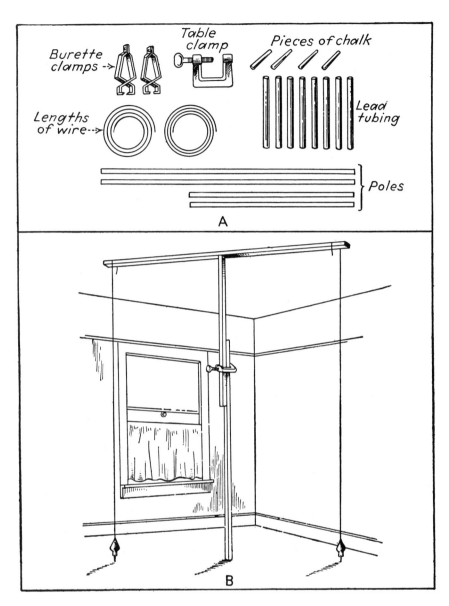

FIGURE 13.2. N. R. F. Maier's pendulum problem. The task was to use the objects provided in (a) to construct two pendulums which would swing in such a way as to make two chalk marks at specified points on the laboratory floor. Diagram (b) illustrates the successful solution. In the original experiment, only 9 of 105 subjects were successful. Of those, 8 were first given the hint that the pendulum should be hung from the ceiling, and then were also shown how to clamp two boards together, how to make a pendulum from clamps and wire, and how to wedge one board in place with another one held at right angles. (From Crafts, L. W., Schneirla, T. C., Robinson, E. E., & Gilbert, R. W., 1950. *Recent experiments in psychology*. New York: McGraw-Hill, p. 407. Reproduced by permission.)

297

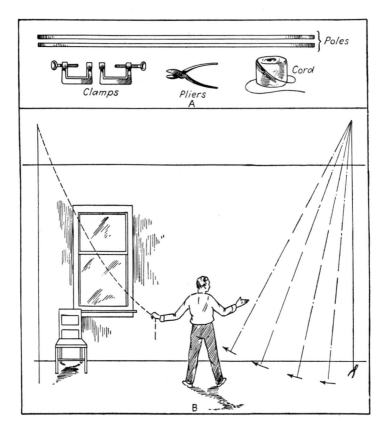

FIGURE 13.3.   Maier's string problem. How do you tie the two strings (b) together, given the objects in (a)? The accepted solution requires setting one string in motion as a pendulum by using the pair of pliers as a weight, holding the other string, and catching the swinging string. In one condition, subjects observed the experimenter accidentally brush the string, to set it in motion. Although the "hint" provided by the experimenter led the subjects to solve the problem faster, many of them were not aware that they had seen the experimenter set the string in motion. (From Crafts, L. W. et al., p. 413. 1950.)

involves exposure to small problems that are solved with less delay, insight involves *mediating processes*. These are explicit in the human and to some degree in the chimpanzee but are inferred in the other animals. The basic idea of a mediating process should be clear from cell assembly theory. Mental activity corresponding to cell assemblies can occur in the absence of overt behavior. The cell assemblies themselves can represent situations that can be imagined to occur; they can represent words describing the situations under study, or even pictures (mental images) of modifications of the situations. That there are two types of mediating processes—words and pictures—is consistent with the ideas (developed in chapter 6) about separate verbal and imagery memory systems. By manipulation of the environment as represented by mediating processes, the trial-and-error processes of overt learning observed by Thorndike, Watson, and Pavlov can occur in a completely symbolic or representational way, without the environment being physically modified at all.

The early behaviorists objected to the assumptions of thought (or mediating processes) because they had no clear record of its relation to behavior; they thought they could explain behavior without it. The following example illustrates the close relationship between behavior and thought in a problem-solving situation. It illustrates something else as well: Now that the existence of mediating processes is well established, and their structure is better known, they can be simulated using a computer. In specific problem-solving situations computers can imitate the output of human verbal or symbolic mediating processes that occur while a behaviorally observable problem is being solved.

Astronauts and Aliens. The problem of astronauts and aliens is classic.[2] Five astronauts and five aliens on one side of Mars want to cross to the other side. They have a space sled with a capacity of five. Unfortunately, if ever there are more aliens than astronauts in one place the aliens will dehydrate the astronauts and use them as snacks. This means that at no time can there be more aliens than astronauts on either side of the planet, or in the space sled that goes back and forth between the two sides. How can all the astronauts and aliens be transported to the other side, without any astronauts being dehydrated (Fig. 13.4)?

Figure 13.5 illustrates the "problem space" for this puzzle. The problem space is the interconnected chain of all possible legal moves (moves that do not violate the rule of more aliens than astronauts in any one place). As a matter of fact, people make very few illegal moves while playing this game. Although the problem space includes both the start (move A) and the solution (move Z), a series of legal moves that fails to solve the problem can be established by going into an endless loop (for example, moves A, D, F, I, E, B, A, etc.). Of course, a player may simply give up.

How do people play this game? The answer was sought by designing a computer program to simulate the number and sequence of moves made by a sample of subjects in completing the problem. The rules of the program were the same as those stated earlier; never more aliens than astronauts in one place, and up to five beings of either kind in the space sled at one time. First, protocols were collected that listed the actual moves made by a sample of 25 subjects who were simply instructed to solve the problem, and another sample of 25 who were

---

[2]Formerly missionaries and cannibals.

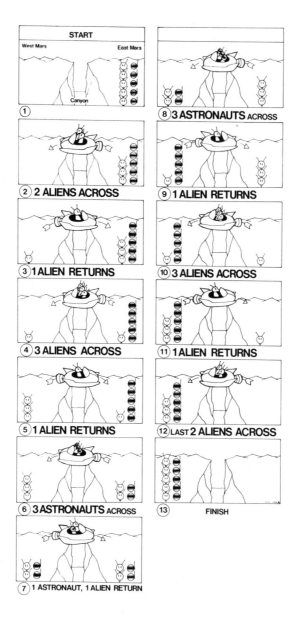

FIGURE 13.4. Astronauts and aliens (formerly missionaries and cannibals). How to get five astronauts and five aliens from East Mars to West Mars in a space sled that holds at most five beings? If ever there are more aliens than astronauts on either side of the planet or in the sled, the aliens will dehydrate the astronauts with unfortunate consequences. The thirteen steps from start (everyone in East Mars) to finish (everyone in West Mars) are displayed in columns from top left to bottom right.

300

told that the solution involved a stage (move L in Fig. 13.5) where there would be three aliens together on one side of the planet, without the space sled. In another part of the experiment, subjects were given two successive trials at a solution, and performance was compared on the first and second trials.

The computer program that successfully simulated human behavior in the game has three strategies. In one, the *balance strategy*, a move was favored that maintained the balance of astronauts and aliens on either side of the planet. For example, move A-D (Fig. 13.5) would be preferred over A-B or A-C. Unfortunately this strategy is unsuccessful. It can lead to an endless loop of the form A-D-F-G-J-G-F-D-A-C-F-G etc. The second strategy is the *means-ends-strategy*. This is the strategy of moving the maximum number of astronauts and aliens across the planet on odd-numbered moves, and the minimum number of astronauts and aliens back on even-numbered moves. The moves dictated by this strategy eventually succeed in solving the puzzle. A third strategy is to avoid moves that have been made before. This is the strategy which prevents loops, or repetitive series of unsuccessful moves.

Simulation of human behavior almost always involves probability (see chapter 8). The computer is programmed on each trial to choose a strategy and select the appropriate move with a certain probability. The probabilities can be programmed to vary over trials, simulating a gradual change from one strategy to another during the course of play. In the astronauts and aliens problem, the successful computer program began with three strategies: random moves, the balance strategy, and the means-end strategy. It was programmed to increase the proportion of times it used either the balance or the means-end strategies, instead of random moves, as play continued. It was also programmed to increase the proportion of trials on which it chose the means-end strategy instead of the balance strategy as play progressed and to increase the number of trials on which it would check to avoid previous moves as the play progressed. With this program, the computer simulation succeeded in matching the statistical properties of the subjects' play: the average number of moves, as well as the actual distribution of moves to solution.

The computer circuits, of course, do not imitate the neural circuits with which this problem is solved by the human. But the logical structure of the program carried out by the computer may very well resemble the logical structure of the problem as it is solved by human subjects. Human subjects may postulate a balance or a means-end strategy; they may gradually switch to the means-end strategy, and they may gradually increase the number of moves on which they check for, and avoid, loops. When these tasks are performed by computer, the

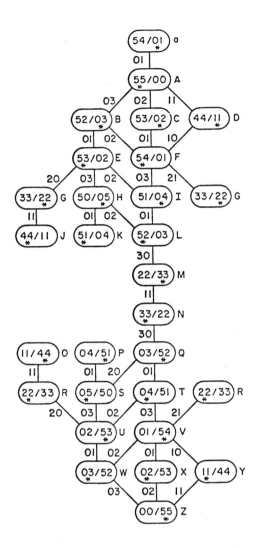

FIGURE 13.5.   The problem space for astronauts and aliens. This is a chart of all of the legal moves in the game. The ovals represent the simultaneous positions of astronauts and aliens on either side of Mars. The numbers to the left of the slash represent the number of astronauts (first digit) and aliens (second digit) on East Mars. The numbers to the right of the slash represent the number of astronauts (first digit) and aliens (second digit) on West Mars. The position of the asterisk represents the location of the space sled on either East or West Mars. The numbers between one oval and the next represent the number of astronauts (first digit) and aliens (second digit) being carried in the space sled. The lines connect successive positions which can be reached by transporting astronauts and aliens in the space sled. Each unique position is labeled by a capital letter. The successful solution extends from position A (all astronauts and aliens on West Mars) down in a line to position Z (all astronauts and aliens on East Mars). (From Simon, H. A. & Reed, S. K., 1976. Modeling strategy shifts in a problem-solving task. *Cognitive Psychology, 8,* 86–97.)

sequence of moves leading to a solution resembles the sequences produced by human subjects. The computer's "mediating processes," which are the program rules telling it what to do on each trial, are produced by electronic circuits. Human "mediating processes," which are not necessarily verbal, are produced by neutral circuits.

Insight and Mental Organization

Insight takes another form when the problem is more immediately visual. The chess board illustrated in Fig. 13.6 contains pieces arranged realistically as they might be during a game. Suppose the board is briefly exposed to view and then removed. How many pieces could you accurately replace on a blank board? It has been demonstrated many times that the number of pieces of a realistic game position that can be recalled after a brief look increases as the viewer's level of chess skill increases (Simon & Chase, 1973). Recall the discussion of chunking in memory in chapter 6.

The chess expert "chunks" the chess position visible on the board into a few very familiar positional units: common configurations that have occurred frequently during the expert's years of play. Very speculative estimates put the number of these different perceptual "chunks" at something close to 50,000 for the expert player. For the expert, remembering a board means remembering several of these 50,000 well-rehearsed chunks. The individual pieces do not form the basis of the chess expert's memory; the familiar configurations do.

One corollary of this theory can be tested by exposing both expert and novice chess players to boards arranged in random nonchess configurations, where the pieces occupy positions they could not occupy according to the legal moves in chess. Under these conditions, expert and novice perform equally poorly, remembering on the average about four of twenty pieces. There are no chunks to remember based on previous experience. All the configurations are equally new and bizarre to the chess player, and previous experience is irrelevant in organizing them.

Thus, experience in solving chess problems (the definition of chess expertise) is accompanied by specific skills in organizing memory for chess positions. But skill in chess goes beyond recognizing familiar positions—it involves making the best response to the positions as well. Here, too, a familiar notion can be used to explain the high-level skill of playing chess—discrimination learning. The expert who can recognize 50,000 different situations and combinations has also learned a chess move appropriate to each of these situations. He has learned what some theorists call a *production system*, consisting of 50,000 discriminable perceptual situations and probably about 50,000

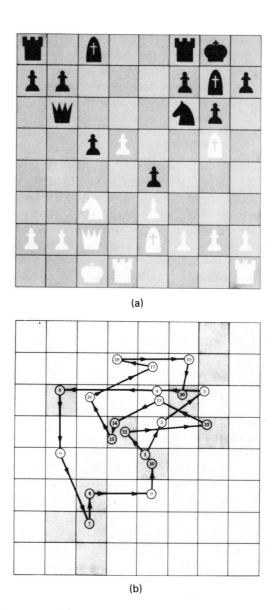

(a)

(b)

FIGURE 13.6. A chess position. Chess experts, exposed briefly to a position like the one in (a), can remember correctly almost all of the pieces and their places, whereas chess novices remember very few pieces and places correctly. In (b), the locations of the most active pieces in (a) (pieces with the greatest immediate potential for attack or defense) are shaded, and the first 20 successive fixations recorded from an expert exposed to this position are indicated by numbered circles connected by arrows. Notice that the expert concentrates fixations on the active positions. From Simon, H. A. and Chase, W. G. (1973). Skill in Chess. *American Scientist, 61,* 394–403.

different responses, one to each situation. Undoubtedly the chess expert's skill grows through a process analogous to that of monkeys exposed to successive similar problems of learning set (chapter 2). Each succcessive problem of the same type that the monkey encounters is learned faster than the last. Thus successive learning of different problems of the same general type benefits from positive transfer from the learning of previous problems of that type. So the basic skills of a chess master consist in the highly learned discrimination of perhaps 50,000 separate positions, which may be found in various combinations at any one time during a game of chess, and appropriate individual responses to those situations. Is chess, then, simply a mechanical response based on extensive previous learning? At its simplest, for the expert, yes. A chess master can simultaneously play chess with many inferior opponents, spending perhaps a few seconds on each move of each game in rotation, and win almost all the games played. In this kind of competition the skill is quite routine. But when two masters are matched, how do they play? Neither author is a chess master, so the answer must come from the literature rather than from experience. The chess master explores the possible consequences, perhaps three, four, or five moves ahead, of the situation of the game at any time. The master knows the probable responses and consequences of similar situations in previous matches; as well as the idiosyncrasies of the opponent. Thinking (no more than 3 minutes per move, on average, is permitted in a tournament game) involves weighing these alternatives for one of several (perhaps only two) moves being seriously contemplated at any one time.

Paradoxically, the novice plays in exactly the same way. The difference between the novice and the master is the difference between a beginner's acquaintance with the familiar positions and moves of chess, and the 50,000 or more positions and responses that can be identified by the master. As a result, the novice's predictions based on familiarity with the situation are less accurate, recognition of the situation and the move may be faulty, and choice of move in any situation may be less effective than the expert's—and so the game is lost. There are also individual differences in the ability or motivation to acquire and use knowledge of chess. But disregarding individual differences, the differences in chess skill between novice and expert appear to be in the ability to discriminate chess positions and to respond effectively to them. Both the novice and the expert "think" in the same way: they use mediating processes to project the environment of the chess game ahead two, three, or four moves: but the expert, on the basis of a more complete recognition of the chess configurations and the possible responses, does it better.

Insight and Thought

Learning is clearly a prerequisite to the kinds of behavior observed when the chimpanzee gets the banana by standing on a box or when the human succeeds in drawing marks on the floor with chalk and string (Fig. 13.2, 13.3). But the learning does not express itself through overt responses to immediately present stimuli. Instead, its role is to develop the mediating processes that make insight possible. Similarly, learning in chess is not shown as an immediate response to the stimulus of the chessboard; its effect on mediating processes is demonstrated by the expert's ability to chunk the chess pieces in memory. Its effect is to make the mediating processes—the looking ahead for several moves that characterizes thinking in chess—more effective when carried out by the expert than by the novice.

We hypothesize that the mediating processes underlying thought operate on the principles of cell assembly theory. They are "closed neural loops" in which excitation persists for longer than would be possible by simple reflex action in the nervous system.

The general process of problem-solving thought is imagined to be something like this: First, a goal is established. This is, of course, true in all formal verbal problem solving, but we assume it to be true for nonverbal problems as well. The goal is represented by a mediating process and may itself arise from a motivational state, some aspect of the environment, or some combination of the two (as with incentive stimuli and motivational states, see chapter 11).

The present environment is also represented mediationally. Comparison of the goal with the present environment reveals in what respects the two differ, and it is perception of these differences that leads to the next stage. Possible actions or behaviors are represented mediationally, and the effects of carrying out an act are anticipated. The anticipated outcome of the act is compared with the goal to generate another perceived difference between the environment after the act, and the goal. If the discrepancy between the anticipated outcome and the goal is less than the discrepancy between the present state and the goal, then the action is carried out; if the anticipated discrepancy is greater than or equal to the present discrepancy, the action is not carried out. The probability of an action is based on its ability to reduce the discrepancy between the goal and the present environment. This in fact is the basic outline of the theory of thinking proposed by several authors (Miller, Galanter, & Pribram, 1960; Newell & Simon, 1972). It has been applied to machine computation to solve problems that can be expressed formally and where operations and measurements of the kind described can be carried out unambiguously. This theory outlines a program for solving problems, but it does not explain how the problems are actually described or how the mediating processes are actually modeled. Techniques for simulating problem solving on computers use a variety of means to carry out programs that are basically similar to the program outlined here, and we believe that this process also characterizes the responses of humans and other animals to problem situations as well.

COMMUNICATION AND LANGUAGE

The term *communication* broadly comprises three levels of behavior: (1) reflexive, or nonpurposive, behavior, exemplified by the social insects and by the emotionally tinged danger cries of mammals; (2) purposive behavior, clearly evident in some subhuman mammals, but nevertheless falling short of language; and (3) language itself, which appears to be exclusively human but which humans share to some degree with chimpanzees. These are, however, broad categories, and it would be unwise to think of them as sharply distinct from each other.

Reflexive Communication

Social insects live in highly organized colonies in which the behavior of one animal must be coordinated with that of the others if they are to survive. The coordination is so good that one can hardly help thinking of it as intelligent and purposive, but as far as is known it is not. For example, the individual worker ant responds automatically to stimuli from other ants, and by her behavior in turn stimulates them to respond in such a way as to promote the life of the colony, without thought processes or any anticipation of the long-term effects of the behavior. Similarly, in one wasp species, the larvae in need of food extend their heads from their cells, which stimulates the workers to provide them with food. In various species of ants, odor determines whether a worker is admissible into the colony; if a true member is given a strange odor, she is attacked and killed by other workers; but if a stranger is given the colony odor, she is unmolested. In some species the nest entrance is guarded by a soldier who blocks it with her large head; when a worker approaches, to enter or leave, she strokes the head or abdomen of the guard, who then moves backward and permits her to pass. The ant is capable of learning, so this behavior may be of the order of a conditioned reflex rather than an unconditioned reflex, but in either case it is sensorily controlled.

In much higher species that communicate purposively, there still may be many examples of an almost equally reflexive and unintelligent, or nonpurposive, level of communication—particularly in the context of fear or hostility. We will return to these examples in the discussion of purposive communication, because they provide a contrast that makes purposiveness, when it does occur, more recognizable. Before doing so, however, let us look briefly at an extremely interesting example of communication in bees.

The worker bee who has encountered a food source at a distance from the hive is able to give other bees the direction and distance to the food by means of the "dance" she performs on a vertical comb in the hive when she returns. She climbs the comb with a peculiar waggling movement, making a number of rotations as she climbs. The angle of climb corresponds to the angle between the direction of the sun and that of the food source. The number of turns corresponds to the distance (fewer turns when food is farther away). Other workers watch her closely and thereafter fly more or less directly to the food (Frisch, 1950).

Such behavior has been called "the language of the bees," which is simply a figure of speech. Though the *effect* of the behavior is the same as if the bee possessed a sign language, it has not been shown that any purposive element is present in it.

Purposive Communication Short of Language

Now let us consider some purposive forms of communication in higher animals and compare them with some nonpurposive ones.

The essential distinction is whether the "sender" acts in such a way as to affect the "receiver's" behavior and modifes the communication according to its effect (or lack of effect). In purposive communication, the sender remains sensitive to the receiver's responses. A dog that wants to be let out may go to the door, turning his head at first and looking at his owner. If at this point the owner gets up and starts toward the door, the dog simply waits. If not, after a moment or two the dog barks—the bark being more restrained than when the dog hears a stranger outside. If nothing happens then, the barks become more vigorous. The behavior is effectively adapted toward achieving a change in another with a minimum of effort and stops as soon as this objective is attained. A caged chimpanzee begging for food beyond his reach similarly adapts the means to the end, making begging gestures with the hands as well as vocalization. The purposive aspect of the behavior is further confirmed by the use of other means of getting the food, such as a stick, if they are available. The begging act is one of a repertoire of acts, any one of which may be employed depending on circumstances.

The alarm calls of Vervet monkeys are another example of purposive social communication. These monkeys make at least three distinct alarm calls: one for leopards, one for eagles, and one for snakes. Eagles, of course, attack from the air, whereas leopards and snakes attack from the ground. When the monkeys hear the eagle alarm call, they are likely to look up and run down out of a tree and under the cover of dense brush. The leopard alarm call is likely to make them run up a tree (or higher up, if they are already in a tree) to avoid the leopard's ambush. And snake calls are likely to make them look to the ground. This happens both when predators are actually present and in field experiments when previously recorded alarm calls are played back to the monkeys.

The accuracy of giving the call increases with age. Infants, juveniles, and adults all give the alarm calls, but infants give the eagle alarm call when almost any bird flies over and will even give the alarm for a falling leaf. Juveniles used the same call more discriminatingly: they give it mainly when raptors (hawks, owls, and eagles) fly near, rather than when other birds are seen, but they do not reserve it exclusively for the eagle, their chief avian predator. Adults are highly selective in their use of the eagle call: it is reserved almost exclusively for the eagle.

Although we do not know in detail how this kind of behavior develops, it is like the development of children's speech in that sounds come to be used in specific situations. It is not known whether the calls occur initially without learning, or whether they are first learned and then perfected, by a process involving imitation, reinforcement, or both. We also do not know if the calls are purposive in requiring a specific response from a specific individual. But they are certainly purposive in a practical sense because they serve to alert (and so protect) the entire troop of monkeys, which in turn protects the individual monkey.

Language

Humans exhibit behavior that parallels both of the preceding classes (a cry of pain or a look of disgust may be reflexive, and some purposive gestures and sounds may be at no higher level of complexity than a chimpanzee's begging). But we also demonstrate a kind of behavior that with one apparent exception is not known to occur in any other species. This is *language*. Language includes sign language, as well as spoken and written words, so the chief distinction of language is not the ability to make the sounds of human speech.

Language is a high level of communication because of the *varied combination* of the same signs (words, pictures, gestures) for different purposes. The human child uses separate words singly or in new combinations to influence others' behavior, as well as using the words in the arrangement in which they were originally heard. We do not have to analyze long sentences to see the 2-year-old's use of four words to form the propositions "I thirsty," "I not thirsty," "Mommy thirsty," and so on.

The criteria for language, then, are (a) that it is usually purposive communication (although the purpose may be private, as in talking to oneself), and (b) that two or more items of the behavior are combined in one way for one purpose and recombined for other purposes. These criteria apply to sign language as well as speech. In ordinary circumstances, the chimpanzee, who makes free use of gesture to invite contact, to threaten or to beg, never seems to combine two gestures, such as in pointing first to an object and then pointing to the place where it should be put.

LANGUAGE LEARNING AND DEVELOPMENT

Chimpanzee Language?

We have already stated the hypothesis that the brains of humans and other primates are organized similarly; that they allow for mediating processes: and that activity of mediating processes is responsible for thought. In humans there are two kinds of mediating processes that enable objects to be imagined before they are perceived and actions imagined before they are carried out: pictorial mediators and verbal or symbolic mediators. Until recently it was believed that only humans could acquire symbolic mediators. However, using a variety of techniques, several researchers have reported that carefully trained chimpanzees can acquire and use symbolic mediators that resemble human language. Although symbols are not naturally acquired by chimpanzees, after extended teaching by humans, some chimpanzees have been taught to use symbols in a way approaching the way humans use words.

Three different approaches have been tried in an attempt to teach language to chimpanzees. Several early efforts were made to train young chimpanzees literally to speak. Some chimps were able to make sounds and to use them in a purposeful way when naming people, like "mama" or "papa" or when pointing out objects like "cup" (Kellogg, 1968). The next effort to train language in a chimp took advantage of their much more versatile hands. R. A. Gardner and B. T. Gardner trained a female chimp, Washoe, to make signs that approximated some of those used in the American Sign Language, a standard language in use among deaf people in the United States. The Gardners were able to document Washoe's use of such signs as "sorry," "hurt," and "up," among others.

Later studies of the films of Washoe, and of other chimps raised under similar circumstances, left uncertain the distinctiveness and specificity of various signs. A very different approach was taken by researchers who trained chimps with a completely artificial language. David Premack (1976) used plastic tags with magnetic backs stuck on a blackboard in sequences with distinctive meanings, either by a trainer or by the chimp Sarah (later joined by Peony, Elisabeth, and Walnut).

An example of Elisabeth's language is displayed in Fig. 13.7. The sentence, written by the trainer, means "Elisabeth give apple (to) Amy." Elizabeth was able to follow this command and others considerably more complex expressed in the plastic "words." Sarah (and the other chimps) were not spontaneous in their use of "words." The plastic symbols were always used as part of a training session in conversation

FIGURE 13.7.   Elizabeth at school. Elizabeth is giving an apple to Amy, her trainer. Behind the chimpanzee is the magnetic blackboard with symbols displayed. The symbols on the blackboard are interpreted from top to bottom as "Elizabeth give apple Amy." From Premack, D. (1976). *Intelligence in Ape and Man.* Hillsdale, NJ: Lawrence Erlbaum Associates.

with one of the human trainers. Both the trainer and Sarah had access to the magnetic blackboard, and Sarah had access to a limited set of the plastic symbols, from which she had to choose the correct items in the correct order (sentences were written from top to bottom) to obtain either real rewards (fruits, cookies) or the approval of the trainer. Much of her learning was by imitation: if it was intended to teach her a new sentence like "Sarah take cookie," the trainer would first spell the sentence on the magnetic blackboard and then give the plastic pieces to Sarah, who was taught by repetition and encouragement to place them on the board in the same positions in order to be allowed to take the cookie.

Although much of Sarah's repetitive learning seems to have been simply that—repetition of responses in anticipation of reward—the subtlety with which she could communicate with and about these plastic words suggests that she was treating them as artificial symbols for real actions and objects and that she used them in ways similar to the way humans use words. For example, Sarah could (using only the plastic symbols that were her "words") answer correctly the two questions: "Is red the color of an apple?" and "Is red the shape of an apple?" In addition, she could name the physical properties of an object referred to by its name, just as we can. For example, using only the plastic symbols, Sarah could answer questions like, "What is the color of an apple?" with the sentence, "Red color of apple," (Fig. 13.8), and she could correctly answer a sentence like "What is the shape of a cookie?" with the sentence, "Square is the shape of a cookie." She also learned, by careful instruction, both to produce and to respond to correct sentences employing the verbs *cut, draw, insert, take,* and *give;* the qualifiers *all, some,* and *none;* the adjectives *same* and *different,* and the names for many food objects, things, and people. Another animal, Peony, spontaneously used the two symbols for same and different (which were normally used as part of sentences as well as for labeling comparisons among real objects) in the ways described in Fig. 13.9.

This work required constant and attentive tuition. Not all of the chimpanzees learned as much or as easily as Sarah, and even Sarah did not use this new medium of communication for the spontaneous exchange of ideas. Nevertheless, she was coaxed into manipulating symbols in a way that showed (a) she had assigned clear and specific meanings to the symbols, (b) she could recognize instructions to herself and produce instructions to others with these symbols, (c) she could answer questions about some symbols with other symbols; and (d) she could answer questions about the real world with the symbols. Whether or not this is "language" is unimportant. It is important to

Synonymous Sentences

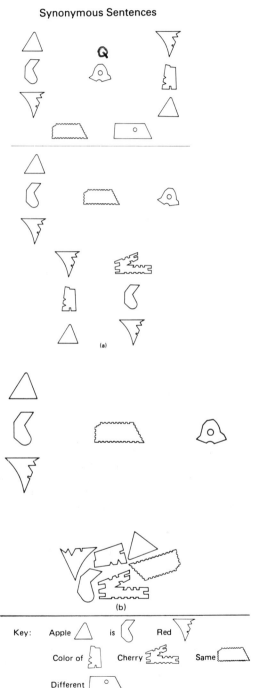

FIGURE 13.8. Sarah's lessons in equivalent sentences. The symbol Q is a question: Sarah has learned to replace it with a symbol or expression that makes the entire construction "correct." For example (referring to the key at the bottom of the figure) in the top panel, Sarah is asked: " 'Apple is red' 'question' 'red color of apple'." Two choices are supplied at the bottom of the panel, the symbols standing for "same" and "different". Sarah correctly replaces the "question" with the "same" symbol. In the second panel, Sarah is asked " 'Apple is red' 'same' 'question'." She correctly replaces the "question" symbol with the construction on the bottom left, "Red color of apple", even though the construction on the bottom right "Cherry is red" has more symbols in common with the first sentence. And in the final panel, Sarah is required to construct the sentence equivalent to "Apple is red" rather than choose between two alternatives. From Premack, D. (1976). *Intelligence in Ape and Man.* Hillsdale, NJ: Lawrence Erlbaum Associates.

313

FIGURE 13.9. "Same-different" formats invented by Peony. The top section shows the random arrangement of the five items—two spoons, one lump of clay, and the words "same" and "different"—as they were thrown out before the subject. The four sections below show the different arrangements Peony imposed on the material. From Premack, D. (1976). *Intelligence in Ape and Man.* Hillsdale, NJ: Lawrence Erlbaum Associates.

recognize the extent to which the symbolic competence of one chimpanzee has been enlarged by attentive training with a totally artificial system of visual communication.

Human Language Learning

A comparison of human and chimpanzee language learning demonstrates the great difference between the two species in ease of attaining a form of symbolic communication. Children learn to speak over a period of years, not without specific tuition, but in ordinary cases without coaxing, without special rewards, and without institutions designed to teach them to speak. Then most children go on in a more formal way to learn written communication, which is partially interchangeable with spoken communication and makes possible permanent symbolic records in place of the temporary communication of speech, or in the case of the deaf, of signing.

Human speech begins with the babbling sounds of the infant, which develop between one and two years of age into the sounds interpreted as proto-words: for example, "ba," "ma," "ha" for "ball," "mother," "hot"; then it develops into clear single-word utterances, into two-word utterances at about 2 years of age, and finally into the short sentences of juvenile speech.

Two aspects of this development require comment: (a) learning the meaning of individual symbols or words, and (b) constructing meaningful combinations of symbols or words. At first, sounds are referred to a large number of acts or objects in the natural world, and the distinction between acts and objects is not always clearly maintained. For example, a child saying "light" may be asking for the light to be turned on, may be responding to the light when it is turned on, or may simply be directing attention to the light. This is a form of language activity that occurs without the need for specific reinforcement and is as natural to children as playing with locks without a specific reward is to chimpanzees. As children grow older, they narrow the meaning of the sounds they make to more specific situations and learn a correspondingly larger number of sounds. Infant speech at about 18 months contains many clear sequences of sounds, each of which has a specific meaning sufficient for the task at hand—words like *mommy*, *daddy*, *out*, *light*, and the like. The study of development and refinement of meaning for specific sounds (and, later, written words) is called *semantics*, and the semantic content of language is the references language makes to things outside itself, either directly or through other symbols in the language.

The second interesting feature of children's speech is the construction of word sequences. As soon as a child (at about 18 months) begins to combine words, the sequence, as well as the individual words, conveys meaning. Thus, meaning is conveyed by more than the semantic content of each word: it is conveyed by the ordering or other structural relationship among the words. This aspect of language is called *syntax*, or the study of its structure.

A most interesting process in English syntax is *substitution*. We illustrate it because it presents a general problem that characterizes almost all attempts to combine information by animals, computers, or human beings. Suppose that our typical child has learned two sentences: "Johnny do it" (meaning to adult onlookers that whatever is happening, Johnny wants to participate in it), and "Play train" (Johnny wants to play with a toy train set). Grammatically, the first sentence (Johnny do it) contains a subject, Johnny, and a predicate, do it, indicating an action. In the second sentence, there is an action word, play, and a modifier, train, which indicates what is to be played with. A typical sentence that combines the meaning of both utterances is "Johnny play train," which could be taken as a request of a more specific nature than either of the previous two. Notice how the subject of the first sentence is combined with the entire second sentence, which substitutes for the unspecific "do it" predicate of the first sentence. In this case, the combination of two separate, meaningful sentences requires the elimination of the more general predicate of one, and its replacement with the more specific predicate indicated in the other. Thus, in general, the growth of language is accomplished not just by stringing together longer and longer sequences of meaningful combinations of words, but by the selection from among available strings of those parts that match, and the selective deletion of overlapping parts to form a compressed unit with an intelligible meaning.

The ability of children and adults to combine and to delete meaningful subunits into longer meaningful sequences is taken as an indication of the importance of syntax in both the production and understanding of language. According to Chomsky (1965) the meaning of a sentence is determined by reference to a simple model in which all of the grammatical variety that characterizes adult speech—the use of passive rather than active verbs, the posing of questions, the elimination of subject and modifiers in imperatives like Move!—is understood by carrying out grammatical changes that express the utterance in its simplest syntactic form: something like reanalyzing the sentence, "Johnny play train" into its constituent parts: Johnny do (play train).

Ours is a clearly incomplete account of the enormous effort that has gone into formulating theories both of word meaning (semantics) and of the role of context and structure in conveying meaning (syntax). Because languages are either natural (human) or artificial (chimpanzees or computers, depending on whether the artificiality is in their application to other species or to machines), the study of language structure has become an important subspecialty both of psychology and of computer science, particularly that branch of it which is concerned with the use of computers to solve problems in a way that parallels human thought (artificial intelligence).

Another major problem in understanding language concerns active and passive voice and how the child becomes able to change from one to the other. No grammatical rule can be formulated to cover all possibilities. Taking into account some aspects of perception and of nonverbal thought makes the active–passive relation easier to understand.

It was emphasized in chapter 12 that a perception is a sequence, not a single static process, and the same object or event may be perceived in different sequences of part-perceptions. Now suppose I am a 6-year-old who observes a playground battle between Annie and Billy. Suppose also that I am attending to Annie when this happens. My perception then runs as follows: I perceive Annie; I see her attacking; I see the contact with Billy and Billy's disturbance. When asked by the teacher, my report is: "Annie hit Billy." But suppose instead that I had been attending to Billy when war broke out. My perception would then run as follows: I perceive Billy; I see a blow and Billy's upset; I see the source, Annie. Now my verbal description of the event would be, "Billy was hit by Annie." The same event can be seen in two ways, one naturally giving rise to the active voice, the other to the passive voice.

This example shows how sentences may be transformed from active to passive and vice versa. Given the sentence "Annie hit Billy" to change to the passive voice, one need only reconstruct the scene in imagery (which also is sequential in structure), attending first to Billy, and make a verbal report in the form that readily results: "Billy was hit by Annie." This does not explain the semantic rule by which the transformation is made, but it does illustrate the attentional basis of the transformation.

The examples in this discussion have been made as simple as possible, and it is perhaps wise to remind the student that nothing about human behavior is as simple as these examples may suggest. The discussion is meant to show how the problem of language may relate to other aspects of behavior, theoretically, and to draw attention to a possible line of cognitive theory for dealing with language, avoiding the extremes both of nativism and empiricism. No simple theory of learning can account for the phenomenon of language. There is evidently a major hereditary determinant of the course of its development; but we have no good idea of what this is or how it has its effect, and the only way to find out is to explore the various possibilities offered by theories of learning. When we find out what is not learned, we have found out what is innate.

HUMAN PROBLEM SOLVING: A REVIEW

We know human problem solving in two contexts: first, as it is studied in the psychological laboratory; and second, as it occurs in the daily life of ordinary people. Unfortunately, the two are not always closely related, and there are some characteristics of real-life solutions that cannot be observed in the controlled experiment—or, at any rate, have not been observed so far. To learn something about these aspects, we turn in the following sections to a consideration of scientific thought.

Animal studies have already shown us that thinking need not depend on language (since animals do not normally have language but do have fairly complex mediating processes). Human studies allow us to go further: not only are there important steps of thought that occur without language, they cannot be put into language after they have occurred. This may be as true with simple problems (adding 8 and 2) as with the complex thought of the mathematician. The flash of insight that occurs in scientific thought can be without warning and without any recollection of the steps of inference immediately preceding. Suddenly the answer is there, and that is all. There are evidently links in the chain of thought that are quite "unconscious"—and not unimportant.

This process is also illustrated in the laboratory by a relatively difficult problem whose solution, when it is found, is simple. It is the two cord problem posed by Maier (1930) and described in Fig. 13.2. When the subjects failed to see the solution, the experimenter "accidentally" brushed against one of the strings and set it swinging, whereupon a number of the subjects solved the problem promptly, but without any realization that they had been steered to the solution. For them, the solution had arisen spontaneously, and they were unaware of a decisive factor in their thinking. Habit in thinking is both an advantage and a disadvantage. A habit to solve in one way blinds one to other solutions; but one's habitual solution may work efficiently, and it would be very inefficient indeed not to have ready-made procedures to apply to common problems. Daily life would hardly be tolerable if every time you wanted to wash your face, for example, you had to return to first principles, examine your ideas for possible misleading assumptions and make sure again that the use of soap and water is a good way of removing dirt. In most of the problems of everyday life, the accustomed solution is still the efficient one. But it is not always so, and the trick is to know when to stop and take a fresh look at a problem, to discard the present solution and seek a better one.

It is not always easy to identify one's tacit assumptions or to change them even when one knows what they are and that it is time to make a reassessment. It can be very difficult to do so in science when the assumption is a long used, and useful, theoretical conception. Laboratory studies have shown that the more confirmations an assumption has had, the less likely it is to be abandoned, even though it is no longer working. In some of these experimental situations, human subjects have been incredibly blind to alternative methods and approaches when a set was established to deal with problems in one particular way that has worked with other, apparently similar, problems in the past.

This is the case with the small, artificial problems used for experimental purposes and is even more pertinent for the complex problems of science. Here a further obstacle may be encountered. The theoretical idea that must be given up, or changed, may affect wider matters. It was difficult for the physical scientist about 1900 to deal with the problem of radioactivity, because the solution required changed assumptions about the atom, changes involving the whole structure of physical and chemical theory. Even when the troublesome assumption is identified and the problem is solved, it may be difficult for someone else to accept the solution. If it affects our view of the cosmos, for example, and the place of humans in it, then there may be a fight to the bitter end to suppress Galileo's ideas about planetary motion, or Darwin's theory of man's origins, or Freud's view of human nature.

Discovery, Invention and Logic

Refusing to accept a cogent argument because one does not like it is illogical but not necessarily stupid. We tend to identify "good" thinking and intelligence with the use of logic, but some doubt about this conclusion should arise when we find intelligent people acting in an illogical way. In laboratory experiments, for example, it is not uncommon for a subject who is baffled by the problem to return repeatedly to try something that has failed before—even when he remembers that it has failed. This is puzzling in an intelligent subject—as long as we think of problem solving as solely a logical process. But is it? It may be recalled that the airplane was invented despite mathematical proof that a heavier-than-air machine could not fly, and as we will see shortly there are records of other highly successful problem solving by great scientists who also departed at times from the use of logic. Of course, the same scientists are eminently capable of using logic when they choose to (e.g., in demolishing an opponent's argument).

Here we should distinguish between two modes of thought: (a) *discovery*, or *invention*, the production of new ideas, and (b) *verification*, the process of testing, clarifying, and systemizing them. When an apparent absence of logical thought is observed in a competent problem solver, it is usually mode (a) that is operating, not mode (b). With this distinction, the aimless or futile moves of the baffled problem solver become more intelligible. When the thinker is completely stuck, having tried everything, logic is of little use. What can be done? One possibility is to leave the problem for a while, hoping that different mediating processes will be active when the problem solver comes back to it (this, in fact, is a recommended procedure, which often works); or one may continue to react almost at random to the different elements of the situation, manipulating them this way and that, hoping that sensory feedback from one of the moves will "give me an idea." In such a process—which also frequently is successful—logic plays no recognizable role.

What is happening here? We assume that a new perception or new idea is a recombination of mediating processes, and that the mediating processes which occur at any moment are a joint product of the sensory input and of the immediately preceding central processes. The thinker does not know in advance what combination of ideas is being sought but must act more or less blindly, to increase the probability that other combinations will occur besides those that have already done so and that the effective one will be among them. Dropping the problem for a time, trying to forget it by doing other things, can help by permitting changes in the mediating-process activity with which the problem is approached on the next attempt. Turning the problem around, looking at it from every possible aspect, juggling its component parts—even though these moves include repetitions of previously unsuccessful ones—can increase the probability that some sensory event will occur just at the moment when a central process is occurring which, with that particular sensory input, adds up to the idea that is needed for solution of the problem.

This is not to imply that blind manipulation is the only source of new ideas. What we are concerned with here is what happens after the possibilities of logically consistent analysis have been exhausted. Then it becomes, essentially, a matter of waiting for the lightning to strike. There is repeated testimony from great mathematicians and scientists that they have arrived at solutions after deeply immersing themselves in the problem, thoroughly familiarizing themselves with the relevant ideas and phenomena, trying this attack and that without success—and then, often with little warning, the line of solution became evident. A new idea, a new insight, is the adventitious occurrence of a certain combination of mediating processes. It can be prepared for in advance, but it cannot be commanded at a particular moment. Having made available the component parts of the idea (as far as he or she can guess what they may be), the thinker must then, so to speak, be open-minded—avoid a too narrow concentration on a particular line of thought—and wait. The element of chance is inescapable, which means that the waiting may take a long time.

The role of chance (which of course works only for the prepared mind) becomes very evident in another aspect of scientific discovery. It is notorious that many great achievements of experimental science have been made as a matter of accident—but "accidental" discoveries are made by those who are prepared to see the possibilitiies. An early example is the discovery of the magnetic effects of electric current, because a compass happened to be lying near a wire through which Oersted passed a current. Another is the discovery of natural radiation (from uranium salts) because Becquerel kept unexposed photographic film where (as we now know) he should not have. A more recent example is the discovery of penicillin, because Fleming had failed to keep his culture dishes clean. Less earthshaking discoveries than these are a common occurrence in the laboratory—in fact, they are a pillar of ordinary, everyday research. There are few scientists who have not had the experience of setting out to solve one problem and ending up instead with the answer to another, a problem that had not even been thought of when the research began. This is serendipity, finding one thing while looking for another.[3]

Examples of psychological serendipity from the present text: Melzack and Thompson (chapter 7) were looking only for a loss of learning ability when they observed the insensitivity to pain and the personality peculiarities in their isolation-reared Scotties (Fig. 7.5): Bexton, Heron and Scott (chapter 11) were interested in motivation and intelligence-test performance when they discovered hallucinatory activity in the isolated college student (Fig. 11.4); Olds and Milner (chapter 10) were investigating the relation of the arousal system to learning when they found the pleasure areas (Fig. 10.3a), and McKinney (chapter 12) was investigating the ability of athletes to judge verticality in a dark room when he discovered the same kind of disappearance that occurs with stabilized images.

Another point that emerges from the scientific record is that some of the most brilliant successes do not involve any intellectually difficult ideas. Once the discovery is made and the new idea formulated, the whole matter seems obvious—any high school student can understand it, and we wonder how generations of brilliant men could have failed to see it. It is sometimes said that a problem well stated is half solved, and

---

[3]The term serendipity has come into common use in discussions of the scientific method but often, it seems, half jokingly. Joke or no joke, the word is needed to refer to a main factor in fundamental research. The word is well established in the English language, dating from Horace Walpole's The Three Princes of Serendip, 1754. The princes "were always making discoveries, by accidents and sagacity [this describes the scientific case precisely] of things they were not in quest of."

this is often (but not always) so. The true difficulty in such cases is to select the relevant facts and ideas, disregarding the rest. When this is done, the solution may be child's play. To us, who know what the relevant information is, the "problem" is absurdly simple; but this misses the real nature of the problem, which was to select the relevant facts, create the effective new ideas, and get rid of the mistaken ideas of the past that were blinding the thinker.

The great scientist is not always the one who thinks more complex thoughts. He is great frequently because his thought somehow has avoided complexities in which others are bogged down, because he sees the relevant issues and—often with no logical justification except that in the end it works—has pushed apparently contradictory data to one side, leaving them to be explained later.

Two cases illustrate these points. Students of physics today have no difficulty understanding how the mercury barometer works and why it is that water cannot be lifted with a suction pump for more than 34 feet or so. They know that air has weight and can see that it must press down on the surface of a well like a gigantic plunger. If we put a pipe into the well and use a pump to remove the pressure from the surface of the water *inside* the pipe, the water in the pipe will rise—pushed up by the pressure outside—until the weight of water balances the weight of air outside, when it will rise no higher. Galileo failed to find this answer. We may reasonably conclude not that Galileo was stupid, but that his pupil Torricelli, who did find the answer, performed an intellectual feat of the first order by abandoning a principle that others were working with ("Nature abhors a vacuum") and asking whether the facts could be accounted for by the weight of the air. Once it was placed in this context, the question could be clearly and finally answered by the experiments with mercury columns (which are more easily handled in a laboratory than 34-foot columns of water) that gave us the barometer.

The second case concerns the phlogiston and oxygen theories of combustion. It is common to poke fun at the phlogiston theory because even when it was being used it did not take into account certain facts that make no difficulty for the oxygen theory. Actually the phlogiston theory was powerful. It explained much that was unexplained before and introduced new order into the field. We know now that the oxygen theory produces a greater order, but when Priestly and Lavoisier were arguing the matter (Priestly, though he himself had discovered oxygen, supporting the phlogiston theory), there were also facts that denied the oxygen theory completely. Logically, one might say, both theories should have been abandoned. In fact, each scientist was confident that evidence contradicting his position would be found faulty and his own theory validated. Lavoisier was right;[4] Priestley was wrong. But the point here is that both men, highly capable and critical thinkers, selected the data that supported their own theory and refused to accept contrary evidence.

From another point of view, of course, neither man was illogical. Each was thinking in terms of a total picture of the future, when more would be known. No scientist would for a moment consider a theory really satisfactory, or "true," if he or she thought that the evidence would always be opposed to it. It is a persistent characteristic of scientific thought that it deals with what is going to happen, or might happen, as well as with those things that have happened already. We saw in chapter 8 that a test of significance may depend logically on asking whether two sets of data (two samples) have been drawn from one population that does not yet exist, or whether one must conclude that they have been drawn from two separate populations, also nonexistent. Scientific thought largely deals with an imagined world where logic and order and predictability prevail (or, in nuclear physics, an ordered lack of predictability), and this fact must be taken into account when evaluating an apparent lack of logic by a Lavoisier or a Priestley.

Where formal analysis and logically formulated inference really come into their own is in the testing and communication of ideas. The thought process produces ideas, as we have seen, more or less unpredictably and at random. Many of these ideas have a short life, not being "attractive" or "interesting"—that is, the new combination of mediating processes does not have the capacity to persist and set off further series of mediating processes. Other combinations interact more strongly with the ideas resulting from the period of preparation and thus persist because the new combination of mediating processes excites other mediating processes, which in turn reexcite the new combination—the thinker continues to "think about" the new idea. This is the point at which the powerful tools of logically consistent analysis make their contribution to thought. They are the means of discovering error and of winnowing the multifarious ideas produced in thought.

As to formal logical analyses, the use of syllogism and systematic induction, it seems likely that these are never used except in trying to pin down error in an opponent's argument or to convince skeptics of the clarity of one's own reasoning. In other words, their primary

---

[4]The difficulty for the oxygen theory disappeared when chemists developed methods for distinguishing between gases such as nitrogen and carbon dioxide, neither of which supports combustion, or hydrogen and carbon monoxide, both of which are inflammable. But Lavoisier died (on the guillotine) before these advances were made and thus never knew how the obstacle would be overcome.

function is communication. It seems quite clear that the propositions "All men are mortal" and "Socrates is a man," from the classic example of a syllogism, do not occur in thought as two separate processes. A neurologist finding a case of hemianopia would never say to himself, (1) This is hemianopia, (2) What causes it? (3) All hemianopias are caused by injury to the visual pathways, (4) This man must have an injury in his visual pathways. But he might very well say so if he had to convince a skeptic.

Similarly, scientific generalizations or laws are not arrived at by a slow process of accumulating cases and gradually formulating the idea with increasing confidence as the number of cases increases. Instead, the conclusion is likely to be formulated on the basis of one or two cases, and the remaining cases are gathered in the light of that idea, as a means of testing it or of convincing others of its value. Both humans and animals have a way of generalizing from one specific type of experience to others; the generalization may either be supported by further experience or it may be extinguished. An example is Pavlov's dog, which generalizes from one sound to others but, being fed following only one sound, eventually stops responding to other sounds. This is a simple experimental analogue of the procedure of the scientist who leaps to a tentative conclusion concerning a new phenomenon ("I wonder whether it could be caused by. . . .) but finds that the idea is not confirmed in later observations. All this implies that although the generalizations of science do not arise by induction, as that term is used in logic, they must survive the test of an essentially inductive method.

CONSCIOUSNESS

We can start by trying to clear up an important point. In this book, conscious describes a person or other higher animal in a normal waking state and responsive to the environment. Consciousness is the state of being awake and responsive, or the state of the brain's activity at such a time. This is the way the terms are used in objective psychology.

In psychoanalytic theory, however, and in popular language, "conscious" has a quite different meaning. There are conscious ideas and unconscious ideas. Here the term does not describe a state of the whole mind, but a part of the mind—the part one knows about. There is a great difference between the two meanings. It is one thing to say that I am conscious of the world about me. It is another thing to say that an idea is conscious, meaning that I am conscious of it and implying that I can introspect and be aware of some of my mental activities but not of others.

The idea that human beings have an unconscious mind, a separate part of the mind that acts independently of the conscious part of the mind and whose actions are not known to the conscious part, was developed by the philosopher Herbart in the early 19th century. This may be a conception useful in a subjective psychology, which assumes the possibility of introspection and direct awareness of one's own mental processes. Modern objective psychology has good reason to conclude that introspection does not exist (see chapter 1). Therefore the mind is not able to observe itself directly. There is no conscious self in this sense (that is, no part of the mind that we are conscious of or observe directly), and hence there is no need to speak of an unconscious.

In psychoanalytic theory, the unconscious is capable of perceiving complex social situations, being jealous or hostile and making someone act accordingly without consciously knowing why. Such powers imply that the unconscious has separate mechanisms of thought parallel to those of the conscious mind. In effect, the unconscious is discussed as if it were a separate mind that competes for the control of behavior (and often wins).

But if we go this far, we must go further. It is not only our disreputable thought that we do not know directly. There is plenty of evidence from scientists, poets, and musicians that new ideas have on occasion come to them suddenly, already worked out. They are new and creative, so the working-out must have been done by the unconscious. In mathematical discovery, it is the beautiful, harmonious, elegant idea that is likely to be powerful. J. Hadamard (1954), the eminent French mathematician, basing his argument on the analysis of another great mathematician, H. Poincaré, has concluded that the unconscious is the real creator in such discovery and that it has great powers of esthetic judgment. The mental processes in question are not known to, cannot be described by, the person in whose mind they occur.

When we add to this, however, that the most ordinary mental acts are in the same class, are not observable by introspection, and by the same logic must also take place in the unconscious mind, the concept of an unconscious mind begins to be absurd. For example, the mechanism that enables a subject to say "ten" when he is shown a 9 and a 1 if he has one set, but "eight" if he has another set, was shown by Oswald Külpe (1910) and his students to be unobservable by introspection. That is, ordinary arithmetical calculation must be done by "the unconscious." *All* mental mechanisms are in this class, a fact that may help the student to see why objective psychology (a) considers that all mental processes are "unconscious" in the sense that they are not reportable or known directly by the subject but must be studied theoretically, and (b) consequently denies that we need to talk about a *separate* unconscious mind.

Behavioral Signs of Consciousness

In other respects also the term consciousness must be used with care. For some people it refers to something that is not part of the physical world, implying dualism (chapter 1). The terms could be avoided in scientific discussion, except that we would at once have to invent another one with the same meaning to designate the normal state of the waking adult of a higher species, as contrasted with the state of a person under anesthesia or in concussion or in deep sleep, and to make a distinction between the level of neural function in higher and lower species. "Conscious" and "consciousness" are useful terms, if used cautiously. The behavioral difference between consciousness and unconsciousness is not simple, as we can see by taking some examples, which also clarify our whole discussion.

Our first pair of examples shows that responsiveness, by itself, is not enough to demonstrate consciousness. First, in comparing a conscious and an unconscious animal, one might think that the only difference is that one animal responds to stimulation and the other does not. But this is not accurate. Reflex responses can be obtained from a person in a coma, who is considered to be unconscious. Also, the reflexes of breathing and heart action continue in unconsciousness, or else death follows at once. Some reflexes disappear, and others are altered, but the unconscious organism is not wholly unresponsive or inactive. Second, vigorous reflex activity can be elicited from the tail end of a "spinal" dog (i.e., one in which the spinal cord has been severed at the level of the neck) which is likewise not considered to be conscious.

Some people attribute "consciousness" to any living thing, plant or animal, but scientifically there is no justification for ascribing consciousness to sensitive plants (such as the Venus flytrap, which makes a reflexlike response to trap insects that alight on it) or bacteria or houseflies or earthworms or jellyfish. These are simply organisms whose behavior is entirely reflexive, as is the behavior of ants, bees, and termites—social insects whose behavior is very remarkable but has not been shown to be more than a reflexive (or sense-dominated) adaptation to the environment.

On the other hand, it is not possible to avoid the inference of consciousness in such higher animals as the chimpanzee or rhesus monkey—or in the dog or cat, though we do not consider these latter to be quite as high in the scale of psychological complexity. None of these animals has a natural language, which is not a necessary sign of consciousness. (This point is also clear when one identifies consciousness in a stranger without hearing him speak a word—a common occurrence.) The higher animals, then, share some feature of human nonverbal behavior that leads us to classify them as having consciousness, and this nonverbal feature is not shared by the ants and bees.[5]

The distinction we are discussing is evidently related to the distinction between sense-dominated behavior and behavior in which thought—or complex mediating activity—takes part. We have seen that there is probably no absolute distinction between these two classes of behavior. Accordingly, we can make a distinction between conscious higher animals and unconscious lower ones without supposing that these are two quite separate classes. There is a continuum of higher and lower species; at one end consciousness is clearly in evidence, at the other, it is not. There is no need to try to dichotomize, to determine at just what point consciousness appears in this hierarchy. Let us agree that the presence of consciousness is not demonstrated by reflex responsiveness alone, a conclusion which implies that mediating processes are required as a minimum. We can then go on to see what other complications are involved without treating this as an all-or-nothing question.

Similarly, consciousness in humans can be impaired in various ways, and there is no good purpose to be served by trying to say just what the impairment must be before we decide that the subject is not conscious. Is the sleeper who is dreaming, but unresponsive to the world about him, conscious or not? Is a man conscious after a blow on the head, if he can talk intelligently about himself but does not know where he is or how he got there and later cannot even recall being helped to the hospital (Boring, 1961)? In either case, some of the processes normally present in the conscious subject are present; others are absent or impaired. But these are in-between cases, and we do not need to classify them in one or the other category.

However, it is worthwhile paying some attention to them, because they tell us something about normal consciousness. Evidently consciousness is not a single function but a group of functions, rather loosely associated, so that one can be decreased or abolished while

---

[5]D. R. Griffin has reviewed many examples of the kind cited here, and he concludes that the behavior observed in many species of animals, including invertebrates, exhibits purposiveness. See Griffin, D. R. (1984). Animal thinking. *American Scientist, 72*, 456–464.

another is not greatly affected. Normally, one feature of consciousness is immediate memory (memory for the immediate past), whereby people remember what they were just thinking about and can recite much of it on request. They remember what was said and done and do not unnecessarily repeat an action that is already complete or bore their listeners by telling the same joke twice at the same sitting. Normally, people perceive most of what goes on around them, unlike the sleeper, though they may not give any overt sign of perceiving; but if they are deeply involved in a book or a TV program, they may actually be less responsive to other stimuli than one who is dozing.

Evidently the state of consciousness varies greatly from one time to another, even in normal people. This variability, in degree of responsiveness and in what the organism is responsive to, is, in fact, one of the marks from which we infer consciousness or the capacity for consciousness. If at times higher animals are unresponsive to the environment (even when their eyes are open and the EEG shows a waking pattern), at other times they prowl restlessly about or seek ways of manipulating, and being excited by, the world around them. Further, when the animals are responsive, the aspects of the environment to which they respond differ greatly from time to time. That is, the interests of the higher animal are variable.

At times, of course, interest is determined by biologically primitive needs. At one time the animal is motivated sexually, at another time by hunger; and this degree of variability is as characteristic of the lower animal as of the higher animal. But when these needs are fully met in the higher animal, other complex motivations appear. Given activity in the arousal system, the thought process appears to be intrinsically motivated; and the complexity of behavior that emerges when no primitive need is present is an excellent index of level in the psychological hierarchy.

Self-consciousness

Rats, dogs, cats, and monkeys are aware of their environment and respond to some of its abstract properties: feeding time, the location of dangerous dogs, the limits of the troop territory, who is dominant, and who is submissive. Humans and chimpanzees are certainly aware of another part of their environment: themselves. Gallup (1970) showed that chimpanzees recognize themselves as unique animals by demonstrating that they respond to their own mirror image. Human self-reference is evident. The world includes "I" as well as "you." Some of our own personal characteristics are perceived as a part of the environment, and some of these characteristics can actually be manipulated, as can other parts of the environment, to solve problems. This is what happens when we self-consciously adopt a "sincere attitude" in talking to someone whom we want to convince.

Self-consciousness, in the everyday sense of the word, means being aware of oneself as a part of the environment. This does not mean that what we experience of ourselves corresponds to what others experience of us. "Self-consciousness" in this commonsense meaning is obviously incomplete.

Many pages have been written about the meaning of the conscious "I," but our argument here is short; "I" does not represent all the biological operations by which the brain works, but rather some of the *results* of these operations fed back to the brian as information (correct or incorrect) about oneself. My knowledge of myself is based on the same kind of information that I receive about the rest of the environment.

In no sense do we directly observe the functions of the biological system which produces our behavior. We experience some of the *products* of that system: movement, proprioceptive and kinesthetic sensations, pain, and other effects such as speaking, writing, singing, playing the piano, thinking. And we experience some of these products more or less as we experience the speaking, writing, singing, and piano playing of others. We have an incomplete knowledge of other people and a similarly incomplete knowledge of ourselves. We are incompletely "self-conscious," and the working of our biological mental apparatus is not directly observable by us.

SUMMARY

The preceding chapters have touched repeatedly on thinking as an aspect of motivation, perception, or some other topic, but here we are concerned with thinking for its own sake.

Insightful behavior in dogs, chimpanzees, and humans is demonstrated when the solution to a problem has not been learned through prior experience and often when the solution occurs after a delay following unsuccessful efforts of an entirely different kind. Insight can be studied experimentally in both animals and humans, and in humans a verbal protocol can be collected to aid in understanding the mediating processes that accompany solution. Successful problem-solving behavior is accompanied by the reorganization of mediating processes, which is demonstrated by a changed capacity to remember the relevant aspects of a problem. The entire problem-solving process can be conceptualized as a mediated effort to reduce the discrepancy between a goal state and the present state of the organism; this approach characterizes computer-based problem-solving programs as well as human problem-solving processes.

Different kinds of communication exist throughout the animal kingdom. The simplest is reflex communication, where both the stimulus leading to the communication and the communication itself are determined by species-specific behavior. Many species engage in purposive communication short of language: begging, aggressive and reassuring calls, and threat indicators. Many of these communications can be specific to changes in the environment and show more flexibility than the reflexive species-specific communication. Language involves symbolic communication: the use of arbitrary symbols (aural or visual), which can be rearranged and which have different meanings in different combinations. By careful tuition, some chimpanzees have been taught a rudimentary form of artificial language based on visual symbols. Chimpanzee language is not spontaneous, and chimpanzees show far less aptitude for their limited language than do human juveniles, who learn spoken language without formal tuition and who use it spontaneously.

Two facets of language are semantics, the study of how symbols come to have their meaning, and syntax, the study of the effect of symbol order, variation, and permutations on meaning. Rudimentary semantics and syntax are observable in the artificial chimpanzee languages. An increase in the complexity of both syntax and semantics can be traced over the course of development of human language. Syntactic substitution is one of the earliest syntactic operations, and finding substitution rules is a universal problem in both human and machine syntax.

Human problem solving is by no means a self-conscious process. The mental activity that accompanies it is not available to introspection, and the results are frequently unexpected even to the problem solver. Problem-solving activity is a clear example of the fact that consciousness does not imply self-awareness of mental activity: humans (and other animals) possess an awareness of self that is qualitatively like their awareness of the rest of the environment: they can experience themselves as objects as well as actors in the environment.

GUIDE TO STUDY

Be able to describe the difference between insight and conventional trial-and-error learning. Understand the use of verbal protocols in research on problem solving. Be able to explain the evidence suggesting that successful problem solving is partly a problem in discrimination learning, and be able to outline a conceptualization of problem solving as a goal-seeking and difference-reducing process.

Explain the difference between purposive communication and language. Is language exclusively human? What are the differences between the use of symbols by chimpanzees and the use of symbols by humans?

What is the substitution problem in syntax? Is problem solving a rational process that can be described in formulations?

To what degree are we aware of our own mental processes in problem solving, and in general? How does this book treat the word *consciousness*? How can human and primate self-awareness be explained?

NOTES AND GENERAL REFERENCES

First, a group of references that have general value for the study of human thought:

Conant, J. B. (1951). *On Understanding Science*. New York: Mentor.

Ghiselin, B. (1952). *The Creative Process*. New York: Mentor. Testimony from scientists and nonscientists about the way in which their creative ideas were achieved.

Hadamard, J. (1954). *The Psychology of Invention in the Mathematical Field*. New York: Dover. Most readable. Not a technical presentation, but fascinating comments on the development of mathematical insights.

Kuhn, T. S. (1970). *The Structure of Scientific Revolutions*, 2nd ed. Chicago: University of Chicago Press. A widely known book that outlines the illogical nature of shifts in scientific thought and defines the "paradigm" as a protective set of assumptions shared by working scientists.

Leeper, R. (1951). Cognitive Processes. In S. S. Stevens, (Ed.), *Handbook of Experimental Psychology*. New York: Wiley.

Newell, A., & Simon, H. (1972). *Human Problem-Solving*. Englewood Cliffs, NJ: Prentice-Hall. A text about cognitive psychology which emphasizes the kind of analysis necessary for computer simulation of thought.

Ray, W. S. (1967). *The Experimental Psychology of Original Thinking*. New York: Macmillan. Part I is a review of the literature; Part II is a collection of papers, including the famous report by Henri Poincaré of how he made his mathematical discoveries.

Woodworth, R. S., & Schlosberg, H. (1954). *Experimental Psychology*. New York: Holt, Rinehart & Winston. Chapter 26 is an admirable account of thought and problem solving.

Language

Chomsky, N. (1967). The formal nature of language. In E. H. Lenneberg, *Biological Foundations of Language*. New York: Wiley. (Appendix E).

Gardner, R. A., & Gardner, B. T. (1969). Teaching sign language to a chimpanzee. *Science,* *165,* 664–672.

Hebb, D. O., Lambert, W. E., & Tucker, G. R. (1971). Language, thought and experience. *Modern Language Journal, 55,* 212–222. The argument against a one-sided emphasis on heredity.

Kellog, W. N. (1968). Communication and language in the home-raised chimpanzee. *Science, 162,* 423–427. A summary account of the earlier experiments in teaching language to chimpanzees.

Lashley, K. S. (1951). The problem of serial order in behavior. In L. A. Jeffress (Ed.), *Cerebral Mechanisms in Behavior.* New York: Wiley.

Lenneberg, E. H. (1967). *Biological Foundations of Language.* New York: Wiley. A valuable book, though it may seem to overemphasize innate factors. It also contains an appendix by Chomsky, whose views, if extreme, are important and have led us to see the true dimensions of the problem of language.

Premack, D. (1976). *Intelligence in Ape and Man.* Hillsdale, NJ: Lawrence Erlbaum Associates. Thorough account of a series of studies of the use of an artificial language with chimpanzees.

Seidenberg, M. S., & Petitto, L. A. (1979). Signing behavior in apes: a critical review. *Cognition, 7,* 177–215. Points out the serious difficulties in interpreting ape "hand signing" as language.

Seyfarth, R. M., Cheney, D. L., & Marler, P. (1980). Monkey responses to three different alarm calls: evidence of predator classification and semantic communication. *Science, 210,* 801–803. Description of the use of alarm calls by vervet monkeys, and of a field experiment in which the use of these calls was tested.

"Language of the Bees"

Frisch, K. v. (1950). *Bees: Their Vision, Chemical Senses and Language.* Ithaca, NY: Cornell University Press. The report was subjected to experimental criticism by:

Wenner, A. M., Wells, P. H., & Johnson, D. L. (1969). Honey bee recruitment to food sources: olfaction or language? *Science, 164,* 84–86. This criticism was itself criticized experimentally by:

Gould, J. L., Henery, M., & MacLeod, M. C. (1970). Communication of direction by the honey bee. *Science, 169,* 544–553. At present, then, Gould et al. hold the field: Bees do communicate.

Other References

Birch, H. G. D. (1945). The relation of previous experience to insightful problem-solving. *Journal of Comparative Psychology, 38,* 367–383.

Boring, E. G. (1961). *Psychologist at Large.* New York: Basic Books. This autobiographical account includes, on page 39, the incident in which Boring was knocked down and experienced post-traumatic amnesia.

Gallup, G. (1970). Chimpanzees: Self-recognition. *Science, 167,* 86–87. Evidence that chimpanzees recognize themselves in a mirror.

Kohler, W. (1951). *The Mentality of Apes.* New York: The Humanities Press.

Maier, N. R. F. (1930). Reasoning in humans: I. On direction. *Journal of Comparative Psychology, 10,* 115–153.

Maier, N. R. F. (1931). Reasoning in humans: II. The solution of a problem and its appearance in consciousness. *Journal of Comparative Psychology, 12,* 181–194.

Miller, G. A., Galanter, E., & Pribram, K. (1960). *Plans and the Structure of Behavior.* New York: Holt. A book that predates the modern era of research in cognitive science and artificial intelligence but expresses principles that are still of value in understanding the organization of thought.

Simon, H. A., & Chase, W. G. (1973). Skill in chess. *American Scientist, 61,* 394–403. An article describing the chess memory experiments discussed in this chapter. An example of the wide-ranging work of Simon, a Nobel-prize winning behavioral scientist who has achieved recognition for his work in the psychology of economic behavior as well as for his work in thought and artificial intelligence.

CHAPTER 14

Psychology and the Scientific Method

This chapter provides a historical background for some aspects of modern psychology. It considers the advantages and the disadvantages of using neurological ideas to understand mind and behavior. It also considers the difficulties of psychology as an objective science. How are we to know what goes on in the minds of others, and how indeed are we to understand ourselves?

Psychology moved toward experiment about 1860, after a long history of philosophical speculation. From the first, the new approach was quantitative. G. T. Fechner, a German physicist, is credited with being the first experimental psychologist. He set out to measure sensations. He could measure the intensity of a physical stimulus, which he wanted to relate to the mental intensity of sensation. He concluded that the intensity of a sensation was proportional to the logarithm of the intensity of the stimulus. This is the *Weber-Fechner law* (Weber, a physiologist, had preceded Fechner in this field). The law in this form is not completely satisfactory, but Fechner's results convinced others that mental measurement is possible. Systematic work also was undertaken on the measurement of *reaction time*—the time needed to respond to a simple stimulus, such as putting on the brake when you see a light turn red—and people began to think of psychology in a new way, as an experimental science.

It was Fechner's work that inspired Hermann Ebbinghaus with the idea of measuring memory, and with Ebbinghaus, whose work is described in chapter 2, we come in 1885 to the beginning of an important chapter in modern psychology. The next major step was made in 1911 by Thorndike with the cat experiments described in chapter 2. Darwin's influence now began to be felt, and psychology took its place among the biological sciences. Darwin (1872) saw that behavior evolves along with the evolution of bodily structures and expressed this conclusion in *The Expression of the Emotions in Man and Animals*. The book, however, had little effect on psychologists, who were still preoccupied with a very different set of ideas.[1] G. B. Romanes, a friend of Darwin's, tried to make an evolutionary study of intelligence using second-hand evidence, but the atempt was not successful. Lloyd Morgan—very critical of Romane's methods—undertook experiments on animal learning. None of this got much attention in the psychological world. Capable as they were, Romanes and Morgan did not depart far from traditional lines of thought: Morgan, for example, assumed that learning requires consciousness. Thorndike, however, was a radical and asked radical questions. He got the wide attention that Romanes and Morgan did not get.

Thorndike's questions may not seem radical now, but they did in 1900. They earned him a certain amount of scientific abuse and stirred up others to find new experimental evidence to show that his answers were wrong. Do animals think, or do they merely learn mechanically? Does learning consist only of S-R connections? Why are some responses learned and others not? What is the function of reward? These were questions that were central in psychological thought, especially in the 1930s and 1940s.

Thorndike was radical only to psychologists. John B. Watson was a radical to a still wider audience, whom he outraged by asserting that mind and consciousness and thought do not really exist. In 1913 Watson founded a movement called Behaviorism, on the principle that psychology is the study of behavior, not of mind. Pavlov had completely excluded consciousness from consideration in his animal work; but he insisted that what he was doing was physiology, not psychology and in this earlier work did not concern himself with human behavior at all. Watson attacked the idea of human consciousness directly. He thought that mind is a collection of habits, nothing more: images, verbal responses, and consciousness were myths. In some of what he claimed, Watson was intentionally overstating his case, but he also

---

[1]See Hebb, D. O. (1968) "Concerning Imagery" for the possibility that imagery exists at different levels of vividness, more or less sensory, with cell assemblies of first-order, second-order and so on.

meant some of it. His views were widely ridiculed, even though they were better thought out than those of some of his critics. He was right in rejecting introspection as a method of study. His idea that thinking is a series of muscular reactions had some value. This is the idea that thinking consists mostly of subvocal speech—talking inaudibly to oneself—or in the case of a deaf-mute, movements of the fingers. Each movement of the vocal organs produces proprioceptive feedback, which is the stimulus for the next movement, and so on: the *motor theory of thought*. Sensory feedback does play an important part in thinking, and in general Watson's views were not so silly that they could be easily disposed of. He was cleaning house, getting rid of ideas that had been uncritically taken for granted. Some of those ideas were brought back later but only when supported by solid evidence.

During the period influenced by Watson and other behaviorists— 1925–1950—the study of animal learning was at a peak. Here the white rat had the central position, and a maze path was what he had to learn. Some work was done with primates, but mostly it was the white rat learning to traverse mazes such as those shown in Fig. 14.1. Some studies of visual learning were being made, using discrimination apparatus like the one shown in Fig. 14.2d. It is incredible that until 1930 it was thought to be an established scientific fact that the dog and the rat could discriminate between objects of different sizes and between different brightnesses, but could not perceive visual patterns. The reason was that in apparatus like that of Fig. 14.2d, the patterns to be discriminated were put *above* the door, where the animal paid no attention to them and did not learn. We now know that learning is prompt when the patterns are put *on* doors, where the animal must push against them. The discovery was actually made in a different apparatus, like that in Fig. 14.2c, where the rat must jump against the pattern he chooses and so pays attention to it. All mammals have pattern vision, and so have birds, as may be readily shown in the Skinner box.

THE ROLE OF NEUROLOGICAL IDEAS

In the development of psychology as an experimental science, theoretical ideas about the nervous system have played a significant part. Theory, like rum, is a good servant and a bad master—we have emphasized both the importance of theory and the importance of not believing it—and the proposition applies as much to neurological theory as to other theories. Let us now see what value this particular intoxicant has had, and what its limitations are.

FIGURE 14.1.   Mazes used to study various aspects of the behavior of laboratory rats. The maze in the upper left-hand corner was used to study the "mental processes of the rat" in 1900; the upper right-hand maze was used to study choice behavior in 1930; the lower left-hand one to study short-cuts in 1979, and the one in the lower right to study exploratory behavior in 1976. (From Olton, D. S., 1974. Mazes, maps and memory, *American Psychologist, 34,* 583–596. Reproduced by permission.)

The S-R formula was the cornerstone of early psychology. It was based on a purely physiological conception of the operation of neural paths leading from sense organ to muscle or gland and of the stimulus producing immediate responses by this means.

But the S-R formula was an oversimplification in neurology as well as psychology. It was a guiding principle, or "paradigm," in psychology for about 50 years (roughly between 1910 and 1960). A scientific paradigm is a set of principles or ideas that are generally accepted as a context for scientific work (Kuhn, 1970). Because psychologists thought that the nervous system operated on S-R principles, they developed behavior theories that conformed to these principles.

The benefits that psychology got from the S-R concept are clear. All

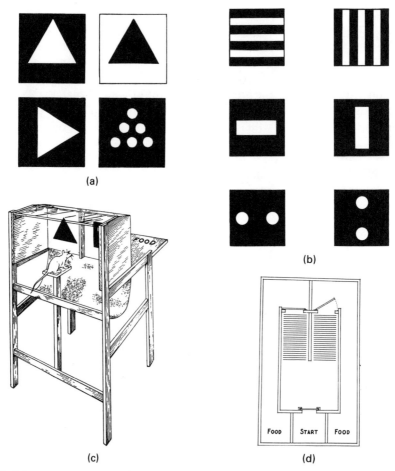

(a)

(b)

(c)   (d)

FIGURE 14.2. Discrimination training apparatus and stimuli. The device at the lower left (c) is a Lashley Jumping Stand: On each trial the rat must jump towards one of two doors. If he chooses correctly, the door opens and he receives food; if he chooses incorrectly, the door remains closed and he falls into the net. The device at the lower right (d) is a Yerkes discrimination box. On each trial, the rat leaves the start box, chooses either the right- or left-hand alley, and pushes against the door at the end. If he chooses correctly, the door opens and he receives food; if he chooses incorrectly, the door remains closed and a mild electric shock is administered through the grid floor.

At the upper left (a) are stimuli for studying the concept of triangularity. Rats trained on the triangle in the upper left will not generalize to any of the remaining three figures; chimpanzees will generalize to the black upright triangle or the white rotated one, children will generalize to all three shapes. In the upper right (b) are stimuli for studying the concept of horizontality. Rats trained in the Jumping Stand to discriminate between the top pair of figures will generalize to both the middle and the bottom pair. Jumping Stand after Lashley from N. L. Munn, *Handbook of Psychological Research,* New York: Houghton Mifflin; Yerkes Box from Lashley, K. S. (1935). *Comparative Psychology Monographs.*

338

of Pavlov's work, still of fundamental significance for psychology, was cast in this mold. Thorndike's attempt to explain problem solving in S-R terms showed us how to attack the theoretical problems of learning. Thorndike and Watson between them achieved the first comprehensive theory of behavior, all by consistent use of the S-R formula.

The S-R principle omitted thought, intelligence, insight, expectancy—any mental activity that we now think about in terms of mediating processes—and so was inadequate. But it was still a great achievement. It did explain much that had not been explained before, and, equally important, it led to new and important experimental problems. Thorndike's clear statement that animal problem solving is all trial-and-error learning to repeat successful responses (because they are rewarded) formulated an equally clear experimental problem for L. T. Hobhouse (1901): Can we find cases of problem solving in which the successful response is not learned but instead comes suddenly? The result was the first insight experiments (by Hobhouse), later followed up by Köhler (1927; see chapter 13).

When Thorndike and Watson and Pavlov were establishing S-R theory, the nervous system was thought to be a set of paths running from receptor to effector, some longer and less direct (i.e., through the cortex, in learning), but all one-way streets—no back connections, no feedback within the system, no loop circuits in which an excitation could maintain itself without sensory stimulation. The self-reexciting paths of Fig. 4.7b described in chapter 4 had been described by the great Spanish anatomist Ramón y Cajal, but physiology paid no attention to them. For physiologists as much as for psychologists, all neural transmissions had to be straight through, from sense organ to muscle or gland. The alternative possibility that some other activity might go on inside the brain seemed to be denied by the facts. For the hard-shell behaviorist especially, to speak of consciousness or of any thinking except Watson's motor thinking was to talk dualism—and dualism was totally unscientific.

Thus theoretical development was at an impasse until R. Lorente de No again demonstrated Ramón y Cajal's closed circuits and this time got the attention of physiologists and psychologists. In 1948, Norbert Weiner drew the attention of engineers to closed-loop feedback principles in his widely read book on cybernetics. Engineers saw the usefulness of feedback in buillding machines sooner than psychologists saw the usefulness of feedback in explaining behavior. But feedback is now, several decades after Weiner's book, better appreciated in psychology.

All theory needs to be treated skeptically. This applies particularly to neurological theory, because psychology tends to become so dependent on it. The time to be especially skeptical is when a theory says that something cannot be so. Our knowledge of neural function is far from complete, and theories based on it must therefore be incomplete and may quite possibly contain gross errors. Understand and use the theoretical ideas that have been developed in the preceding chapters, but—once again—maintain your capacity for disbelief.

Limits on Neurologizing: Psychological Constructs

Some aspects of behavior may never be dealt with in neurological terms alone. The simplest behavior of the whole animal involves a practically uncountable number of firings of individual neurons and muscle cells: for example, as the animal moves out of the starting box in a maze, or as you read a line of this text. There is currently no possible way of keeping track of more than a few of these cells. To try to describe mental activity by individual neural firing would be like trying to describe a storm by listing every raindrop and every tiny movement of air.

We must have units on a larger scale to describe behavior. To describe the storm, the meterologist speaks of showers or centimeters of rainfall (instead of the number of raindrops), systems of low and high pressure extending over hundreds of kilometers (instead of the pressure of each cubic centimeter of the atmosphere), and so forth. For the understanding of behavior, we can use neurological concepts such as a volley of impulses, the level of firing in the arousal system, or the occurrence of widespread summation in the cortex. But the intricacies of brain function are such that this still does not take us far enough, and we reach a point where the use of psychological conceptions of still greater complexity becomes inevitable.

To discuss what goes on inside a rat's head as he runs the maze, for example, we use such terms as "hunger," "expectancy," "stimulus trace," and "the stimuli of the choice point." Such constructs have little direct reference to the neural function. They were invented and subsequently refined in the context of studying behavior, and their use does not depend on first knowing how the brain fucntions. Instead, we can learn about how the brain functions *from the behavior,* beginning with these psychological constructs. Perception, for example, can be discussed from this point of view. The behavior of the child who calls a sea urchin a ball when he sees it for the first time tells us that sight of the sea urchin must excite some of the same activity in the brain that sight of a ball does. We do not as yet know what the activity is, but this kind of information is an important guide in our study of the neural processes of perception. In the meantime, we use the psychological construct, "perception of similarity." When eventually we learn in detail what the neural processes are, we may still find that they are as complex and variable as the raindrops in the meteorologist's weather system and that, just as the meteorologist needs his large-scale construct of a weather system for convenience in thought and communication, so we as psychologists will continue to need such constructs as the perception of similarity.

There are, broadly speaking, two ways of knowing about the functioning of the brain and of mind as the highest level of brain function. One is physiological and anatomical; the other is behavioral. The physiological tends to be more *molecular*, or fine grained, dealing with units rather than the whole, concerned more with the trees than with the forest; the behavioral tends to be more *molar*, large scale, looking at the forest rather than the trees. Both kinds of information about brain function are essential. One adds to or may correct the other. Logically, the physiological and anatomical data have priority in the analysis of brain function, but conclusions drawn from these data alone may be incomplete and may be corrected by evidence from behavior.

The theory of cell assemblies is based on behavioral work and on an attempt to coordinate the physiological-anatomical evidence with the behavioral. The behavioral evidence says that thoughts or intentions can last for seconds, perhaps minutes, whereas the single loops that Lorenté de No described might reverberate for much shorter periods (perhaps a tenth of a second). If a number of loops worked together, however, the reverberation might last longer. How would they work together? If a learning process is involved, making synaptic connections between the individual loops and combining them into larger systems, perhaps evidence of this learning could be found in infancy. From this kind of question some of the experiments on early experience and Factor IV (chapter 7) originated. The structure of the nervous system is by now well enough known for mathematical descriptions of hypothetical cell assembly processes to be developed. The predictions made from these mathematical theories can be compared, qualitatively at least, to the data from psychological experiments. The evidence does not yet guarantee that this approach is right, but it is promising (Grossberg, 1980).

"Cell assembly" and "mediating process" refer to the same function (chapter 4), the first being a hypothesis concerning the way in which the second might work. Cell assembly refers to a bridging conception, relating the mediating process—known from behavior—to brain function. Physiological psychology makes hypotheses about the nature of psychological constructs on the assumption that the hypotheses may have clarifying value, but it does *not* try to dispose of all psychological constructs.

Psychology is not a branch of physiology. We cannot escape the need for large-scale units of analysis, nor the need for the special methods of behavioral study on which such analysis is based. It may seem that neurological entities are somehow more substantial, more "real," than psychological entities, that the study of nerve impulses is a more scientific affair than the study of anxiety or motivation. This is entirely mistaken. It may be that the "probable error" of a psychological conception is larger than that of the neural conceptions of anatomy and physiology. That is, our conceptions may need more revision and sharpening, but they are not less related to reality. The forest is as real as the trees, a shower of rain as much an entity as the drops that compose it. There must be different levels of analysis in natural science, from the microscopic (or submicroscopic) to the large-scale macroscopic. At any given level, "reality" consists of unanalyzed units whose existence is taken for granted as the basis for analyzing the next higher level of complexity. Otherwise we should have to deny the reality of the raindrops as well as of the shower, for the drop is "only" a group of molecules. Such reasoning would lead us to the ultimate conclusion that the only fit objects for scientific discourse are the subatomic particles of nuclear physics—this page would not exist as an entity, nor would you who are now reading it.

THE INFERENCE FROM BEHAVIOR

We have no choice about the liaison between psychology and neurology. Psychological ideas, even those that seem furthest from any talk about neuron and synapse, are inextricably involved with ideas about sensation and how the brain works. Similarly, we have no choice about the objective method, whether we like it or not. Direct self-observation, of the mind by the mind, does not exist.

How is the inference about mental states made from behavior? We can begin by seeing how we find out what the world looks like and sounds like to others, animal or human.

What Others Perceive

Ingenious methods have been developed for studying animal perception. Pavlov (1928) showed that the dog's auditory range goes up to 40,000 Hz (the human's upper limit in practice is about 15,000) and also obtained a remarkable discrimination between tones of 1000 and 1012 Hz. Not only does the dog have a wider auditory range than humans, his discrimination of fine differences also is very good indeed—as good as one could expect in humans.

By using the same methods, one can show that the dog distinguishes between temporal patterns of sound. The dog can readily be conditioned to respond to a series such as 500 Hz, 600 Hz, 400 Hz, and not to respond to 600 Hz, 500 Hz, 400 Hz, just as the human being distinguishes between two simple "tunes." Furthermore, the dog will also respond to the series 550-660-440 Hz, which has the same pattern as the first series, but not to these new stimuli in another order, just as people recognize a familiar tune in a new key. We recognize the tune, the auditory pattern, rather than the particular notes that make it up.

This is the method of *transfer*, which has been used extensively in the study of the visual world of animals. By means of transfer, for example, it has been shown that the laboratory rat has a good perception of horizontal and vertical, but not of triangularity. In the jumping stand (Fig. 14.2c), the rat is first trained to discriminate between the two top diagrams of Fig. 14.2b, rewarded with food for choice of the horizontal stripes (top left) and punished for choice of the vertical (very mild punishment: falling about 20 centimeters into a net). Then he is tested with the second pair of diagrams and transfers his response to the single horizontal bar, even though it has a different size and shape. The rat shows that he perceives the difference: on the first test trial, he hesitates long before responding; with the training diagrams, he chooses promptly. We can conclude that the rat perceives both similarity and difference between the test cards and the training cards. The similarity is not merely in the horizontal edges and the vertical edges, but something more generalized, for now he will transfer his response also to the horizontal pair of circles though they do not contain even a horizontal line. As far as we know, the rat's perception of the horizontal is very like man's.

With regard to triangularity, the rat still shows some similarity to the human, but this is evidently a more complex process and the rat's limitations become clear. If we train a rat to discriminate a triangle from a square, for example, we can make the diagram bigger or smaller and still obtain the discrimination. However, if we rotate both diagrams 45°, the discrimination breaks down; that is, the response does not transfer to a rotated triangle. Or if we train the rat to discriminate an erect triangle from an inverted one, we find that he does not transfer his response to black triangles after training with white, nor does he transfer to triangular masses of small circles (Fig. 14.2a). In other words, his perception of the original triangles was not as generalized as that of humans, and it seems clear that the rat does not see a triangle as a triangle, as one of a distinctive, unified class of figures, separate from squares, circles, rectangles, and so on.

The Meaning of Verbal Report

It may seem easier to find out what a human subject perceives than what an animal does: You need only ask for a description, a verbal report. But this is true only if you and your subject have much experience in common. In principle, a human verbal report is behavior that functions the same way as that of a laboratory rat seeking food behind differently marked doors. In both cases we must (a) find out what events the subject is sensitive to or is capable of responding to; (b) see what events are discriminable; and (c) find out what events are discriminable but are sometimes confused, and so may be similar. The only saving of effort with human subjects is that we need not train them in advance but can make use of the fact that they have already learned to make verbal responses to common objects. Unfortunately, ordinary language does not resolve all of the confusion about what is and what is not experienced as alike.

You may have a friend to whom you respond with the name "Jack"; you also have a contraption for changing tires on a car to which you give—apparently—the same name. But this does not mean that "Jack" looks like a "jack." It only means that you have learned to make the same response independently in two different situations.

There are many such complications of learning in the adult, which is one of the reasons for special caution in drawing inferences from human behavior. (It is easier to keep track of the past learning of a laboratory animal).

Human verbal behavior is enormously complex; the mental machinery that controls and produces it is even more complex. Psychology has only begun the task of working out these complications. Verbal behavior is, nevertheless, still behavior, and the principles by which the inference is made are clear, being of the same kind as in the (slightly) simpler case of an animal's performance on a Lashley jumping stand (Fig. 14.2c) or in a Skinner box (Fig. 2.5).

The Reliability of Report

Inference from behavior is only inference. Inference from a verbal report is most reliable when it is supported by all the other behavior of the subject and when it is in accord with reports from others. If I stick a needle into a subject's finger and he says Ouch! and pulls his hand away, I can infer from his two responses, verbal and manual, that he felt pain. But I *also* know that other people in like circumstances, receiving a needle-puncture, say they feel pain. I have two kinds of evidence on which to base my inference: the immediate behavior of this subject and what I know about human beings in general. But what about other cases, in which pain is reported but no injury can be observed?

One interesting example is pain in what is known as the *phantom limb*, which happens often enough so that we can talk confidently about it—although if ever there was a case of a genuinely private experience, this is it. The amputation of a leg does not stop the patient from having "sensations" from the leg. Since the leg is not there, this experience is imagery or hallucination. Careful investigation shows that it occurs in almost all (probably all) cases when the loss occurs after the age of 6 or 8 years (Simmel, 1956). The unanimity of report—even from subjects who never heard of such a thing before, who are not just saying what they think they should say but are puzzled by the experience—provides a solid basis for accepting the phenomenon. Furthermore, in 10% to 15% of the cases, the patient also suffers pain in the phantom limb. The patient characteristically complains of cramp: for example, that the "toes" are twisted or curled up tightly. Our evidence here is only the verbal report, but when we are dealing with a subject who has not heard of the possibility of experiencing cramps in nonexistent toes, the inference can be made with reasonable security.

An opposite case is when we know the imagery to be present but it cannot be reported by the observer. In discussing afterimages (chapter 12), we said that it is fairly common for the subject who first looks for the negative afterimage not to see it. It was suggested that the failure may be the result of learning to pay no attention to afterimages. Everything we know about the human eye and nervous system tells us that the afterimage is there—so we do not trust the subject's report, urge him to look again—and he reports it.

To Know Your Own Mind

It has been emphasized that self-knowledge, knowing what is going on in your own mind, has to be achieved by the same sort of inference that tells us what is going on in someone else's mind. These inferences may be the same in principle, but they are different in practice. An inference about oneself is both harder and easier to make than an inference about someone else: harder because it is difficult or impossible to see your own behavior as a whole; easier because you have private evidence that is not available to other people.

In some respects other people have an advantage in knowing *your* mind. A close friend may realize before you do that you are worried, tired, or irritable. The difference in your behavior—restlessness, not paying attention to the conversation or to things that usually interest you, giving sharper answers—may be easily seen by someone who knows you well, but you may not see these behaviors with the same ease. To you it may seem that it is *other people* who have changed, who have become more boring or more irritating than usual, just as the deaf man complains that nowadays people mumble instead of speaking clearly. These examples show that self-knowledge is not always superior to other's knowledge of yourself.

But not in all respects. Private evidence does exist to aid self-diagnosis. The onset of a headache when you have learned that headaches make you irritable may enable you to avoid an argument and conceal your irritability completely. Others may recognize your hunger when you eat greedily, but you know hunger in advance from stomach sensations or just because food cooking smells particularly good. Your own sleepiness may be detected in sensations from the eyelids, with no betraying signs to others.

So much is obvious. The next step, almost as obvious, concerns imagination, illusion, and memory. Some people say they have no visual or auditory memory images. However, we do know that they have a mediating process that acts in the same way: an internal sensory representation that functions like an image and must have originated as images do, in the act of perceiving.[2]

"Imagination" is a popular term commonly used when an internal sensory representation is mistaken for a real event. I hear a noise as I read, go to the door and find no one in sight, and conclude that I "imagined" the noise. The test, here as in other cases, is whether or not all the evidence agrees. In the example given, the visual and auditory experiences conflict (I hear something, but nothing can be seen). In chapter 12, some cylinders were perceived to be of different size, although when measured they were the same size (Fig. 12.5). The conclusion in both cases is that the apparent differences are illusory. In both cases (imagination and illusion) one is inferring *from the appearance of the external world* something about the operations of one's own mind. The conflict in sensory information is crucial. If I hear voices but can find no one in the room when I make a factual as well as a visual exploration, and if I do not believe in spirits, I must conclude that the

---

[2]Darwin, in this book, was particularly interested in the evolutionary significance of facial expressions indicating fear, aggression, submission, etc. This is still a matter of interest. W. E. Rinn (1984) has reviewed the neural mechanisms of human facial expression.

voices are hallucinatory: something happening in me, not outside. The afterimage is recognized as an internal sensory representation because it moves as the eyes move, does not disappear when the eyes are closed, and is not followed by tactual sensation when I reach out to touch what I am (apparently) seeing.

And this line of thought explains something else. In the isolation experiments (Bexton, Heron & Scott, 1954) one student reported that his mind seemed to have left his body. A test pilot reported that at high altitude he seemed to be outside his plane, looking in at himself, a puppet at the controls. Such reports become intelligible if the subject in either case hallucinates seeing himself and if the hallucination is more vivid than the sensory representation of ordinary experience and has the full sensory quality that the eidetic image seems to have. The observer, then, seems to be looking at himself. To see your body at a distance you—the real you—must have left the body. If you do not believe in a soul that can wander in the void while you are still alive, this must be a disturbing conclusion to come to. A yogi, with a different theory of existence, could properly conclude that the true self had been freed from the husk of the body. For the rest of us, the explanation can be found in our knowledge of the nervous system.

SCIENCE AND PSYCHOLOGY

For many philosophers, psychiatrists, neurologists, and social commentators, the effect of science and scientific methods on psychology has been calamitous. They feel that in experimental psychology we have lost our humanity, that we are made into a sort of biological machine. To deny human beings a soul and equate mind with an activity of matter, to make consciousness nothing but nerve impulses running to and fro in the brain, when nerve impulses are nothing but chemical disturbances, is for those people obviously nonsense. They *know* that mind and consciousness are not like this. What answer should be made to their criticism?

Part of the answer is that psychology is still engaged in laying foundations. We are still discovering new complexities of mind and behavior, and if scientific understanding is still inadequate it does not necessarily mean that we are searching for understanding in the wrong direction. It may mean only that we have much further to go. To equate mind with an activity of matter does not necessarily diminish mind but may elevate matter. Instead of reducing the spirit to the level of dull, inert matter—as we conceive matter to be—it may imply that matter is something different.

Modern psychology has not degraded humanity. It has not denied us choice. Those who suppose that determinism denies choice have not understood the nature of the problem. Modern psychology has not made us meaner, more despicable creatures; quite the contrary. Earlier psychologists had no rebuttal to the hedonistic theory that we are moved only by the search for pleasure and the avoidance of pain, but a biological and evolutionary psychology easily shows that this is not so. Humans are generous as well as selfish, kind as well as cruel (chapter 11), and how they are brought up may determine which aspect predominates. The mind that was known by introspection (supposedly) was incredibly flat, not even suggesting the complexities of thought shown us by Piaget or the complexities of language shown us by Chomsky (see chapter 13). In modern psychology, humans are interesting and entitled to respect.

It may be difficult to accept the idea that your consciousness of the world about you is based entirely on a pattern of nerve impulses in your brain, but the only test of the idea, as a working assumption in a scientific investigation, is whether it works, whether it helps to organize existing knowledge and leads to the discovery of further knowledge. Science deals in preposterous ideas, preposterous when they are new, that is, and because they constitute a change from existing ideas. Once they are accepted and familiar and have become part of "common sense," we may forget how absurd they seemed at first. No one today talks about the absurdity of saying that matter is a form of energy, and vice versa—not today, when nuclear energy is a reality. Other scientific ideas have seemed equally absurd in the past. Galileo laughed at Kepler's suggestion that the moon and the oceans may have some attraction between them, to account for the tides; Newton found the Royal Society openly skeptical of the preposterous proposition that white light is simply a mixture of the colors of the rainbow; no good defense can be offered for the idea that the sun does not rise or set, that instead the earth is revolving and carrying us through space at a speed up to 1600 kilometers an hour. There is no defense for these ideas, that is, except that they work and have led us to new understanding and new knowledge.

If, then, in psychology you encounter ideas that clearly contradict common sense, this may be a sign not that the ideas are bad but that psychology is following in the grand traditions of science. We have hardly begun to understand the human mind. If the ideas with which we are working at this stage seem implausible, they can only be expected to become more so as the study of behavior progresses. With good fortune, psychology may eventually achieve that degree of implausibility—and fertility—that now characterizes the longer established sciences.

SUMMARY

Modern psychological theory has been preoccupied with the problem of learning, a field opened by Ebbinghaus and made of central theoretical importance by Thorndike, Pavlov, and Watson. Until about 1930, this theory was very directly influenced by ideas about what the nervous system could or could not do. Since then, a number of highly capable psychologists have developed a psychology that on the surface at least is independent of anatomy and physiology. Neurological knowledge was evidently a stimulant to psychological thought earlier and is still so, though it seems clear that psychology cannot be reduced to neurophysiology.

A major problem for the objective study of mind is to know how the "inference from behavior" is to be made, to know what is going on in someone else's mind, what is going on in one's own mind. The present chapter considers how we can tell what the world looks like to an animal or another person and discusses the difficulties that arise in the interpretation of a verbal report. It proposes that in learning what goes on in one's own mind, one utilizes one's own behavior, just as if one were observing someone else: private evidence of sensations from one's body, and internal sensory representation—imagery or a functional equivalent thereof.

GUIDE TO STUDY

Relate the various topics discussed in the first part of this chapter to what was studied in earlier chapters.

Can you see why it is said that the S-R formula is a physiological idea and how it would be possible to forget this notion if no mention of the nervous system is made?

Why is Thorndike described as more radical than Lloyd Morgan? What did Hunter have to tell the physiologist of 1915?

How would you set out to learn whether a pet dog can recognize his master or mistress visually?

What problem has a colorblind person in telling others how the world looks to him?

Can you invent a test of your own for seeing whether people who lack visual imagery have some "functional equivalent"—something that serves the same purpose?

Compare the discussion of the mind–body question in the final section of this chapter with the treatment of the same question in chapter 1.

Add to the examples of scientific ideas that seemed preposterous when first proposed or perhaps still do.

NOTES AND GENERAL REFERENCES

Historical

Boring, E. G. (1950). *A History of Experimental Psychology.* New York: Appleton-Century Crofts. Commonly considered the standard work, and beautifully clear in its exposition, this book is thoroughly misleading in its emphasis on the modern period: on Wundt and Titchener in particular, neither of whom left behind him any discernable contribution to psychological knowledge. Boring says that Ebbinghaus left no deep imprint on the psychological world, and refers to Thorndike only as one of the professors at Columbia—and these are the two men who made modern psychology what it is!

Esper, E. A. (1954). *A History of Psychology.* Philadelphia: Saunders. A wholly different approach, concerned with the physiological basis of psychology; stimulating but spotty, and giving no real account of the development from Ebbinghaus and Romanes to Watson, Lashley and Skinner.

Hobhouse, L. T. (1901). *Mind in Evolution.* New York: Macmillan.

Murphy, G. (1948). *Historical Introduction to Modern Psychology.* New York: Harcourt Brace. More catholic but less detailed than Boring: psychology as seen by a perceptive man in 1928 (date of the first edition).

Other References

Bexton, W. H., Heron. W., & Scott, T. H. (1954). Effects of decreased variation in the sensory environment. *Canadian Journal of Psychology, 8,* 70–76.

Hebb, D. O. (1968). Concerning imagery. *Psychological Review, 75,* 466–477.

Humphrey, G. (1951). *Thinking.* New York: Wiley. See pages 122–131 for the evidence that highly trained introspectors working with Titchener at Cornell really described objects and not the sensations that objects give rise to.

Kuhn, T. S. (1970). *The Structure of Scientific Revolutions, 2nd ed.* Chicago: University of Chicago Press. Kuhn argues in this book that new scientific ideas—even "correct" ones—play no role in "normal science" until the accumulated defects of the previously accepted ideas are too great to ignore, at which point everyone accepts the new ideas in a very short time. This may help to explain the extreme longevity of the S-R formulation in psychology in spite of its numerous and easily perceived defects.

Pavlov, I. P. (1928). *Lectures on Conditioned Reflexes.* (Trans. H. L. Gantt). New York: International Publishers.

Rinn, W. E. (1984). The neuropsychology of facial expression: A review of the neurological and psychological mechanisms for producing facial expression. *Psychological Bulletin, 95,* 52–77.

Simmel, M. L. (1950). Phantoms in patients with leprosy and in elderly digital amputees. *American Journal of Psychology, 69,* 529–545.

Weiner, N. (1961). *Cybernetics: Or Control and Communication in the Animal and the Machine, 2nd ed.* Cambridge, MA: MIT Press. The first edition of this book, which appeared in 1948, explained clearly to the general scientific public the mathematics of negative and positive feedback loops. Weiner anticipated the development of mathematical models for psychological processes like the perception of similarity.

Glossary

Note: this glossary is, as the term might imply, a set of *glosses* (explanations or comments) on certain words in the text. This is not a dictionary, and for adequate definitions – as far as they are provided at all – the student must consult the text itself. What follows is meant to be a ready and informal guide for the reader in trouble.

a priori assumption   what one takes for granted, does not question, but uses as a basis for questioning other propositions.

absolute refractory period   when the neuron, immediately after firing once, will not fire even with strong stimulation (about 1 msec in duration).

accommodation   In vision, change in the curvature of the lens to focus on the retina and make a clear image.

addiction   acquired artificial homeostatic need; not a simple habit. (The man who can't quit smoking, or who needs his morning coffee, is addicted to nicotine or caffeine – but "addiction" is now a dirty word and people who should know better say these aren't addictions, just habits. A fine example of using language to conceal distasteful truth from oneself.)

adrenal gland   an **endocrine gland** near the kidney. the inner part (medulla) secretes adrenalin, the outer part (cortex) a complex of hormones, including cortisone.

adrenalin   also known as epinephrine, a hormone secreted by the adrenal gland which acts both on the arousal system and on smooth muscle.

afferent   conducting toward the CNS or toward higher centers in CNS.

all-or-none principle   the mode of action in which a neuron spends all its accumulated energy if it fires at all, the intensity not varying with the strength of stimulation (the frequency, however, does vary).

alpha rhythm   a regular (approximately 10 cps) wave pattern in the EEG, found in most subjects when they are relaxed with eyes closed.

altruism   "other-ism," tendency to act for another's benefit as if the other were oneself – i.e., helping without getting anything in return.

ambiguous figure   visual presentation that is seen alternately as two quite different objects.

ambivalence   simultaneous presence of almost equally strong but opposing motivations: e.g., to fight or to run away, to mate or to fight.

ameba a one-celled animal, especially *Amoeba proteus,* which moves by flowing in one direction with the rest of the tiny drop of fluid protoplasm following after.

amputee a bastard word referring to a person who has had an amputation (surgical removal of part of the body).

analogical changing gradually, not by jumps, contrasted with digital (the difference between a ramp and a set of steps).

androgen male hormone.

anesthesia "without sensation," in its literal meaning and in local anesthesia; with general anesthesia, there is loss of consciousness too.

animism the theory that living things are inhabited by a spirit of some sort.

anxiety continued fear of a specific event without means of escape; or fear due to some disordered function of the brain, in which case, of course, there is no external threatening object to run away from.

aorta the great artery from the heart.

aphasia a general disturbance of language, which may take different forms, with speaking, understanding speech, reading and writing all usually affected to some degree.

aqueduct a narrow passage connecting the third and fourth ventricles. (A block here is what causes hydrocephalus or "water on the brain," in children.)

arousal wakefulness, alertness, vigilance, excitation or excitability; at high levels, emotional disturbance.

arousal function the general excitatory effect of sensory stimulation, as distinct from its function as a guide to response.

arousal system a network of neurons in the brain stem, of which the reticular formation is the main component; activity of the system is necessary for consciousness and wakefulness.

association cortex all cortex that is not specialized motor or sensory cortex; the term is a survival from an earlier day, when messages from the different senses were supposed to meet here and become associated.

association of ideas classical term for what might be called today S–S learning or a connection between mediating processes.

attention a state or activity of the brain predisposing the subject to respond to some part or aspect of the environment rather than other parts.

auditory area cortical tissue specialized for hearing, inside and on the lower lip of the sylvian fissure.

autonomic nervous system a primitive motor system controlling activity of "visceral" structures (including smooth muscle everywhere, not only in the body cavity).

average see **mean.**

averaged evoked potential [AEP] the arithmetic mean or average of many evoked potentials recorded from a cell or population of cells and linked to an external stimulus event.

axon the fiber that constitutes the sending end of the neuron.

basilar membrane structure in the cochlea, in the inner ear, on which are found the receptors for hearing.

behavior technically, the observable activity of muscle and glands of external secretion (but more broadly defined by some writers).

Behaviorism (with capital *B*) originally the S-R psychology of J. B. Watson that excluded mental events from consideration, but now sometimes used (with small *b*) to include all objective psychology.

behavioristic (with small *b*) reference to psychological methods using only public evidence, especially behavior, as distinct from subjective or introspective psychology.

beta rhythm fast, irregular small waves in the EEG, characteristic of mental activity (loosely, waves of 12 cps and faster).

binocular involving both eyes.

biological clock figurative reference to one of the physiological systems that maintain the 24-hour cycle in behavior (alternation of sleep and waking), the 12-month cycle (hibernation), etc.

blind spot   region of no vision in the field of each eye (not coinciding in the two eyes, so there is no blind spot with both open), corresponding to the point in the nasal retina where the optic nerve gathers together and leaves.

brain stem   the part of the neural tube that is inside the skull, to which cerebellum and cerebrum are attached; in effect, a prolongation of the spinal cord inside the skull.

break-off phenomenon   Clark and Graybiel's description of certain indescribable experiences of solitary pilots at high altitudes.

brightness constancy   the tendency of an object to appear of the same degree of lightness or darkness, despite changes of illumination.

buck fever   referring to the classical situation in which the novice hunter suddenly sees a deer and makes no move to shoot: paradigm of certain social situations.

CA   chronological or actual age, as contrasted with *mental age (MA)*.

carotid artery   in the throat, the main supply of blood to the brain.

catatonic schizophrenic   a psychotic individual whose distinguishing symptoms involve stupor, rigidity, negativism, or unusual or bizarre posturing, sometimes with rapid alternation between extremes of excitement and stupor.

caudal   referring to the tail end (the head end is cranial).

caveat emptor   Latin for "let the buyer beware"—or in theoretical matters, don't be too trusting.

cell assembly   a hypothetical reverberating system, supposed to be the basis of a mediating process (a mediating process might consist of two or more cell assemblies, however).

cementing action   figurative reference to the idea that reinforcement may act directly to strengthen an S-R connection.

central fissure   a cleft in the cortex running from the midline almost down to the **sylvian fissure** and separating the motor (in front) from the somesthetic cortex (behind).

central nervous system   the brain and spinal cord, excluding the autonomic nervous sytem and peripheral nerves, but including the retina and the optic nerve (this part of the brain got stretched out and nearly detached).

central process   an activity within the CNS as distinct from S-R transmission through the CNS.

central tendency   in statistics, the average; the single value that best represents the set of numbers in question.

cerebellum   a mass of tissue above the fourth ventricle, at the lower end of the brain stem.

cerebral hemispheres   the two halves of the cerebrum, not really hemispherical.

cerebrospinal fluid   bathes brain and spinal cord, and fills the central hollow in the cord and the four **ventricles** of the brain.

cerebrum   the swollen anterior end of the neural tube and the seat of mind (more or less: mental function needs also the lower brain stem, but development of the cerebrum makes the difference between higher and lower animals).

chimerical   unreal, not practical politics, refers to wild-goose undertakings.

chunking   the ability to relate new memories to old memories so that the new memories can be organized in easy-to-remember ways; associating memories with each other through connections with established knowledge.

circadian   applied to 24-hour biological rhythms and sometimes by extension to other effects of **biological clocks**.

clinical   naturalistic, when referring to a method of research in which phenomena of illness are observed as they occur and are not induced experimentally.

CNS   central nervous system.

cochlea   the snail-like bony structure that contains the basilar membrane and the receptors for hearing.

coding   patterning of nerve impulses that distinguishes two sensory inputs though they travel on the same afferent fibers; the patterning may be in the frequency (e.g., slow and irregular vs. fast and regular) or in the different combinations of afferent fibers that are active.

cognitive learning   includes some effect on mediating processes.

cognitive theory   refers to a line of thought, more or less opposed to **learning theory**, that emphasizes thought processes.

color blindness   partial or complete inability to distinguish hues as such.

commissure   a bundle of fibers connecting corresponding points on the two sides of the CNS.

communication   social behavior varying in complexity from reflex to language.

comparative psychology   the study of behavior which uses a comparison of species as a source of knowledge; not a synonym for "animal psychology," in which only a single species such as the rat may be studied.

conditioned reflex and **conditioned response**   see **CR**.

conditioning method   see **Type-S** and **Type-R conditioning**.

cone   light-sensitive cell in the retina, usually fatter than the other such cell, the rod; the cone's specialty is acuity in daylight conditions, and color vision; the rod's, twilight vision.

confidence interval   the range of scores within which an observation is expected to occur a certain percentage of the time. The usual intervals are specified for 90, 95, and 99 percent of all the observations.

consciousness   refers both to the state of being normally awake and responsive, and to the complex thought processes guiding the behavior of the higher animal when he is awake and responsive.

consolidation   in learning, some process necessary for continued retention (i.e., for long-term memory).

constancy of the IQ   a supposed fixity found only in the healthy young adult. The IQ declines in old age, and varies greatly in growing children if there are variations of the stimulating environment.

constitutional variables   the genetic inheritance of the individual, plus any influence on growth processes, plus any traumatic or toxic influence.

consummatory   see **preparatory-consummatory**.

contiguity   as a behavioral term, temporal contiguity only: the occurrence of two events simultaneously or close together in time.

contiguity theory   the idea that contiguity is sufficient for learning, without **reinforcement**.

control group   used in a control procedure.

control procedure   obtaining results as they would occur without experimental manipulation, for comparison with experimental results (to see whether the experimental procedure makes any real difference).

convergence   in vision, change in the angle between the directions of the two eyes so that both loook at the same point.

copulation   mating.

cornea   the transparent outer surface at the front of the eyeball.

corpus callosum   a large bundle of nerve fibers interconnecting the two cerebral hemispheres of the brain.

correlation coefficient   measure of the degree of relation between two variables; plus 1, perfect correspondence; 0, none; minus 1, perfect inverse relation (top score on one corresponds to bottom score on the other).

cortex   the outer layer of the cerebrum or of the adrenal gland (cerebral cortex, adrenal cortex).

cortical sensory area   a specialized area of the cortex whose primary input is from one of the sensory systems [e.g. visual, auditory, etc.].

cortico-thalamic, cortico-diencephalic   describing paths between cortex and thalamus or hypothalamus.

cps   cycles per second (in sound, the number of "waves" or pulsations per second: middle C is 256 cps).

CR   stands for both conditioned reflex and conditioned response; "reflex" referring to the operation of the S-R connection, "response" to the end result, the motor act.

cranial   referring to the cranium or skull, and to the anterior end of the nervous system.

creativity   the capacity to produce new ideas (which everyone has, though the term is often used to imply only the production of high-powered ideas by the great artists and thinkers).

CS   conditioned stimulus.

cue function   the guiding or steering role of sensation, as distinct from its effect on **arousal**.

death mask   cast of a face made after death: the object of Fig. 11.2 was a plaster-of-paris cast made from a wax death mask of the chimpanzee Lita.

decortication   removal of all or nearly all the cerebral cortex.

delayed conditioning   conditioning situation in which there is a long interval between reinforcement and what is learned.

delayed-response procedure   the subject is shown food in one of two containers, but is allowed to choose between them only after a period of delay (e.g., 20 sec).

delta rhythm   large slow waves, 2 to 5 cps, in the EEG; characteristic of deep sleep and of brain damage.

dendrites   the fibers at the receiving end of the neuron.

dependent variable   see **independent variable**.

depolarization   of a neuron, the movement of positive ions inward, so that there is no longer a difference of potential between the inside and the outside of the neuron.

diencephalon   the front end of the brain stem, consisting mainly of thalamus and hypothalamus (there are also epithalamus and subthalamus, but they don't amount to much).

digital   stepwise, not gradual; contrasted with **analogical** (a digital computer works with digits, and obtains its results simply by counting, an analogical computer does not).

discrimination method   presentation of a positive and a negative stimulus object simultaneously, choice of the positive one being rewarded.

disinhibition   the temporary increase in the strength of a conditioned response [CR] due to the presentation of a novel but irrelevant stimulus.

dispersion   variability, the extent to which individual values differ from the mean or other central tendency.

disuse   lack of practice; the cause of forgetting that occurs merely by the passage of time. See **retroactive interference**.

divergent conduction   conduction by two or more neurons from one locus to different loci, as distinct from parallel conduction, where the neurons which start together end together.

dorsal   the side near the animal's back.

dorsal root   the sensory part of a spinal nerve (as the nerve nears the cord it divides into two branches, the dorsal and ventral roots).

dualism   the assumption that there are two kinds of existence or two kinds of being, spiritual and physical, or ideal and material; on this assumption, mind is not part of the brain's activity (which is physical).

early experience   the sensory stimulation of infancy, normally the same, in large part, for all members of a species.

ECS, ECT   electroconvulsive shock, electroconvulsive therapy: electric current passed through the head, producing a momentary convulsion.

EEG   electroencephalogram, the record of "brain waves," changing potentials in the cortex measured by electrodes attached to the scalp.

effector   muscle cell or an individual cell in glands of external secretion.

efferent   conducting away from higher centers in the CNS and toward muscle or gland.

eidetic image   exceptionally vivid memory image of short duration, found in a small fraction of children, rarely in adults.

electroencephalogram   EEG (q.v.).

embryo   see **fetus**.

EMG   electromyogram, a record of muscle potentials; like the EEG, but from muscle instead of brain.

emotion   special state of arousal accompanied by mediating processes which tend to excite behavior maintaining or modifying the present state of affairs.

empirical   related to experience, the practical rather than the ideal, what works rather than what should work (theoretically). Binet's procedure was justified empirically, not theoretically; i.e., it worked but was not theoretically defensible at the time.

endocrine gland   one that secretes into the blood or lymph stream as distinct from one (such as kidney or sweat gland) that secretes outwardly ("external secretion").

endogenous depression   a marked and relatively persistent sadness or loss of interest or pleasure in usual activities, often accompanied by change in weight, sleep disturbance, fatigue and other somatic complaints. The biochemical origin of the disorder is often emphasized rather than the presence of a clear environmental cause.

estrogen   one of the female hormones producing sexual responsiveness (heat).

estrus   a period of sexual responsiveness in the female.

ethology   the study of behavior by zoologists—in principle, comparative psychology, but with emphasis on the problems of instinctive behavior and evolution.

eustachian tube   connecting middle ear with mouth, permitting air pressure in the middle ear to stay at the same level as in the surrounding atmosphere.

expectancy   mediating-process activity occurring in advance of the stimulating situation of which that activity would be the perception: anticipatory imagery or ideation, aroused by association.

experience   sensory stimulation.

experimental group   the group you do something to (contrasted with **control group**).

experimental neurosis   an apparently neurotic disorder produced (especially in the dog) by an insoluble problem.

extensor muscle   one that straightens the joint, thus extending the limb; opposed to **flexor**.

extinction   producing the disappearance of a habit by removing reinforcement.

facial vision   a mistaken early term, used before the phenomenon was understood, for the auditory perception of a nearby surface by means of echoes.

facilitation   stimulation of one neuron by another, which may or may not fire the second neuron.

"Factor IV"   the effect of early experience that is normal for the species.

familial   hereditary, something that "runs in the family."

fatigue   in the neuron, refers to the difficulty in firing again after having transmitted an impulse, due to the refractory period and to excess sodium ions that accumulate within the cell after repeated firings at a rapid rate.

feedback   in behavior, sensory stimulation resulting from a response; either sensation from the movement itself, or the change of external stimulation as the moving hand touches another surface or as the eye in its new angle of regard sees different objects (e.g.).

feedforward   refers to a situation where the action of neurons at one point in a neural circuit exerts an influence upon the acitivity of neurons at a later point in the circuit.

fetus   unborn young in the latter part of pregnancy; before that, an embryo.

fibril   a fine branching of axon or dendrite.

figure-ground relation   the figure (constantly changing in ordinary perception) is what one perceives at the moment, the rest of the visual field being ground (i.e., background).

fissure   a cleft in the wrinkled cortex.

flexor muscle   one producing flexion, bending of the joint of a limb, and thus retraction of the limb; opposed to **extensor muscle**.

form board   a nonverbal intelligence test for children; the subject is required to place a number of blocks of different shapes in corresponding holes in the board.

fovea   central retinal area, the region in which daytime acuity is highest.

fraternal twins   born at the same time but not the product of one fertilized ovum, and thus no more closely related (in terms of genetics) than two children born at different times.

frequency histogram   a graphic representation of a frequency distribution in which the range of scores appears in order across the bottom of the graph, and the number of scores falling within each range is indicated by the height of a bar drawn above the range.

frontal lobes   the two front halves of the cerebrum, anterior to the central fissure.

frustration   failure to reach an expected goal or reward.

ganglion cells   in the retina, the neurons that send their axons to the central structures of the brain, forming the optic nerves.

generalization spontaneous transfer of response or response tendency, established with one stimulus object, to other objects in the same class.

gin a trap, not a drink. "O Thou, who didst with pitfall and with gin/Beset the road I was to wander in . . ."

glia cells supporting, and presumably a nutritive accompaniment of neurons.

goal the end result of an activity or the result toward which an organism strives.

gonads sex glands: testicles in the male, ovaries in the female.

gray matter closely packed cell-bodies, as distinct from white matter, which is closely packed connecting fibers.

ground see **figure-ground relation**.

GSR galvanic skin response; a change of electrical resistance in the skin, related to sweat-gland activity and an indicator of arousal.

gustatory area taste area: not discussed in the text, but lying at the foot of the somesthetic area inside the sylvian fissure.

gyrus the protruding part of a wrinkle in the cortex.

habituation becoming less and less excited by some stimulation. (If the alarm clock loses its capacity to wake you, or the sound of a plane overhead no longer catches your attention, you have become habituated).

hallucination exceptionally convincing imagery, such that the subject believes that he is perceiving, or would believe it if he did not have other contractory information.

hammer, anvil and stirrup the three bones of the middle ear (tribute to the poetic imagination of the old anatomists).

heat period of sexual responsiveness in the female of lower species, in which the behavioral difference between being in or out of heat is clear-cut.

hemianesthesia loss of sensation in all of the right half, or of the left half, of the body.

hemianopia a loss of vision, resulting from damage to one occipital lobe, in which a person can see nothing to one side of the point upon which he/she is fixating. Damage to the left lobe results in blindness in the right visual field and vice versa.

heredity in mammals, the process of transmitting characteristics through the genes by the union of the sperm and ovum.

higher animal one characterized by more complex behavioral mechanisms; in some contexts, vertebrate as opposed to invertebrate (roughly); in others, mammal as opposed to non-mammal, or again ape, porpoise and man as opposed to other mammals.

higher process mental process, mediating process, characteristic of the higher animal only; not reflexive.

hippocampus primitive cortical structure, in man lying near the tip of the temporal pole.

holding the capacity of the brain to receive an excitation and transmit it to muscle or gland after some appreciable period of time.

homeostasis maintenance of a constant internal environment, chemically and physically.

homosexuality preference for sexual activity with one of the same sex; an almost exclusively human trait—with the exception of male porpoises, on two or three occasions, the *preference* has not been observed in lower animals; male-male or female-female sexual behavior occurs, but only in the absence of a receptive animal of the opposite sex.

hormone substance secreted into the blood stream by an endocrine gland.

hunger tendency to eat determined by mediating processes (ideas of getting and eating food); not equivalent to a lack of food, since one may need food and not be hungry, or be hungry and not need food.

hyperactivity a disorder of childhood characterized by the inability to maintain attention for long periods of time and the inability to inhibit inappropriate responses in situations which call for restraint. Associated problems in learning and relating to peers are often present.

hyperpolarized a state in which there has been a change in voltage rendering the inside of a nerve cell membrane more negative relative to the normal resting membrane potential; results from inhibitory synaptic transmission.

hypothalamus the lower half of the diencephalon, the highest level of reflex function (with the possible exception of the cerebellum).

idea the classical name for what we would call a mediating process today, a single mental activity. As ordinarily used ("the idea of going home," "the idea of having green hair," or "I have an idea that . . .") the term must refer to a complex set of mediating processes.

ideation a loose designation of the presence of ideas or mediating processes, which commits one to no theory of the nature of mental activity.

identical twins not necessarily identical, except genetically: differences in their uterine environments may produce significant physical differences even at birth.

imagery the occurrence of mental activity corresponding to the perception of an object, but when the object is not presented to the sense organ.

imprinting a lasting social attachment to, or identification with, the species to which the newly hatched bird is exposed.

impulse nerve impulse, or "propagated disturbance."

independent variable one that is varied by the experimenter to see what the effect is on another, the dependent variable (i.e., the independent variable is treated as causal). In a study of rat intelligence the experimenter might use animals of different ages, different heredities and different early experiences: these would be independent variables, and maze-learning score might be the dependent variable.

inhibition technically, an action by one neuron that reduces the probability that another will fire; loosely, any suppression of activity.

inhibitory neurons nerve cells found throughout the CNS whose function it is to block or suppress the transmission of impulses by making other neurons temporarily difficult to excite.

inner ear fluid-filled labyrinth, with two sensory functions, that of the cochlea (hearing) and that of the vestibular apparatus (movement and balance).

insanity a legal term, roughly equivalent to psychosis, but a patient may be psychotic and not insane (i.e., he can still manage his own affairs though he might be better off if someone else did).

insight activity of mediating processes leading to solution of a problem, but especially the reorganization of such processes, with sudden success.

instinct that which controls instinctive behavior (*not* opposed to learing, *not* separate from intelligence). A term not currently in good standing in psychology because of its connotations. (OK if used according to directions.)

instinctive behavior species-predictable behavior at a more complex level than the reflex.

intelligence A the innate potential for cognitive development.

intelligence B the second sense in which the term intelligence is commonly used. It refers loosely to a general or average level of development of ability to perceive, to learn, to solve problems, to think, to adapt.

interneurons nerve cells located entirely within the gray matter of the spinal cord and serving to interconnect other spinal neurons.

internuncial connections paths or fibers in CNS that are neither afferent nor efferent ("lateral" connections between points at about the same level).

intrinsic motivation doing something for its own sake, not in order to get something else (which would be extrinsic motivation, or work for an extrinsic reward).

introspection direct observation of one's own mental processes (figuratively, "looking inward").

inverted-U curve rising to a peak in the middle of the range, then declining – specifically, a reference to a supposed relation of cue to arousal function implying that behavior is most efficient with a moderate degree of arousal.

ion a positively or negatively charged chemical particle.

IQ intelligence quotient, an index of rate of mental development as compared to the average of the population. IQ = MA/CA $\times$ 100.

iris the colored tissues surrounding the pupil of the eye.

IRSO "internal representation of sensory origin": a reference in this text to something that functions like an image, but does not seem to be sufficiently sensory to be recognized as imagery.

item in test construction, a single question, problem or task.

kinesthesis sensation of movement, either from receptors in muscle and joint, or from the vestibular apparatus of the inner ear.

knowledge some modification of central processes which affects the response that may be made in any of a number of situations in the future.

labyrinth the fluid-filled canals of the inner ear.

language purposive communication, not necessarily verbal, at a level of complexity known only in man (with the possible exception of one specially trained young chimpanzee).

latent learning learning without overt response at the time the learning occurs.

law of effect Thorndike's principle of reinforcement: a habit is strengthened if the response is followed by satisfaction, weakened if followed by discomfort.

learning modification of stimulus-response relations, present or potential, resulting from sensory stimulation (including the stimulation of reinforcement). Theoretically, a change in S-R connections or in the connections of mediating processes; also theoretically, fundamentally a synaptic change.

learning set a learned, generalized approach to a problem situation which leads to more rapid learning of successive problems of a similar type.

learning theory a special term, not equivalent to "theory of learning," that refers to a line of thought emphasizing the S-R formula, cautious in its approach to thought (whereas cognitive psychologists rush in).

limbic system a set of primitive structures in the brain, believed to be the seat of emotional feeling.

limen the poiint at which a stimulation becomes capable of causing excitation, as the stimulation becomes stronger or as it varies in frequency, etc. (thus man's upper limen for sound is about 15,000 cps—above this, he does not hear sound, below it he does).

lobotomy an incision into a lobe (the frontal lobe, in brain operations for mental illness or intractable pain), as distinct from lobectomy, which means the removal of a lobe.

long-circuiting formation of an S-R path through the cortex.

long-term memory relatively stable long-lasting memory; i.e., hours, days or years.

m meter(s).

MA mental age.

macro-molecule a very large organic molecule.

manic-depressive psychosis a psychotic disorder featuring marked alternations in mood from extreme euphoria and excitement to profound sadness.

massed trials learning or extinction trials presented at short intervals until learning or extinction is complete. See **spaced trials**.

maturation physical maturation is bodily growth, including neural development; psychological maturation, which is what is actually observed in normal circumstances, includes also the effect of early experience.

mean the arithmetic mean, an average determined by adding all the values and dividing by the number of values.

median an average determined by arranging the numbers in order and then taking the middle one.

mediating process in modern theory, the element of thought, capable of holding an excitation and thus of bridging a gap in time between stimulus and response.

memory technically, retention of any learning; used popularly to refer only to what the human subject can recall or report.

memory image imagery for complex material at some time after perceiving it.

mental referring to **mind**.

mental age the age of which the subject's level of intellectual function is characteristic. A child with an MA of 7 performs at the level of the average seven-year-old.

mental retardation significantly below average intellectual functioning with associated impairment in adaptive behavior and social adjustment. Begins before the age of 18.

midbrain a short section of the brain stem immediately posterior to the diencephalon, surrounding the aqueduct.

middle ear   air-filled cavity where three small bones transmit vibrations from eardrum ("tympanum") to the flexible membrane of the oval window, and thence to the fluid of the inner ear.

mind   a loose reference to the processes inside the head that control behavior in its more complex manifestations.

mirabile dictu   Latin, meaning "wonderful to relate."

mnemonic   having to do with memory: a "mnemonic device" is some aid to memory.

molar   as applied to theoretical conceptions, dealing in larger units, less concerned with fine detail (see **molecular**).

molecular   as applied to theoretical conceptions, fine-grained, small scale (contrasted with **molar**).

monism   the assumption, in opposition to **dualism**, that there is only one kind of existence and thus the assumption that mind is a part or aspect of the brain's activity.

monotonous   unvarying (monotony is not a mental state but a state of the external environment).

moon illusion   apparent difference between the size of the moon or other objects when seen near the horizon (or horizontally) and when seen near the zenith.

monozygotic twins   genetically identical twins who develop from the same fertilized egg (zygote).

motivation   tendency of the whole animal to be active in a selective, organized way ("selective," because not any kind of activity but a particular kind, at any one time, dominates).

motor area   a cortical region having relatively direct connections with efferent neurons in the cord; stimulation of the area produces movement in the corresponding part of the body.

msec.   millisecond(s): 1/1000 sec.

myelin sheath   a fatty white covering of many (but not all) nerve fibers, insulating one from another.

nasal retina   the half of the retina nearest the nose.

natural selection   Darwin's conception. Nature "selects" the stronger and better equipped animal to carry on the species, by killing off the weaker one or not giving it an opportunity to mate.

negative adaptation   habituation (q.v.).

negative afterimage   visual aftereffect in complementary colors: black after looking at white, green after looking at red, etc.

neural circuit   a closed pathway of interconnected neurons that leads back into itself; a loop of connected neurons.

neural tube   the original embryonic hollow tube which develops into the nervous system; or, in the adult, the spinal cord and brain stem.

neurology   study of the nervous system: in one usage, the diagnosis and medical treatment of neural disorder, but also used more broadly to include neuroanatomy and neurophysiology.

neuron   the individual nerve cell. Distinguish between neuron and **nerve**, the latter being a bundle of the branches of neurons.

neuroscience   the sciences that emphasize the study of the central nervous system.

neurosis   ill-defined term referring to less extreme forms of personality disorder.

neurotransmitter   the chemical substance involved in the electrochemical communication between neurons; the substance by which neurons transmit information.

nerve   a bundle of axons or dendrites or both outside the CNS. (Such a bundle inside is a "tract," "lemniscus," "fasciculus," etc.)

nerve impulse   the electrochemical disturbance that travels from cell-body to the end of the axon, the means by which the nervous system conducts excitations from one point to another (e.g., from spinal cord to muscle).

nonsense syllable   meaningless short syllables invented by Ebbinghaus for the study of learning and memory: e.g., dom, zik, ral.

nonspecific afferents   fibers leading to the cortex via the arousal system, where inputs from different senses are pooled; thus the excitation that reaches the cortex is not specific to any one sense.

nonspecific projection system   consists of the ascending reticular activating system plus other nonspecific afferents: NPS or **arousal system** for short.

normal probability curve   a distribution which, it is assumed, many biological values (such as men's heights or women's chest measurements) approximate. Obviously an idealized conception.

noxious stimulation   damaging, or such as normally causes pain.

NPS   nonspecific projection system or, for convenience, **arousal system**.

nucleus   a term with several meanings depending on context; a nucleus is a nub or kernel or central mass: thus a cell has its nucleus, a cell-body may be referred to as a nucleus, and a thalamic or hypothalamic nucleus consists of a cluster of cell-bodies.

null hypothesis   the working assumption, in comparing two groups, that they come from the same population (i.e., their difference does not represent a true difference but results from sampling only): assumption normally made to see whether it can be disproved.

objective psychology   based on public or objective evidence, as contrasted with subjective or introspective psychology; behavioristic.

occipital lobe   the posterior end of the cerebrum.

olfactory area   there is no olfactory area.

one-trial learning   the total acquisition of a skill or forming of an association after only one trial or exposure to the stimuli.

optic chiasm   where the optic nerves meet, intertwine, and sort out the fibers that go from each eye to both sides of the brain.

ovum   egg, the cell produced by female mammals as well as by birds: the bird's is much larger since it must carry with it enough nutriment to last through the period of gestation.

pain   refers to two things, a distinctive sensory event and an emotional reaction thereto.

paradigm   a clear representative example (of a mode of thought or of experiment).

parallax   different appearance of an object (or in astronomy, a difference in the pattern of stars) as seen from two points in space.

parallel conduction   where transmitting fibers are laid down side by side, and thus can support each other's action at the synapse with summation, producing reliable transmission to the next level.

paralysis of terror   loose reference to the ineffectual behavior that may accompany strong arousal.

paranoid schizophrenic   a psychotic individual who has systematized delusions or hallucinations which are persecutory or grandiose in content. The individual may also be quite anxious, angry, argumentative and sometimes violent.

parasympathetic nervous system   the two divisions of the autonomic nervous system found at each end of the neural axis, cranial and caudal, and more or less opposed in their action to that of the **sympathetic** division of the **autonomic nervous system**, which is found in the middle regions of the cord.

parietal lobe   the cerebrum on one side, from the central fissure back nearly to the posterior pole of the brain, and above the sylvian fissure.

partial reinforcement   feeding only on every fifth or tenth trial or on some other scheme by which the animal makes a number of responses for one reward.

perception   activity of mediating processes initiated by sensation.

perceptual constancy   the tendency for a perception to remain stable under varying external conditions.

perceptual isolation   procedure minimizing patterned stimulation and thus perception; sometimes referred to as sensory deprivation, but this would imply eliminating sensory input, which can't be done except for vision.

perceptual learning   modification of perception resulting from prior perceptions.

phantom limb   the somesthetic hallucination of the presence of a limb or some part of the body after it has been amputated.

phenylketonuria   a genetically transmitted disorder characterized by a deficiency of the liver enzyme phenylalanine hydroxylase which creates a disturbance in the metabolic process resulting in profound mental retardation unless phenylalanine is largely restricted from a child's diet.

pheronome   a chemical substance produced by an animal that acts as a stimulant, especially to members of the same species.

phi-phenomenon   perception of apparent movement (as in moving pictures).

photomicrograph   photograph from a microscope slide.

pleasure area   one of the regions of the brain whose stimulation is rewarding: the animal will repeat any action that is followed by such stimulation.

polarization   of a cell membrane, the presence of positive ions on one side, negative ions on the other.

population   in statistics the body of numbers of measurements or events – often a hypothetical body, indefinitely large – of which one considers the numbers one has to be a sample.

positive afterimage   visual aftereffect not in complementary colors (see **negative afterimage**).

positive feedback   neural transmission within a circuit of nerve cells that sustains or increases the activity of those cells.

practice effect   the effect on performance resulting from prior exposure to a task [e.g., displaying improved performance on a test the third time it is taken].

preparatory-consummatory   Sherrington's conception of two stages in satisfaction of biological needs, the second being unconditioned reflex (courtship is preparatory, copulation is consummatory; seeking food is preparatory, chewing and swallowing is consummatory).

presynaptic-postsynaptic   when neuron *A* excites neuron *B* (at a synapse, of course), *A* is presynaptic, *B* is postsynaptic.

primary reinforcement   reinforcement by satisfaction of a biological need – in practice, usually the escape from pain, or food or water for a hungry or thirsty animal.

private evidence   sensations and imagery arising in oneself and so not available information for others.

proactive interference   forgetting that is a weakening of learning caused by *prior* learning. See **retroactive interference**.

probable error   deviation from the mean or true value which would occur in 50 per cent of one's measurements.

proprioception   kinesthesis: sensation from active muscles and from joints, supplying information about limb position and movement of parts of the body, and sensations of movement from the vestibular apparatus.

psychoanalysis   refers to both a theory of mental illness and a form of **psychotherapy**, originated by Freud.

psychological construct   a named conception invented for dealing with a particular class of data.

psychological maturation   see **maturation**.

psychosis   ill-defined term referring to the more extreme disorders of personality.

psychotherapy   psychological treatment of mental illness, a form of re-education rather than treatment by drugs, electric shock, etc.

public evidence   data which, for scientific purposes, might be recorded by any competent observer – i.e., objective as distinct from private or subjective or introspective evidence.

pupillary   related to the pupil of the eye; pupillary reflexes, contraction or expansion in response to changes of illumination.

purpose   mediating processes controlling purposive behavior.

purposive behavior   behavior partly under the control of expectancy, the present action being such as to produce a desired goal or suitable to an expected future state of affairs, not determined merely by their present state.

pyramidal tract   a bundle of efferent fibers, mainly those connecting the motor cortex with motor centers in stem and spinal cord.

range   in statistics, the distance from the lowest to the highest value; usually expressed by saying the range is from (low value) to (high value), or vice versa.

reaction time   technically, the interval between presentation of a stimulus and initiation of the response.

receptor   a sensory cell.

reentrant pathway   a closed circuit in which re-excitation or "reverberation" can occur: e.g., *A* excites *B*, which excites *C*, which re-excites *A*, and so on.

reflexive   characterized by immediacy and reliability of response to stimulation, as in either unconditioned or conditioned reflex.

reinforcement   any event following a response that increases the probability that the response will be made again when the same situation recurs. (This is the general sense: see also **primary reinforcement**.)

reinforcement theory   the idea that learning does not occur without reinforcement (see **contiguity theory**).

relative refractory period   period following the **absolute refractory period** when the neuron will fire but only with strong stimulation.

reliability   consistency of measurement by a test, expressed quantitatively as the correlation between two measurements.

Renshaw cells   inhibitory interneurons located in the spinal cord.

response   any overt or covert behavior including, muscular and glandularl behavior which can be observed with electronic instruments. The word is often extended to cover the actions of neurons as observed electronically.

retina   the light-sensitive structure at the back of the eye, containing rods and cones and connecting fibers.

retinal angle   as a measure of visual size, the angle formed by lines drawn from the center of the lens to each end of the retinal image; in effect, the angle between lines drawn from the eye to the two extremes of the object (a 1-inch line four feet away has about the same retinal angle as a 2-inch line eight feet away).

retinal disparity   difference in the images on the retinas, due to the different positions of the two eyes.

retroactive interference   forgetting caused by interference between what is learned and subsequent learning, as distinct from **disuse**, and from **proactive interference**, which is an effect of learning that was done earlier.

retrograde amnesia   forgetting of the events that happened just before a blow on the head, or the like.

reverberating circuit   same as **reentrant pathway**.

rod   slender light-sensitive cell in the retina. See **cone**.

salivary reflect   mouth watering, which dogs are good at. ("Any dog conditioned well/ Slobbers when you ring a bell.")

sample   in statistics, one's actual data, regarded as drawn from a population of data.

satiation   having enough; with respect to eating, a suppression of hunger.

savings method   measure of retention (memory) which compares the number of trials required to relearn with the number in the original learning.

schizophrenia   ill-defined but clinically recognizable form of psychosis.

SD   standard deviation.

secondary reinforcement   stimulation that has accompanied **primary reinforcement** in the past and has acquired some reinforcing value.

selectivity   the capacity to choose among the vast array of stimuli and responses confronting an organism.

semantics   the study of the development and refinement of the meaning of symbols; sounds, words, etc.

semicircular canals   part of the vestibular apparatus of the inner ear, involved in the perception of head movements.

sensation   activity of receptors and specific afferent pathway.

sense-dominated behavior   behavior fully controlled by sensory events which by themselves elicit the complete pattern of response; reflexive behavior.

sensory area   a cortical region specialized for one sensory function by receiving fibers from the sense organ; e.g., visual area, auditory area.

sensory dominance   full sensory control of behavior, without modulation by mediating processes.

sensory preconditioning   refers to Brogden's procedure in which two sensory events are first associated, whereupon one can substitute for the other in a CR.

serendipity   discovering what one was not looking for, while looking for something else.

set   a state or activity of the brain predisposing to rapid response or to one class of response when others would have been possible (with other sets).

shaping up   Skinner's procedure in which the desired pattern of behavior is gradually developed by rewarding any approximation to it, then a closer approximation, and so on.

short-term memory   immediate memory of limited capacity which lasts only for a brief time, a few seconds to a few minutes.

"significant at the 5 per cent level"   (or 1 per cent, etc.): a result that would be obtained by chance only once in 20 times (or 100 times) and is thus assumed not to be due to chance. (Samples differ, experimental and control groups are samples, and thus expected to differ: the statement says that a mere sampling difference of this size would only occur once in 20 times, so the probability—19 to 1—is that something else made the difference. At the 1 per cent level, the probability is 99 to 1.)

similarity   some degree of perceived identity in objects that are also discriminable.

size constancy   the tendency of objects to appear of the same size, despite changes of distance.

skeletal muscle   striate muscle that moves the parts of the skeleton—limbs, chest wall, hips—in contrast particularly with gut muscle, etc.

Skinner box   apparatus for Type-R conditioning, in which pressure on a lever or a button, etc., is rewarded.

smooth muscle   muscle lacking the striations of limb muscle, etc., and slower acting; found in gut, walls of blood vessels, etc. See **striate muscle**.

somatosensory area   regions of the cerebral cortex, especially the postcentral gyrus, responsible for receiving various types of bodily sensations, such as touch, pressure, etc.

somesthesis   body sensation, including touch and temperature from the skin, pain, pressure and kinesthesis.

somesthetic area   cortex posterior to the central fissure specialized for body sensations.

spaced trials   learning or extinction trials with long intervals between them. See **massed trials**.

spatial integration   coordinated activity in different parts of the body at the same time. (Usually combined with **temporal integration**.)

species predictable   characteristic of normal members of a species, and so predictable from knowing with what species you are dealing: e.g., speech in man, nest-building in robins.

specific energy   an old conception: that distinguishable sensory inputs must somehow be distinctive. It is now believed that they are on different input lines, or are **coded** differently on the same line.

specific nerve energies [law of]   doctrine that sensory neurons transmit impulses which are specific to the modality which they represent, regardless of the nature of the stimuli; each nerve is capable of reacting in a certain way only [e.g., any stimulation to a sensory neuron in the auditory system will lead to a sound not a sensation of light or pressure].

speech areas   cortical tissue with a special importance for language; the principal regions are the cortex around the posterior end of the sylvian fissure and the foot of the motor cortex, all on the left side (in the great majority of cases).

spinal cord   part of the CNS, a thick cord of neural tissue in the spinal column responsible for the relay of information to and from the brain as well as for a number of reflexive behaviors.

split-brain preparation an animal with a deep vertical incision in the brain, separating most of it into two (left and right) halves.

S-R stimulus-response.

S-R formula the conception of response as following stimulation immediately and as predictable from it (i.e., the formula describes reflexive behavior).

stabilized image a visual image that remains at the same point on the retina, achieved by prevention of the slight movements of the image on the retina which result from the normal tremor of the eye muscles in looking at an object.

standard deviation statistical measure of dispersion, obtained by squaring the individual differences from the mean, adding the results together, dividing by their number, and taking the square root of this result.

standard error of the mean the standard deviation of the distribution of the sample means; an estimate of the amount that an obtained mean deviates by chance from the true mean.

stereoscope device showing one picture to one eye, a slightly different one to the other, in such a way that one sees a single picture in three dimensions.

stimulus external energy acting on a sensitive cell (receptor or neuron); in careless language, a stimulus object or event.

stimulus object (or event) something in the environment that gives rise to a stimulus (food is a stimulus object; its chemical action on tongue receptors is a stimulus).

striate muscle under the microscope marked with striations distinguishing from the **smooth muscle** of the gut, etc.

subvocal referring to movements of larynx, etc., corresponding to speech but without sound.

summation on the neural level, the adding together of two or more nerve impulses over time or space creating greater depolarization in a postsynaptic neuron. One the behavioral level, the reinforcement of the action of one stimulus by that of another [e.g., two dim flashes of light summing their effects thus producing a response].

syllogism a formal mode of deductive thought.

sylvian fissure a great cleft in the side of the brain, slanting slightly upward from front to back.

sympathetic nervous system the central division of the **autonomic nervous system,** active especially in emergency or emotional situations; closely related to **arousal.**

synapse the point at which one neuron makes functional connection with another neuron and the place at which, it is assumed, the fundamental change of learning occurs.

synaptic knob an enlargement of the axon at the point of contact with another neuron. (Also known as **bouton terminal,** or end-foot.)

synaptic vesicle a small, saclike structure found in the presynaptic ending of a neuron; contains the neurotransmitter substance.

synesthesia the association to a sensory experience of another sensory memory, often in a different modality [e.g., the association of colors with sounds], so that a present sense experience evokes a related sensory memory at the same time.

syntax the structural arrangement or organization of words in language.

taboo formalized avoidance, or a combination of detestation or fear with approval or worship, considered in the literature to be characteristic of primitive societies. We have them too, full-blown.

temper tantrum peculiar pattern of behavior commonly seen in ape and human children, involving self-injury, with the apparent purpose of influencing a parent (e.g.). Loosely, any outburst of frustrated rage.

temporal integration coordinated or organized sequence of activities — strictly speaking, a series of actions by the same effectors, but usually involving spatial integration as well, a coordination of different effectors.

temporal lobe the protrusion of the cerebrum below the sylvian fissure.

temporal retina the half of the retina next to the temple, away from the nose.

thalamus the upper half of the diencephalon, mainly afferent in function.

thiamine a vitamin, part of the B complex.

threshold limen (q.v.).

tract a distinctive bundle of nerve fibers inside the CNS.

transfer generalization; the making of a response, learned with one stimulus object, to other such objects. "Transfer of training" more broadly refers to the effect of earlier on later learning (positive transfer is learning accelerated by having learned something else earlier).

translucent permitting the passage of light but not pattern vision.

trauma injury ("psychic trauma," injury to the soul").

twilight vision "scotopic" as contrasted with "photopic" vision; occuring in very low illumination, when human visual acuity is best two or three degrees off center, because there are no rods in the foveal area, only the less sensitive cones.

two-point limen the distance between two skin stimulations that is necessary for them to be perceived as two, not one.

tympanum the eardrum.

Type-R conditioning no specific CS or UCS is used (as in Type-S), but the response to be conditioned is rewarded when it happens to appear.

Type-S conditioning a neutral stimulation, the CS, repeatedly followed by the UCS (e.g., food), results in the capacity of the CS to elicit responses.

UCR stands for both unconditioned reflex and unconditioned response (cf. **CR**). The abbreviation UR is also used by some writers.

UCS unconditioned stimulus, one able to elicit the response without need of a prior learning process to establish the connection. Some writers use the abbreviation US.

umweg problem one in which the subject must turn away from the goal he can see, in order to reach it (umweg, German for "indirect").

unconscious in a subjective psychology, the unconscious is part of the mind of which one is not directly aware.

universe statistically, the total population of cases from which samples can be drawn.

ventricle one of four cavities in the brain filled with fluid, important anatomical landmarks.

vertebrates animals with a spinal column, excluding thus the octopus, the ant, and the spider.

vestibular apparatus sense organ excited differentially by head movements; part of the inner ear, and including the three semi-circular canals.

vigilance readiness to respond to stimulation: arousal, wakefulness, alertness.

visual area cortex specialized for vision, in man at the occipital pole of the brain.

visual depth distance from the eye.

visual field the part of the environment seen at any moment, extending horizontally for more than 180°, for the normal human subject with both eyes open.

visual texture organized detail in the visual field, the fine detail diminishing with distance and larger objects becoming smaller.

volition the will, an old-fashioned conception that we might still use. "Free will," absence of sense dominance.

voluntary behavior behavior not under complete sensory control but determined by the interacton of sensory and central processes.

Weber-Fechner law a principle of psychophysics which states that the intensity of sensation equals a constant times the logarithm of the intensity of the stimulus.

white matter CNS tissue mainly composed of fibers, not cell-bodies.

Author Index

Subject Index